A Primer in Christian Ethics

How does Christian belief and practice relate to living well amid the difficulties of everyday life and the catastrophes and injustices that afflict so many today? In his introduction to Christian ethics, Luke Bretherton provides a new, constructive framework for addressing this question. Connecting the theory and practice of Christian moral and political thought to contemporary existential concerns, his book integrates classic sources and approaches to the pursuit of wisdom with contemporary liberationist and critical voices, while making the relationship between human and nonhuman life a central focus. As well as addressing a broad range of ethical questions, Bretherton situates moral formation and the pursuit of human and nonhuman flourishing alongside a concern for spirituality, pastoral care, and political struggles to survive and thrive in the contemporary context. Written for those seeking a place to start, as well as seasoned scholars, Bretherton's book provides an innovative ethical framework that moves beyond many of the impasses that shape current moral and political debates.

LUKE BRETHERTON is the Robert E. Cushman Distinguished Professor of Moral and Political Theology at Duke University. He is author of *Christ and the Common Life: Political Theology and the Case for Democracy* (Eerdmans, 2019), *Resurrecting Democracy: Faith, Citizenship and the Politics of a Common Life* (Cambridge University Press, 2015), *Christianity and Contemporary Politics* (Wiley-Blackwell, 2010) – winner of the 2013 Michael Ramsey Prize for Theological Writing – and *Hospitality as Holiness: Christian Witness amid Moral Diversity* (Routledge, 2006). Alongside his scholarship and teaching, he writes on topics related to religion and politics in the media; hosts the Listen, Organize, Act! podcast; and is involved in forms of grassroots democratic politics in both the United Kingdom and the United States.

A Primer in Christian Ethics

Christ and the Struggle to Live Well

LUKE BRETHERTON

Shaftesbury Road, Cambridge CB2 8EA, United Kingdom

One Liberty Plaza, 20th Floor, New York, NY 10006, USA

477 Williamstown Road, Port Melbourne, VIC 3207, Australia

314–321, 3rd Floor, Plot 3, Splendor Forum, Jasola District Centre, New Delhi – 110025, India

103 Penang Road, #05-06/07, Visioncrest Commercial, Singapore 238467

Cambridge University Press is part of Cambridge University Press & Assessment, a department of the University of Cambridge.

We share the University's mission to contribute to society through the pursuit of education, learning and research at the highest international levels of excellence.

www.cambridge.org
Information on this title: www.cambridge.org/highereducation/isbn/9781009328975

DOI: 10.1017/9781009328982

First published 2023

A catalogue record for this publication is available from the British Library.

Library of Congress Cataloging-in-Publication Data
Names: Bretherton, Luke, author.
Title: A primer in Christian ethics : Christ and the struggle to live well / Luke Bretherton, Duke University, North Carolina.
Description: First edition. | Cambridge, United Kingdom ; New York, NY, USA : Cambridge University Press, 2023. | Includes bibliographical references and index.
Identifiers: LCCN 2022061981 (print) | LCCN 2022061982 (ebook) | ISBN 9781009328975 (Hardback) | ISBN 9781009329026 (Paperback) | ISBN 9781009328982 (epub)
Subjects: LCSH: Christian ethics.
Classification: LCC BJ1251 .B735 2023 (print) | LCC BJ1251 (ebook) | DDC 241–dc23/eng/20230405
LC record available at https://lccn.loc.gov/2022061981
LC ebook record available at https://lccn.loc.gov/2022061982

ISBN 978-1-009-32897-5 Hardback
ISBN 978-1-009-32902-6 Paperback

To Caroline

Contents

Acknowledgments

This book is a work of gratitude. It would not have been written but for all the students over many years, across two continents, who taught me how to think better and state more clearly what I was talking about when I taught them. My own education in Christian moral and political thought consisted of reading a series of classic, mostly European texts from which I was to derive how to do something called Christian ethics by a process of mimesis. This approach has an ancient warrant and many merits. But it proved inadequate when teaching those either in ordination training, already running ministries and missions of various kinds, or involved in on-the-ground forms of civic and social work. Simply teaching classic texts as an introduction to Christian moral and political deliberation was too far removed from the existential questions they wrestled with and needed to think through. Lives, pastoral integrity, and the health and well-being of communities insistently pressed themselves into the classroom. What students asked of me and what I was struggling with myself needed an alternative approach. I have experimented with different ways of teaching Christian ethics over the years. Most of them were attempts to address the specific needs and context of the students I was charged with helping to understand the moral and political dimensions and implications of Christianity as a way of life. The approach adopted in this book is the one I've found the most generative and straightforward. As I outline in the introduction (Chapter 1), it is built on a set of questions that philosophers and theologians have asked when trying to give an account of what it means to live well: namely, what is going on? What is to be done? And how then shall we live?

As well as being a testimony to the students I have taught, this book is also the fruit of conversations with colleagues over many years. Those I am grateful to for wisdom and insight are too numerous to name here. However, I do owe a specific word of thanks to those who have commented on either chapters or drafts of the whole manuscript. For direct input into the writing of this book, I am grateful for feedback from Christopher Beeley, Peter Casarella, Ellen Davis, Peter Sedgwick, Patrick Smith, Warren Smith, Janet Martin Soskice, Brittany Wilson, Wylin Wilson, and Norman Wirzba. For critical feedback on specific chapters, I am grateful to Richard Chartres on Chapter 6; James Alison, Natalie Carnes, Roberto Che-Espinoza, Sean Larsen, and Eugene Rogers on Chapter 12; and to Darrel Cosden, James Featherby, Philip Lorish, and Andrew Lynn on Chapter 13.

A particular debt of gratitude is owed to Stanley Hauerwas and Jonathan Tran who have patiently engaged with multiple drafts of the manuscript. In some ways, this book is a testimony to a rolling conversation and set of arguments with Stanley over this past ten years, for much of which we had adjacent offices.

I am privileged to have accompanied a remarkable set of doctoral students at Duke from whom I have learned a great deal and whose questions, concerns, and agitations directly inform this book. I am deeply grateful to have kept company with Jackson Adamah, Emily Dubie, Matthew Elia, Matthew Elmore, Michael Remedios Grigoni, Nathan Hershberger, Matthew Jantzen, Ryan Juskus, Brett McCarty, Alberto La Rosa Rojas, Kaitlyn Scheiss, and Isaac Villegas. This book is a testimony to our shared deliberations.

While writing the book, I was part of a weekly Bible study group with Sarah Jobe, Ryan Juskus, Casey Stanton, Lauren Winner, and Felipe Witchger. The insights from our exegesis are woven into this text in many places. I give thanks here for the friendship, prayer, and support they provided, particularly during the COVID-19 pandemic when most of this book was written.

For their crucial editorial work and guidance, I am immensely grateful for the labors of Judith Heyhoe and Jana Riess. The text is much improved as a result of their ministrations.

Finally, my thanks must go to Caroline, Gabriel, and Isaac for their support and encouragement. Without them I could not do this work.

1 Introduction

Christ and the Struggle to Live Well

On August 26, 1572, Peter Ramus was stabbed to death in his study, his body thrown out the window, mutilated, and then cast into the Seine. He was one of thousands killed over a period of a few days in Paris and then over several weeks as the violence spread beyond the city. This bloodletting came to be known as the St. Bartholomew's Day Massacre. The reason for the massacre was ostensibly a conflict between Catholics and Protestants. But it also had to do with court intrigue, mob violence, the settling of scores, and a sporadic civil war that had begun a decade earlier.[1] Ramus had become a Protestant around the same time as the civil war began. He grew up poor and as an adult worked as a servant and soldier. But at his death, Ramus was a well-known if controversial humanist scholar, mathematician, theologian, and philosopher. Ramus defined theology as teaching "the art of living well."[2] This also serves as a good summary of what ethics tries to teach. Just as the material of carpentry is wood, the material of ethics is the question of what it means to live well.

Ramus's work is little read today and there is nothing unique about the manner of his demise, since many suffer equally brutal deaths. Yet there is something emblematic about both. The pain-filled and contradictory space between Ramus's definition of theology and his death for having the wrong kind of theology is the place from which Christian moral and political reflection must now speak. For one thing, Ramus was a victim of the "wars of religion," which are consistently used to berate Christianity as at best hypocritical and at worst a source of evil. But beyond this polemical context, Christians must necessarily wrestle with what it means to proclaim the good news of Jesus Christ when that very proclamation has been allied with so much suffering and death. They must also ask what it means to pursue the art of living well in the midst of brutal chaos and oppression. And they have to think through how righteousness and justice can be pursued while keeping company with those who grieve.

Like Ramus, we live amid seismic changes. For example, the advent of the Internet and the increasing use of artificial intelligence are reshaping friendship, work, and politics, raising basic questions about the relationship between humans and technology. Similarly, the fundamental structures of life from DNA to the planet itself are being changed through human intervention, which generates existential questions about what it means to be human and how the relationship between humans and nature should be ordered. Crises caused by repeated flooding, fires, heatwaves, and pandemics demand that we reorganize our ways of life, while conflicts over moral, political, and religious differences are bitterly polarized and can turn violent at any moment. In such a context, the assumed ways of doing things no longer necessarily fit the world we live in. And as Ramus did in his day, many are now questioning long-established ways of doing things or challenging customary forms of belief and practice. At such inflection points, it is imperative to discern whether our moral intuitions and frames of reference are adequate for the new situation or whether they need recalibrating or even rejecting. This demands ethical deliberation.

The need for ethical reflection can be brought on by many kinds of change or conflict that generate a sense of crisis.[3] One is a shock, such as a natural disaster, which is beyond human making. A second is a shock, such as a financial or political crisis, which emerges from within human systems. A third are events or movements that convert what is chronic but normalized within existing systems – lack of affordable housing, poor schooling, mass incarceration, pollution – into a matter that needs to be urgently addressed. Other causes are more slow-burn processes involving gradual change, such as cross-cultural encounters generated by patterns of migration that provoke reflection on what we value and why. Is our attitude to certain clothing and behaviors (e.g., women wearing a burqa) based on moral disagreements or cultural differences? Are our judgments about those not like us based on claims about what is just, right, and good, or are they racist? Disagreement and friction leading to deeper questions also occur through changes within cultures and traditions. Christians are increasingly caught between what are taken to be Christian habits of belief and practice and prevailing norms in Western societies, especially as these societies become more plural. This dissonance necessarily provokes ethical debate and reflection. Debates over gender and sexuality are a good example: changes in the broader culture provoke questioning and revision in some churches even while other churches actively oppose these changes. As an introduction to Christian ethics, this book addresses the contemporary context in which conflict, crises, and fundamental changes abound.

Change is not the only prompt for ethical reflection. The reverse also takes place: ethical reflection can cause change. As in Ramus's day, any account of "living well" necessitates asking difficult questions about what needs to change in order to make life better. Asking questions about what needs to change is based on the realization that my life or the life of others is not all that it could be; to thrive, we will have to face head on the need to change. And this brings me to ask questions about, on the one hand, how to live truthfully and meaningfully in the midst of suffering, scarcity, and oppression; and on the other hand, to ask whether my well-being is built off the dispossession or oppression of others. If it is, then my life needs to radically change. To draw on scriptural motifs, ethical reflection necessitates asking what it means to live righteously in Babylon – *and* what it means to live righteously if it turns out we are the Babylonians. For in as much as we might identify with the prophets or a figure of liberation like Moses, we must also be ready to recognize ourselves as standing in the place of Pharoah.[4] As an overview of Christian ethics, this book takes up both standpoints.

WHY A PRIMER? AND WHY THIS PRIMER?

This book is born out of over twenty years' experience teaching introductory courses in Christian ethics on two sides of the Atlantic as well as running workshops for churches and organizations in various contexts on related topics. I try to distill here the ways of understanding Christian ethics that I've developed through preparing these courses and discussing the questions and perplexities around what it means to live a moral life that arise in either the classroom, the church hall, or the pub. It also emerges out of my involvement in and research on the intersection of Christianity and politics, extending my account of faithful witness by situating it within a broader understanding of ethics.

Overall, this book explores what it means for Christians to speak and act faithfully, hopefully, and lovingly in the contemporary Western context. It is written for people trying to work out what it means to live ethically amid the struggles and indignities of everyday life and the personal and political catastrophes and injustices that afflict those around us. I hope that what follows helps generate wisdom and passion for how to live well as moral and political animals who confess Jesus Christ as Lord while facing head on the difficulties and tragedies of this life.

A distinctive feature of the book is that it combines what is often held apart. First, it synthesizes moral and political theology, attending to how the ethical, economic, and political dimensions of living well go together and refract each other. In doing so, it positions political theology as a subspecies of Christian ethics.[5] Second, it draws on and integrates classic sources of Christian moral and political thought with contemporary liberationist and critical voices. Finally, it makes central how a moral life goes beyond the relationship we have with other human beings; how we relate to nonhuman ways of being alive is also fundamental. It is striking that none of the introductory texts I have used over the years make the relationship between human and nonhuman life a central focus. Rather than seeing nonhuman life as integral to every area of human moral and political existence, ecological ethics tends to be treated as a distinct question. Indeed, most introductory texts view the environment as either a platform on which humans perform their moral and political life or a resource for that life. This book disrupts such human-centered approaches and their long history in moral and political reflection. However, rather than being a book on environmental ethics, it situates ecological concerns within a broad introduction to how Christianity addresses fundamental questions about the nature and purpose of living a good life.

As a primer, this book provides vocabulary and concepts for ethical reflection: without the appropriate linguistic and conceptual tools, our ways of being alive cannot be described and analyzed in ethical terms. It also tells stories and gives examples that frame, make sense of, and exemplify a moral life. Ethical reflection involves telling stories about what it means to be human, what a good life involves, how and why moral failure occurs, and what evil looks like. These come in the form of myths, parables, testimonies, case studies, news reports, plays, novels, and films. I've chosen stories that help make sense of the world in ethical terms and enable us to narrate our own lives in morally coherent ways.

As a primer, this book is a kind of guide. Like any good guide, it narrates a landscape while at the same time charting a specific path. And so it presents a distinctive perspective and argument about the meaning and practices of a moral life. A primer can also refer to a devotional manual. This book comes under that heading as well, aiming to help the reader understand theologically what it means to speak and act together as moral and political animals and how such action contributes to worship and discipleship. It is also a primer in the chemical sense of the term: that is, a catalyst meant to spur wider reflection and engagement with moral and political questions. As such it is a first word. It does not cover the whole intellectual history of Christian moral and political reflection over several millennia. Nor does it speak to every contemporary issue or ethical concern. Nor can it cover every figure mentioned or question raised with the depth they invite. Rather, I aim to provide an initial orientation toward the difficult and costly pathway to discovering faithful, hopeful, and loving ways of being alive with the people and in the places where we live and move and have our being.

As a primer, the book contributes to a venerable and still vibrant stream of guides to living well. In the contemporary context, some turn to ancient philosophies such as Stoicism to provide a "school for life." Others look to indigenous sources of wisdom. And many turn to other religious traditions such as Buddhism or Islam for their guidance. Like all guides to living well, the frameworks of this book are specific to a particular tradition, and, from that starting point, it makes truth claims about what it means to thrive as a human. However, in the very particularity of its confession, the book also contributes to a wider dialogue of wisdoms about what it means to live well amid confusing and turbulent times.

WHAT IS CHRISTIAN ETHICS?

Dylann Roof walked into Emmanuel African Methodist Episcopal Church in Charleston on June 17, 2015, and murdered nine people while they met for Bible study and prayer. Their names were Cynthia Hurd, Clementa Pickney, Depayne Middleton-Doctor, Sharonda Coleman-Singleton, Susie Jackson, Myra Thompson, Tywanza Sanders, Daniel Simmons Sr., and Ethel Lance. Roof was a White supremacist who killed the congregants for being Black in the hopes of igniting a "race war." His actions were part of a long history and emerge out of wider cultural and institutional processes that produce racism and the ideology of White supremacy.

Roof's actions were evil and a moral response to them needs to name them as such and unambiguously condemn them along with the culture and systems they express. Ethics provides a focal language and set of categories for determining why and how Roof's actions were evil and establishing the parameters of a right response. At a more primal level, confronting a brutal death inflicted by another invokes a need for a vision of life unmarked by violence. Ethics brings such a vision to speech. How then should we hear the statements by many of the families of the victims at his bond hearing who forgave Roof and asked God to have mercy on his soul? Nadine Collier, the daughter of seventy-year-old Ethel Lance, said: "I forgive you. You took something very precious from me. I will never talk to her again. I will never, ever hold her again. But I forgive you. And have mercy on your soul. You hurt me, you hurt a lot of people, but I forgive you."[6] Collier was *not* exonerating, absolving, or letting Roof off the hook. But she did forgive him.[7] What did that mean? Was it just? Was it moral? What vision of life did it invoke?

I remember reading Collier's and the other statements at the time and feeling simultaneously shocked and full of wonder. I also found myself worrying about how they would be heard. My worries were confirmed as social media went berserk and op-ed columns flowed. Some pointed to the vexed matter of how forgiveness by Black folks helps perpetuate systemic racism by enabling White Americans to bypass their complicity in it.[8] However, while caught up in this dynamic, the words were neither reducible to this history nor nullified by it. Others said Roof could not be forgiven: what he did was unforgiveable.[9] These reactions point to how forgiveness is a strange and hard word to hear as a response to evil. The vision of life forgiveness speaks of is difficult to see and make sense of in a violent world. But forgiveness is an even harder word to say. Indeed, practicing love in the face of evil is the hardest of all things to do even as it raises disquieting moral and political questions. Yet making sense of, rendering legible, and advocating for such spiritually, emotionally, and physically costly gestures is the heart of Christian ethics, even as such words and actions cause confusion to some and revulsion to others, both within and without the church.

It may be jarring to introduce a book on Christian ethics with scenes of religious and racial terror. However, any ethic that claims the moniker "Christian" must begin with the life, death, and resurrection of Jesus Christ. And to do that is to reckon with the scriptural portrayal of God as revealed in one whose birth is marked by massacre and fugitivity, whose life is subject to imperial subjugation, whose ministry is under constant surveillance and physical threat, and whose death is one of brutal execution. Scenes of violence are the backdrop and foreground for Christian reflection on living well. It is the job of Christian ethics to reflect on and name what it takes to render sacred a world shaped and scared by such scenes. It brings to speech both the painful realities of crucifixion and the seemingly impossible possibility of crucifixion redeemed through resurrection.

At its core, Christian ethics is a way of naming the purpose and practice of living well, even in the most difficult circumstances and challenging times. To discover wisdom about how to live well takes careful reflection. Ethics is the name given to that process of reflection. Indeed, at its most basic, the term "ethics" refers to intentional and rigorous reflection on what it means to flourish as human beings in relationship with the world in which we participate. Another way to put this is to say that ethics is the formal mode of deliberation on morality, understood as the ways and means of living a good life with others over time. *Christian* ethics is born out of careful consideration of the meaning and purpose of life with God, with each other, and with the rest of creation, and how to live a life that is true to and directed toward this meaning and purpose. However, Christian ethics is not just about how to live a good life amid conditions of finitude and fallenness. It is also a mode of reflection on what it means to inhabit the Gospel. In giving an account of the moral life, it tries to take seriously with my body, energy, time, friendships, family, work, and every other aspect of what it means to be alive, the revelation that Christ has died, Christ has risen, and Christ will come again. Christian ethics is thus also about seeking holiness.

In this book, I use the term "Christian ethics" as a synonym for a cluster of other, parallel terms, each of which has a particular history of adoption, but which I take to be addressing the same set of concerns. These include moral theology, theological ethics, Christian social ethics, social theology, and, within certain frameworks, constructive theology, practical theology, and political theology. As formal modes of inquiry, all these terms can be distinguished from Christian discipleship. That said, reflection on living well cannot and should not be separated from matters of spirituality, worship, and pastoral care. This is an insight shared by ancient Greek and Roman philosophers, the authors of monastic rules, and those who penned penitential manuals. All emphasized the centrality of spiritual exercises to living a good life.[10] Aligned as it is with the pursuit of holiness, Christian ethics seeks to describe and communicate the form, character, and implications of Christian confession for different ways of being alive in specific contexts. In doing so, it combines questions of biblical interpretation, doctrine, mission, ecclesiology, liturgy, pastoral care, and everyday practice; in other words, it concerns the work of the church. Christian ethics is then a form of theology – and despite academic divisions, there can be no hard and fast distinction between Christian ethics and other aspects of theology. But, echoing Ramus's definition, it is theology dense with the lives of people trying to live well, in all their wonder, frailty, and folly. As theology with the people in it, it is faith seeking practical wisdom about how to love God, neighbor, and all creation over time with others.

A basic assumption of Christian ethics is that a true, good, or flourishing life cannot be reduced to individual happiness. We are not individual atoms bouncing against each other but mutually vulnerable, interdependent creatures. We cannot survive without others. And to thrive depends on being embedded in some kind of loving and just form of common life. Our individual flourishing is symbiotic with the flourishing of a wider ecology of human and nonhuman relations.[11] As already suggested, a Christian account of "living well" must also reckon with how flourishing in this age before Christ's return is always in some sense wounded and ambiguous. Our ability to live well is inevitably cobbled together amid asymmetries of power, histories of harm, and the looming presence of wickedness and evil.

A key scriptural term for flourishing is *shalom*. This is a Hebrew word that denotes wholeness, prosperity, peace, well-being, and a state of blessing for the community as a whole, including the soil, plants, and animals with whom humans share a life.[12] Shalom is the bringing to fruitfulness of creation, whose sheer existence God declares "very good" (Gen 1:31).[13] By implication, a truly good, meaningful, shalom-like way of living cannot be one built on the domination and exploitation of others or of the rest of creation. Therefore, to ask "what is the good life?" or "what does it mean to live well?" necessitates asking about the interpersonal, structural, ecological, and spiritual conditions of human flourishing – that is, how we may participate rightly and truthfully in relationship with God, other humans (both like and unlike us), and the rest of creation – and what institutions and practices enable such participation to be fruitful in a context shaped by idolatry and sin. Answering such questions is at once a theological and practical matter.

Christian ethics asks about the nature and form of the flourishing or shalom-like life in the light of the life, death, resurrection, and ascension of Jesus Christ. On a theological account, to inhabit the cosmos fruitfully, we must be transformed so as to participate in Christ more fully. However, such transformation does not give rise to only one way of life. Rather, it generates myriad ways of being alive, each with their own way of bearing witness to reality as structured and ordered in and through Christ, the one through whom all things are made and in whom all things are reconciled to God.

The temptation for Christians is to ask questions about how everyone else but themselves are trying to live well. Yet Scripture teaches the difficult truth that God's judgment comes first and foremost to the people of God. So, to be faithful, Christians must ask hard questions about what it means to be church and whether or not Christians are really embodying love and justice. This necessitates reckoning with the question of what it means for the church, if it is to be a faithful witness, to think its existence against itself. We have to address the complicity and centrality of Christianity in the formation of bad and evil ways of shaping life with others, such as systems of industrial extraction, colonialism, and slavery. In other words, we have to reckon with the ways in which Christianity not only betrays its own best insights but is often its own worst enemy. This is always the condition of the people of God. Membership demands wrestling with sin, idolatry, and complicity in the creation of systems and histories of domination and abuse. Exodus is a response to the crisis brought on by Joseph, who designed the very system of debt bondage that Israel needed liberation from. The prophets arise to condemn the religio-political system that was set up to enable the people to keep the covenant. Jesus calls out the whitewashed sepulchers of his day whose earnest prescriptions for holiness are revealed to be complicit in systems of oppression. As the genealogy of Matthew's Gospel makes clear, God's Word comes to us through fallible and fallen people and from often horrific sources that include sexual violence, deception, war, mass deportation, and betrayal. Christian ethics continues this response, offering fragile, contingent words of faith, hope, and love amid the still smoldering ashes of history. But, like Nadine Collier's word of forgiveness, such words can be difficult to hear and even more difficult to say. Moreover, there is a specific responsibility for Western Christians to reckon with what it means to be part of a history that generated the particular ways our current world worships death and curses that which gives life.

THE TASKS OF CHRISTIAN ETHICS

Christian ethics involves three primary tasks. First, it develops ways of understanding what is going on in the context of a specific form of life (e.g., being American) and/or in an area of concern (e.g., medicine) and/or in relation to a particular problem (e.g., care of the suffering and dying).[14] Second, it offers wisdom for how to act faithfully, hopefully, and lovingly in response to a specific form of life, area of concern, or issue. This wisdom contributes to displaying what a Christian vision of human flourishing entails as situated in and attuned to a particular context. In doing so, it also displays the practical reasoning needed to judge why this rather than that action better inhabits such a vision. Third, it gives an account of what it means to live well with others in this time and place and what needs to change in order to make such a life possible.

This threefold task involves assembling the resources through which we may understand better what is going on (i.e., what we are currently doing and what we are trying to achieve when we speak and act together as moral and political animals). It also entails discerning and communicating ways in which Christians might bear witness to what the healing and fulfillment of a specific form of life or area of concern might entail. The most common ways of going about these tasks involve interpreting the Scriptures, excavating the social and intellectual histories of the Christian tradition and its contexts of formation, and analyzing the "signs of the times" through engaging diverse philosophical frameworks, theoretical critiques, literary and artistic works, and forms of scientific analysis and social scientific descriptions (e.g., anthropology, sociology, economics, etc.). All these are drawn on in an ad hoc way to give an account of what is going on, form the basis for coming to a judgment about what to do and how to do it, and advocate for particular ways of organizing life together. The focus can be either the everyday, such as how we grow our food, what counts as food, and with whom we should eat; a vehemently contested issue like abortion; or a structural and systemic condition such as capitalism. As a mode of reflection, ethics is not a science but an art. As an art, its proper measure is its capacity to illuminate our moral and political experience and commitments – a somewhat diffuse object of analysis – and how these do or don't connect to our descriptions of who God is and who we are in relation to God.

It makes a difference where ethical analysis begins from: with theory or practice; from an elite, top-down perspective or that of the marginalized; with the church or the world. The approach I lay out in this book is committed to a way of knowing that begins with reflecting on existing forms of life and their histories of formation: that is, with putting practice before theory. But not over and against theory. Rather, it is a question of putting first things first. Stated technically, I advocate a more inductive than deductive approach to moral reasoning. The basis of this approach is an incarnational understanding of truth: the truths of revelation are participative events and relationships to be encountered and inhabited and not things or ideas to be possessed. Moreover, the accuracy of our apprehension of God's self-revelation in Jesus Christ is not, ultimately, verified by whether we espouse this or that statement of faith or dogma but by the quality and depth of our love of God and neighbor.

This brings me to a broader point: political and moral judgments are discovered, not made. We do not impose meaning on the world by an act of will. The universe is not a blank slate passively waiting to receive the meaning humans assign it. Rather, it is pregnant with the meanings and purposes given creation by God. Just as our participation in friendships precedes and is the basis of our accounts of it, so we discover the meanings and purposes of creatureliness through a process of participating in and naming them. This discovery and articulation take place in and through the interlaced pathways, places, relationships, and events that form us. It is through this meshwork of physical, biotic, social, and spiritual relations, and the communicative webs between them, that we hear and respond to the Word of God. Moreover, we are constituted through this lifeworld: it generates us and we help generate it in an ongoing process of communication.

On this kind of account, we do not develop a concept of friendship that is then either applied to people we meet or merely demonstrated by the friendships we form. Rather, friendship is a social reality God makes possible that we in turn discover together with others, how we name it emerging through that discovery in an iterative way. Likewise, we cannot try to get our theology or worldview straight in the abstract and then apply it to the world around us. Nor can we begin with the church, as if the church is a distinct social reality wholly separate from the world. Nor can we investigate the world using social science and then reflect on that "reality" theologically, as if theology was a wholly second order activity and the world had an autonomous existence independent of the flow of divine communication and the ongoing historical impact of Christian institutions and practices. Rather, reflection on God and reflection on social and political life, and the implications of one for the other, emerge together as we discover their reality through participating in both. For example, the New Testament writers drew on political terms to articulate what it meant to be the church: the Greek word *ekklēsia*, which came to mean "church," originally meant a political assembly. This and many other political terms proved crucial to saying something about the nature and form of divine-human relations. Conversely, participation in ecclesial practices enabled new kinds of moral and political judgment to be made, generating new understandings of what it means for humans to flourish: in Christ, we become citizens of the kingdom of God and thereby relativize all earthly political identities. It is a task of Christian ethics to display how talk of God and talk of moral and political life are mutually constitutive and refract each other, and how, for better or worse, this interrelationship shapes *both* the church and the world.

In recognition of the fallen and fallible nature of human knowledge about what is true, good, and beautiful, a condition of ethical reflection is cultivating humility. Too often, however, attempts to do ethics are expressions of pride. They are born out of a desire to either establish an inerrant answer or create a one-size-fits-all blueprint for moral rectitude. Neither of these approaches ever begin by asking what is going on. This is not only foolhardy; it degrades ethics into a mode of social control. By contrast, a properly Christian ethics begins with the attempt to discover *with others* what God is doing *today*. If that process of discovery is to be faithful rather than foolish, it entails rendering ourselves vulnerable to God and neighbor. When we deploy strategies of invulnerability and coercive control, we refuse to discover and bear witness to what the Spirit is doing among these people in this place. Instead, we have predetermined what a moral life looks like, overidentifying it with one specific cultural form or historical set of experiences. Such a move denies how loss, vulnerability, and lack of control are central to the experience of acting faithfully, lovingly, and hopefully with and for others. Instead of rendering ourselves invulnerable through predetermined ethical checklists that put our ideological programs before the lives and loves of the people around us, we must find ways to identify with Christ and thereby disidentify with the idols and systems of domination with which we are entangled. Hence the need for humility: the disposition that allows space and time for God and neighbor to communicate, each in their own way, and for ourselves to act from "sober judgment" (Romans 12:3).

We are always already participating in the reality of God's creation and its eschatological fulfillment; the question is the extent to which our lives and actions are in tune with and bear witness to this participation. Part of being a human creature situated in a reality we did not make is that we don't choose or control either the hour we are born; the political economy we live in; or the values, languages, and landscapes that shape our existence. We can respond to these realities in a number of ways. We can deny the reality of where we find ourselves, retreating from it into an enclave of our choosing, constructing a small world that reflects things we like and keeping out the things and people we don't like. We can accommodate ourselves to the world we find ourselves within, simply going with the flow and conforming to its ways. Or we can confront what is going on, refusing its inevitability while discerning what is good and what is bad, what needs abolishing and what needs recovering, saying yes to this and no to that as we figure out how to live well with others in the midst of where we find ourselves and the evils we confront. This book takes this last approach.

In summary, I take the task of Christian ethics to be threefold and have organized the book around these three elements. Part I is about listening to and describing the world around us, exploring how we cannot act in a world that we cannot describe. The act of naming, describing, or giving an account of what is going on is not neutral. Rather, description inherently entails evaluation, and any evaluation reflects certain commitments (albeit often tacit or implied) about what it means to live well. Moreover, for description itself to be moral, it must meet certain conditions. So Part I examines a Christian understanding of what it means to describe the world in moral terms and how that process of description itself can be accountable and moral by listening to creation, Scripture, strangers, those crying out for liberation, and ancestors – Christian or otherwise. I contend that rather than the more familiar appeals to the modern "quadrilateral" of revelation, reason, experience, and tradition, it is a combination of these expanded points of reference that are the primary sources of authority from which to derive judgments about right and wrong.

In relation to the widely used quadrilateral, it is neither clear what is meant by each term, what to do with them, nor how they can be distinguished from each other. For example, revelation, reason, and experience are not independent variables that can separated out from tradition. Rather, they are each part of and conditioned by traditions of belief and practice that shape how to understand and make use of them in theological reflection on moral matters. Or to take another example, citing experience as a ground of authority inevitably raises questions about whose experiences count (the privileged or the marginalized? The individual or the community?) and what kind of experience is relevant (historical or personal? Spiritual, physical, or emotional?). In addition to these questions, there are hotly contested debates in philosophy and psychology about what is meant by the term experience and theological debates about whether experience is the basis of revelation or whether revelation necessarily overturns experience, which as inherently sinful cannot guide moral discernment. In contrast, while there is much overlap, the sources of authority discussed here are more immediately identifiable, distinct, and able to be acted on. They are also more theologically cogent.

Doing Christian ethics does not just involve listening to and then describing reality so we can rightly orientate ourselves in relation to the world around us. It also requires making a judgment about what to do and how to do it in order to live well. This entails discerning how, when, and where to act alongside evaluating the form, character, and purpose of such action. So Part II reflects on what is to be done by examining the personal, social, ecological, and spiritual conditions of moral agency. This entails reflecting on the means through which we judge and act well – namely, commands, rules, virtues, and practical wisdom – alongside what inhibits or wrecks our capacity to judge and act well – namely, sin, idolatry, and evil.

Doing ethics cannot just focus on individual speech and action. It must also reflect on how our forms of life give rise to structures and systems that either build up or break down human and ecological flourishing. In short, being moral is always already a social, political, economic, and ecological task as much as it is a personal one; with this in mind, Part III addresses the question of how to live well with others over time. Ethics must articulate an understanding of the character, quality, and purpose of the intimate, material, and political relationships needed to form moral communities in which the flourishing of each is interdependent with the flourishing of all, especially the weak and vulnerable and the ecologies from which life itself is woven.

Parts I, II, and III of the book follow the basic questions philosophers and theologians have always asked when reflecting on the nature of the moral life, namely, what is going on? What is to be done? And how should we live together? But this division is a heuristic one. In practice, the three tasks of Christian ethics are interwoven. In being called to love God and neighbor (which includes loving both human and other kinds of creatures) we must reflect on the reality we encounter and participate in, listening well by asking what is going on. We must deliberate toward a moment of action with these people, in this place, at this time, asking what is to be done. And we must come to a judgment about what actions will contribute to forming and sustaining more just and loving forms of common life with others by asking how we should live together.[15] In asking these questions, we discover ways of answering the basic question ethics asks, namely, what is the good life. These three questions are thereby a curriculum for learning the "art of living well."

NOTES

1 Barbara Diefendorf, *The Saint Bartholomew's Day Massacre: A Brief History with Documents* (Boston: Bedford/St Martin's, 2009), 1–36.

2 "*Theologia est doctrina bene vivendi.*" Petri Rami, *Commentariorum de religione Christiana. Libri quatuor* (Frankfurt: A. Wechel, 1576), 6.

3 My use of "crisis" draws on an older definition of the term that means both a point of decision and a judgment. This usage draws on its Latin and Greek meaning and is found in the New Testament (e.g., Luke 11:32; John 3:19).

4 Karl Barth, *The Epistle to the Romans*, trans., Edwyn C. Hoskyns (New York: Oxford University Press, 1968 [1933]), 353.

5 In many ways this book can be read as a companion to Luke Bretherton, *Christ and the Common Life: Political Theology and the Case for Democracy* (Grand Rapids, MI: Eerdmans, 2019).

6 *The Guardian*, June 19, 2015. www.theguardian.com/world/2015/jun/19/charleston-south-carolina-shooting-dylann-roof-victims-statements (accessed July 15, 2021).

7 For a discussion of what was meant by this statement and the array of responses expressed by the victims' families other than forgiveness, see Herb Frazer, Bernard Edward Powers, and Marjory Wentworth, *We Are Charleston: Tragedy and Triumph at Mother Emmanuel* (Nashville, TN: Thomas Nelson, 2016), 163–177.

8 See, for example, Kiese Laymon, "Black Churches Taught Us to Forgive People. We Learned to Shame Ourselves," *The Guardian*, June 23, 2015, www.theguardian.com/commentisfree/2015/jun/23/black-churchesforgive-white-people-shame.

9 See, for example, Roxane Gay, "Why I Can't Forgive Dylann Roof," *New York Times*, June 23, 2015, www.nytimes.com/2015/06/24/opinion/why-i-cant-forgive-dylann-roof.html.

10 See Pierre Hadot, *Philosophy as a Way of Life: Spiritual Exercises from Socrates to Foucault*, trans., Michael Chase (Oxford: Blackwell, 1995).

11 "Flourishing" as a term in moral and political thought is taken up by a wide spectrum of thinkers, ancient and modern. These range from contemporary ecological and feminist philosophers such as Donna Harraway, Alexis Shotwell, and Chris Cuomo to figures from the Christian tradition, such as Thomas Aquinas. My usage of the term draws from across this spectrum.

12 Alongside *shalom* can be put *tsedaqah* (righteousness) and *yeshu'ah* (salvation), which combine to signify a intricate notion of creational flourishing.

13 Much hangs on whether this proclamation of goodness is understood to mean that all that is good is already given at the point of origin and

disclosed over time (it is protological) or whether this proclamation is eschatological such that the goodness of creation is only realized at the eschatological fulfillment of time (it is teleological).

14 Tacit here is H. Richard Niebuhr's admonition that the first question of Christian ethics is "What is going on?" See *The Responsible Self: An Essay in Christian Moral Philosophy* (New York: Harper & Row, 1963), 60–61. See also Stanley Hauerwas, *Peaceable Kingdom: A Primer in Christian Ethics* (Notre Dame: University of Notre Dame Press, 1983), 102.

15 How I develop this framework has decidedly Protestant accents; that said, it overlaps and resonates with the "see, judge, act" approach initially developed by Joseph Cardijn (1882–1967), the Belgian Cardinal and founding figure of the democratic movement, Catholic Action. Cardijn's approach has its roots in Thomistic moral theology and was adopted into Catholic social teaching as a way to frame the relationship between theology and practice (*Mater et Magistra* [1961], #236), and provided the basis for Vatican II's influential "Pastoral Constitution on the Church in the Modern World" (*Gaudium et spes*, 1964). It also directly influenced the threefold paradigm developed by Latin American Liberation Theology, and subsequently *Mujerista* theology, of becoming aware of reality, taking responsibility for reality, and transforming reality. See for example, Ignacio Ellacuría, *Ignacio Ellacuría: Essays on History, Liberation, and Salvation*, ed., Michael E. Lee (Maryknoll, NY: Orbis, 2013), 80; and Ada María Isasi-Díaz, *La Lucha Continues: Mujerista Theology* (Maryknoll, NY: Orbis, 2004), 98–101. As will become apparent, there are parallels and overlap between this latter approach and the one developed in this book.

PART I Describing Well

A dear friend who had stage four cancer told me how few, if any, of her friends and family were prepared to take the time to listen to what she was going through and enter into the reality of her situation. Existing as she did on a precipice between life and death, she felt alone and unheard. Instead of listening, friends and family rushed to offer either platitudes or crazy cures (eating kale being a memorable one) or find reasons that explained away what was going on and thereby dissolved their own dis-ease. Her situation demanded paying attention to what was actually going on, however uncomfortable or bewildering it was. I struggled. It is difficult – indeed, it is a work of faith, hope, and love – to confront the perplexities and tragedies of a human life head-on or absorb unsettling truths about ourselves, what (or whom) we cherish, and the world we live in. Rather than choose delusion as a strategy of avoidance, faithful witness calls us to bear with reality as a prelude to its transformation. And that begins with listening.

To truly engage in a process of listening to discern what is going on is challenging. It is often even harder to abide with and respond faithfully to the reality discerned, as many times we don't like what we hear. As we see around us today, rather than confront the truth, it is easier to turn to the fantastical in the form of conspiracy theories, or find solace in reductive and often highly polarized pictures of the world, or make bad faith arguments that swap difficult truths for pleasing falsehoods, or lose ourselves in one of the myriad technologies of distraction that compete for our attention. Yet taking the time to listen is vital if we are to describe what is really going on and tell the truth about ourselves and the world we live in.

Listening is foundational for how we come to be as moral and political animals. However, prioritizing listening does not exclude the other senses. Rather, we are, in one sense, "all ears." Listening is a physiological and material process, not just a mental one. It witnesses to an orientation of openness, reception, and attunement to God and creation, an orientation that can involve each of our five senses. Encountering God and neighbor is as much about what and how we touch, smell, taste, and see as it is about how we listen.[1] So I am using listening as a metaphor and symbol for those actions and modes of attention – for example, savoring and beholding – and dispositions – for example, humility – that enable loving attunement to be realized, and which in turn enable more generative ways of inhabiting and bearing witness to reality.[2] Listening is a stand in for the kind of open hearted attention that is a prelude to good action.

That said, there is a theological case to be made that listening has a symbolic priority. Listening should be the most basic act for the people of God. God's address – the Word – is heard before it is read, seen, smelled, or touched. The opening of John's Gospel – "In the beginning was the Word" – alerts us to how creation is born out of an act of communication we must hear before we can respond. Through hearing and responding, the Word becomes our flesh. The fourth-century theologian and bishop, Ambrose of Milan, echoes this primacy of hearing in relation to the formation of the people of God. Quoting the *Shema* (Deut 6:4–6), which is the fundamental prayer of Israel, Ambrose exhorts: "The law says: Hear, O Israel, the Lord thy God.' It said not: 'Speak,' but 'Hear' .... Be silent therefore first of all, and hearken, that thou fail not in thy tongue."[3] This initiatory act of listening forms the people of God and models the way Christians are to relate to each other and the rest of creation. The philosopher Simone Weil draws out the importance of listening as fundamental to being orientated rightly to others and the world around us when she says: "The effort which brings the soul to salvation is like the effort of looking and listening."[4] Weil understands attention as a paradoxical stance of receptive attunement or "passive activity," the quality of which form us as persons capable of receiving grace.

Weil's insight is echoed by the German theologian and martyr, Dietrich Bonhoeffer. Bonhoeffer exhorts us to realize that:

> The first service one owes to others in the community involves listening to them. Just as our love of God begins with listening to God's Word, the beginning of love for other Christians is learning to listen to them. God's love for us is shown by the fact that God not only gives us God's Word, but also lends us God's ear. We do God's work for our brothers and sisters when we learn to listen to them.[5]

For Bonhoeffer, listening with the "ears of God" is the necessary precursor to being able to proclaim the Word of God because those who do not listen to others, or who presume to already know what the other person has to say, will soon no longer listen to God.[6] Moreover, as Ambrose, Weil, and Bonhoeffer indicate, listening is not just an individual act but also a communal, ecclesial one. The church hears the call of God and neighbor, then responds by way of its life together.

Listening is not just a theologically pregnant act. It is also a moral gesture. It is a refusal to treat others merely as *biology* that I make use of for my own benefit and instead responds to others as having a *biography*. Those before me are people who have meaning and purpose, a story to tell, and a voice independent of me that needs to be heard and responded to. In sum, listening is vital to deepening our moral conversion in relation to God and neighbor and thus our ability to discover the right or just judgment to be made with these people, at this time, in this place.

Who or what do we listen to in order to rightly hear what is going on and thereby discern how to respond rightly? The answer I give here is that in Christian ethics it is imperative that we listen to creation, Scripture, strangers, those crying out for liberation, and our ancestors. Together these sources help us discover who we are, where we have come from, and where we are going (and thereby describe reality). They are marker points through which we find our moral bearings. Extending Ambrose, Weil, and Bonhoeffer, in what follows I explore how listening to creation, Scripture, strangers, the oppressed, and our ancestors enables discernment of who is the neighbor to be loved and how to contribute to and uphold where we find ourselves as a common world in which all may flourish. In the process, we discover what it means to hear and respond to the Word of God in tangible and granular ways.

If listening is the first gesture in becoming morally orientated, it is not the last one. Having first listened, we must then name what is going on, giving language to what we hear. As with listening, how we name things or people is itself a moral act. It makes all the difference in the world to name someone as a combatant or a civilian, an illegal alien or an asylum seeker, a rioter or a protester. Each description calls forth a different response. Description is both a way of morally categorizing something or someone and determining how to respond appropriately.[7] The reverse is also true. George Orwell, in his dystopian novel *1984*, portrays a society in which state authorities intentionally strip language of its descriptive power, replacing everyday terms with "newspeak" – a reduced and truncated way of talking with a very limited vocabulary. As a result, certain ways of naming the world and ways of being human become unimaginable and thence unintelligible. In contrast to "newspeak," ethics is a way of enriching how we name human experience, bringing to speech and rendering imaginable and legible ways to live well. As Orwell clearly saw, our descriptions and narratives situate us in particular geographies and histories and in relation to others in distinctive ways. How we describe the world sets the stage for moral agency: the ability to act and the kind of action that is called forth depends on how we describe an issue or problem. So alongside setting out who and what is to be listened to in order to tell the truth about ourselves and the world, Part I examines how the ways we name and narrate that world can affect the quality and character of our moral life.

NOTES

1 Encounter really does involve all the senses even if many contemporary Christians tend to privilege sight and hearing. For a historical example of the place of smell in fostering a Christian moral and political imaginary, see Susan Ashbrook Harvey, *Scenting Salvation: Ancient Christianity and the Olfactory Imagination* (Los Angeles: University of California Press, 2006).

2 By positing the ethical subject as one who listens, I depart from a modern focus on the ethical subject as either one who speaks or communicates well (Jürgen Habermas, Stanley Cavell), or who sees well (Iris Murdoch, Stanley Hauerwas), or a variation of seeing, notably, one who recognizes the other (Emmanuel Levinas, Paul Ricoeur, Charles Taylor). Likewise, a focus on listening departs from a critical focus on ocular forms of domination, notably the panopticon and surveillance (Michel Foucault), the spectacle (Guy Debord), and the male gaze (Laura Mulvey).

3 Ambrose, "On the Duties of the Clergy," *Nicene and Post-Nicene Fathers, Second Series*, vol. X, eds., Philip Schaff and Henry Wace, trans., H. De Romestein (Edinburgh: T&T Clark, 1989), 2. Ambrose directly connects listening and "active silence" to faithful witness and the building up of the church.

4 Simone Weil, *Waiting for God* (New York: HarperPerennial, 2009), 126.

5 Dietrich Bonhoeffer, *Life Together*, ed., Geffrey Kelly, trans., Daniel Bloesch and James Burtness, *Dietrich Bonhoeffer Works*, vol. 5 (Minneapolis, MN: Fortress Press, 1996), 98.

6 Bonhoeffer, *Life Together*. For Bonhoeffer, the practice of confession best embodies the importance of listening because it positions Christians toward each other and toward the world as forgiven sinners, that is, as those who have been freed to serve and bear with each other and their neighbors from a position of humility and hope (108–118).

7 Description involves combinations of stories, categories, concepts, distinctions, propositions, and identifying characteristic features. I tend to use description as an overarching term but on occasion distinguish between narrative and description in recognition of how, as Oliver O'Donovan puts it: "Narrative presents reality as events in time, description presents it as formal relations. The two depend on each other." Oliver O'Donovan, *Entering into Rest: Ethics as Theology*, vol. 3 (Grand Rapids, MI: Eerdmans, 2017), 171.

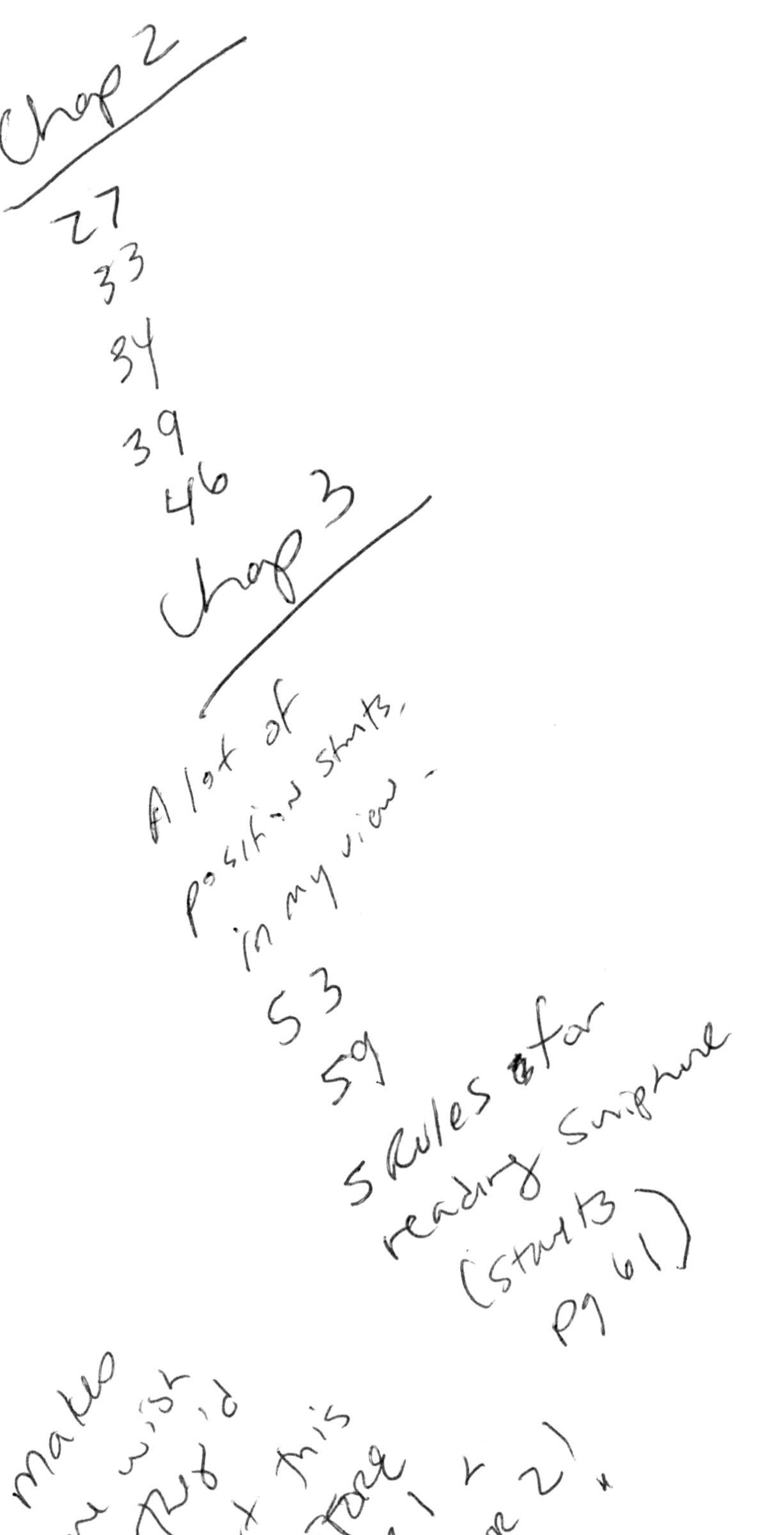
Chap 2
27
33
34
39
46
Chap 3
A lot of positive stmts, in my view.
53
59
5 Rules for reading Scripture (starts pg 61)
makes me wish I'd put this BEFORE YR 1 & YR 2!

2 Listening to Creaturely Life

James Rebanks's grandfather took pride in the careful way he watched and judged what was occurring each day with the land and livestock he farmed. Rebanks writes that when his grandfather stood looking over a gate, "he was figuring these things out by close and thoughtful observation." In a meditation on the changing nature of the relationship British farmers have with the land they till and the animals they keep, Rebanks notes that this kind of deep attention is disappearing. "Managing animals the traditional way required specialist knowledge and judgment, and skilled people to care for them and understand their needs." In an age of factory farming, such expertise "didn't scale up easily for mass production." As Rebanks puts it:

> Animals came in different sizes and shapes, and they matured at different times. Farmers slaughtered, preserved and cooked animal meat when it was available and ready, not every week. It was all a long way from the factory ideal of identical commodities all being ready for the shops at the same time. So, incredibly, farm animals had been made more uniform.[1]

Rebanks summarizes the heart of what this chapter argues. Like Rebanks's grandfather, we learn how to describe the world we are living in through "close and thoughtful observation." We must listen to and learn from creation if we are to know how to live well with and within it. Going beyond Rebanks, I contend that in listening to creation we can also learn something of what it means to be in right relationship with the Creator because in listening to creation, we hear from God. God's communication in and through creation is the basis of the world we discover ourselves inhabiting. Yet we are caught up in systems and structures that do not listen. Instead, they remake the world so it can be controlled and managed to suit human desires. In doing so, they turn us away from both God and creation. My contention is that ethical reflection begins with taking time to listen to creation.

Many cultures throughout history have a sense that a flourishing life involves living in some kind of attunement to, and reciprocal relationship with, nature. They believed that to go against the rhythms and cycles of the earth and moon and to ignore how we inhabit a shared world with animals and plant life was a recipe for disaster. As the American agrarian writer and poet, Wendell Berry (b. 1934), puts it: "The idea is variously stated: we should not work until we have looked and seen where we are; we should honor Nature not only as our mother or grandmother, but as our teacher and judge."[2] There is a deep wisdom in this insight. Sustaining life requires careful attention to the environmental conditions and relations that make life possible. However, part of our current predicament is that we inhabit forms of life engineered to seek mastery over nature and other species, rather than live in a reciprocal, mutually adaptive relation with them. Like intensive factory farming, such an orientation ignores how we need certain kinds and quality of relation with the places we inhabit to flourish. Most obviously there is the need for breathable air, clean water, nourishing food, secure shelter, and regular means of warmth. If what makes these possible are destroyed or rendered toxic, we cannot survive let alone thrive. But as humans, we also need more intangible goods such as intimacy and a sense of meaning and purpose. Ethical descriptions should seek to hear and then name the reality of what it takes to participate in nature – or what, in a Christian lexicon, should always be called "creation" – in ways that promote flourishing.

Scripture asks us to contemplate creation in order to understand the ways of the Lord. To take but one instance, Paul's speech depicted in Acts 14:17 frames nature itself – the rains and seasons – as a witness to God, a witness to be learned from. Building on this kind of injunction, early theologians such as Origen, Gregory of Nyssa, Augustine, and Maximus the Confessor envisaged *both* the Bible *and* nature as arenas of divine address. Each was best read and understood in dialogue with the other so as to attain knowledge of and communion with the triune Creator and rightly participate in the divine economy of creation.[3] Knowing God through Scripture requires learning from creation and knowing creation truly necessitates coming to know God revealed in Scripture. This interplay continued with cathedral builders who combined scriptural and natural imagery in their architecture to reveal the glory of God, manuscript illustrators who drew nature to open out Scripture, and was given voice by medieval mystics like Hildegard of Bingen and the tradition of Hexaemeral sermons on the six days of creation. It continues today in the work modern poets like Jane Kenyon and agrarian writers like Berry and Ronald Blythe. As Pope Francis puts it, echoing both St. Francis and Romans 1:20, to be faithful to Scripture is to be invited to see nature "as a magnificent book in which God speaks to us and grants us a glimpse of his infinite beauty and goodness."[4]

If anything, the call of God in creation comes first.[5] And as with the text of Scripture, the call of God is inseparable from how creation itself speaks in its own voice. As will be seen in Chapter 3, there are parallels between how both creation and Scripture should be heard. Listening to Scripture is not first and foremost about finding the right technique for interpreting the text but cultivating forms of contemplation that shape us and our ecclesial communities so as to be able to read the world around us as a labor of love through which Christ and the Holy Spirit are at work. Listening to creation involves much the same dynamic. Rather than see nature as a resource to be turned into commodities, it entails ways of attending to and participating in creation so we recognize the nonhuman as a fellow worshipper of God.

BEYOND THE NATURE-CULTURE BINARY

A key theme in the dominant modern stories told about the relationship between humans and nature is that nature is something wholly distinct from culture. Indeed, modern understandings of nature tend to operate with a binary division between nature and culture, assuming that to become fully human we must transcend "nature" by freeing ourselves from its limits. Culture is the overcoming of nature. We see this played out in the use of technology and science as a means to transcend the limits of time and space through faster travel, drugs to help us think better, and phones that can be used anywhere to communicate with anyone at any time. From a theological perspective, however, the vital distinction to be made is neither between nature and culture, nor between what is material and what is spiritual, but between creation and Creator. One thing we see happen in modernity, and what in many ways makes modern life plausible and possible, is that culture comes to be understood as the realm subject to human determination. Conversely, nature becomes seen as that which we can't change or is beyond control (an ever shrinking area). This is an oppositional and binary conception of the distinction between nature and culture. In such a conception culture is not about enabling humans to participate in and fructify creation. Instead of culture being a means of cultivation it becomes a mode of extraction.

Many premodern conceptions of the cosmos entail a sense that the world around us provides meaning to those who participate in it and has ends we must attend to if we are to flourish. A good example are natural law frameworks developed by ancient Greek and Roman philosophers and then extended by Jewish, Christian, and Islamic thinkers. In such an approach, the "book of nature" is "read" to glean wisdom about what it means to live well.[6] Part of the shift into the modern period was a rejection of this kind of approach to ethics. In its place the cosmos came to be understood in mechanistic, wholly material, and morally neutral terms. Understood in those terms, it cannot disclose to us any sense of how we should live. Indeed, instead of the world around us giving us a sense of meaning and value, we ascribe meaning and value to it. The cosmos is now a universe: that is, a flat, meaningless, and inert thing on which we impose meaning. Most modern ethical frameworks assume this way of describing the world, operating as they do within a form of philosophical naturalism.

They work with a fact-value distinction and envisage ethics as about imposing meaning and value on a morally neutral universe (a realm of facts) that in and of itself can reveal nothing about how to live well and sets no limits to what humans can or cannot do to nature. This is the ethical equivalent of the shift from how Rebanks's grandfather viewed the animals he observed to the way factory farming treats animals. Within such frameworks, there is no need to listen to nature so as to learn how to live well. Nature is merely a resource that humans instrumentalize to fuel their moral and political lives. "It" has no intrinsic or divine meanings and purposes to be discovered. Those who invest in this approach justify it as the means by which we free ourselves from nature (understood as meaningless matter) and thereby gain freedom from necessity. Science and technology are then deployed in order to transcend nature, which is understood as a realm of unfreedom.

Tragically, by asserting our freedom over and against creation we end up destroying ourselves. The German sociologist, Ulrich Beck, identifies this dynamic as one whereby the means that were meant to alleviate and free humans from necessity (industrialization, science, urbanization, capitalism, bureaucracy, etc.) become the main sources of hazard and risk that threaten the very basis of human life. At the micro level, we see this danger in the way antibiotic drugs that have facilitated industrial scale farming have also led to strains of microbes resistant to antibiotics. At the macro level, we find it in climate change, nuclear and biological warfare, and zoonosis leading to pandemics. The ecological crisis is central to the development of Beck's work, which was in part inspired by the Chernobyl nuclear reactor disaster in 1986.[7] His work points to how our anthropocentric and technocratic quest for freedom *from* nature becomes the basis for cataclysmic forms of self-destruction and, at a more prosaic level, our alienation from and wholly extractive relationship with the natural world.

The reality is that contrary to philosophical and scientific naturalism, humans do not impose meaning on the world by an act of will. The universe is not a blank slate. Rather, we discover the world and its meanings and purposes through immersion in the interlaced pathways, places, patterns of life, and events that form our lifeworld. We are like fish in the sea: we are immersed in an environment on which we depend. It is the water we swim in, which flows through us, and in which we flow. Poison the water and we die. Frameworks that suggest we stand over and above nature are a fantasy. Our lifeworld, our judgments, and our visions of the good emerge in and through relations *with* nonhuman ways of being alive.

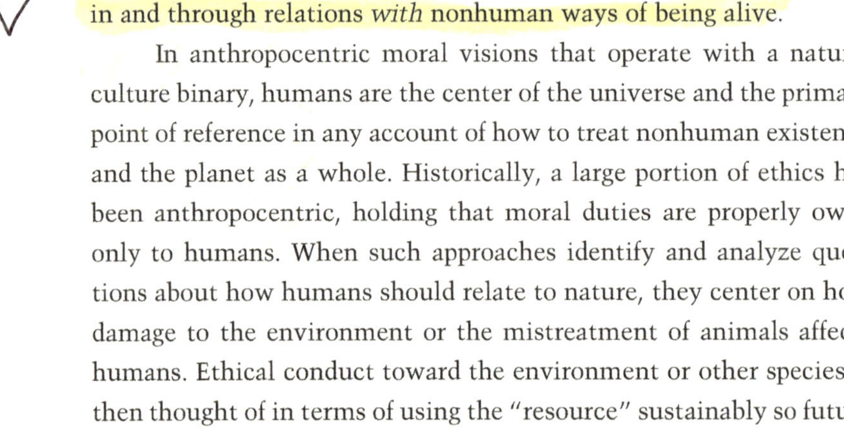

In anthropocentric moral visions that operate with a nature-culture binary, humans are the center of the universe and the primary point of reference in any account of how to treat nonhuman existence and the planet as a whole. Historically, a large portion of ethics has been anthropocentric, holding that moral duties are properly owed only to humans. When such approaches identify and analyze questions about how humans should relate to nature, they center on how damage to the environment or the mistreatment of animals affects humans. Ethical conduct toward the environment or other species is then thought of in terms of using the "resource" sustainably so future generations or other parts of the human world don't suffer. The primary goal of anthropocentric approaches is the flourishing of humanity and, only secondarily, the good of nonhuman ways of being alive. A significant move in much recent environmental ethics challenges anthropocentric approaches. In what follows I build on that work.

A METABOLIC VISION OF MORAL AND POLITICAL AGENCY

As we've seen, human beings cannot act morally and politically apart from and without the biotic life on which we depend to even exist. Creation constitutes the flow of communication we live and move and have our being within and through. Nonhuman creation acts on us just as we act in relation to the rest of creation. Consequently, our immorality and idolatry bring ruin upon nonhuman life just as much if not more so than upon human communities.[8]

In response, we need a way of imagining and narrating – describing – a single reality born out of the interaction of divine, human, and nonhuman forms of being and becoming. This cuts against the dominant ways of thinking and talking about ethics that either separate talk of morality from talk of God or envisages the moral life as somehow independent of the rest of creation. In other words, to ask about the good life necessitates asking about the interspecies, ecological, and cosmic conditions of creational flourishing. A conception of human flourishing necessitates accounting for the symbiotic relationship between humans, other species, plants, and the microbial world and understanding how the material conditions of human flourishing are interwoven with those of nonhuman flourishing.

Historically, ethics has tended to focus on the individual and communal conditions for moral agency. The moral subject was an individual agent understood as responsible for actions that caused effects. As already noted, much ethical reflection focused on the processes and structures that either detract from or contribute to *human* flourishing. But interpersonal and structural problems are also ecological problems. And the individual is part of a meshwork of relations and systems in which there is not necessarily a discrete and identifiable set of causes and effects for which I am directly responsible. For example, does my purchase of a computer directly cause the environmental destruction and terrible labor conditions involved in mining the rare earth metals that are vital to the computer's production? Not directly, but I still participate in the systems and structures that produce these conditions. I may not be directly culpable, but I am still a willing participant in perpetuating them and thereby, in some inchoate way, still responsible. Standard accounts of moral agency struggle to make sense of this long-chain or networked kind of responsibility. So how should we act when our actions are dependent on nonhuman ways of being alive and participate in histories, structures, and systems (both ecological and human made) beyond our control? My answer to this question is that instead of focusing on discrete actions, Christian ethics must address how the conversion of the soul cannot be separated from the cultivation of the soil and the cure of our social, economic, and political life together (the city). They are mutually constitutive. To take seriously the mutually constitutive relationships between soil, soul, and city, we need to reimagine human agency in ways that neither make humans the center of value nor envisage humans as the only bit of creation that has moral status and agency. In short, we must develop a non-anthropocentric moral imagination. This book tries to model what this might look like in practice, but the basis of my constructive proposal is a *metabolic* conception of agency.

A metabolic conception of moral agency is one in which a person is always already dependent on and participating in a form of life and situated within a meshwork of symbiotic relationships that constitute the agency of the person and the context of their actions.[9] I use the term "metabolic" to name this description of agency because it names a vibrant, interactive, communicative process. The technical definition of metabolism is a chemical or physical process that occurs within and through a living organism resulting in the breakdown, synthesis, or transformation of things in order to maintain or generate life. It can also refer to the complex flows of energy and materials across ecosystems that maintain life at a larger scale. If human societies are included in these cycles and systems of communication and exchange, the concept of metabolism as applied to our moral and political life begins to make sense.[10]

I am extending the term to frame how we imagine agency directed to flourishing. "Metabolic" in this sense points to how ordered, generative communication – *logos* – is constitutive of *being alive*, both in the sense of life being itself and life becoming vibrant and blossoming. It attends to how there are distinctive ways of being alive – rabbits and chimpanzees have their own ways of organizing life together that are distinct from what humans do – but, at the same time, human and nonhuman interact to produce shared worlds that can either enable the flourishing of all or hasten the destruction of each.

In a metabolic conception of agency, there is no clear line between either "nature" and "culture" (or "ecology" and "political economy"), as the person is both absorbing and constituting both at the same time. For example, as Elizabeth Wilson notes, when breast-feeding, a child absorbs affection *and* nutrition, *both* of which help form neural pathways, bone structure, and relational capacity, all of which are vital for the ability to act well with and for others.[11] Or viticulture is as much to do with the kind of soil, sunlight, and vines as it is with modes of producing and consuming wine. Likewise, beekeeping entails interspecies exchanges and mutual adaptation that enable the pollination of fruit trees, harvesting honey, and the flourishing of bee colonies that are vital to the political economy of agriculture and food systems. Even the seemingly abstract, cognitive processes of reflection and interpretation are themselves metabolic and physiological activities that expend and in turn generate energy.

Human agency depends on how ecologies of nonhuman life, human cultures, and political economies are enmeshed. A negative example is lead in paint, which affects emotional states and cognitive capacities as it poisons the body. It is also unequally distributed, affecting poor, predominantly African American neighborhoods in the United States disproportionally in comparison to predominantly white suburban ones – so its absorption is a cultural, economic, and political process as much as a biological one. Another negative example is how diseases such as cholera and tuberculosis move along the fault lines created by poverty itself produced by human policies and the moral and ideological commitments these enact.

ON BEGINNING IN THE MIDDLE

A metabolic view rejects both passivity and determinism, pointing to how our presence and action directly impact our environment in either creative or destructive ways. It also cuts against a view of agency as mastery, countering that we are *not* in control of our environment and that human beings are *not* initiators of something from nothing. We do not create *ex nihilo*; only God does.[12] Rather, human agency operates in the middle term, bringing to the fore what is already there, both affected by and affecting what is happening.[13] Humans as agents draw on the potentialities and energies of other things to distribute, promulgate, render, tend, and direct the flow. Rather than control and initiate, better words to describe what we do include: collect, preserve, repair, adapt, catalyze, craft, and cultivate. Through such actions we build a place to dwell, making use of what is already there. If that dwelling place is to be one that blesses rather than curses by making that place fruitful, then the quality and character of relations between human and nonhuman ways of being alive is central.

Metabolism is a dynamic process – always *in via*. Human life begins by drawing on the body and blood of our mother and continues even after death as our body decomposes and is absorbed into the soil or is burnt and dispersed as ash. A metabolic view of agency therefore speaks to how we are not the beginning and end point for our moral and political life; rather, we begin in the middle of a process that exists before and continues after us. And by not privileging one aspect of agency – the mind, character, will, or desire – metabolism encompasses the person as a biospiritual whole. It can thereby include those with intellectual disabilities, the suffering dying, and the embryonic. To act metabolically does not require consciousness, even while conscious action can intensify more directed modes of metabolic change.

Theologian Willie Jennings connects the dynamic of being alive – understood as existing in the middle term – with the question of what it means to be the people of God. He frames it in terms of "second reading"; that is, reading after and learning from what was sensed and discovered first by others not like us. He states:

> "Second reading" in this regard is the way of the creature that attends carefully to the ways of other creatures listening and learning from them of the reality of this world and of God's life with the world. This is a process fundamentally governed by the pedagogy of joining we learn as gentiles entering the story of Israel. It is also a pedagogy offered to biblical Israel in the New Testament where they were invited to join the lives of gentiles in new and revolutionarily intimate ways.[14]

Through the pedagogy of joining and being second readers, Christians should then (but too often don't) learn to listen to and learn from fellow inhabitants – whether human or nonhuman – and other readers of particular places whose experience of that place is either more primary or attends to it in ways beyond or outside of our experience. This includes not just other species and prior inhabitants but also, as will be explored in later chapters, our own ancestors. To understand what is going on, we must hear what has already been discovered from those who came before us, whoever they are and wherever we may be.

A metabolic, middle-term conception of agency attends to the relationship between past and present in ways that can be masked when ethics focuses exclusively on the responsibilities and actions of the individual. For example, within conceptions premised on the autonomy of the individual and sovereign exercise of their will, one response to slavery in the United States is to say, "I am not personally responsible for slavery. I did not enslave anyone, so why should I be held accountable for it?" or "My family had not even migrated to the Americas then and were themselves poor, so what has slavery to do with me?" Agency is locked in the present and envisaged as existing independently of history and place. But, like radioactive isotopes after a nuclear explosion, slavery has an afterlife with long-term toxic effects. These operate at a physical and social level that shape the moral and spiritual life of the country. Epigenetics teaches that trauma and deprivation in one generation can shape physical development and responses in later generations.[15] Likewise, the Americas are still metabolizing slavery ecologically, socially, economically, and politically in ways that affect everyone who lives there, including the ways White supremacy is baked into structures such as education, prison, and financial systems. This political economy needs transforming to account for how structural racism and the legacies of slavery systemically disadvantage some, rendering them more vulnerable to exploitation, even as it advantages others in unseen ways. Then there is tacit and intentional racism that operates at an interpersonal and affective level through feelings of aversion between whites and peoples of color and between different peoples of color (i.e., colorism). Then there is how the intersections of racism and capitalism structures our sense of place and ecological relations. For example, the soil quality in North Carolina and much of the Southeast of the United States is negatively determined by the lasting effects of plantation and industrial farming practices that depended on slavery and, subsequently, the exploitation of minoritized farmworkers. The afterlife of slavery in the organization of life together is such that whether we intend it or not, skin color structurally advantages some to the detriment of others. We cannot step outside of or ignore how our present is constituted through physically and socially poisonous histories. Attempts to either willfully forget, wash our hands of, or address these histories through simplistic moral judgments generate further harms in the present. Their afterlife, for example, in ongoing racism, points to how violence and violation become inscribed into the very fabric of life together and can be metabolized in ways that acknowledge and seek to convert this reality or, like toxins in food systems, concentrate and intensify its destructive effects.

The world around us is communicated to us through myriad interactions including with food, families, governmental structures, air quality, and worship, and in turn absorbs our actions and outputs, from our excrement to our words and deeds. A metabolic view of agency thereby speaks to how ethical reflection cannot focus only on the individual or the community or solely on structures. Neither can it separate human relations from ecological ones. Rather, it must attend to how a good, true, or flourishing life emerges *between* all these elements. In short, we are complex creatures entangled in a broader web of life.

A healthy metabolism involves continuity and change over time. It requires the maintenance of equilibrium (homeostasis), while combining this with the ability to grow, change shape, and adapt without breaking apart (morphogenesis). A flourishing human, ecclesial, or political body requires a dynamic interplay between homeostasis and morphogenesis. This enables such a body to live and act as a contingent, historical, time-bound form of life caught between continuity and change and constituted through a meshwork of ecological, human, and spiritual relations and the communications between them.

A THEOCENTRIC UNDERSTANDING OF CREATION

The metabolic view of human agency set out here is neither biocentric nor anthropocentric but theocentric. What does that mean? If humans are the center of all things, then nature is undervalued (an anthropocentric account), but if nature simply replaces humans (biocentric and ecocentric accounts), then humans are undervalued.[16] In biocentric moral frameworks, humanity is merely a knot in the broader assemblage of life on this planet, and it is the whole biosphere, not humanity, that is the center of value. By contrast, rather than the biosphere, ecocentric accounts make particular ecosystems the center of value. Anthropocentric, biocentric, and ecocentric approaches are morally myopic: anthropocentric accounts generate the exclusion of nonhuman creation from moral consideration, while biocentric and ecocentric accounts entail the devaluation of humans in moral reflection. By contrast, if God is the center of what determines value (a theocentric account), then both human and nonhuman forms of life can be properly valued, and both are answerable to God. Moreover, love and justice for both involves proper participation in communion with God and the recognition that God acts in relation to both, while each in their own way responds to God. Thus, we must ask how nonhuman life should participate in human society, how human society should participate in and adapt to nonhuman ways of being alive, and how both may enjoy communion with God.[17]

A theocentric account moves beyond a conflict paradigm to one of coexistence, emphasizing the need for mutual adaptation between human and nonhuman forms of life. One example of this in practice comes from James Rebank's farm where I began the chapter. In response to industrialized, extractive, and dehumanizing farming practices, he describes how he changed his own approach to farming, introducing a process of "rewilding" that mixes agriculture with fostering biodiversity.[18] Rebank is part of a wider movement for regenerative agriculture in the United Kingdom that itself is part of a worldwide agroecology movement that integrates work for environmental and social justice.[19] A further example comes from regenerative, "nature based solutions" to urban design. These replace gray infrastructure of concrete and steel with "green" and "blue" infrastructure such as wetlands, woods, parks, and ponds. These are used to address issues like flooding, air pollution, and heat islands that are simultaneously public health, social equity, quality of life, and environmental problems.[20] Such approaches seek to create "garden cities" that are both biophilic and people friendly.

On a theocentric vision, humans are neither masters of creation (i.e., we cannot treat creation as if we have total control over it), nor its custodians (i.e., creation is not dependent on us). But the alternative to these patterns of relationships is not to preserve creation as pristine. Human activity understood as the cultivation of a garden should, quite properly, seek to fructify creation and so enable the wonder and goodness of what God has created to shine forth as part of fostering reciprocal relations and forms of mutual adaptation. This kind of reciprocity is affirmed and fulfilled in the Eucharist: Christ did not take the raw materials of grain and grape, but wine and bread, the products of human labor and creativity, and used them as an anticipation of the coming eschatological fulfilment of all creation.[21] What is received is freely and joyously offered back as thanksgiving within an ecology of mutual blessing. In other words, it is metabolized in ways that fructify and increase life.

In a theocentric account, the individual is not collapsed into the system; humans have a particular and specific value and agency within the whole. There is a distinctive quality and character to how humans metabolize creation, particularly through our practices of care and communication. One such is cooking. Humans need to cook their food and animals do not.[22] Cooking points to the specific ways in which humans depend on the care of others to live. But cooking is not just about getting the right nutrients so our brains and bodies can function. Cooking creates a common life. It generates solidarity, intimacy, and festivity. Cooking sustains our cultural life and its shared meanings and purposes (e.g., a Thanksgiving or Christmas feast). It can also be a spiritual act that makes God's love tangible and tasty.[23] In cooking we survive and thrive, both at the same time. Cooking thereby points to how our material life is never just about existing; it is always suffused with meanings and purposes beyond simply surviving.[24] When I cook lasagne according to my mother's recipe, I not only physically nourish the bodies of family and friends, I also tend a memory of home in a new country and provide for a shared life together.

As with cooking, human metabolism is a deeply agentive process that has a dense and active sociality. Our bodies don't passively absorb the substances in our environment. Instead, metabolism is an active process through which we endure, cope with, sometimes resist, and often times navigate our environments, all while constantly interpreting the flow of signs and signals – whether biochemical, linguistic or otherwise – that constitute our relations with our surroundings and other species. For example, what, where, and how we eat is a metabolic process that simultaneously entails action and responses while being dependent on and affecting a prior meshwork of physical, biological, social, economic, and political relations. And as with nutritious, tasty cooking and convivial eating, knowledge of the world must be animated by love if wise and good ways of participating in reality are to be generated.[25]

A metabolic view of agency allows for the inclusion of unseen forces whether emotional, physical, incorporeal, nonhuman (e.g., microbial), or angelic that bear on human agency and faithful witness. With a metabolic approach, we acknowledge that humans are not the only agents. Responses to COVID-19 illustrate this point: the virus was neither visible nor something humans could control, but at the same time, what we did in response made a difference to what happened and how it affected social, political, and economic life.

A metabolic understanding of human moral and political agency is a way of constructively addressing two intersecting crises of the contemporary context: the crisis of the human and the crisis of the moral agent. The boundaries of who counts as human, and thus whose moral and political agency deserves recognition, is always vehemently contested. More often than not, those judged as less than human are brutalized and exploited. But today, the concept of humanity itself is increasingly in question even as the need for a conception of shared humanity grows more acute. The ability to edit human DNA, the capacity to merge humans and machines at a cellular level, and the prospect of artificial intelligence that shares characteristics of human consciousness have led some to ask whether there will emerge different kinds of humans or even posthumans. The sense of humanity as a singular phenomenon also becomes blurry when we realize how humans are not self-sufficient as a species but biologically symbiotic with other forms of life, particularly the microbiome. Moreover, the quality of these symbiotic relations directly affects what are taken to be specifically human capacities, notably higher level reasoning. A metabolic conception of the *imago dei* is vital to address these emerging questions.

THE *IMAGO DEI*: A METABOLIC VIEW

Metabolism provides a direct link to broader patterns of biotic life. While humans metabolize the world around us in specific ways, metabolizing is a mode of agency we share with all animate life. This is in keeping with the vision of what it means to be human depicted in Genesis. To be human/*adam* is to be made of the soil/*adamah*: that is, the ground all animate life and inanimate things share. But to be this kind of creature is also to be Spirit-breathed soil (*nephesh ḥayyah*), a condition shared with all animate life (Gen 2:17, 19; Ps 104:27–30; Eccl 3:18–21). In origin, *nephesh* denotes breath and appetite, that is, that which is the seat of physical and social vitality and desire. In the Hebrew Scriptures/Old Testament, it is used to signify the nexus of will, desire, and agency, hence it is usually translated as "soul." One way of understanding *nephesh hayyah* is to see it as situating humans among the animals. But the broader interpretation given here is more likely: within the agrarian context from which the text emerges, the soil is known to be teeming with life. On this reading, humans are the fruit of and depend on this Spirit-breathed soil. Humans share creaturely standing with all life, not just animals. This shared standing is reflected in how Israel is to live in reciprocal relations with both animal and nonanimal life.[26] For example, just as the soil and the trees give generously of their fruit (Lev 25:19, 26:4; Deut 11:17), so humans are to respond generously to the land, giving the land sabbath rest and acting with respect to the created world around them (Lev 25:2, 26:34–35). Failure to treat the land with respect causes the land to mourn and requires repentance by Israel (Is 24:4–6; Jer 4:28; Hosea 4:3; Amos 1:2).[27] The land itself stands as a witness to the covenant (Joshua 24:22–28). As biblical scholar Ellen Davis puts it:

> When humanity, or the people of Israel, is disobedient, thorns and briars abound (Gen. 3:17–19); rain is withheld (Deut. 11:11–17; 28:24); the land languishes and mourns (Is. 16:8; 33:9; Hos. 4:3). Conversely, the most extravagant poetic images of loveliness – in the Prophets, the Psalms, and the Song of Songs – all show land lush with growth, together with a people living in (or restored to) righteousness and full intimacy with God.[28]

Humans do not merely share biology with nonhuman forms of existence. They also share a biography. The command to "fructify" life (*peru urebu*, Gen 1:28) should be heard in this light. It both calls forth more life as such and for life that yields fruit through the cultivation of blessed (i.e., shalom-like, peaceable, flourishing) forms of life with and for human and nonhuman others.[29] It is true that only in and through communion with another human can what it means to be *human* be named and lived out. However, to move from merely surviving to thriving, Adam and Eve must also live with and for creation. This pattern is repeated in the life of Israel and comes to fulfillment in a young Jew, who as the new *adam*, is the one through whom and in whom all creation is reconciled.

This creational vision is echoed at Pentecost, which is not solely about the birth of the church through gentiles being grafted into Israel; it recapitulates the act of Genesis (Joel 2:20–29; John 20:19–23; Acts 2:1–21). At Pentecost, the Spirit once again breathes on (wind) and energizes (fire) *adamah*: creation is renewed through the transfiguration of earthly distinctions and the healing of life wrecked by sin. This renewal is mediated and symbolized by the formation of a new communion of persons that represents the first fruits of the new creation (Rom 8:22–23).

As at Pentecost, through Christ, in the power of the Spirit, we become more porous to the rest of creation and to God in ways that enable us to respond more faithfully, hopefully, and lovingly.[30] This is enacted at the Eucharist where we metabolize bread and wine along with the presence of God and the communion of saints.[31] The Eucharist embodies a richly metabolic vision of salvation and sanctification at work in a text like John 6:22–59. In the text, Jesus exhorts his listeners, saying that unless you

> eat the flesh of the Son of Man and drink his blood, you have no life in you. Those who eat my flesh and drink my blood have eternal life, and I will raise them up on the last day; for my flesh is true food and my blood is true drink. Those who eat my flesh and drink my blood abide in me, and I in them. (vs. 53–56)

As the disciples note, this is a difficult teaching. It conjures up images of cannibalism and vampires. Unless, that is, we understand it in the context of being born again (John 3:1–10). As theologian Natalie Carnes notes of the Gospel of John:

> Language of birth abounds in these first few chapters: the rebirth metaphors for conversion, the descriptions of Jesus as the only-begotten Son of God, the baptisms of and by Jesus. Images of wombs and mothers and waters of parturition seep into the book, enlivening descriptions of conversion and new life. Birth, as metaphor and image, is everywhere.[32]

In John 3, Jesus identifies himself as a mother pregnant with new life.[33] He invokes how every human being comes to life through a metabolic process of feeding on flesh and blood. The placenta feeds the child through the blood of the mother while removing waste and harmful substances. And the nutrients of a woman's flesh and bones – calcium, etc. – are vital for the child's growth and development. Christ's body does likewise.[34] And like crucifixion understood as a moment of birth (John 16:20–23), pregnancy is fraught with risk and pain, yet no one comes to life without the metabolic process of feeding on the flesh and blood that gestation entails. Salvation is literally and symbolically a metabolic process of gestation and birth, a process Christians recall and participate in at baptism and eucharist.[35]

Ultimately, the picture of the fulfilment of all things in Christ is one of cosmic eschatology where there is not a separation out of human and nonhuman creation but their transfiguration by the presence of God. The church is to bear witness to a messianic banquet (i.e., the priesting of creation in feasting and fellowship) and the new Jerusalem (i.e., a garden-city that signifies the healed and harmonious inter-relationship between human political economies and nonhuman ecologies). Any theological account of human flourishing must of necessity include concern for the flourishing of nonhuman creation. Conversely, no conception of what a flourishing environment might entail can be a true account if it excludes an account of human flourishing.

As reflected here, listening to Scripture in tandem to listening to creation helps ensure we tell a story about nature as creation. Learning to describe nature as creation through listening to Scripture leads in a very different direction to either anthropocentric, biocentric, or ecocentric accounts. In its matrix of song, poetry, story, and law, Scripture teaches us how to desire and relate to the world around us in ways that properly understand what we are experiencing and how it should be valued. It invokes a theocentric vision that calls us to understand that the worth of creatures and creation is not in the eyes of the human beholder but in the eyes of the divine beholder, the author and sustainer of all things. It is the Creator who declares what we see as good, not humans. All of life is a gift to be received from God. All life has intrinsic value independent of any human scheme of valuation, centered as these are on the utility, market price, or beauty of nature. The value of life is bestowed by God and this is a value that is to be discerned and respected. For example, Job 40:15–24 calls us to behold the Behemoth, an ugly creature not under human control, a creature that is different, "other," and yet is interdependent with humans as part of creation. Scripture reveals how God calls humans into being as creatures created for communion and as such is vital for learning to describe reality. But how can we best hear the testimony of Scripture? It is to that question I now turn.

ACCOMPANYING READINGS

Thomas Aquinas, *Summa Theologiae* I–II, Questions 91, 93, 94, 95. A classic statement of natural law as an account of the moral life situated within a framework that takes it as a given that the cosmos has something to teach us about how to live well.

George "Tink" Tinker, "Creation, Justice and Peace: Indians, Christianity and Trinitarian Theologies," *American Indian Liberation: A Theology of Sovereignty* (Maryknoll, NY: Orbis, 2008), 36–56. Tinker sets out a participative, trinitarian, theological understanding of the relationship between ecology and justice that builds on the wisdom of his ancestors.

Larry Rasmussen, "The Sacred and the Commodified," *Earth-Honoring Faith: Religious Ethics in a New Key* (Oxford: Oxford University Press, 2012), ch. 9. Rasmussen considers how we describe the environment we live in and how that affects the ways we treat creation.

Pope Francis, *Laudato si'* (2015). Available online via www.vatican.va. This papal encyclical provides a theology of creation care and critique of what Pope Francis calls the "technocratic paradigm" that dominates most modern, Western moral and political visions.

Mari Jørstad, *The Hebrew Bible and Environmental Ethics: Humans, NonHumans, and the Living Landscape* (Cambridge: Cambridge University Press, 2019), ch. 2. Jørstad opens up a compelling way to read how nonhuman creation is an active agent and participant in divine-human relations in the Hebrew Scriptures/Old Testament. She develops this in dialogue with anthropology and moral philosophy.

NOTES

1 James Rebanks, *English Pastoral: An Inheritance* (London: Allen Lane, 2020), 133–134.
2 Wendell Berry, *The Art of the Commonplace: The Agrarian Essays of Wendell Berry*, ed., Norman Wirzba (Oxford: Oxford Publicity Partnership, 2002), 240.
3 See Paul Blowers, *Drama of the Divine Economy: Creator and Creation in Early Christian Theology and Piety* (Oxford: Oxford University Press, 2012), especially 313–335.
4 *Laudato Si'* §12.
5 As the Nigerian New Testament scholar Teresa Okure puts it, "Life as the starting point and abiding context of hermeneutics is not only important; it is the reality that imposes itself .... The biblical works themselves are records of people who struggled to understand the meaning of their life in relation to God." Teresa Okure, *To Cast Fire upon the Earth: Bible and Mission Collaborating in Today's Multicultural Global Context* (Pietermaritzburg: Cluster, 2000), 196–197. And echoing Augustine, Oliver O'Donovan puts it thus: "The call to learn the world is, of course, a call of God; it echoes the Creator's will for us as expressed in his creation .... God's call reaches us only *through* the created world and as we participate in it." Oliver O'Donovan, *Finding and Seeking: Ethics as Theology*, vol. 2 (Grand Rapids, MI: Eerdmans, 2014), 100.
6 Natural law is a term used to describe those moral norms or rules that best enable humans to conform to the created order. These norms are not obvious but are available to all humans who reason rightly upon the experience of being human such that they formulate ways of living according to their nature (i.e., that conform to the true order of things). Indeed, the ability to discern and conform to the created order (known in natural law theories as the eternal law) by means of reason is the distinctive attribute of humans as animals. The basic presupposition behind natural law is that nature is not formless and so conforming to and fulfilling its form constitutes the right way of ordering human life because it is in sync with the form given to creation by God. To be unnatural is to live as if there is no form or pre-given shape to creation. The discussion of natural law in classical philosophy, and later, Judaism, Christianity, and Islam is one way of thinking about and discussing the question of what the

proper shape or form of life consists of, given that humans do not live in a formless void.

7 Ulrich Beck, *Risk Society: Towards a New Modernity*, trans., Mark Ritter (London: Sage, 1992).

8 See, for example, Genesis 6:5–13, where human violence and wickedness brings ruin upon all the earth.

9 The metabolic account set out here has parallels with patristic theologians such as Lactantius and Gregory of Nyssa, who emphasized the interrelationship between the physiological and the spiritual. See, for example, Gregory's *The Great Catechism* (chapter 37) in which his discussion of the Eucharist and the renewal of our humanity through becoming the body of Christ involves an analogy between metabolizing bread and becoming bread and Christ becoming bread and us becoming Christ.

10 For example, the term "metabolic rift" is now used by environmental sociologists and ecologists to describe a breakdown in the relationship between humans and ecological systems, generated by the demands of capitalism and colonialism, which leads to their mutual fragilization and possible collapse.

11 Elizabeth Wilson, *Gut Feminism* (Durham, NC: Duke University Press, 2015).

12 God creates existence. Humans are creative animals and can make new starts and innovate, but all such action takes place within the realm of existence created by God. It is therefore always already and only ever working with and developing what already exists. Developed by numerous theologians, this is also a fundamental insight of the creeds, which in the Nicene formulation declares: "We believe in one God, the Father almighty, maker of heaven and earth, of all things visible and invisible."

13 I am grateful to the philosopher Jane Bennett for the concept of the middle term. Jane Bennett, "Only Zeus is Free," Bi-Annual Facing the Anthropocene Luce Lecture, Duke University, Durham, NC, October 14, 2019.

14 Willie James Jennings, "Reframing the World: Toward an Actual Christian Doctrine of Creation," *International Journal of Systematic Theology* 21, no. 4 (2019): 388–407 (394).

15 Rodrick Wallace and Deborah Wallace, *Gene Expression and Its Discontents: The Social Production of Chronic Disease*, 2nd ed. (Cham: Springer, 2017); and Eva Jablonka, "Cultural Epigenetics," *Biosocial*

Matters: Rethinking Sociology-Biology Relations in the Twenty-First Century, eds., Maurizio Meloni, Simon Williams, and Paul Martin (Chichester: Wiley-Blackwell, 2016), 42–60.

16 Biocentric accounts draw inspiration from a range of sources including earth science, systems theory, and indigenous cultural insights. Their focus on life as an interconnected web resituates humans as part of a larger whole. No one organism can claim supremacy over anything else, for all are needed to support the ecosystem. Biocentric approaches emphasize the need to restore a lost harmony between humans and our ecological environments. However, there are pessimistic versions of such an approach that envisage the planet as a self-regulating system that has no need of humanity and will regulate itself in ignorance of humanity's fate. In other words, we can destroy ourselves, while nature blindly carries on.

17 The encyclicals *Laudato Si'* (2015) and the Post-Synodal Apostolic Exhortation *Querida Amazonia* (2020) by Pope Francis articulate just such a holistic, theocentric vision.

18 Rebanks, *English Pastoral*, 191–277.

19 In the United Kingdom, this movement is represented by organizations such as the Landworkers Alliance. Worldwide, it is given expression by La Via Campesina.

20 An example of this approach developed at scale is Singapore's Green Town and ABC Waters Programs and its wider "Green Plan 2030." www.greenplan.gov.sg (accessed September 9, 2021).

21 Luke 22:16, 19.

22 See, for example, Sonia Ragir, "Diet and Food Preparation: Rethinking Early Hominid Behavior," *Evolutionary Anthropology* 8 (2000): 153–155.

23 Norman Wirzba, *Food and Faith: A Theology of Eating* (Cambridge: Cambridge University Press, 2011), xii.

24 This is a point Reinhold Niebuhr makes with great force in *The Children of Light and the Children of Darkness: A Vindication of Democracy and a Critique of Its Traditional Defence* (Chicago: University of Chicago Press, 2011 [1944]), 61–63. Niebuhr points to how meeting basic needs and forms of cultural production are sutured together in a way that can produce both beauty and brutality.

25 The necessary intersection of love and knowledge in generating true participation in reality as marked by right relations with God, neighbor, and creation is an ancient one. See, for example, Augustine's *On Christian*

Doctrine, I.22–29. Following Jürgen Moltmann, we might call this an epistemology of communion. As Moltmann puts it:

To be alive means existing in relationship with other people and things. Life is communication in communion. And, conversely, isolation and lack of relationship means death for all living things and dissolution even for elementary particles. So if we want to understand what is real as real, and what is living as living, we have to know it in its own primal and individual community, in its relationships, interconnections and surroundings.

When directed to participation in Christ, the aim of such integrating and holistic thinking is "to generate the community between human beings and nature which is necessary and promotes life. And here 'nature' means both the natural world in which we share, and our own bodily nature. As a network and interplay of relationships is built up, a symbiotic life comes into being." Jürgen Moltmann, *God in Creation: A New Theology of Creation and the Spirit of God*, trans., Margaret Kohl (Minneapolis, MN: Fortress Press, 1993), 3.

26 See also *Laudato Si'* §67.

27 Mari Jørstad, *The Hebrew Bible and Environmental Ethics: Humans, NonHumans, and the Living Landscape* (Cambridge: Cambridge University Press, 2019), 8, 48–98.

28 Ellen Davis, *Scripture, Culture, and Agriculture: An Agrarian Reading of the Bible* (Cambridge: Cambridge University Press, 2009), 8.

29 Heinz-Josef Fabry, "*Para*," *Theological Dictionary of the Old Testament*, vol. XII (Grand Rapids, MI: Eerdmans, 2003), 81–83.

30 An important development in twentieth-century theology was the recovery of a trinitarian doctrine of God in which the perichoresis or interpenetration of Father, Son, and Holy Spirit is constitutive of God's nature. Aligned with this development is an emphasis on *theosis* or how, through Christ and the Spirit, humans participate in divine communion. What is less attended to is the way the rest of creation participates in divine communion and how creation has its own intra-creational form of perichoresis. My account of metabolism points toward the perichoretic, mutually constitutive relationship between different parts of creation, which, through Christ and the Spirit, participate in Trinitarian communion as creation.

31 As a matter of technical sacramental theology, metabolism refers to the change undergone by the Eucharistic elements when they are consecrated and stands between transubstantiation and a merely symbolic view of divine presence in the elements.

32 Natalie Carnes, *Motherhood: A Confession* (Redwood City, CA: Stanford University Press, 2020), 3.

33 On the long-standing tradition of envisaging Jesus as the mother of the church, as giving birth to eternal life, as nursing the faithful like a mother nurses a child from his blood and milk (understood as whitened blood) at the Eucharist, and as female flesh (Jesus' body does womanly things like bleed and give birth), see Janet Martin Soskice, *The Kindness of God: Metaphor, Gender, and Religious Language* (New York: Oxford University Press, 2007), 84–99; and Caroline Walker Bynum, *Jesus as Mother: Studies in the Spirituality of the High Middle Ages* (Los Angeles: University of California Press, 1982), 110–169. On how in Scripture blood that is gendered male cleanses and delivers, whereas blood that is gendered female defiles, and how Jesus's incarnation inverts this symbolic order, see Eugene Rogers, *Blood Theology: Seeing Red in Body- and God-Talk* (Cambridge: Cambridge University Press, 2021).

34 Sarah Jobe, *Creating with God: The Holy Confusing Blessedness of Pregnancy* (Brewster, MA: Paraclete Press, 2011), 91–103. For a parallel meditation on this theme, see Carnes, *Motherhood*, 11–24.

35 In keeping with John 16, the conception of the crucifixion as a moment of birth is central to a trinitarian conception of salvation. As Soskice notes: "The death of the Son, then, and separation of God from God in the cry of dereliction on the Cross, give way to a new birth, the *ekstasis* which is the mission of the Spirit. It is through the Spirit that there is resurrection and the Church born to newness of life." And as she goes on to say: "All three Persons, figuratively, give birth – the First Person as Unoriginate Origin begets the Son and gives the Spirit, the Second as Son 'makes' God the Father and 'gives birth' to the Church on the Cross, and the Holy Spirit, the Lord the Giver of Life, animates the Church in the world." Soskice, *The Kindness of God*, 117–118.

3 Listening to Scripture

Does Scripture have anything to say about whether genetically modified crops are moral? Can the Bible provide an answer to whether it is legitimate to possess nuclear weapons in order to deter an enemy? Underlying these specific questions are two broader ones: How can Scripture help address contemporary issues? And can it provide answers to moral questions that go beyond what Scripture teaches?

These are not just modern questions. They are present in Scripture itself. For example, Paul's letters are themselves reflections that go beyond the Scriptures as he received them to address questions that arose in specific contexts. This is displayed in 1 Corinthians 8 where Paul wrestles with whether it is licit for Christians to eat meat produced as part of a pagan sacrificial system. In the passage, Paul commends a particular, love-oriented, Christ-centered approach to practical moral reasoning (*syneidesis*), generating nuanced ethical teaching that is able to distinguish between primary and secondary matters. Echoing Paul, my contention in this chapter is that Christian ethics is not about the rote repetition of what Scripture says, nor does it demand reperforming Scripture like a script. Rather, Christian ethics enables faithful participation in the reality Scripture announces.

Grappling with Scripture is a necessary condition of *Christian* moral reflection. But Christian moral reflection extends beyond what Scripture addresses and draws on other sources as well, including, for example, science, philosophy, art, and history. Moreover, divine communication is not restricted to Scripture. We can hear God's call in visions (e.g., Julian of Norwich's "shewings"), in the face of the poor (e.g., Francis of Assisi's encounter with a beggar), through listening to creation, and myriad other means. In trying to understand the relationship between ethical deliberation and Scripture, we must wrestle with the following: Scripture by itself is not enough to know how to live well, but we cannot live lives of faithful witness without reference to Scripture.

Scripture is an authoritative basis on which to make theological judgments about creaturely flourishing. As Black liberation theologian James Cone puts it: "Christian theology exists only as its language arises out of an encounter with the biblical story."[1] Scripture is the primary basis on which theological claims about how to live well are authorized and validated. Or to use a more traditional formulation, Scripture is the "norming norm" or measure that provides criteria by which to interpret and determine the meaning and purpose of what we are metabolizing.

To say Scripture is authoritative is to claim that this collection of texts is a means through which to know and encounter the triune God. What's more, it's a means through which to understand *everything else* in relation to God. God's ongoing self-communication occurs in and through this text – particularly, God's self-revelation in Jesus Christ. Scripture authorizes truthful speech and righteous action through enabling us to hear and respond to the living God.[2] In short, Scripture is the servant of God's Word, while the church names those who hear and respond to God's Word. It follows that the interpretation of Scripture is, at its best, a participation in God's teaching.

If a fundamental task of Christian ethics is listening to Scripture, we must first understand what kind of text we are listening to. To see the Bible as a rule book or equivalent to a car manual is to misunderstand what one is reading. The Bible is first and foremost a pathway to contemplating God and participating in God's ongoing communication.[3] By meditating on these texts, by wrestling with them, by coming under their judgment, by digesting them, we encounter God and are formed into the kind of people who can see, touch, taste, and smell the world around us in creaturely and neighborly ways rather than sinful and idolatrous ones. Through dwelling with and metabolizing these texts, we gradually come to imagine, envision, reason, and communicate with each other in more faithful, hopeful, and loving ways and can thereby make wiser moral and political judgments about how to flourish.

SCRIPTURE AS TESTIMONY AND CONFESSION

The standard way to name the Scriptures as a text is to call them a "testimony," as in the Old and New Testaments. Scripture is the testimony of God's self-revelation – the self-disclosure of God. This implies that while God may indeed be transcendent, infinite, and beyond our human capacity to comprehend or categorize, God nevertheless makes Godself known in a way that humans can apprehend and speak about. Scripture is first and foremost the testimony to that revelation. Through hearing and being instructed by this testimony, we too can encounter God.

But Scripture is also, at one and the same time, a confession of human speech and action in response to God. As a set of texts, Scripture is both a profession of faith in response to a prior divine call and an expression of that call. The text is the fruit of this call-and-response relationship and mediates it in an ongoing way. It is creaturely communication ordered to and serving divine communication. The influential Swiss theologian, Karl Barth (1886–1968), formulates the dynamic relation between Scripture as divine address and Scripture as human speech as one in which divine inspiration does not imply the infallibility of human words. Rather: "It means that the fallible and faulty human word is as such used by God and has to be received and heard in spite of its human fallibility."[4] This means that, to use Barth's judicious phrasing, we can acknowledge Scripture's "capacity for errors" even as the Bible is taken to be divinely inspired.[5] Contrary to modern notions of "inerrancy" but in keeping with the majority of the Christian tradition, Barth is bringing to the fore the logic of the Council of Chalcedon (451 CE) and using it as a framework for Scripture. In a way analogous to how the Council confesses that Jesus is fully human and fully divine, Scripture fully participates in both divine and human forms of communication.

To affirm this is to walk a middle path between two dangers: so emphasizing the fallibility of Scripture that undermined is any sense of how, in these texts, God's address can be heard; or, conversely, so emphasizing the divinity of Scripture that its fallibility is obscured.

It is important to remember that, like all forms of human language and communication, Scripture comes to us as speech after Babel. It simultaneously connects and divides us. In doing so, it participates in histories of confusion, conflict, and domination that all human communities endure and perpetuate. And each community of readers brings to the text their own specific histories of suffering and oppression, which are then taken up in further readings, which may be reparative of some wrongs but, as themselves fallen and fallible, may also generate further wounds. Yet just as God providentially provides clothes for Adam and Eve in response to their fallen sense of being naked and ashamed, so Scripture is a providential response to the ways divine address is heard and responded to in a fallen world. And just as the New Jerusalem is depicted as without a temple since God is present throughout, so there will be no need of Scripture in the new creation: God's presence will not need the mediation of human words.

Scripture itself testifies to its own limits: even as it mediates God's word, like John the Baptist, it points beyond itself to one who is God's Word. Part of what I lay out here is how to understand the penultimate, fallible nature of Scripture constructively without either ignoring Scripture entirely in ethical reflection or – as one of America's founding fathers, Thomas Jefferson, did – editing out the bits of Scripture that don't suit our particular moral sensibilities.

Although the Bible is fallible and fallen human communication, it is, nevertheless, the primary archive of how to speak and act in the light of God's prior action with and for us. It gives us not simply pathways for how we might respond and live but also patterns for how to speak, reason, and tell stories together in order to confess who God is and who we are in relation to God. As *human* speech, Scripture has multiple voices and contains many ways of confessing (poetry, histories, proverbs, etc.). And alongside elements of consensus, it also has conflicts that unsettle and disturb any sense of being able to fully grasp or contain what it means to confess who God is. The contemporary Roman Catholic theologian, Mathew Levering, helpfully coordinates the simultaneously divine and human instruction we receive from Scripture as follows: "God the Teacher may teach more through the human teachers' words than the human teachers know, and so God's teaching is not in conflict with the 'messiness' of human teaching. The great variety of the forms of human teaching in the biblical texts thus enters into and enriches the encounter with God the Teacher."[6]

As testimony and confession, Scripture is the basis of a shared realm of meaning and action. Through its testimony and confession, it calls forth further interpretation and judgments about what is to be valued and why. It is also generative of a community that apprentices its members in ways of reading, interpreting, and attending to God's testimony through liturgy, creeds, doctrinal treatises, sermons, hymns, festivals, cathedrals, and other means. Echoing the earlier quote from Cone, as forms of written, sung, and enacted theology, these means are themselves responses to Scripture. They further open out, through their own agreements and disagreements, what it means to witness to God's prior testimony. These confessions take embodied form through further performances and iterations, including prayers, dreams, meditations, poems, plays, pictures, meals, and pilgrimages. Scripture as confession thus gives birth to innumerable other confessions that are themselves frail and fallen responses to as well as participations in divine communication. To echo Barth, it is through these fallible human words that we hear God's divine address.

Understanding Scripture as divine address means that the primary reason for reading Scripture is not to extract moral principles or ethical paradigms to then apply. That may seem counterintuitive given that I've placed "listening to Scripture" as one of the foundations of Christian ethics. However, my point is that reading Scripture for moral principles or ethical paradigms is reductive. The primary point of listening to Scripture is to cultivate intimacy with God.

As such, hearing Scripture cannot remain at the level of intellectual consent. It must involve embodying a pattern of life shaped by interaction with Scripture as part of participating in God's ongoing communication. Coming to hear the Word of God through Scripture redirects our desires and leads us to reevaluate our priorities, goals, and commitments. The true test of our exegesis is neither the sophistication nor the inerrancy of our exegesis but whether it helps generate and sustain persons and communities whose character bears witness to the love of God.

SCRIPTURE IS NOT A REVEALED MORALITY, BUT AN ANGEL WITH WHOM TO WRESTLE

The Bible is the primary point of reference for understanding what it means to confess Jesus Christ as Lord and, in its various forms, is the one thing shared by all Christians. But to understand what such a confession might mean among these people, in this place, at this time, it cannot be the sole interlocutor. Another way to say this is that the Bible is most helpful as a description both of who God is and the way the world is. But as a source for telling us what to do about that in practice, its scope is limited. To use a distinction introduced by the American Protestant ethicist, H. Richard Niebuhr (1894–1962), the Bible is a *revealed reality* and not a *revealed morality*. This distinction is in keeping with the basic nature of Scripture as revelation or *apokalypsis* that unveils what is really going on and makes manifest the glory of God so that we might be changed into God's likeness from one degree of glory to another (2 Cor 3:18). This does not mean that the Bible is without direct moral instructions and exhortations that provide guidance for today. It clearly does. Rather, this distinction suggests that alongside how Scripture is a means of divine address, another primary and basic connection between Scripture and ethics is how the Bible furnishes its readers with ways of learning to describe and narrate the world truly. Rather than giving us a definitive, once and for all list of "do's" and "don'ts," the Bible serves to apprentice us in a Christian moral and political vision.

As a revealed reality, the Scriptures should shape how we name and narrate the world around us. We cannot know what words like "god" or "good" or "evil" or "oppression" mean independently of how these come to be defined by the life of a young Jew who wanders about with a ragtag group of disciples, teaching, healing, exorcising, eating with despised people, crying over Jerusalem, all while being constantly harassed and surveilled by the authorities, and who eventually dies on a Roman cross and is resurrected three days later. In short, we must somehow allow the meanings of these words to be recentered around the life, death, resurrection, and ascension of Jesus.

The difficulty of interpreting Scripture is itself a means of training us in how to hear God and be transformed. As the Cappadocian theologian, Gregory of Nyssa (c. 335–c. 395), notes, "Christ trained his disciples' minds through sayings veiled and hidden in parables, images, obscure words, and terse sayings in riddles."[7] Building on Gregory of Nyssa and the work of the feminist biblical scholar Phyllis Trible, we can picture Scripture as an angel with whom to wrestle.[8] Like Jacob wrestling with a stranger who is somehow also God (Gen 32:22–32), contending with Scripture can leave us wounded and blessed, both at the same time. Texts can trouble us, unsettling our relationship with God, ourselves, and others, but we should not let go of them until we are blessed. We must hold on past any sense of paralysis, disgust, or desire to withdraw that some texts, particularly violent texts, can invoke. For Jacob, the wrestling resulted in a name change (from Jacob to Israel) and a physical difference: the stranger injured Jacob's hip, and he walked ever after with a limp. As it did with Jacob, the act of wrestling changes us. The struggle enables us to enter into ever-deeper readings of Scripture, readings that take time and patience to emerge. As with Jesus's arresting parable about prayer, we must persevere like the tenacious widow who keeps petitioning the unjust judge until she receives justice (Luke 18:1–8).

In the wrestling we discover God's living presence beckoning us on, even as, paradoxically, what is often revealed is God's hiddenness and how God's presence can be found in apophatic darkness. As with those who accompanied Jesus on the road to Emmaus and who failed to recognize him, God can be present when we don't understand what is going on in a text. And just as Jesus's companions recognized him and at that very moment, Jesus disappeared, so, paradoxically, God can become hidden at the point of revelation (Luke 24:13–35).[9] Conversely, in the reading, praying, preaching, and singing of Scripture, the church as a body hears and inhabits the world – even in its places of desolation and trauma – as open to the transformative love of God and neighbor. It can come to understand and embody how the world is not merely dust but also, as the Psalmists and Prophets proclaim, a song of praise (e.g., Ps 148; Isa 44:23). Scripture is not then a code of beliefs and behaviors to be subscribed to (a revealed morality). Neither is hearing the word of God about listening to a set of facts or ideas. Scripture is to be contemplated, prayed, preached, and wrestled with so as to convert our ways of describing and inhabiting the world around us. And in turn, through this Spirit-led struggle, we become wiser and more adept at when and how Scripture may be spoken and acted on in ways that bless rather than curse.

Like the burning bush, which manifests divine presence in vegetal form, Scripture is vibrant, glorified, Spirit-filled matter. The long tradition of associating the four Gospels with the four creatures depicted in Ezekiel 10 that are at once angelic, human, and animal speaks to how the texts are more than material. Whether as a scroll, book, or screen, Scripture shimmers with presences and energies that bring new life through reading, hearing, and singing it. As Augustine exhorts us: "So for the time being treat the Scripture of God as the face of God. Melt in front of it."[10] Like Moses before the burning bush or Ezekiel before the Cherubim, to encounter the Holy Spirit's wonder-working presence in the text, we need bodily and affective ways of listening. The somatic and sensory dimensions of how we read and hear Scripture are key to how we become infused with Scripture and hear the call of God through it. Our posture, voice, and manner all play a part. Like a good meal, the craft of reading, interpreting, and understanding Scripture involves desiring, ruminating, savoring, and digesting. And while it can be done alone, it is best done in company, like a really good meal or a feast. This is reading as a sacramental and liturgical act.

Part of reading the Bible in company means including previous readers and, echoing Chapter 2, recognizing we come to it as second readers. For this we need some sense of the history of how texts have been read in the past, for better and worse. We read in the company of our ancestors as part of a community of memory. Paradoxically, such memories – even difficult memories of how Scripture has been utilized to wound the world – can nurture hope. Reading Scripture as part of a community of memory means learning to see certain kinds of readings as destructive and certain texts as requiring caution: we need to interpret these in relation to other texts and in concert with other voices. Such listening is at the same time a way of learning to have hope that things can change, that covenantal faithfulness can be renewed despite the sins of the past.

To build on the point that we read as second readers who are part of a community of memory, we always receive scriptural passages within wider arguments about what they mean. Whether we are conscious of it or not, none of us is coming to a text "clean." Some awareness of the history of the reception of biblical texts should make a difference to how they are read in relation to contemporary moral and political questions. So, for example, it matters for how we read Deuteronomy and Joshua to know how they have been used as a justification for projects of settler-colonialism and genocide.[11] The experience of contemporary Palestinian Christians is but one example.[12] Ignoring this history means tacitly sanctioning it.[13] Likewise, a failure to read the story of Lot cursing his son Ham without attending to how this story was used to justify modern, racialized chattel slavery makes one an inept reader, while acknowledging that history sensitizes us to how our own readings may justify grotesque evil. Positively, attention to previous readings can open up and challenge contemporary assumptions we bring to a text, enabling us to hear it in new ways or make abstruse texts come alive. For example, the story of Jephthah and the sacrifice of his unnamed daughter in Judges 11 can seem an obscure "text of terror" best hurried past.[14] Yet for early modern political thinkers like the hugely influential Thomas Hobbes and John Locke, this was a text that spoke to the relationship between sovereignty and citizenship and who is sacrificed for the sake of political stability. It's a question that, as the political theorist Danielle Allen shows, still torments contemporary politics, even if it is often unacknowledged.[15]

FIVE RULES FOR READING

Reading the Bible so as to learn how to describe the world around us as suffused with the presence of God is easier said than done. In practice, do we seek proof texts; that is, find verses that conveniently support our prior view? Or do we cherry pick what verses to read while avoiding those bits we find uncongenial? Or do we read in a literalistic way, ignoring the context and chronology of a text so as to read a contemporary concern into it? Here it is important to distinguish literalistic from literal readings. "Literalism" denotes a flat, functionalist, and presentist way of reading that assumes the meaning of a text is immediately obvious, singular, and static. By contrast, while there are various uses of the term "literal" in the history of biblical exegesis, literal or plain-sense readings of Scripture necessitate attending to the inherently multilayered and figurative meanings of scriptural texts and the instabilities between them. As a number of theologians argue, the theological ground for this is God, who as the first author and cause of Scripture intends many meanings to be present in one passage so as to reflect divine understanding that comprehends everything all at once.[16]

Literalism, proof texting, and cherry picking generate ideological readings that simplify and constrain who God is and who we are in relation to God and each other. As ways of reading Scripture, they overlook the diversity of views in Scripture, discount the wider passage an individual verse comes from, set aside the cultural context the passage is situated in, and ignore traditions of reception that have shaped how we hear and understand the text. In doing so, they neither keep time with the text nor give the text any time. Instead, they work on a kind of aggregate model: the more verses I can stack up in favor of my position the more likely it is I will "win"; or my position is the most fully "Christian," "scriptural," or "sound."

Literalism, proof texting, and cherry picking are demonstrably irreverent, bad faith ways of reading Scripture that ignore what Scripture itself teaches about patterns of good reading. While their simplicity sounds appealing, they flatten Scripture, thereby masking its meaning. What are needed instead are ways of reading that, like listening to jazz, abide with the cuts and breaks of Scripture, taking note of its competing rhythms, timescales, and discordant notes. These puncture our settled sensibilities and ways of understanding God, who we are, and the times we live in. To abide with Scripture so we can hear God speak through both its harmonies and its atonal qualities requires a patience and humility that literalism, cherry picking, and proof texting refuse.

There are nourishing ways of reading Scripture that combine plain sense, critical, and spiritual readings but don't require sophisticated "hermeneutics" – that is, methods and theories for interpreting the text. Outside of formal hermeneutical theories, there are rules for reading that help ensure that how we listen to Scripture is accountable to the text itself, that the text reads us rather than we read what we like into the text, and that our readings are orientated toward loving God and neighbor. These rules have an ancient warrant. In the fourth century, the African theologian Tyconius wrote a set of seven rules for interpreting Scripture that were taken up and discussed by Augustine, among others. Echoing Tyconius, the five rules I present here are not exhaustive but do draw together a range of reflections on how to approach Scripture as an authoritative source of instruction for vision and wisdom about moral and political matters.

1 *Rule of the Canon*

We cannot pick and choose which bits of Scripture to listen to. As a community of listeners, the church inherits the whole of the canon, not this or that text. When attending to Scripture in order to describe reality we must attend to the whole of it, even the bits we find uncomfortable or even unconscionable. Taking seriously the full canon as Scripture requires different kinds of reading. It can involve close readings of specific texts or even words. It includes reading against the grain and paying attention to what is not said or who is not present in a text. Conversely, it means noticing who is present but often unnoticed; for example, the way Miriam is a leader alongside Moses, one whose leadership the prophet Micah proclaims as equal to Moses and Aaron (Micah 6:4). It can be vital to notice how a text resists making sense – what seems foolish or confused can confound what seems wise. But it also means taking seriously that when a topic is mentioned or a theme recurs in a book, testament, or overall, that demands due weight. Most obviously, over 2,000 verses point to God's concern for the poor and for justice. There is a parallel concern for idolatry. Accordingly, Christians should be centrally preoccupied with poverty, justice, and the nature and form of idolatry.

2 *Rule of the Part in Relation to the Whole*

A variation on the first rule is reading texts in relation to a broader, overarching account of God's purposes – or at least, broader constellations of beliefs, themes, or narratives in the Scriptures. To put this another way, we should not read verses in isolation but connect them to wider patterns that run through individual books and the Bible as a whole and situate particular texts in dialogue with texts from elsewhere in the Bible (or intertextually).

Scripture gives us a polyphony of voices. Like a film montage, Cubist portrait, or a reredos panel of icons behind an altar, Scripture provides different angles on and depictions of a complex reality that is not reducible to a single picture or voice even while there are threads and seams that connect them. The four Gospels are the most obvious example of this dynamic. Each brings its own emphasis to a shared reality and, in the process, can generate disagreement and conflicts with the other renderings. Compare, for example, the different birth narratives in Mathew and Luke and how John and Mark don't have birth narratives at all. That said, there are limits. While the Gospel of John is different from but in keeping with the synoptic Gospels, gnostic and other versions are not.[17] They sound so jarring as to be telling an entirely different kind of story, one out of keeping with the rest of Scripture. While not straightforward, putting the part into conversation with the whole is an important discipline for faithful reading as it allows both difference and relation to be brought into view.

An important way to put the part in relation to the whole is synthesis. Synthesizing does not mean homogenizing texts, ignoring or downplaying any disagreements between them. On the contrary, it includes highlighting those tensions and disagreements so as to evaluate how a particular text should be weighted in relation to a broader synthetic understanding. For example, how should Paul's admonition that there is no longer male and female in Christ (Gal 3:28) be related to the specific advice that women should keep silent in churches (1 Cor 14:34–35)? Or prohibitions against eating blood (Gen 9:4–5; Lev 17:10–14; Deut 12:16; Acts 15:20) with instructions to drink the blood of Christ (Mark 14:22–24; John 6:54–56)? Synthesizing entails developing a broader interpretative framework as a means to coordinate and prioritize different passages even while recognizing the tension and disagreement between them. That said, it is important to recognize the limits and shortcomings of any synthesis we might construct.

There are two modern versions of synthesis in widespread use today. The first is to look for overarching themes or motifs: for example, love, liberation, or covenant. These themes or motifs are then ways of connecting different texts as well as applying them in the present: for example, the use of either liberation or covenant as ways of analyzing and ordering contemporary political relations. While this is a helpful strategy for relating the part to the whole, the danger is that such themes are abstracted from the text and separated from their context and so tend to flatten everything to fit a single theme.

A second form of contemporary synthesis is to read particular texts within an overarching narrative, for example, of creation, fall, and redemption. Individual passages or books are understood as making sense within an overarching story that runs through the Bible. That story tells us we are created good, but something is fundamentally wrong with the human condition; we find ourselves always-already alienated from God, from each other, and from creation but unable to change this condition. But God through Israel and Jesus Christ enables humans to be reconciled and enjoy communion with God, with each other, and with creation; however, we still await the fullness of that reconciliation and communion to be shown forth at the fulfillment of history when Christ returns. Misconceptions arise when we omit some part of this story or overemphasize one aspect at the expense of another. By extension, Scripture informs the Christian life by giving us stories through which to interpret our story and make sense of it: I narrate my story after the pattern and in the light of the story Scripture tells about reality.

The problem with a narrative approach is that it assumes a single, cohesive story that lies behind different texts and can thereby generate inattention to the particularities of a specific text. For example, Song of Songs, Proverbs, Ecclesiastes, and Job sit awkwardly in this overarching narrative of creation, fall, and redemption. While a theologically generative and important way of relating the part to the whole (and one I use myself), narrative approaches tend to place unity in the wrong place. The unity of Scripture lies with the triune God to which the texts testify, not in the coherence of the story it tells. Moreover, its narrative is unfinished and there is always more to be said.

3 *Rule of Christ*

The rule of Christ is not a heavy-handed Christomonism where every text is really about Jesus; this would collapse the polyphony of Scripture into a single note. Rather, Christ is a marker for orientating our interpretations. This is especially important when drawing on the Hebrew Scriptures/Old Testament for moral and political reflection in a Christian key. As indicated at the outset of this chapter, Paul models a way of reading Scripture through the rule of Christ. His ways of doing so – particularly figurative reading – went on to shape how much Patristic and medieval exegesis developed. What Paul points to is how Scripture must be read anew in the light of Christ's life, death, resurrection, and ascension. For example, Levitical laws are read in dialogue with who God is revealed to be in Christ. Part of the way Christ serves as a reference point is attending to how Jesus is himself portrayed as reading Scripture. For example, how does Jesus read Leviticus? Luke portrays Jesus as reading Leviticus 19:18: "You shall not take vengeance or bear a grudge against any of your people, but you shall love your neighbor as yourself: I am the Lord." This is taken to be a summary of the law and interpreted through the parable of the Good Samaritan (Luke 10:25–37). Overall, Jesus is portrayed as showing how he cannot be understood apart from the Hebrew Scriptures and, at the same time, how his death and resurrection open up the Hebrew Scriptures in new ways (Luke 24:13–35). This echoes how the Gospels in general receive and interpret Scripture (for example, how John's Gospel reads and reinterprets Exodus).

The rule of Christ also calls us to be readers of Scripture in fellowship with people from other communities and traditions. Christ listened with great care to Syrophoenician and Samaritan readers and interpreters who did not confess or read in the same way as he did, and yet their readings stand as a witness to who God is no less than the words of Jesus (Matt 15:17–27; Mark 7:21–31; John 4). The rule of Christ thereby calls us to read with and alongside others who read Scripture very differently from us and to abide with and learn from these readings (especially Jewish and Islamic readings).

4 *Rule of Slow Reading*

Read the text closely and with care. Do not presume to know what it says. Listen. One approach that embodies slow reading is the practice of *lectio divina*, which entails prayerfully reading a sentence or passage repeatedly. As a practice it makes time to notice different meanings in the text, for the Holy Spirit to speak through the text, and to become aware of God's presence mediated by the text.

5 *Rule of Love*

Taking his lead from Matthew 22:34–40, a discussion of how to rightly order love of God and neighbor, Augustine developed this influential rule about the interpretation of Scripture. As he puts it:

> So if it seems to you that you have understood the divine Scriptures, or any part of them, in such a way that by this understanding you do not build up this twin love of God and neighbor, then you have not yet understood them. If on the other hand you have made judgments about them that are helpful for building up this love, but for all that have not said what the author you have been reading actually meant in that place, then your mistake is not pernicious, and you certainly cannot be accused of lying.[18]

Augustine uses the metaphor of a walker who strays from a path but ends up in the right place to explain how even if we don't exactly follow the primary meaning or plain sense of a text but end up developing an interpretation that fosters love of God and neighbor, then that interpretation is in the spirit if not the letter of the Scriptures. Augustine's broader point is that exegesis is less about what a particular text says and more about what God is trying to teach us, here and now, about what it means to love God and neighbor so that we may more fully participate in that love.

The technical issue at stake is that interpretation is not one gesture. It entails two movements: rendering the text intelligible *and* discerning its significance for our life. Both these movements require virtue. In the terms that medieval exegesis emphasized, the rule of love makes primary the spiritual (or anagogic) as well as the moral meanings of a text. A more subtle point to be drawn from Augustine's discussion is that without the rule of love we can end up enjoying the exegesis of Scripture for itself divorced from its true end as a means to enjoy God. I sometimes recall Augustine's insight when those who take a proof texting approach start firing verses at me to prove a point or when wading through a particularly turgid and technical piece of academic biblical criticism.

SCRIPTURE IS NECESSARY BUT NOT SUFFICIENT

Ethical reflection can begin with any of the sources of authority discussed in Part I, but each will lead inexorably to Scripture, for Scripture is the source of the narratives and descriptions that enable the naming of the world in relation to God. For example, we could begin with tradition, but faithful participation in a Christian tradition is fostered by engagement with the canon of Scripture and a set of debates about how to be a Christian. But it also leads beyond Scripture as it involves active interrogation of what it means to be in symbiotic relations with nonhuman ways of being and becoming (creation), dialogue with those from other traditions with whom a common life must be forged (strangers), hearing experiences of suffering and domination (the afflicted and oppressed), and attending to how the community of memory made sense of and responded to Scripture (ancestors). Each of these sources of authority needs the other if our descriptions are themselves to be moral. At the same time, and in the same breath, all these points of reference are means of grace through which we hear God's call.

I expand here on this last point that hearing God requires more than just listening to Scripture. Listening to Scripture must be done alongside listening to strangers (Chapter 4) and the cries of those calling out for liberation (Chapter 5) if we are to respond faithfully, hopefully, and lovingly to what we hear. If we are hearers of Scripture but refuse to listen to strangers, then we refuse to seek understanding from what we fear or find strange or don't know. And that is not just foolish but unfaithful. Faith seeking understanding is the basis of theological wisdom. And if we hear not the cries of the suffering and oppressed, we are deaf to what needs changing – including the need to change our own hearts and minds. We must not be like the pious slavers who read their Scriptures diligently but failed to hear the cries of those they enslaved, whipped, and lynched, and so catastrophically failed to hear in these cries the crucified Christ's own cry of dereliction (Matt 27:46; Mark 15:34). By contrast, deep listening to the cries for freedom and songs of simultaneous lament and joy voiced, for example, in spirituals, blues, jazz, soul, and hip-hop can shatter the way racialized visions govern the order of things, opening the way to a more faithful hearing of Scripture.[19] However, while listening to Scripture, strangers, and those crying out for liberation is vital, we must also listen to those who came before us – our ancestors – and from whom we received the faith and the ways of life, stories, and language we use to make sense of the world. Another way to put this is the need to listen to the traditions that shape us (Chapter 6). It is to the need to read Scripture in the company of strangers that I turn in Chapter 4.

ACCOMPANYING READINGS

Gregory of Nyssa, "Preface [Prologue]," *Homilies on the Song of Songs*, trans., Richard A. Norris Jr. (Atlanta, GA: Society of Biblical Literature, 2012), 3–13. This provides a classic account of figurative and spiritual ways of reading Scripture and how such readings help cultivate a virtuous life.

Dietrich Bonhoeffer, "Christ, Reality, and Good. Christ, Church, and World," *Dietrich Bonhoeffer Works*, vol. 6, *Ethics* (Minneapolis, MN: Fortress Press, 2005), 47–68. Bonhoeffer offers a meditation on the relationship between the revelation of God in Jesus Christ that we receive in Scripture and the implications of this revelation for how we may participate in a non-dualistic understanding of reality as a unified whole.

Delores Williams, *Sisters in the Wilderness: The Challenge of Womanist God-Talk* (Maryknoll, NY: Orbis Books, 1993), chs. 1 and 6. Rejecting any notion of vicarious suffering (e.g., penal substitution) or that suffering can be redemptive, Williams provides a trenchant critique of dominant ways that divine-human relations and the ethical task are understood through a close reading of Hagar's story. In a number of ways, these two chapters incorporate the rules outlined here in operation.

R. S. Sugirtharajah, "Desperately Seeking the Indigene: Nativism and Vernacular Hermeneutics," *The Bible and the Third World: Precolonial, Colonial and Postcolonial Encounters* (Cambridge: Cambridge University Press, 2001), ch.

6. Sugirtharajah, a leading postcolonial biblical scholar, critically reviews "vernacular hermeneutics" as a way to engage in intercultural readings of the Bible that attend to local and indigenous literary, cultural, and religious heritages.

Ellen Davis, "Critical Traditioning: Seeking an Inner Biblical Hermeneutic," *The Art of Reading Scripture*, eds., Ellen Davis and Richard Hays (Grand Rapids, MI: Eerdmans, 2003), 163–180. Davis outlines a constructive approach to interpreting the Bible, particularly what she calls its "repellent texts," that is both critical and attentive to the ongoing life of faith.

Peter Ochs, "The Bible's Wounded Authority," *Engaging Biblical Authority: Perspectives on the Bible as Scripture*, eds., William P. Brown (Louisville, KY: Westminster John Knox, 2007), 113–121. In this essay, Jewish philosopher and theologian Peter Ochs meditates on how to read Scripture as an authority that both wounds and heals us. He closes with his own set of rules for reading and sets out what he calls "textual reasoning" as a practice of slow reading.

NOTES

1 James Cone, "Biblical Revelation and Social Existence," *Interpretation* 28, no. 4 (1974): 438.

2 The Anglican theologian John Webster (1955–2016) articulates this in a formal way, stating: "The definitive act of the church is faithful hearing of the gospel of salvation by the risen Christ in the Spirit's power through the service of Holy Scripture. As *creatura verbi divini*, the creature of the divine Word, the church is the hearing church." John Webster, *Holy Scripture: A Dogmatic Sketch* (Cambridge: Cambridge University Press, 2003), 44.

3 My concern here is the relationship between Scripture, moral formation, and ethical deliberation. I bracket the broader question of the relationship between becoming the people of God and Scripture.

4 Karl Barth, *Church Dogmatics: The Doctrine of the Word of God*, vol. I/2, trans., G. T. Thomson and Harold Knight (New York: Scribner's Sons, 1956), 533.

5 Barth, *Church Dogmatics*, I/2, 508.

6 Mathew Levering, *Participatory Biblical Exegesis: A Theology of Biblical Interpretation* (South Bend, IN: University of Notre Dame Press, 2008), 70.

7 Gregory of Nyssa, *Song of Songs*, trans., Casimir McCambley (Brookline, MA: Hellenic College, 1987), 37.

8 Trible connects the analogy between reading Scripture and Jacob wrestling with a stranger to a further image, that of the people of God on the verge of

entering the promised land and Moses setting before them both blessings and curses. It was for them to choose which they would follow. Likewise, as Trible puts it: "The Bible sets before us blessing and curse, good and evil, and it tells us to choose. It doesn't make the choice for us. The text that in one setting can be a blessing, in another setting can be a curse." Phyllis Trible, "Wrestling with Scripture," *Biblical Archeology Review* 32, no. 2 (2006): 51.

9 Hiddenness is not the same as absence. The ways in which divine presence can be veiled and unveiled, and at other times, God can be present and absent are rich themes in Scripture taken up by mystical and other theologians.

10 "Sermon 22," *The Works of St. Augustine: Sermons, (20–50) on the Old Testament III/2*, trans., Edmund Hill (New York: New City, 1990), 47.

11 See Laura Donaldson, "Joshua in America: On Cowboys, Canaanites, and Indians," *The Calling of the Nations: Exegesis, Ethnography, and Empire in a Biblical-Historic Present*, eds., Mark Vessey, Sharon Betcher, Robert Daum, and Harry Maier (Toronto: University of Toronto Press, 2011), 273–290.

12 On this, see Naim Ateek, *Justice and Only Justice: A Palestinian Theology of Liberation* (Maryknoll, NY: Orbis Books, 1989).

13 For a constructive reading of Joshua in relation to contemporary moral concerns see Davis, *Opening Israel's Scripture*, 130–141.

14 Phyllis Trible, *Texts of Terror: Literary-Feminist Readings of Biblical Narratives* (Philadelphia: Fortress Press, 1984).

15 Allen uses this story in dialogue with Hobbes and Locke to frame a contemporary discussion of who is sacrificed and who loses what for the sake of liberal democracy in North America. Danielle Allen, *Talking to Strangers: Anxieties of Citizenship Since Brown v. Board of Education* (Chicago: University of Chicago Press, 2004), 37–49.

16 A parallel between plain sense/literal readings and literalism is how both read by forgetting context and chronology. The former does so within an eschatological temporality whereby the text is a means of reading the present from the past and the future simultaneously, thereby opening up the now as a moment of participation in the communion of saints in communion with God. Literalism, by contrast, remains tethered to the present, ignoring rather than suspending context and chronology, in order to read the text through the grid of contemporary concerns and frames of reference.

17 That said, marked by the apocrypha, there is a blurred line between what is canonical and what is not that resists final closure of what texts should be read together.

18 Augustine, *Teaching Christianity (De Doctrina Christiana)*, trans., Edmund Hill (Hyde Park, NY: New City Press, 1996), 129 (I.36).

19 This is a point drawn from Frederick Douglass's autobiographical reflections on the role of slaves' music and songs for understanding slavery as a system. As Paul Gilroy notes, this music "was not simply a matter of African cultural life reasserting and renewing itself. For him, the music and the social relations it created supplied the favored means to assert and examine the humanity of the slave population that was being dehumanized by the government of the plantation." Paul Gilroy, "The Black Atlantic and the Re-enchantment of Humanism," The Tanner Lectures on Human Values, delivered at Yale University, February 21, 2014.

4 Listening to Strangers

Some years ago, I was involved in a community organizing coalition called London Citizens and its response to the financial crisis of 2007–2008. The coalition, which addressed issues ranging from street safety to the need for a living wage, was made up of churches, mosques, synagogues, trade unions, schools, resident associations, and universities. In the wake of the crisis, the coalition engaged in a process of listening to the folk who were part of the membership institutions to hear how the crisis, and the economic recession that came in its aftermath, was affecting them and what issues needed to be addressed. What became clear was that many were negatively affected by extortionate rates of interest charged by credit card companies, banks, and subprime lenders who at the same time were being bailed out by taxpayers' money. Jewish and Muslim members knew exactly what to call what was happening: it was usury. To my shame, and despite having written extensively on political and economic questions, I had never thought about debt and usury and their role in creating and perpetuating injustice. But in conversation with my Muslim and Jewish neighbors I was provoked to revisit the Bible and the Christian tradition to discover what they taught about debt and usury. Listening to the cries of those negatively affected by the financial crisis demanded a response. Listening to non-Christian "strangers" provided wisdom and a beginning point for further theological reflection that led me to listen to Scripture and the Christian tradition in a new way.

This experience poses the following question: Can we listen to creation and Scripture by ourselves, or do we need others not like us to be able to really hear what is going on? Without keeping company with strangers do we end up in a kind of groupthink conflating what is moral with what is widely accepted or popular? In short, what is the role of the stranger, "the other," those not like "us" in truthful description? It is this question that is the focus of this chapter. As my experience with London Citizens illustrates, one vital way to counter the dynamics of either groupthink, parochialism, or simply doing what is conventional is through listening to and learning from strangers. But listening to strangers is not merely a prophylactic against self-deception. It is also a fundamental way to be morally oriented to and metabolize reality: encountering and understanding others is a beginning point for wisdom about what is true, good, and beautiful.

THE STRANGER AS SOURCE OF FEAR AND WONDER

Theology and philosophy both begin with a sense of wonder (*thaumazein*) about and open attention to what we fear, what is different, and what we don't understand. There is no theology or philosophy without an attempt to comprehend the unknown, without faith seeking understanding. How we relate to what we don't know and don't understand – whether it is divine or just different – defines whether we are moral and wise or not. Do we ignore and repress what we don't know and don't understand, thereby remaining ignorant, or seek to engage it and understand better what or who is strange? But then what is the right way to order and respond to others, to what we don't understand, to that which fills us with either fear or wonder?

Having just discussed the importance of listening to Scripture, it is important to attend to its call on this point. Scripture counsels separation from idolators and sinners. But idolators and sinners are not the same as strangers. Quite the contrary. As Hebrews exhorts: "Do not neglect to show hospitality to strangers, for by doing that some have entertained angels without knowing it" (Heb 13:2). Often it is the one who presumes faithfulness who is the idolator and sinner, while the stranger is a means of grace by which the self-righteous may come to repentance. Moreover, Scripture teaches that the people of God need to listen for the authoritative word that comes from outsiders. This is exemplified in the story of Balaam (Num 22–24), a foreign prophet who hears the voice of God unmediated by Israel and delivers what is a blessing that could easily be heard as a curse. The pattern for this is Melchizedek, the outsider in the book of Genesis who bears the blessing and word of God to the covenanted so that they can know better how to go on. In the New Testament, Melchizedek is read as a type of Christ (Heb 7). And throughout the Gospels, Christ is the ambiguous figure that we meet as both a stranger to be welcomed and the host who welcomes. He is discovered at the center *and the periphery*. Jesus himself exhorts his followers to be open to the word of life coming from strangers, and he models what this openness looks like, whether he is relating to Samaritans, Syrophoenician women, Centurions, children, or the marginalized. Scripture's teaching may be summarized as follows: Christians by themselves turn strange; they need strangers to keep them Christian.

Beyond scriptural imperative is the sheer fact of plurality. Wherever we live and whatever our structural location, encountering strangers and what we find strange is just part of life. Culture, religion, ethnicity, socioeconomic position, ideology, gender, sexuality, and geography are but a few of the many divisions by which we encounter difference, that in turn can invoke dread or wonder. To be moral requires addressing the inevitable reality that we encounter all sorts of people not like us, whom we don't understand, and with whom we disagree. How to respond lovingly and justly to the other – the stranger, the enemy, the one not like me – is a central moral challenge for any form of life, at any time, in any place.

In the contemporary context, the fact of plurality takes the particular form of living in multifaith, multicultural, morally diverse societies that are also socioeconomically and racially divided. This context poses the question of how to keep faith with my distinctive commitments while also forming a common life with neighbors who have a different vision of life than I do under circumstances in which we may be structurally divided and unequally located. I address the latter part of this situation in Chapter 5. In this chapter, I focus on the question of how our own roots, our sense of what counts as home, identity, or belonging – that is, what makes us distinctive and particular – should be ordered in relationship to those we find strange. This is a key question for Christian ethics, and one I take up again in Chapter 14. It is key because creating and sustaining a loving and just common life between "Christians" and "non-Christians" – or church and world – is a central concern. In terms of Christian ethics, therefore, we have to consider how a Christian way of being alive takes account of those we find strange, those we fear, and those we regard as enemies of "our" way of life.

As I mentioned at the start of this chapter, it was listening to strangers and those crying out for liberation that profoundly redirected my understanding and description of what was going on during the 2007–2008 financial crisis. This process of listening involved two key elements: first, having my walls down so as to be in a place to hear from others not like me; and second, putting my roots down by digging into Scripture and traditions of Christian belief and practice. Too often, though, Christians either put their *walls up*, refusing to listen to and learn from strangers, or in the name of being open to others, put their walls down but pull their *roots up*, not engaging Scripture or their traditions. In my experience, bringing walls down generated a desire to put my roots down, the two emerging simultaneously, which then enabled bridges to be built through discovering points of connection and shared concern that formed the basis of a common life in which difference was brought into reciprocal relation. The practical outworking of this collaboration was a successful campaign for responsible lending practices by banks.[1]

Listening to strangers, however, requires a particular kind of relationship. If we are listening, we are not silencing, oppressing, or killing others. If we are listening, we are in some kind of mutual relationship. If we are listening, we are building institutions and structures that enable not just the usual voices to be heard, but also the voices of the least, the lost, and the last, valuing them as having something to say. If we are listening, we are not pretending to be in control or trying to determine the outcome before the conversation begins. Instead, we are trusting that wisdom is to be found not just among those we understand or like or who are like us but also among those we find strange or even scandalous.

THE STRANGER AS LIKE AND UNLIKE ME

When listening to strangers in order to discern what is going on, do we begin by listening for the ways we are *like* them or the ways we are *unlike* them? Neither is necessarily wrong, but each approach has certain limitations and can generate specific kinds of problems. Both starting points are born out of concern for justice; that is, how to justly respond to the fact of plurality by giving strangers what is due to them. Frameworks that begin with an analysis of how humans are the same or what they have in common speculate that, despite different ways of life, underneath it all, the other is like us. Such frameworks appeal to what are presumed to be universal sets of values or human commonalities while bracketing cultural differences. Versions of this move in the contemporary context include human rights and humanitarianism. Within Christianity, Judaism, and Islam some version of natural law is a primary instantiation of such a framework. However, natural law, along with other approaches that emphasize our common humanity, such as human rights, tend to be anthropocentric. The metabolic vision outlined in Chapter 2 is an alternative framework that attends both to what humans share and how our humanity is constituted through relationship with nonhuman ways of existing.

Alongside the problem of anthropocentrism, a further problem attends moral frameworks that begin with how humans are the same. The claim to be the same is based on premises that obscure how others are different. A primary way this manifests itself is through the generation of categories that predetermine how to interpret others. For example, I determine that all humans are rational, but I set the terms and conditions of what constitutes rationality. When others do not meet my criteria of what is rational, I thereby judge them to be less than human. In such instances, a moral concern for recognizing the humanity of others, combined with an asymmetry of power used to enforce a specific worldview forces others to conform to an account of what it means to be human that is at a minimum alien to them but can also be destructive of their way of life. European colonialism, justified as a civilizational project to make the "savage" truly human, is a paradigm instance of just such a process of imposition and destruction. To appear and be valued as fellow humans, the colonized must reorder how they live so as to appear human according to the classifications of the colonizer.

In contrast to moral frameworks that begin by exploring how humans are the same, the alternative is to presume the other is not like us, but "we" must try to understand "them" in relation to their own customs and language if they are to be given what is their due. While difference is recognized at the outset, the ways of the other are not seen as random, outlandish, or incomprehensible (i.e., they do not live in chaos). Rather, their form of life has an intelligible order that must be understood in its own terms of reference if we are to understand them and how they might see us. Without such an attempt at understanding, no realm of shared meaning and action can emerge. Beginning with difference entails an act of moral imagination rather than speculative reasoning. Difference-oriented frameworks most often emerge at close quarters when the need to negotiate a common life with strangers is existentially pressing.

Yet attending to the "otherness" of the other has its own problems. Such a move can exoticize strangers, rendering them objects of fantasy or titillation rather than beings with whom we might share a reciprocal common life. The postcolonial theorist Edward Said names one example of this dynamic "Orientalism."[2] The other becomes simultaneously a source of fascination and fear. They are portrayed as both a source of vitality, authenticity, and strength, and, in contrast to the decadent and corrupt ways of "our" civilization, they represent a way to reconnect to what is real and true. At the same time, the other represents a form of life that is less than or a potential threat to "our" civilized way of life. White suburban teenagers mimicking the dress and language of "gangsta" rappers as a way to "keep it real" while simultaneously trading in racist stereotypes is an example of this dynamic.

THE STRANGER AS THE BASIS OF ETHICS

A focus on moral reflection generated through encounter with others has become a central focus for much of contemporary ethics. That preoccupation is born in part out of a suspicion that Western moral philosophies that emphasize our common humanity are not neutral in how they understand what it means to be human. They posit a vision of the human as a rational, autonomous, self-reflexive subject that is far from universal while depending on a very limited understanding of reason. It is increasingly recognized that different cultures have very different conceptions of the moral subject, and reason itself is always determined by structures of power that shape who counts as reasonable and what counts as rational. Instead of looking to our capacity to reason as the quality that makes and connects us as humans, we should look to particular forms and practices of relating. This is a move exemplified by a number of contemporary philosophers and critical theorists who argue that the basis for being moral is not a shared rationality, but a radical receptivity toward others not like "us."[3] In short, instead of ethics beginning with the injunction to know thyself and then extending that self-knowledge to others; it begins with knowing thy neighbor and through their eyes coming to understand oneself in relation to others.

On this kind of other-orientated approach to ethics, the stranger presents a crisis to how I have constructed the world. Such a crisis can be constructive: the encounter with and reception of others not like me is the beginning of ethical reflection and thus a moral life. But this is necessarily an unstable and open-ended process, as we are always in danger of reconstituting a closed circle of relations that excludes some even as it includes others.

An other-orientated approach does not depend on seeing the other as the same as me. To draw analogies between ourselves and another – to love your neighbor as yourself – is to force our own categories on the other. In that view, what looks like me is what counts. In place of envisaging the other as like me, we need to accept an other's own self-definitions on the presumption that the other is not like me at all: there is an absolute difference that cannot be overcome. The French philosopher and literary critic Jacques Derrida (1930–2004) goes so far as to suggest that the only truly ethical relation is one in which I completely empty myself and, at the threat of annihilation of myself, host others who define themselves through their own terms of reference. Radical openness to others requires we suspend any ethical judgment, refusing to discriminate or even recognize a difference between the psychopathic killer and the homeless stranger in need of succor. All are to be welcomed, so that ethics becomes a kind of subjection or self-sacrifice. This may seem extreme, except that there is a common way of interpreting the highest ideal of Christian love (*agape*) exactly in terms of self-emptying, unconditional, disinterested, and self-negating sacrifice. The obvious danger with an emphasis on radical receptivity is that we become passive and accept everything and everyone. There is no reciprocity; we are simply acted upon. Indeed, the notion that a moral relation with others should involve some form of reciprocity or mutuality is precisely what Derrida and some interpretations of agapic love are suspicious of. They insist that the only truly moral relation is one that suspends all judgment and expects no return.

Neither defining the other as somehow the same as me, nor suspending all norms and ethical judgments, nor total, unconditional acceptance of others exhausts all the options for how to frame moral relations with strangers. There is a third, christologically defined option beyond absolute otherness and relative sameness. Benedict of Nursia, one of the founding figures of Western monasticism, taught monks to always welcome the stranger as if they were Christ. It is Christ who defines and gives us the criteria to discern who is the stranger to be welcomed and who is to be challenged or resisted. We can recognize the other as neighbor not in relation to ourselves but first and foremost in relation to Christ (i.e., a theocentric rather than anthropocentric horizon). An example of this in action comes from the Belgian town of Geel.

Echoing St. Benedict's rule, since at least the thirteenth century, perhaps earlier, the villagers of Geel have welcomed and cared for vulnerable strangers. Initially a place of pilgrimage and healing for those considered insane, for 700 years villagers have provided a place of sanctuary and care for the disabled and mentally ill in their homes. Some were short-term guests, others joined households for a lifetime. Originally overseen by the church, the system was incorporated into the state provision of social care from the mid-nineteenth century onwards.[4] The village has helped inspire a wider, global movement for decentralized, mutual, non-commercial, non-bureaucratic forms of home-based foster care exemplified by the work of Shared Lives Plus in the United Kingdom. Another example of how hospitality to strangers can be a pathway to holiness was the welcome and protection of thousands of Jews by the villagers of Le Chambon-sur-Lignon in the French Massif Central during the Fascist Vichy regime and then under Nazi occupation during World War II.[5] Led by their Protestant pastor, André Trocmé, himself committed to nonviolent civil resistance, the villagers organized not only the protection but also enabled the escape of many Jews to neutral Switzerland. As in Geel, they and those they protected formed common households and a community of shared risk and belonging.

A moral life consists of more than passive receptivity. The philosopher Simone Weil's notion of attentiveness is better than receptivity as a way to conceptualize the kind of openness to others that moral relations require.[6] Loving attention or attunement involves active contemplation, beholding, or hearing rather than simply receiving. Such attention involves elements of expectation, reverence, keeping faith, longing, and hope. Contrary to Derrida, this requires neither suspending moral judgment nor denying the expectation of a return. Rather, attention is premised on them. Moreover, we don't just contemplate either God or others. Like acts of hospitality by those who lived in Geel and Le Chambon, we must also respond. Through call and response, a shared realm of meaning and action is constituted between ourselves and another. Loving attention seeks fulfillment in practices of response that give rise to a mutually constituted common life in which each becomes responsible for the other. For example, in the shared household of Geel and Le Chambon, each party took a risk and each took responsibility for the other. Something is wrong if either side over-determines the character and quality of the common life that emerges. Terms for that over-determination include abuse, exploitation, and domination.

BEING MORAL AS BECOMING OTHERWISE

Loving attention enables us to become "otherwise." Beyond its standard meaning as acting differently or in another way, I extend it to mean becoming wise and insightful about those who act or live differently but with whom we can build a fruitful common life.[7] Becoming otherwise does not involve becoming like or identical to the other, or even identifying with the other. The differences between us are not erased or overcome. Rather, it entails a movement from knowing *about* to learning *from* to eventually knowing and being in relationship *with*. This requires a kind of conversion. Becoming otherwise means that I move into another, often narrow pathway for being alive so that "I" no longer interpret and experience reality only in terms defined by my experience, history, and classifications. What feels like "common sense" is no longer defined by me and those who are like me. Instead, it emerges through a mutually constituted common life between friends, strangers, and enemies. Chapter 14 explores what it means to cultivate such a common life in practice through politics.

Ethical frameworks that focus solely on the place of the other rather than the life that exists *between* us assume an absolute separation between oneself and another, a clear autonomy. In contrast, on a metabolic view of being alive, we are always already entangled in and constituted through the lives of others. Both autonomy and absolute difference are fantasies. The issue is the quality and character of our relations with others, not whether we should or can relate. Other focused approaches to moral concern tend to assume a gap between the self and the other that needs to be overcome or simply accepted. But relations of one kind or another exist whether we like or intend them. The real question is not whether to relate but how to care for the relationships from which our life is woven. And here a strong parallel and overlap can be made between the approach I am developing here on theological grounds and what is known as an "ethic of care."

Originating in the work of Carol Gilligan and Nel Noddings, and subsequently developed by feminist philosophers, an ethic of care is an increasingly influential strand of moral theory. It begins from the starting point that all humans need to receive and give care to live and that we are embedded in relations that need ongoing care from us if we are to live well. From this beginning point, Joan Tronto and Berenice Fisher define care as "everything that we do to maintain, continue and repair our 'world' so that we can live in it as well as possible. That world includes our bodies, our selves, and our environment, all of which we seek to interweave in a complex, life sustaining web."[8] For Tronto, rightly caring for the world requires four elements: *attentiveness* to what is going on so that real needs can be identified; taking either personal or collective *responsibility* for these needs; *competence* in the mode and manner of care given (rather than either good intentions or simply being seen to do something, the care given must actually provide in some way what is genuinely needed); and lastly, *responsiveness* to the person or context and the specificity of the need in ways that address the vulnerability and particularities of those cared for.[9] Absent any one of the characteristics and the action itself ceases to be a form of good care.

An ethics of care points to how any conception of human freedom and flourishing must take seriously the ways humans are inherently entangled in relationships with and for others. At the same time, even as we recognize that our lives are woven from the lives of others, there is also always both a certain opacity and excess to those others with whom we relate. Echoing Tronto's criteria of good care, we do not and cannot claim to fully know and understand another, even close kin, so to be responsible we always need to be attentive and responsive to others in order to treat them lovingly and justly. To presume to understand and know how to relate is to presume too much (it also forecloses the possibility of being surprised). Conversely, to seek to understand what we don't know and be open to its wonder is a mark of both wisdom and faith.

As humans who come to be through relations with others, we are the same as all other creatures, we are more like some persons than others, and we are also like no other person. Each person is unique. This basic structure of a human being is at once assumed and affirmed in the incarnation of Jesus Christ. Like other humans, Jesus is a human animal; Jesus, as a historical person, is more like some than others; and Jesus is unique, able to disclose to us more than we can imagine about what it means to be a human creature in relationship with other forms of creatureliness. The example of hospitality toward strangers illustrates how good care is grounded on this threefold pattern. To welcome the other is to recognize one who is the same as me. Yet to welcome the other is to be in a place of welcome and thus in relationship with others who are more like me than the "stranger" who is welcomed. However, to truly welcome another is to welcome one who is like nobody else, affording them the concrete respect that communicates recognition of their particularity. In short, hospitality demands recognizing the other as being simultaneously like me, *un*like me, and wholly unique. This is true of all forms of neighbor love.

FREEDOM AS FRUITFULNESS VS. FREEDOM AS CHOICE

An other-oriented moral life demands that we think more carefully about our conception of freedom. Modern ethics – Christian or otherwise – is rightly concerned with what inhibits the free expression or choice of the individual, whether that is because of physical suffering or political oppression. But a conception of freedom centered on individual choice is problematic. As Bonhoeffer notes:

> In the language of the Bible, freedom is not something that people have for themselves but something they have for others .... Freedom is not a quality a human being has; it is not an ability, a capacity, an attribute of being that may be deeply hidden in a person but can somehow be uncovered .... To be more precise, freedom is a relationship between two persons. Being free means "being-free-for-the-other," because I am bound to the other. Only by being in relation with the other am I free.[10]

Bonhoeffer's conception of freedom as "being-free-for-the-other" is grounded in the Gospel message that in Christ, God is free for creation, becoming creation so that creation may once more be free for God.[11] Freedom on this account is constituted through the relationship between God, humans, and the rest of creation. Freedom is the quality and character of the relationship between us, and thus the forms of life that articulate and sustain these relations are the condition for the possibility of my ability to act freely.

Individual agency is dependent on others and determined in part by things we did not make, such as night and day and our digestive system. Autonomy – or better, my ability to act purposefully – is dependent on and constrained by a meshwork of prior relations and factors that make possible the ability to act. On a theological account, it is not so much a lack of choice that is the enemy of purposeful action; rather, it is giving oneself over to forms of authority or desire that constrain purposeful action directed to flourishing. I can't act for my good, God, or the good of my neighbor because I am consumed by lust or fear or some other tyrannical appetite or made subject to the tyranny of another's lust for power and control over me. Cultivating freedom entails the ability to resist and redirect my own appetites or those of another in order to be able to purposively act in a way that is directed to mutual flourishing and shared responsibility. Conversely, action that does not pursue love of God and neighbor is not free; it is directed to either the subjection of the self to sin or the sinful subjection of others through some form of domination or abuse. Or as James Cone puts it: "As long as man is a slave to another power, he is not free to serve God with mature responsibility. He is not free to become what he is – human."[12]

An alternative to imagining freedom in terms of individual choice and unconstrained autonomy is to understand freedom in terms of fruitfulness. Freedom is the ability to metabolize, grow, and overflow beyond our immediate capacities. That which inhibits growth or flourishing is oppressive. The Holy Spirit is the source of true freedom as the Spirit brings new life, and so the ability to grow into what we are created to be and will become. This Spirit-filled life is ecstatic and exuberant in its qualities, generating an excess or superabundance – fruit – that can bring nourishment or vitality to others.

Growth or fruitfulness is not aimless, random, or arbitrary. We cannot choose just anything and still become fruitful creatures who germinate life in others. Fruitfulness necessitates a teleology; that is, a sense of the good into which growth is ordered and participates. In Christian terms, the ultimate good we seek is communion with God who is the source and fulfillment of all being. If we are not growing up into God – and thereby fulfilling what it means to be a human creature – we are collapsing into nothingness. That's still a kind of movement but not one that generates life. Immorality is the dissipation of good relations, which happens when we seek after that which brings nothingness, while oppression is a stunting of growth or a refusal to let others flourish. As we will see in Chapter 8, freedom as fruitfulness is what it means to fulfill Jesus's command to love God and neighbor (John 15:1–15; Col 1:3–14). To turn away from others, or act toward them in such a way that destroys the possibility of fruitful encounter, is to turn to nothingness and unfreedom.

This account of freedom as fruitfulness emphasizes the quality and kind of relationships we have and the need to become otherwise as defining features of a moral life. It thereby rejects a common underlying logic that characterizes much ethical thought; namely, copying, becoming the same as, or identifying with an ideal. Within frameworks that emphasize identification over interrelationship, there is a fixed ideal or singular way of doing things, a standard we all must approximate in order to count as ethical. This hallowed ideal or condition represents all that is true, good, and beautiful. Failure to approximate or mimic the ideal is to be rendered false, bad, and ugly. If we adopt this understanding of ethics, we reduce morality to a hierarchy of status with some representing the ideal, some approximating the ideal, and others representing its inversion. Inevitably, certain kinds of bodies and people are coded as incapable of fulfilling the ideal and are thereby excluded from the realm of what counts as true, good, and beautiful. Indeed, the ideal requires its inversion to make sense: what we identify as "black" becomes the necessary negative quality against which what we identify as "white" makes sense as the ideal. To be true, good, and beautiful is to be identified with what is considered "white." In the same way, "savage" is used to legitimize those who understand themselves as civilized, and "queer" sanctifies what is perceived as "straight."[13] This goes along with a linear sense of moral development: one is either developing into or departing from the ideal; over time, one either moves up or down the hierarchy. By contrast, on my metabolic, relational account, becoming moral is an interactive, dynamic way of being alive that can only be discovered over time with others who are not like me through fruitfully metabolizing the relationships within which I am entangled. Christologically, being alive in ways that bring blessing rather than a curse – that is, ways that care for and cultivate rather than render toxic or destroy – is about participation in and relationship with the ascended Christ in the power of the Holy Spirit. However, being in relationship with Christ is not about conformity to a contingent, culturally determined, fallen archetype of an ideal human falsely identified as representing God. Rather than conforming to a preexisting ideal or being located on a fixed hierarchy of value to which everyone must conform, discovering what brings flourishing requires becoming otherwise if it is to be fruitful. One way to specify what it means to be fruitfully otherwise is through an ethic of care involving attentiveness, responsibility, competence, and responsiveness.

In summary, a moral way of being alive demands attention to others not like "us" yet with whom our lives are interwoven in seen and unseen ways. But in listening to strangers, both near and far, we must reckon with how the strangers we listen to are structurally located. In Christian ethics, a further specification of listening to strangers is the need to prioritize listening to the poor and structurally marginalized. It is this "preferential option for the poor" that I examine in Chapter 5.

ACCOMPANYING READINGS

Benedict, *Rule of St Benedict*, chapter 36, "Of the Sick Brethren," and 53 "Of the Reception of Guests." The Rule appears in various editions and is available online. Benedict argues for the centrality of welcoming the stranger to the cultivation of a Christian moral life, which is understood as necessarily lived in community.

Sandra Sullivan-Dunbar, "Human Dependency, Justice, and Christian Love," *Human Dependency and Christian Ethics* (Cambridge: Cambridge University Press, 2017), 1–26. Sullivan-Dunbar analyzes the interrelationship between the universal and particular dimensions of love and justice and the nature of equality through beginning with how humans come to be through a web of dependent and communal relations of care.

Nicolás Panotto, "A Critique of the Coloniality of Theological Knowledge: Rereading Latin American Liberation Theology as Thinking Otherwise," *Decolonial Christianities: Latinx and Latin American Perspectives*, eds., Raimundo Barreto and Roberto Sirvent (Cham: Palgrave Macmillan, 2019), 217–237. Panotto reviews different decolonial epistemologies that center the "other" and thereby challenge colonial/modern/Western monopolies of power and knowledge, advocating instead for diverse approaches to being alive. He then draws on these frameworks to "deepen and radicalize" Latin American Liberation Theology as a project.

NOTES

1 For a detailed account of this story and the theology of debt and usury it generated, see Luke Bretherton, *Resurrecting Democracy: Faith, Citizenship and the Politics of a Common Life* (Cambridge: Cambridge University Press, 2015).

2 Edward Said, *Orientalism* (New York: Vintage, 1979).

3 Thinkers who emphasize encounter with and responding to the "other" as the ground of ethical reflection and formation include Martin Buber, Emmanuel Levinas, Paul Ricoeur, Jacques Derrida, Judith Butler, Luce Irigaray, Enrique Dussel, and Jean-Luc Marion. A key critical concern of such reflection are conceptions of the self as somehow fully autonomous and oriented toward securing itself and the world in terms established by itself, thereby refusing the call or claim of others and how the self is constituted through relations with others.

4 Jackie Goldstein and Marc Godemont, "The Legend and Lessons of Geel, Belgium: A 1500-Year-Old Legend, a 21st-Century Model," *Community Mental Health Journal* 39, no. 5 (2003): 441–458; Henck P. J. G. van Bilsen, "Lessons to Be Learned from the Oldest Community Psychiatric Service in the World: Geel in Belgium," *BJPsych Bulletin* 40, no. 4 (2016): 207–211.

5 Philip Hallie, *Lest Innocent Blood Be Shed: The Story of the Village of Le Chambon, and How Goodness Happened There* (New York: Harper & Row, 1979).

6 Simone Weil, "Reflections on the Right Use of School Studies with a View to the Love of God," *Waiting on God*, trans., Emma Craufurd (London: Fontana Books, 1950), 66–76.

7 The call to become otherwise is exemplified in strands of decolonial theology. See, for example, Nicolás Panotto, "A Critique of the Coloniality of Theological Knowledge: Rereading Latin American Liberation Theology as Thinking Otherwise," *Decolonial Christianities: Latinx and Latin American Perspectives*, eds., Raimundo Barreto and Roberto Sirvent (Cham: Palgrave Macmillan, 2019), 217–237.

8 Joan Tronto, *Moral Boundaries: A Political Argument for an Ethic of Care* (New York: Routledge, 1993), 103. For a direct engagement with an ethics of care in Christian ethics see Sandra Sullivan-Dunbar, *Human Dependency and Christian Ethics* (New York: Cambridge University Press, 2017).

9 Tronto, *Moral Boundaries*, 127–137.

10 Dietrich Bonhoeffer, *Bonhoeffer Works, vol. 3, Creation and Fall: A Theological Interpretation of Genesis 1–3*, ed., John de Gruchy, trans., Douglas Stephen Bax (Minneapolis, MN: Fortress Press, 2004), 62–63. Note this passage is quoted by Gustavo Gutiérrez in his seminal book *Theology of Liberation: History, Politics, and Salvation*, rev. ed. (Maryknoll, NY: Orbis, 1988 [1973]), 24.

11 Bonhoeffer, *Creation and Fall*, 63.

12 James Cone, *Black Theology and Black Power*, rev. ed. (Maryknoll, NY: Orbis Books, 1997), 39

13 The actuality of those whose way of being alive are designated "black," "savage," or "queer" are not captured by the system of representation that stigmatizes them in this way. Framed in terms of stereotype and stigma such forms of life are illegible to and thereby indigestible by that structure of value. As that which is outside the system, as that which has no real measure within it, these illegible ways of being alive are at once seditious and provide resources of resistance and alternative ways of being alive to the status quo. The church is at times and should be just such a form of life that is in excess of, never fully digestible by, and partly illegible to any instantiation of the earthly city.

5 Listening to Cries for Liberation

Everyday life gives us ample opportunity to pay attention to ethical questions, particularly those related to exploitation and suffering. For example, consider the issues related to the sourcing, selling, and preparation of our food. When I go to the grocery store, how aware am I of the living conditions of the chickens whose flesh I buy and the working conditions of those who processed the meat? How conscious should I be of the terms and conditions given to the farmer who owns the chicken plant by the conglomerate that buys the chicken and sells it on to the supermarket? Are they so burdened with debt that they harbor suicidal thoughts? Should I ask whether those who stack the shelves or work at the checkout lane are paid a living wage? Can I recycle the packaging the chicken comes in? Do I cook and eat the chicken around a table with others, or by myself in front of a computer screen while anxiously catching up on emails? Do I say grace before I eat, giving thanks for the life and labor of those who made it possible for me to eat this piece of chicken here and now?

Becoming a good person or community does not just mean becoming attuned to creaturely life, following Scripture with creative fidelity, and being hospitable to strangers. We must also attend to how the everyday things we do to make a life, such as buying and cooking chicken, either nourish or diminish the lives of others, both human and nonhuman. It means changing how we live so as to ensure that our ways of being alive are not built on systems of exploitation. For many, this entails ensuring we are listening to, learning from, and forming a common life with those who are crying out for liberation. Only when we are doing so can we tell the truth about who we are and the world we live in and therefore be able to act morally and politically with and for others in ways that cultivate mutual flourishing.

ON HEARING WHO IS BURDENED SO SOME ARE NOT

The trouble is that many of us tend to only listen to certain kinds of voices. Our lives are constructed so that we remain oblivious to those crying out for liberation. Those who are materially or politically advantaged in some way, even marginally so, are free *not* to notice how others are afflicted and disempowered by the ways in which the status quo only benefits those who are relatively secure in their position. Those who are prosperous and powerful often suffer from the vice of indifference, inhabiting worlds that reinforce a sense that they deserve what they have. Segregated housing patterns, easy access to credit, better resourced schools, preferential treatment in medical care, and other advantages generate enclaves of unconcern among the structurally advantaged. This indifference generates a myopia about how certain people are socially, physically, linguistically, and legally hindered from living well. Issues of class, sexuality, gender, physical ability, national origin, and race are critical here: when we remain unaware of how certain kinds of bodies are favored by the systems we inhabit, we leave in place systemic disadvantages. We immunize ourselves from realizing how others bear the costs of a way of life that benefits some and disproportionately burdens others. Such indifference is not only unjust; it is also depraved. That is, it actively perverts our moral faculties so that when we are confronted with complicity in injustice, instead of repentance, our reaction is one of aggrieved entitlement.

It is a struggle to puncture the mental and spiritual enclosure that prosperity and a sense of entitlement sustains. As Jesus puts it in the Gospels, it's harder than passing a camel through the eye of a needle (Matt 19:24). Structural advantage is often woven out of the very fabric of our lives and operates in subtle, unseen ways. For example, how we sit, talk, eat, dress, and comport ourselves can express and reproduce socioeconomic class or racial divisions that favor some people over others in access to education, loans, jobs, housing, and the like. Yet, at an instinctive level, those whose behaviors and bodies comport with what is deemed normal or socially correct feel their behaviors are simply good, right, and proper. They assume it is rude not to sit up straight, look people in the eye, and pick up on subtle social cues.

Pointing out to the structurally advantaged how much of their resources either comes to them in unearned ways or requires others to bear its costs often leads to vicious reactions. Such defensive backlash occurs because asking people to acknowledge their participation in an oppressive system challenges the very basis of their way of life. Like the Pharisees and Sadducees, no one likes to think that their way of doing things is part of the problem and bitterly oppose those who force them to confront this possibility. Ignorance is bliss, but to be blissfully ignorant of the deprivation of others is to turn ourselves away from the pursuit of a flourishing life.

The counter to ignorance is cultivating ways of paying attention to who is being impoverished or oppressed. To echo Luke 6, if we are to hunger and thirst for righteousness and justice then we need practices of listening and ways of cultivating virtues such as courage, patience, humility, and hope in order to hear and learn from those crying out for liberation. Without attending to their voices we cannot know what needs changing in order to forge a more generous and just way of life.

As an ascetic discipline, listening to those crying out for liberation is an anti-ideological measure that puts people before program. Ideology, as defined here, does two things. First, it naturalizes and universalizes contingent and contestable concepts of how to order our economic, political, and social life, generating the sense that certain ways of doing things are simply the ways things should be done. Everyone should conform to these standards or practices without asking questions. Hiding the contestability and contingency of a policy or way of doing things normalizes that policy, reinforcing existing modes of exploitation, domination, and unjust hierarchies of value. For example, within White supremacy as an ideological framework, racial distinctions and stereotypes are taken to be "natural" rather than constructed in order to benefit some and exploit others. Their "naturalness" in turn justifies further violent, exploitative, and discriminatory behaviors and policies, both to those doing the discriminating and to the discriminated against.

Second, ideology turns things upside down. It inverts reality, describing the world in opposite terms, in order to direct attention away from whose interests are being served. For example, our data is stored in the "cloud" which in reality is made of vast energy consuming, carbon emitting data processing centers constructed using rare earth metals and other materials extracted from the ground. Or in mainstream economics "security" now means risk and "credit" now means debt. "Trickle-down economics" is said to "lift all boats" and thereby serve the interests of everyone when in actuality it concentrates wealth and political power in the hands of existing elites. In the words of the prophet Isaiah, bitter becomes sweet and sweet bitter; evil is called good and good evil (Isa 5:20). The following are some of the ways in which ideological ways of holding beliefs invert reality: they are reductive, generating simplistic, often binary understandings of reality that thereby distort it; they mask what contests our view of things; they misdirect our attention; and they render invisible or illegible what is actually happening. The impact of ideology is to delegitimize other ways of doing things and perpetuate an unjust status quo.

Ideology as defined here is indexed to idolatry. Idolatry is giving to creaturely things that which only properly should be given to God, namely worship. But it also means rendering the finite into the infinite, the penultimate into the ultimate, the conditional into something unconditional.[1] In other words, idolatry entails inverting reality and distorting the true order of value. When our moral and political descriptions are subject to ideology and thereby reinscribe idolatry, listening to the oppressed is a way to bring accountability. The loss enabled by listening, particularly listening to those crying out for liberation, should drive the mourner of lost idols to engagement with the fragile and often complex world of those struggling to get by and make ends meet.

As a way to counter the ideological overdetermination of how we describe what is going on, listening to the least, the lost, and the last is also a way to address the dynamics of what philosopher Miranda Fricker calls "epistemic injustice."[2] Beyond straightforward questions of stealing, plagiarizing, or exploiting the knowledge of others without giving due credit, questions of epistemic injustice fall into three sets of interrelated issues. The first are questions about who is excluded from existing ways and means of producing and accessing knowledge. For example, medical knowledge as such is good, but women, the working class, and minorities have historically been excluded from its production and distribution. Epistemic justice entails including in its production those who have been unjustly excluded and ensuring fair access for all. Epistemic justice also corrects asymmetries in the authority and credibility of knowers. Historically, the status of what people know has been tied to prejudice and discrimination; or to put this more simply, the testimony of some counts more. For example, the testimonies of women, the working class, or minorities doing "amateur" scientific experiments or giving testimony in a court of law have not carried as much weight as that of white, middle-class men with credentialed knowledge that others are institutionally excluded from obtaining.

A second set of issues is how certain kinds of knowledge delegitimize or inhibit other ways of knowing and making sense of the world. For example, modern medical knowledge about birthing practices excluded and discredited prior, inherited, and experiential knowledge held by women and midwives. In such instances, epistemic justice entails opening out and expanding what counts as valid knowledge and ways of knowing.

The last set of issues relates to how certain ways of interpreting the world and knowledge regimes fundamentally disorder one's relationship to the world while at the same time producing self-interested groupthink and repressing alternative forms of understanding that contest the status quo. For example, modern medicine constitutively reduces the body to biology rather than envisaging the body as a person with a biography situated in a context. This approach in turn views something like obesity as only a medical and individual problem rather than also a structural matter of political economy that for some arises from "food deserts," effects of policies such as redlining that inhibit investment in marginalized communities, poverty wages, and the like. In such cases it's not just that medical knowledge itself is insufficient or incomplete. It's that medical knowledge needs changing so the diagnoses and remedies it generates neither insulate doctors from attending to the social and political realities of their patients nor propagate injustice. Listening in the ways discussed here is a measure to remediate such dynamics as they shape moral and political determinations of how to discern what is going on.

The practices of listening I foreground enable recognizing that our descriptions of reality and the moral and political judgments that flow from these descriptions need testing, that fallen institutions and structures shape what we believe and so our convictions need challenging, and that it is the pursuit of the truth of the situation that matters not my opinion or ideology as reality is always larger than my ideas about it.

POVERTY AS A MORAL AND POLITICAL RELATION

In Scripture and in political life, change for the better begins with a cry. Scripture is full of cries, groans, wails, and shouts. Some of these cries are born of pain, some of fear, and some of wonder and amazement. It is these cries that germinate change and the struggle for new possibilities. This is exemplified in Exodus when God declares to Moses: "The cry of the Israelites has now come to me; I have also seen how the Egyptians oppress them" (Ex 3:9). Listening for those crying out in anguish is vital for any movement toward a more loving and just common life. But, as stated in Chapter 3 and as exemplified in Exodus 3, we need to be hearing the Word of God and the cries of the oppressed *together* in order to pursue faithful, hopeful, and loving change.

If we are hearers of the cries of the poor but not hearers of the Word of God then we cannot fathom either the depth of what needs changing or our own personal need to change. We are like a self-righteous vanguard who lack any humility or sense of our own sinfulness and think that everyone else is the problem. We then refuse to change our own hearts and minds. As Black liberation theologian James Cone frames this twofold dynamic: "Jesus Christ is the Truth and thus stands in judgment over all statements about truth .... There is no truth in Jesus Christ independent of the oppressed of the land."[3]

Like Cone, the Latin American liberation theologian Gustavo Gutiérrez lays out in his work how the prophetic commitment to heed experiences of suffering and poverty must be held together with the contemplative commitment to seek God. Noting how Scripture itself repeatedly and consistently enjoins us to do so, Gutiérrez states that to opt for one "to the exclusion of the other would be to mutilate the Christian message. The great challenge is to maintain a response to both demands, as Archbishop Romero used to say with reference to the church, 'From among the poor, the church can be for everyone.'"[4] Likewise, reflecting on what it means to speak of loving God and neighbor in a world where understanding what this means is fundamentally distorted, Black theologian and philosopher, Vincent Lloyd states:

> [The Christian] may turn inward to prayer, or more broadly spiritual life, as authoritative – *lex orandi, lex credendi*. She may turn outward to marginalized communities, knowing that because God is to be found among the outcasts words about God are refined as she attends to the margins. These techniques work best in concert: on the one hand, challenging idolatry (or ideology); on the other hand, attending to the wisdom of prayer and poverty. The first, alone, leads to onanistic pleasures; the second, alone, accedes to the confusions of the world. Together they correct each other.[5]

For Lloyd, alongside a turn to prayer, listening to, learning from, and identification with the poor is a vital ascetic discipline by which the advantaged may come to understand and rightly order how they love God and neighbor. But who are the poor to be listened to and given a preferential option? And how should we understand the nature and form of poverty?

The term "poverty" is first and foremost a moral and political description. The terms "poverty" and "the poor" are not neutral, technical, or impartial terms. Like words such as "war," "rape," and "murder," they simultaneously name something and make a normative evaluation of it. Language is important. Think about the difference between stating someone has been murdered rather than killed, for example. To call someone "poor" carries a different freighting than saying they merely lack food. Attempts to provide wholly technical definitions – for example, as those living below a "poverty line" – fail to grasp the moral and political dynamics in play. As a moral and political description, the word poverty is laden with a tacit set of claims about what should be valued and what constitutes the right ordering of relations.

Within Christianity, poverty implies four kinds of relation.

Drawing on Scripture as a primary point of reference, the first denotation of the term poverty is *destitution.* Destitution signifies the material lack of basic needs (food, water, shelter, etc.), a consequence of which is economic, political, and social marginality. For example, in the Scriptures, it is the widow, orphan, and stranger who are symbolic of the destitute as they lack even the most basic means of sustenance (e.g., Ps 10:14; Deut 10:18).

Destitution closely aligns with the second denotation of poverty in Scripture, which is *powerlessness.* People in poverty lack agency and become vulnerable to the actions of others, whether these others are rulers, the rich, or foreign powers. Rather than food, shelter, or some other aspect of material provision, combating powerlessness requires the redistribution and just use of power, breaking cycles of dependency, and the reconstitution of the powerless as a people capable of acting for themselves. The most common word for poverty in the Hebrew Scriptures/Old Testament (*'ānî* and *'ānāw*) implies vulnerability to oppression more than material destitution (e.g., Ps 72). The narrative paradigm of powerlessness is Exodus: God liberates the impoverished, downtrodden, and hovel-dwelling Israelites from the yoke of the wealthy, powerful, and palace-dwelling Pharaoh. The "poor of Yahweh" are those who seek justice from God (e.g., Isa 42). But, as Womanist biblical scholar Delores Williams contends, in any consideration of poverty as powerlessness it is also important to look beyond Exodus. Attention must also be given to stories such as that of Hagar and Ishmael that highlight how the marginalized – in this case Sarah – can themselves oppress others in their midst (Gen 21). Williams calls these the "oppressed of the oppressed."[6]

Poverty as powerlessness dovetails with Greek conceptions of the *demos* and Roman notions of the *pauperi*, the *plebs*, and the *populus*. These individuals are not destitute, but they are in a condition of political and thence economic and social precarity. The analogy in the contemporary context is with terms such as "the working class," "minorities," or, in Korean, "the Minjung." A more specific example is the incarcerated: their basic biological needs are met, but they lack any economic and political agency to determine their living and working conditions. Different analytical lenses frame the nature and basis of powerlessness in various ways. Some liberation theologians focus on race while others focus on either class, sexuality, physical ability, or gender as their primary point of reference. For example, queer theologian Marcella Althaus-Reid (1952–2009) contends that unless we begin with the instabilities of how sexuality and gender are constructed, and the way norms about sexual identity and behaviors organize social, economic, and political relations, we are masking *a*, if not *the*, fundamental way in which human life together is ordered and power distributed.[7] By contrast, those who focus on class contend that economic inequality is more basic, determining all other relations, including those of sexuality and gender. Although liberation theologians emphasize different primary aspects of powerlessness – class, race, gender, etc. – they share a focus on the need for liberation from unjust systems of stratification.

The third meaning of poverty in Scripture is *affliction*. The afflicted are those who are either suffering or grieving because of illness, disablement, emergency, demonic possession, accident, or the loss of a loved one. Whether they need solace, pastoral care, emergency aid, healing, or exorcism, the key is to include them within the circle of divine-human relations through the outreach of others who can at least bring comfort if not relief. A key need is active inclusion in a wider community of care and recognition so as to alleviate isolation and the ways traumatic experiences fracture a world and fragment a coherent sense of self. In the Bible, the figure of the leper symbolized affliction. In the contemporary European and American context, it is victims of war, famine, or natural disaster.

The final point of reference in a theologically formed conception of poverty is *humility*. The humble, or "poor in spirit," are like children who are ready and open to receive the Kingdom of God (Isa 61; Luke 18:15–17). But this is the most ambivalent and problematic point of reference in how poverty is constructed within Christian theology. It is problematic because it can be used to valorize poverty as a moral and political status that is spiritually beneficial for those who find themselves destitute and powerless. It can thereby serve to justify or hide structural injustice. Indeed, it is this aspect of a Christian conception of poverty that seems to drive the philosopher Karl Marx's critique of religion. Marx saw religion as a means of legitimizing poverty to elites whose interests are served by the system.[8] He held that in addition to acting as a narcotic and a mask for oppression, religion enabled elites to reconcile themselves to the system. Conceptions of poverty as a blessed state because it is a humble estate have often operated in this way. However, as Latin American liberation theologians contend, cultivating a poverty of spirit is a necessary condition for the encounter with and proper response to other kinds of poverty and the structural conditions that so often produce them.[9]

Poverty of spirit or humility emerges when we recognize what it means to be fallen, frail, and finite creatures who are dependent on God. True spiritual strength and wisdom come through recognizing our poverty as death-bound, perishable bodies in contrast to the resurrected, imperishable body of Christ (1 Cor 15; 2 Cor 12:10). As Augustine and Benedict of Nursia constantly reiterate, humility is necessary to see and hear the truth about ourselves and so be touched by God and neighbor. As those who must cultivate humility, Christians – and especially those who are structurally advantaged – are to contemplate Christ in order that they might be provoked to repentance. Through contemplating the broken body of the suffering servant, they become open to the realization that they have a common life, in and through Christ, with the poor. They also begin to understand their own poverty of spirit through recognizing their own fallenness, frailty, and finitude, and thence their need of others and God. From this place of repentance they can not only begin to hear, see, smell, taste, and touch the lives of "the poor" but also receive from them, recognizing that "we" need them as much if not more than "they" need us. "We" cannot be healed without "them," nor they without us.

As well as having a range of meanings, the term poverty invokes a moral economy of relations between rich and poor, powerful and powerless. Some must be rich so that others may be thought of as poor. That is to say, poverty entails stratification and differentiation of one kind or another. You can be starving and without shelter and yet think of yourself as famished and cold rather than poor. Talk of poverty should always at the same time be a reflection on the meaning of wealth and power. The Beatitudes exemplify this by connecting and contrasting the blessed and the cursed (Luke 6:20–26). Failure to do this constitutes a failure to reckon with the inherently moral and political nature of poverty.

A PREFERENTIAL OPTION FOR THE POOR AND THE EARTH

Liberation theologies advocate a "preferential option for the poor" as a way of disidentifying with seen and unseen patterns of domination and cultivating a poverty of spirit. Experiences of poverty, particularly those of oppression, must be recognized as having a priority as they give a better read on what is really going on. For example, to understand the economy, the experiences and stories of the low-waged and unemployed provide the beginning point for describing what is really happening in a way that spreadsheets and boardroom agendas never will. Likewise, rather than hearing first from those who own, manage, and sell the world, it is better to listen first to those closest to the ground who produce it and bear its burdens. To understand the garden, talk to the gardener not just its owner.

A preferential option for the poor is in part born out of the realization that our readings of Scripture, creation, and other people are themselves in bondage to social and political processes and harmful descriptions from which they need liberation. What is in view in the preferential option for the poor is the need to take seriously the interrelationship between how we are located in relation to social, economic, and political structures; our ways of naming and understanding what is going on; and the need for the conversion of our moral and political reasoning. Yet the priority of the poor and oppressed does not imply they are intrinsically good or their ways of narrating their experience are infallible (i.e., that they can do no wrong because their structural location makes them better humans and their experience is all-determinative). It is a question of putting first things first: whose account of the order of things is given priority when determining the reality of a situation.

The ultimate reason for a preferential option for the poor and oppressed does not, as Gutiérrez notes, "lie in the social analysis that we employ, or in our human compassion, or in the direct experience we may have of poverty." As he goes on to say:

> All of these are valid reasons and surely play an important role in our commitment. But as Christians, we base that commitment fundamentally on the God of our faith. It is a theocentric, prophetic option we make, one which strikes its roots deep in the gratuity of God's love and is demanded by that love.... In other words, the poor are preferred not because they are necessarily better than others from a moral or religious standpoint, but because God is God. No one lays conditions on God, for whom the last are first.[10]

Alongside bearing witness to the nature of God, prioritizing the historical and contemporary experience of the poor is a way of disinvesting in the structures that unjustly advantage some at the expense of others. Abiding with experiences of poverty and marginalization and letting them shape our descriptions of what is going on is also another way we might become "otherwise." Crucial to the development of such wisdom is learning from how those enduring and struggling against conditions that generate their suffering and oppression reflect on and articulate their own situation. A good example of why this is important is the development of Womanist social ethics and the ways in which it exposes the inadequacy of other frameworks. Womanist theologians such as Katie Cannon, Jacqueline Grant, Cheryl Townsend Gilkes, and Emilie Townes recognized that no existing theology provided all the categories needed to make sense of the world as they and other Black women, particularly poor Black women, experienced it. Feminist theology focused primarily on gender, Black liberation theology on racism, and Latin American liberation theology on class. Drawing on the work of earlier figures such as Pauli Murray, from the early 1980s onwards, Womanist theologians argued that a separate approach was needed to make sense of the situation of Black women who live at the intersection of three systems of oppression: one economic (class), one racial (White supremacy), and another gendered (patriarchy). Of late, a new generation of Womanist theologians has added sexuality as a point of reference. Womanist social ethics seeks to uncover and resist the way assemblages of class, race, gender, and sexuality assign negative value. As part of this, Womanists reject any notion that suffering brought on by these oppressions is God's will. Rather, God's will is for the liberation of Black women and, in concert with them, the liberation of all people.

Womanism attempts to awaken everyone to the possibility of richer visions of social relations and enable a way beyond conditions of alienation and exploitation: we are not economic units but living, desiring, social, and embodied creatures whose form of life should enable all people to thrive. Discerning what thriving means entails critically investigating "the conditions and circumstances of daily life." However, as Emilie Townes contends, such investigation must go beyond secular critical theories and attend to how theology both colludes with and reinforces hegemonic discourses while also contesting and overturning them.[11] By focusing on how constructions of class, gender, sexuality, and race deny and distort creative and nourishing forms of common life, both within and outside the church, Womanists seek ways toward love and justice for all people. As Townes puts it: "Because God loves humanity, God gives all peoples the opportunity to embrace the victory of the resurrection. The resurrection moves the oppressed past suffering to pain and struggle and from pain and struggle to new life and wholeness."[12]

East of Eden, listening to cries for liberation must include listening to the groaning of creation. The blood of Abel mixes with the earth from which it came and into which it soaked, and both cry out for justice.[13] "Am I my brother's keeper?" we ask as we extract what we can from land, sea, and air and in that process exploit our brothers and sisters for material gain. For example, what and how we eat is shaped by what and how we produce and consume, further framing how we relate to God, other humans, and the rest of creation. What is cooked, how it is prepared, who cooks and who does not, and how and when food is eaten are all windows into the soul of a society. A political economy is always already a political ecology, a culture a form of cultivation.

A popular theological way of framing what an ethical response to nonhuman creation entails is "stewardship." Stewardship can be used in a way that encourages listening to and responding to the groans of creation. However, in many presentations of this term, stewardship operates as the theological partner to the anthropocentric visions described in Chapter 2. Those who refer to human stewardship of the earth often frame it in terms of lordship, using a particular exegesis of Genesis 1:26 and 1:28 as their warrant. When understood as lordship over creation, there is no need to listen to and learn from creation. However, to understand stewardship in this way inverts its meaning. As biblical scholar Richard Bauckham points out, stewardship as a translation emerges in the seventeenth century as an alternative to the language of dominion, which had become indexed to a project of scientific and technological mastery over creation.[14] But beyond questions about whether stewardship is a good translation of the Hebrew (or an equivalent in English to New Testament and early church uses of *oikonomos* and *oikonomia*), I am not convinced that in the contemporary context stewardship is helpful as a term.

Stewards derive their authority from a sovereign power. They are deputized, on behalf of the sovereign, to care for the lands and household in their charge but which they do not own. The steward's orientation is one of conscientious and prudent use. But while stewardship invokes the need for better, more ethical forms of management, it still assumes humans stand over and above creation.[15] The overall scriptural imperative is very different and far more radical: in keeping with the theological anthropology laid out in Chapter 2, what is required is covenantal fellowship with the rest of creation. Such fellowship entails a fundamental recalibration of our ways of being alive so as to cultivate reciprocal relations with and bless nonhuman creation. In contrast to stewardship, a properly Christian account should envisage humans as being in covenantal fellowship with the rest of creation that culminates in shared worship of a common Creator (e.g., Ps 104; Ps 148; Rev 5:13). To describe the relationship in this way calls forth a very different orientation to nonhuman creation than stewardship does, one that seeks a mutual and symbiotic common life with creation rather than mastery over it. As the hymn to Christ in Colossians 1:15–23 frames it, the Gospel is proclaimed for the healing and redemption of *all* creation as fellow participants in the divine economy which has its origin and fulfillment in Christ.

Rather than stewardship, a more accurate picture of what Genesis speaks of is artisanship and agrarian conceptions of cultivation and pastoral care. Human "rule" (*radah*) over creation in Genesis 1 does *not* call for the earth's exploitation, should *not* generate the alienation of human from nonhuman life, and is *not* anthropocentric but theocentric. Even the negative valence of *radah* as stepping on or subjugating can be that of treading down wine, harvesting, or pruning, which, as any gardener knows, can increase fruitfulness. Rather than lordship, "rule" should imply authoritative, skilled, and creative agency that enacts the prior blessing God speaks over all creation and patiently attends to that creation on which humans depend for life itself.[16] Moreover, in Genesis, ruling is marked by dependency. Humans participate in a blessing and command that was in the first instance given to nonhuman forms of life (Gen 1:22) and is more explicitly enumerated in the language of Genesis 2:15. There, humans are called to *`ābad* (till, serve, work) and *shamar* (keep, preserve, protect, treasure) creation – words commonly associated with keeping the covenant and commandments.[17]

In the scriptural witness, human agency in relation to the rest of creation is indelibly marked by dependency, gift, and the need to be attuned to nonhuman ways of being alive.[18] Human "ruling" or "dominion" is thus paradoxical and severely constrained. It is born out of the reality that humans are entirely dependent on and owe their life to other, prior forms of creaturely life. However, this is not necessarily a reciprocal relation: those other forms of creaturely life do not need humans to survive let alone thrive.[19] This form of ruling is responsive and accountable to a prior and superordinate set of divine and nonhuman claims that determine its scope and purpose. In this regard, to hear the invocation to "rule" in the context of a peasant, agrarian society buffeted by wind, rain, pest, and plague is very different than taking it up in an industrialized, mechanized one and the differentials of power over nature that each makes possible. Humans are to echo God's own skilled, authoritative, and creative action as one who acts out of love; such action is to culminate in rest and delighting in the fulfilment of the true character and quality of creation. But when humans rule outside the parameters of right relationship with God and creation, they curse rather than bless, and their rule turns to misrule or domination.

Ways that curse creation mimic the ancient and modern equivalents to the Babylonian creation narrative, the *Enuma Elish*. This myth depicts creation as the result of a cosmic war in which a god vanquishes an enemy. In the *Enuma Elish*, violence and war rather than love are basic to the cosmic order that humans are to echo in their relations with each other. This dynamic is repeated in the depiction of human-nonhuman relations elsewhere in ancient civilizations. These cultures presented monarchs as image-bearers of the divine charged with ruling over the cosmos in violent ways vis-à-vis animals – for example, in a royal hunt. By contrast, as noted in Chapter 2, Genesis calls forth care and cultivation rather than predation.

Listening to creaturely life, Scripture, strangers, and those struggling for liberation are the north, south, east, and west on a compass that enable us to get our moral bearings. But if these are vital points on our moral compass, we depend on what we learn from those who come before us to assemble the compass and on the Spirit who animates and is the pillar of cloud that our moral journey follows.

ACCOMPANYING READINGS

James Cone, "Black Theology and Ideology," *God of the Oppressed*, rev. ed. (Maryknoll, NY: Orbis, 1997 [1975]), 77–98. Cone wrestles with the relationship between ideology, social context, and telling the truth about ourselves and who we are in relation to God. He advocates listening to and learning from the oppressed as an anti-ideological measure.

Óscar Romero, "The Political Dimension of the Faith from the Perspective of the Option for the Poor (1980)," *Voice of the Voiceless: The Four Pastoral Letters and Other Statements*, trans., Michael J. Walsh (Maryknoll, NY: Orbis Books, 1985), 177–187. Situated in the context of El Salvador, this lecture gives an urgent theological account of the preferential option for the poor and why it is essential for understanding God and the nature of the church.

Arvind P. Nirmal, "Towards a Christian Dalit Theology," *A Reader in Dalit Theology*, ed., Arvind P. Nirmal (Madras: Gurukul Lutheran Theological College & Research Center, 1988), 53–70. Nirmal is a founding figure of Dalit liberation theology. In this seminal essay in its development, he sets out a Trinitarian account of how and why Jesus Christ, as one who hears the cries of the suffering and is himself a suffering servant, identifies with the Dalits.

Emilie M. Townes, "Living in the New Jerusalem: The Rhetoric and Movement of Liberation in the House of Evil," *A Troubling in My Soul: Womanist Perspectives on Evil and Suffering*, ed., Emilie Townes (Maryknoll, NY: Orbis, 1993), 78–91. Through focusing on the experiences of Black women, Townes rejects any notion of suffering as having redemptive value. She distinguishes between pain and suffering, and in ways that are analogous to Nirmal, argues for a movement away from the passive acceptance of oppression to an active transformation of suffering into pain and living into a covenantal vision of the New Jerusalem.

Leonardo Boff, "Liberation Theology and Ecology," *Cry of the Earth, Cry of the Poor*, trans., Philip Berryman (Maryknoll, NY: Orbis, 1997 [1995]), 104–114. Boff outlines how and why a preferential option for the poor necessitates at the same time attending to ecological degradation.

Ada María Isasi-Díaz, "Lo Cotidiano: Everyday Struggles in Hispanas/Latinas' Lives," *La Lucha Continues: Mujerista Theology* (Maryknoll, NY: Orbis, 2004), 92–106. Focusing on the experience of "Hispanas/Latinas," Isasi-Díaz sets out why it is vital for descriptions of reality and any program of change to begin by first listening to the wisdom born out of women's everyday struggles for survival and liberation.

NOTES

1 For a more systematic account of idolatry along these lines, see Robert Adams, *Finite and Infinite Goods: A Framework for Ethics* (Oxford: Oxford University Press, 1999), 199–213.

2 Miranda Fricker, *Epistemic Injustice: Power and the Ethics of Knowing* (Oxford: Oxford University Press, 2007). My brief summary builds on her account of "hermeneutic" and "testimonial" injustice but also extends beyond it. Part of what is valuable about Fricker's account is that it takes seriously the role of social forces in how we obtain knowledge and what knowledge counts without either reducing truth and knowledge claims to a product of power relations, social location, or resorting to totalizing notions such as "false consciousness."

3 James Cone, *God of the Oppressed*, rev. ed. (Maryknoll, NY: Orbis, 1997), 31.

4 Gustavo Gutiérrez, "Option for the Poor," *Mysterium Liberationis: Fundamental Concepts of Liberation Theology*, eds., Ignacio Ellacuría and Jon Sobrino (Maryknoll, NY: Orbis, 1993), 239.

5 Vincent Lloyd, "What Love Is Not: Lessons from Martin Luther King, Jr.," *Modern Theology* 36, no. 1 (2020): 108.

6 Delores Williams, *Sisters in the Wilderness: The Challenge of Womanist God-Talk* (Maryknoll, NY: Orbis Books, 1993), 143–161.

7 Marcella Althaus-Reid, *Indecent Theology: Theological Perversions in Sex, Gender, and Politics* (London: Routledge, 2000).

8 See, for example, Karl Marx and Friedrich Engels, *The Communist Manifesto*, trans., Samuel Moore (London: Penguin, 1967), 92.

9 See Gustavo Gutiérrez, *A Theology of Liberation: History, Politics, Salvation* (Maryknoll, NY: Orbis, 2015 [1973]), 162–171; and Leonardo and Clodovis Boff, *Introducing Liberation Theology*, trans., Paul Burns (Tunbridge Wells: Burns & Oates, 1987), 46–49.

10 Gutiérrez, "Option for the Poor," 240–241.

11 Emilie Townes, "Living in the New Jerusalem: The Rhetoric and Movement of Liberation in the House of Evil," *A Troubling in My Soul: Womanist Perspectives on Evil & Suffering*, ed., Emilie Townes (Maryknoll, NY: Orbis, 1993), 88–89.

12 Townes, "Living in the New Jerusalem," 85.

13 For an early exploration of how a preferential option for the poor necessitates at the same time attending to ecological degradation, see Leonardo Boff, *Cry of the Earth, Cry of the Poor*, trans., Philip Berryman (Maryknoll, NY: Orbis, 1997). This is picked up by Pope Francis who states: "a true ecological approach always becomes a social approach; it must integrate questions of justice in debates on the environment, so as to hear both the cry of the earth and the cry of the poor." *Laudato Si'* (2015), §49.

14 Richard Bauckham, "Stewardship and Relationship," *The Care of Creation: Focusing Concern and Action*, ed., R. J. Berry (Leicester: Inter-Varsity Press, 2000), 99–106.

15 George Mathew Nalunnakkal, *Green Liberation: Toward an Integral Ecotheology* (Delhi: ISPCK, 1999), 259–261.

16 Ellen Davis, *Opening Israel's Scripture* (Oxford: Oxford University Press, 2019), 10–13. One way of framing authority as skilled mastery is the Catholic philosopher Yves Simon's notion of authority as the communication of excellence. Yves Simon, *A General Theory of Authority* (Notre Dame, IN: University of Notre Dame Press, 1962), 133–156.

17 There is a parallel here with John 21 where Jesus's threefold call to Peter to exercise pastoral leadership is framed in terms of tending and keeping God's people.

18 Quoting St. Francis's *Canticle of the Creatures*, Pope Francis frames this in terms of how humans are themselves governed and sustained by "our Sister, Mother Earth." *Laudato Si'*, §§1–2, 6.

19 This point is picked up by Karl Barth who asks:

> Will [human] sovereignty over plants and beasts consist in anything but the fact that he has more to be grateful for than these other earthly creatures not only for his own existence, but for that of the whole earthly sphere which is the indispensable presupposition of his own? Will he be able to exercise and preserve his sovereignty otherwise than by expressing thanks both in his own name and at the same time in the name of all other earthly creatures?

Karl Barth, *Church Dogmatics: The Doctrine of Creation*, vol. III/1, trans., J. W. Edwards et al. (Edinburgh: T&T Clark, 1958), 143

6 Listening to Ancestors

When my father died, my family and I needed a way to house and express our grief, bury his body, and gather with others to remember him. We could not conjure funeral practices out of nothing for ourselves; and even if we could have, we did not have the energy to do so. We were also confronted with having to navigate a vexed and primal moral question: What constitutes good care for the dead? Our tradition gave us words (Scripture and prayers), a ritual process (liturgies and funerary rites), institutions (the church and municipal cemetery), practices (bedside visitation by the priest, last rites, burial and memorial services), and virtues (truthfulness, hospitality, faith, hope, and love) for answering this question. It provided us with moral means to fulfill moral ends in a time of trouble.

My freedom was not constrained by the customary practices, institutions, and beliefs about caring for the dead I inherited and passed on. Rather, my ability to care appropriately for my father in his death and burial needed a tradition so I could be attentive to this person, in this context, at this time. Without it I could only stutter, lacking a way of entering into a shared world of meaning and action with family and friends, both living and dead. Other traditions had other ways of caring for the dead, but my friends who inhabit those other traditions and who came to the funeral could all join in with my way of caring for my dead father. My being situated in the Anglican tradition then enabled us to talk about how our respective traditions shaped our responses to death so we could learn from and be in solidarity with each other.

We cannot metabolize life without shared customs and practices received from our kin about a whole range of activities such as burying the dead, speaking, feeding ourselves, and parenting. We don't get to pick these. We discover ourselves inheriting forms of life that make our life possible. We can work with them, against them, or around them, but work them we must in one way or another. This chapter argues that to be moral, ethical reflection must listen to and learn from the wisdom of ancestors. Such wisdom is both a means of description and a mode of agency. This wisdom is embodied in particular traditions of belief and practice. To formulate moral descriptions requires listening to the wisdom of ancestors mediated through time by particular traditions.

In what follows, I review why tradition came to be understood as the enemy of ethics only to be recovered as the basis of any form of ethical inquiry. The chapter ends by reflecting on the relationship between tradition and critique, contending that tradition is itself a form of critique that provides moral norms that are vital for developing measures of accountability.

TRADITION AS A MEANS OF DESCRIPTION AND A MODE OF AGENCY

To be rightly oriented to reality we must not only look around at where we are today; we must also look back to discover where we have come from and what needs remembering in order to head in the right direction. Paradoxically, looking back is crucial to discerning a way forward, as part of what we inherit from our ancestors is a vision of the world as it should be. And in looking back, we are better able to ask whether we ourselves are being good ancestors to those who come after us. "Tradition" is a common way of naming this shared process of recalling the wisdom of those who have come before us so that we can situate our moral judgments in a longer time horizon than the present. Far from being static, homogenous, or hermetically sealed, traditions are arguments over time about how to fulfill a vision of the good and a way of recognizing the time-bound and memory-dependent nature of all moral commitments. As arguments over time, traditions are internally and externally contested with many voices constituting the tradition as a whole.

Without some kind of connection to ancestral wisdom through a tradition (and a substantive vision of the good they mediate) we cannot describe and narrate the world or our place within it. That is because absent a tradition, we are left without the resources to tell a meaningful story about who we are, where we come from, and where we are going.[1] Moreover, without attending to what is handed on to us as a deposit of faith (*paradosis*), then what counts as rationality, morality, and justice are determined by strength alone (might makes right). Without the kinds of communal forms (e.g., a congregation), social practices (e.g., prayer and worship), and institutions (e.g., denominational structures and seminaries) that communicate a tradition, individuals are left vulnerable to the power of the state and the market. What we inherit from our ancestors in the faith is vital for cultivating our own flourishing and tending a common life with others through time. In short, traditions as mediators of ancestral wisdom provide a crucial means for metabolizing life with the dead, the living, and those yet born.

We are, however, educated to think traditions are bad or we can operate without them. And some nondenominational churches think they don't have a tradition or use tradition as a dirty word. But traditions are like family: they have complicated and often troubled histories. Even if we are unhappy with, alienated from, or in rebellion against them, none of us exist without one. Like the complex, oftentimes fraught interconnections between biological, marital, and adoptive families, we can inherit and participate in multiple traditions simultaneously. For example, the philosopher Simone Weil grew up in France in a Jewish home, was influenced by Marxism and socialism, and then was drawn to Roman Catholicism, and each of these traditions shaped her life and thought.

There is a long and complicated history as to why tradition became a dirty word. The focus of this history is how modern moral philosophy claimed to free itself from tradition, particularly religious tradition. Modern philosophers came to believe that to be moral, ethical injunctions needed to be universal and impartial: that is, relevant to everyone, everywhere, all at once and without favor to some over others. The primary schools of thought that dominate Western ethics are still based on this assumption.

That universalist drive for impartiality arose out of a difficult historical situation. If we wind back to a key moment in the formation of modern, Western moral philosophy and how it emerged from the sixteenth century onwards, we find that a series of crises created legitimate sources of disquiet and fear. The Reformation catalyzed a whole range of political, economic, and social conflicts in which fights over moral and theological questions were a key factor. The story of Peter Ramus I began the book with is but one instantiation of this. Philosophers sought ways of settling these moral, theological, and political disputes without recourse to coercion or conflict. This quest generated two core concerns. First, these thinkers wanted a secure and impartial ground for moral claims beyond the contested ones of basing them on the interpretation of Scripture or personal revelations. There had to be a foundation that transcended the factional claims of different religious authorities. And second, they desired that all moral claims be subject to rigorous critique so as to verify whether they were true and coherent and not based on superstition, irrationality, or coercion. Leading lights of what is often referred to as "the Enlightenment," such as René Descartes (1596–1650), Thomas Hobbes (1588–1679), Baruch Spinoza (1632–1677), John Locke (1632–1704), and Immanuel Kant (1724–1804), all shared these concerns. And all reached for some

account of reason as a universal and impartial basis for making moral claims. Reason – unencumbered by tradition or revelation – would become for them the means by which to ensure moral claims are themselves moral; that is, universal, impartial, and refined by critique. This became the dominant framework for thinking about moral questions and is still the touchstone for moral philosophy today. It gave rise to a whole cluster of modern approaches to ethics that assume we can generate moral claims without recourse to metaphysics, revelation, or traditions of thought and practice.[2] For example, it

is exemplified in human rights discourse, which begins from the assumption that human rights are universal, derived from reason alone, and provide a means of critiquing other kinds of moral and political claims.

WHY ETHICS NEEDS ANCESTORS

The appeal of universalist approaches to ethics is obvious. Their motivating concerns are as present today as they ever were. We still live in a world of conflict and division, and it's comforting to imagine that a single, universal, impartial ethic can light the way. But while the wound such approaches seek to address is real, the poultice applied led that wound to fester rather than heal. A number of subsequent philosophical developments have questioned the neutrality of reason, recognizing that all moral and political claims – for example, about freedom, justice, and equality – emerge from somewhere and sometime. Reason is not some Archimedean point that exists outside of time and space. What is considered reasonable has a history and a geography. What Enlightenment philosophers understood as the universal, impartial ideal was in actuality an attempt to deny how ethical reflection always begins in the middle of an ongoing process of inheritance, tending, and passing on.

Additionally, moral and political claims emerge out of and are rendered plausible by certain economic, political, and cultural processes. A long line of critical theorists from Karl Marx onwards have exposed how, far from being universal, reason is shaped by material social, economic, and political relations. Critical theories ask whether the ruling moral ideas are merely the expression of the ideas and interests of the ruling classes. Within critical theory, moral claims about, say, debt or sex or technology are seen to be generated by something else, mostly cultural or economic modes of production. And what is taken to be reasonable and rational can itself be highly irrational. For example, the creation and proliferation of nuclear weapons are the fruit of a sophisticated and highly rational scientific and bureaucratic process that generates the seemingly cogent yet insane policy of mutually assured destruction that costs billions of dollars a year to maintain and threatens to exterminate life on earth. Ethical approaches that insist they are universal and based wholly on immanent rational foundations mask or deny what critical theories bring into view.

A further development emerges from a line of philosophical thought initiated by the philosopher Ludwig Wittgenstein (1889–1951). Its focus is neither on the rational basis of moral and political claims, nor their historical formation, nor their social, economic, and political production. Instead, it focuses on the importance of language and how moral claims cannot be understood without paying attention to the forms of life within which they are embedded. On this account, there is no rational, autonomous, individual agent who decides what is and what is not moral, independent of historical or contextual factors. Rather, the individual can only discover with and through others what is moral inside the spider's web of signification within which they are situated. Discovering what is moral thereby requires careful attention to what we say, how we say it, the context in which it is said, and the stories we tell about ourselves and the world we live in. If universalizing moral philosophies focus on questions of rational and empirical justification, and critical theories expose how different social, economic, and political structures favor some truths while suppressing others, linguistic approaches seek to understand the form of life that determines the meaning and context of what we take to be true, good, and beautiful. Wittgenstein and his heirs help us see that ethics does not exist in a zone separated from the rest of life, nor does it only relate to special occasions or quandaries, nor is it reducible to a set of abstract ideas or principles that are then applied to life. Ethics emerges out of and demands paying attention to a whole form of life – what and how we eat, speak, dress, etc. – and the ways these practices form us as persons in relation to the world. Or, as Stanley Hauerwas parses this in relation to Christian ethics: the church *is* rather than *has* a social ethic.[3]

Critical theories and linguistic approaches create space for the reappropriation of tradition as a vital component of moral and political thought. They also help make sense of why many contemporary calls for liberation are not framed in terms of modern universalist approaches, whether revolutionary or reformist. Rather, as in the example of indigenous land rights movements in North and South America, they are staged through recovering and preserving indigenous traditions of belief and practice.[4] If moral and political thought has a history and geography (it comes from somewhere), is contingent and contextual (it only makes sense within a form of life that changes over time), and is born out of material conditions that benefit some and not others, then we need to pay attention to different traditions to understand those histories, contexts, and conditions. Far from being irrelevant, traditions provide a means of making sense of the particular rationality of moral and political claims that emerge from and are attuned to specific places, histories, and sets of relations. Conversely, we need some kind of tradition to provide the resources of critique: namely, a moral vision and set of criteria by which to judge the gap between the world as it is and the world as it should be. In the case of indigenous land rights movements, ancestral traditions and practices provide a frame of reference and source of power by which to challenge universalizing state and market interventions – often justified by universalizing moral frameworks, notably utilitarianism – that denigrate and dispossess local people.

TRADITION, NIHILISM, AND CRITIQUE

To understand what is at stake in recognizing the centrality of ancestral traditions to moral inquiry it is helpful to compare two titans of modern moral thought: Karl Marx (1818–1883) and Friedrich Nietzsche (1844–1900). Marx was committed to realizing the same values as earlier thinkers such as Immanuel Kant: his critique was in the service of generating a free, just, and more equal world. What he challenged was the means by which to realize these moral commitments and the form these commitments should take. As such, he advocated for a communist society as needing to replace a bourgeois, liberal, capitalist one. By contrast, Nietzsche called for a fundamental reevaluation of these values. For Nietzsche, notions such as freedom, justice, and equality mask claims to power by the weak who seek to control the naturally strong.[5] On Nietzsche's account, there is no such thing as truth or morality. Even though we are the kind of animal that cannot live without values, the universe we live in is without inherent meaning or purpose and is one in which might makes right. A Nietzschean form of critique intends to expose the contingency, relativity, and essential meaninglessness of moral and political claims, revealing how blood and horror are the basis of all we take to be good.

There is much to be learned from Nietzsche's critique of morality. As one of my teachers used to say, only half-jokingly, Nietzsche was raised up by God to teach liberal Protestants the error of their ways. But in his wake, we are faced with a stark choice. We can commit ourselves to some kind of vision of the good and the sense that we live in a moral universe in which might does not make right and the exercise of unilateral power can be held accountable by speaking truth to power.[6] Or we are one of two things: nihilists committed to being *Übermenschen* – that is, overcoming our limitations and getting what power, vitality, and nobility we can for ourselves and others like us by the strength of our own arms. Or we are nihilists of a different order, what Nietzsche called "the last human"; that is, someone who takes no risks, seeking only comfort, security, and minimal conflict, and in effect, eating, drinking, and consuming in the mall of life before we die, the poor and the environment be damned.[7]

In many ways, we have come to live in the world Nietzsche imagined. It is a world in which we are seemingly forced to choose between being part of the online shopping, social media ogling, and celebrity-obsessed bovine "herd" (Nietzsche's term), or those who seek greatness by worldly achievement, be these scientific, commercial, artistic, or political. While the latter may sound more attractive than the former, none of those achievements has any meaning or purpose for Nietzsche other than to enhance the status of the individual or group doing it. Where moral claims are attached to these heroic feats, they merely garnish rather than guide them. And each of these has altogether more sinister and misanthropic versions: either the fascistic and Ayn Rand–reading versions of the *Übermenschen* that populate the alt-right, survivalist groups, and the upper reaches of Silicon Valley; or the addicted, self-medicating, escapist versions of the last humans dying "deaths of despair."

If we are committed to a non-nihilistic view of what it means to thrive, then we have to articulate a specific moral and political vision of creaturely flourishing. We need an account of a meaningful life that does not instrumentalize others and the world around us for our own security, material well-being, or status. In doing so, it is not enough to mouth abstract nouns like justice, equality, peace, and freedom divorced from particular ancestral traditions through which these nouns are given content. As the philosopher Alasdair MacIntyre argued, given the historicity, contingency, and contextual nature of all such terms – that is, their meanings are neither universal nor impartial nor objective – we must ask whose justice? Whose equality? Whose peace? Whose freedom? And which rationality is being used to justify such claims? And this means we are asking about particular traditions – and the practices, beliefs, virtues, institutions, and political economies that sustain them – and must constructively relate different traditions in order to generate a loving and just common life amid competing claims about the good and asymmetries of power. That is, we need to forge some kind of common life if we are not going to kill, dominate, or drive out those with whom we disagree (something I address in detail in Chapter 14). This is the context in which claims about justice, freedom, and equality are negotiated and within which such claims can be held accountable.

Traditions are necessary to sustain moral forms of life and a peaceable politics but can themselves quickly collapse into forms of legalistic traditionalism. We see this in the "dead faith of the living," whereby an institution unthinkingly and doggedly preserves what was done before by any means necessary.[8] The alternative is creative fidelity to the past so as to tend and pass on the gift that is received from those who came before us. In part, this tending entails drawing on the customary practices and lifeways of people so as to cultivate shared forms of life that are rooted in and attentive to everyday struggles to live well. Creative fidelity to traditions of belief and practice also necessarily involves disciplines of internal and external critique generated through listening to strangers and those struggling for liberation. Such critique helps keep traditions from degenerating into modes of ideology and idolatry.[9]

Likewise, critique must also attend to and serve actual forms of life. If we cannot trade in universal claims and abstract nouns without being in active conversation with our ancestors, neither can we merely denounce and expose whatever we take to be false, corrupt, racist, sexist, etc. without in some way hallowing what we inherit. Critique that does not at the same time tend to and cultivate a form of life through which normative moral claims can make sense either reproduces or clears the way for de facto forms of nihilism that are destroying us and our planetary home. To put this in scriptural terms, where there is no vision the people perish (Prov 29:18, KJV). More prosaically, to speak truth to power in order to hold it accountable requires a commitment to truthfulness and practices of truth telling.

Critique in and of itself is not inherently emancipatory. For example, climate change skeptics serving the interests of the coal and oil industries also practice critique. Critique must be indexed in some way to a vision of creational flourishing as a truth claim about the nature of reality.[10] Without that, critique becomes a highbrow form of conspiracy theory. As the queer theorist Eve Sedgwick argues, if a hermeneutic of suspicion is the *only* mode of description, then it produces a stifling paranoia. For Sedgwick, to sustain what we cherish, we need reparative readings not paranoid ones.[11] Without a definite form of life and a tradition that can help us discern and describe what creational flourishing consists of, we are left naked and alone before the power of the state and the financial markets and without the resources to stop ourselves from becoming mere instruments upon which others play their desires, preferences, and will.

The understanding of tradition and critique I have been developing here in many ways echoes that articulated by the Black philosopher and social critic, Cornel West (b. 1953). He summarizes well the inevitability of tradition and the inherent interdependency between tradition and critique when he states:

> Tradition is to be associated not solely with ignorance and intolerance, prejudice and parochialism, dogmatism and docility. Rather, tradition is also to be identified with insight and intelligence, rationality and resistance, critique and contestation. Tradition per se is never a problem, but rather those traditions that have been and are hegemonic over other traditions. All that human beings basically have are traditions – those institutions and practices, values and sensibilities, stories and symbols, ideas and metaphors that shape human identities, attitudes, outlooks, and dispositions. These traditions are dynamic, malleable, and revised, yet all changes in a tradition are done in light of some old or newly emerging tradition. Innovation presupposes some tradition and inaugurates another tradition.[12]

INDIVIDUALISM, ANTINOMIANISM, AND THE NEED FOR NORMS

The individual is central to modern ethics. We assume it is the individual who is the center of moral concern. We take it for granted that individuals deserve proper treatment, should possess the freedom to express themselves authentically in the world, and have nothing done to them without their consent. These are deep commitments of the modern world that profoundly shape how we think about ethics. Yet it is not at all clear what it means to be an individual or have a self who is the subject and focus of ethical concern and responsibility.

A standard criticism of modern, Western life, one I share, is that it is too "individualistic." This critique is often aligned with the call for more emphasis on community (e.g., communitarianism) or making society the locus of ethical value (e.g., socialism) or focusing on the earth as the point of moral regard (e.g., various strands of environmentalism). Critiques of individualism rightly ask whether the actions and judgments of the individual are the proper subject of ethics and whether making the individual the focus of ethical concern is itself immoral. Yet, if we begin with the relationships between individuals rather than the individual as such, then we are in danger of the collective taking precedence over and oppressing the individual or, as in biocentric accounts, the eco-system having greater value than any particular part. This is also immoral. When doing ethics today we are caught between the rock of individualism and the hard place of either communal or environmental over-determination. So, an underlying crisis, one provoking much ethical reflection in the contemporary context, is determining who or what should be the primary focus of moral concern: the individual, the community, the nation, humanity, eco-systems, or the planet?

The question of whether to make the individual the primary focus of ethical concern is complicated further by even more fundamental questions about whether morality is itself a form of oppression. Another strand of modernity criticism, echoing Nietzsche, points to the historical and cultural relativity of all our moral commitments and the ways in which these commitments can mask systems and structures of domination. Such critiques point to how our modern sense of having a self is a cultural construct resulting from oppressive structures and normative frames of reference: there is neither an "I" that acts and can be held responsible, nor a stable identity that can be expressed and recognized.[13] All is fluid and constructed. Under the weight of these critiques the ideal of a responsible moral subject who has an intrinsic dignity collapses.

The problem goes beyond the relativity and contingency of moral norms. Rather, these critiques pose the question of whether there is anyone – any authentic self or identifiable community – there to be moral. Or is the notion of morality either simply a by-product of a combination of our DNA and the synaptic exchanges in our brain? Some contend that moral norms are nothing more than the froth made by the swirling waters of fiction and fantasy that constitute our consciousness of life. On such a view, morality is a mist that will burn off in the bright light of science and suspicion. What will be revealed is the harsh reality that there is no morality, only a drive to survive and the structures and institutions of power that make might right. On such an account, any form of ethics, Christian or otherwise, is a hoax, a scam, fake news. What really matters is power, not morality. In such a framework, for example, sexual ethics or talk of how to rightly order sexual relations with each other is merely a power grab that masks a mode of domination. There are no good or bad kinds of sexual relations, just endless and meaningless iterations of power and pleasure. Any claim that there can be either moral norms to guide human flourishing or that there are truthful descriptions are treated with suspicion. Within such a view, normativity as such is the problem.

Such an approach can be called "antinomian," by which is meant it rejects any notion of morality or that moral demands are binding in any way. On such a view, there is only critique and never any constructive moral claims. A metabolic view of moral agency and the need to listen to ancestors addresses both the crisis posed by whether the individual can or should be the center of moral agency as well as antinomian frameworks that call into question whether morality is anything more than a power play. It does so by articulating a relational anthropology and showing how and why, on a theological account, all relations are inherently suffused with God-given meanings and purposes. Such an account envisions the individual as a distinct person constituted through the quality and character of relations with human and other-than-human forms of life, both past and present, and as enmeshed within fallen systems and structures that shape us, but which can be reshaped through shared struggle.

ON BEING A GOOD ANCESTOR

Listening to ancestors entails moral questions about what it means to honor our parents or filial piety (the fifth commandment), what the living owe the dead (socially and spiritually), the ethics of memory (e.g., what and who is commemorated), and the connection between the veneration of ancestors and social and familial solidarity. These questions are often vehemently contested.[14] However, rather than focus on them, I close with a reflection on intergenerational ethics framed prospectively rather than retrospectively by asking what it means to be a good ancestor. Being a good ancestor is not the same as acting in ways I think are moral primarily because I am concerned about my legacy. To be concerned about matters of legacy is to look back in anxiety and ask what those coming after me are doing with what I left behind, whether they are acting the same as me, or in accord with my standards or commitments, and if they will maintain what I have done. In contrast, to be concerned with the question of what it means to be a good ancestor is to look forward, asking how can we act now to secure the flourishing of those who will come after us? How can we seed now possibilities that will come to fruition long after we are dead? How can we resource or invest in this practice or institution or craft so that it flourishes in times to come? Ancestor thinking is future-oriented and generative rather than backward-looking and nostalgic. Ethically, the practice of being a good ancestor is covenantal, entailing keeping a covenant with both past and future generations, and constitutes an intergenerational form of neighbor love.

A historical analogy illustrates the point I am making. Medieval cathedrals took hundreds of years to build and last for millennia. The people that built them understood this and also knew that, in order to undertake the work of building a cathedral in their day, they must plant the trees and identify the resources they knew would not come to maturity, in some cases, until a century or more later. Alongside planting, say, a grove of oaks, they also put in place a set of institutional practices and measures – a cathedral chapter, an archive, an endowment, a set of legal frameworks such as a trust – that ensured those living hundreds of years hence had what was needed to do the work well. They were good ancestors to those who came after them, both making the past legible and accessible to those living centuries later and seeding the resources that would enable their inheritors to keep going.[15] In the same way, being a good ancestor means planting now the resources and institutional means to ensure shared goods can be sustained and available long after we are gone but also that such goods are legible and accessible.[16] Such thinking demands a covenantal imagination and an institutional creativity that orients contemporary action in a way that future generations can give thanks for the foresight of those living now. Tragically, especially when it comes to matters of the environment, they are more likely to curse those of us now living.

In Part I of this book, I focused on the vital importance of deep listening as a foundation of Christian ethics. While ethics begins with description born out of listening to God, creation, and neighbor – and through this process of active listening, becoming attuned to the work of the Spirit here and now – it also necessitates a movement from description to judgments about what to say and do if we are to metabolize and bear witness to a flourishing life. Part II of the book takes up this focus by reflecting on the place of commands, rules, virtues, practical reason, and sin in either enabling or disabling moral speech and action. In focusing on moral agency, Part II explores the interpersonal and subjective conditions that enable us to articulate and embody ethical speech and action.

ACCOMPANYING READINGS

Jaroslav Pelikan, "Tradition as Heritage: A Vindication," *The Vindication of Tradition* (New Haven, CT: Yale University Press, 1984), 65–82. This chapter opens with a now-classic distinction between tradition as "the living faith of the dead," as against traditionalism as the "dead faith of the living." Pelikan goes on to expand on this distinction and set out why and how tradition is not opposed to insight and creativity but a condition for it.

Chang-Won Park, "Between God and Ancestors: Ancestral Practice in Korean Protestantism," *International Journal for the Study of the Christian Church* 10, no. 4 (2010): 257–273. Park explores how the religious, ethical, and political conflicts arising between Christianity and Confucian practices for venerating ancestors in Korea were addressed theologically and liturgically over time. The article also exemplifies how ethics is more about a form of life than it is about a set of ideas or principles.

Rachel Muers, "Doing Traditions Justice," *Gendering Christian Ethics*, ed., Jenny Daggers (Newcastle: Cambridge Scholars Publishing, 2012), 7–22. In dialogue with feminist theology and drawing on notions of restorative justice, this essay moves beyond reductive moves to either condemn or exonerate a tradition and instead opens up a way to inhabit a tradition in a reparative way in the face of the injustices a tradition so often inscribes.

Paulinus Ikechukwu Odozor, "Tradition, Rationality, and Morality," *Morality Truly Christian, Truly African: Foundational, Methodological, and Theological Considerations* (Notre Dame, IN: University of Notre Dame Press, 2014), ch. 2. Odozor sets out an account of tradition as central to moral reasoning situated within a discussion of the interchange and conflicts between Christianity and traditional African religions and the complexity of negotiating relations between traditions under conditions of globalization. He points to how each tradition is subject to critique by moral standards within other traditions and how the Gospel poses a limit and test for every tradition.

NOTES

1 Vincent Lloyd puts this more sharply still, saying that absent a tradition, a person is merely an "atomized individual accountable to nothing, fleeing from everything, solipsistically posturing." Vincent W. Lloyd, *Religion of the Field Negro: On Black Secularism and Black Theology* (New York: Fordham University Press, 2018), 75.

2 Iris Murdoch, "Metaphysics and Ethics," *Existentialists and Mystics: Writings on Philosophy and Literature* (London: Penguin Books, 1997), 59–75.

3 Stanley Hauerwas, *Peaceable Kingdom: A Primer in Christian Ethics* (Notre Dame, IN: Notre Dame Press, 1991), 99.

4 See Leanne Betasamosake Simpson, *As We Have Always Done: Indigenous Freedom through Radical Resistance* (Minneapolis: University of Minnesota Press, 2017).

5 Friedrich Nietzsche, *On the Genealogy of Morality*, ed., Keith Ansell Pearson, trans., Carol Diethe (Cambridge: Cambridge University Press, 1994).

6 The moral philosopher Alasdair MacIntyre poses this as a choice between Aristotle or Nietzsche. This is right in so far as the choice is between relativism and some form of a tradition-constituted vision of the moral life, whether that be Buddhist, Stoic, Wiccan, Islamic etc. It is wrong in so far as it *must* be some derivation of Aristotelianism as the alternative. Alasdair MacIntyre, *After Virtue: A Study in Moral Theory* (London: Duckworth, 1994), 109–120.

7 Friedrich Nietzsche, *Thus Spoke Zarathustra*, eds., Adrian Del Caro and Robert Pippin, trans., Adrian Del Caro (Cambridge: Cambridge University Press, 2006); *Beyond Good and Evil* (section 2601).

8 Jaroslav Pelikan, *The Vindication of Tradition* (New Haven, CT: Yale University Press, 1984), 65–82.

9 This extends MacIntyre's influential definition of a tradition as a socially embodied, institutionally mediated argument over generations about the goods the pursuit of which "gives to that tradition its particular point and purpose." For MacIntyre, traditions "embody continuities of conflict." When they become self-enclosed and wholly focused on stability and preservation, "they are dying or dead." *After Virtue*, 221–222. See also, Stanley Hauerwas, "A Story-Formed Community: Reflections on *Watership Down* (1981)," *The Hauerwas Reader* (Durham, NC: Duke University Press, 2001), 171–198.

10 A model for holding tradition and critique together is given by the Black feminist organization Combahee River Collective, which in 1977 articulated a critique of prevailing modes of domination that affected them. Their constructive political vision began with naming their ancestors from whom they had learned – Sojourner Truth, Harriet Tubman, Frances E. W. Harper, Ida B. Wells Barnett, and Mary Church Terrell – and situating their confession ("What we believe") within a longer history of struggle. "Combahee River Collective Statement," 1977, https://combaheerivercollective.weebly.com/the-combahee-river-collective-statement.html (accessed February 23, 2021).

11 Eve Kosofsky Sedgwick, "Paranoid Reading and Reparative Reading, or, You're so Paranoid, You Probably Think This Essay Is about You," *Touching Feeling* (Durham, NC: Duke University Press, 2003), 124–151.

See also Bruno Latour, "Why Has Critique Run Out of Steam? From Matters of Fact to Matters of Concern," *Critical Inquiry* 30, no. 2 (2004): 225–248.

12 Cornel West, *The American Evasion of Philosophy: A Genealogy of Pragmatism* (Madison: University of Wisconsin Press, 1989), 230.

13 A technical term for this is "desubjectivation" and is born out of antinormative and antifoundationalist ways of analyzing agency.

14 The compatibility between Christianity and existing practices for the veneration of ancestors is a common point of tension as Christianity takes form and shape in new contexts through processes of cross-cultural encounter and mission. See, for example, Chang-Won Park, "Between God and Ancestors: Ancestral Practice in Korean Protestantism," *International Journal for the Study of the Christian Church* 10, no. 4 (2010): 257–273. For a constructive theology of ancestors driven by this concern, see Kwame Bediako, "Towards a Theology of Ancestors," *Christianity in Africa: The Renewal of a Non-western Religion* (Maryknoll, NY: Orbis, 1995), 223–230.

15 A parallel but more familiar example is given by James Rebanks who states: "They say that old wheelwrights planted, felled and stored apple trees in a three-generation cycle, so that their grandsons would have sufficient matured trees, and dried wood of the right kind, from which to make the hard wheel hubs they needed. We need to live like that again, thinking longer term and with more humility." *English Pastoral*, 268–269.

16 This can entail radically recalibrating and reimagining such goods and practices and how they might be lived in the wake of one's form of life ending or being destroyed. A case study of just such a reimagining is Plenty Coup, the last Chief of the Crow Nation, as narrated and analyzed by Jonathan Lear, and how Plenty Coup understood what it meant to be a good ancestor to his people in the face of their political, economic, and cultural devastation at the hands of White settlers. Jonathan Lear, *Radical Hope: Ethics in the Face of Cultural Devastation* (Cambridge, MA: Harvard University Press, 2006).

PART II Acting Well

Part I focused on ethics as a mode of description. I argued that ethical descriptions should situate us within and help us respond morally to the world in which we find ourselves. Inherent in ethical description is a determination of the gap between the world as it is and a vision of the world as it should be if we are to live well. Part I set out how we become rightly orientated and able to pursue a vision of a flourishing life through a combination of listening to creation, Scripture, strangers, cries for liberation, and our ancestors. However, while moral description is a first step in ethical deliberation, ethics does not live by description alone. It also necessitates a movement from description to action. We have to say and do stuff with others if we are to live well. Thus, Part II shifts from questions about how to name and envision the world around us in moral terms to focus on the question "what is to be done?" To ask what is to be done is to ask about moral agency: How can and should we act morally? What is the nature, character, and purpose of moral action? And of what does moral action consist?

Theologians and philosophers give different accounts of the nature and basis of moral agency. Some say good action means following the right rules. Some emphasize obeying God's commands as the basis of moral agency. Others envisage virtue as the foundation of moral action. However, against all of these, some say humans cannot act well; since we are sinners all the way down, any capacity to be good depends on God's grace alone. For those people, the real question is how humans can be redeemed from a sinful life in which all attempts to be moral are merely attempts to assert human autonomy over and against God. I will explore each of these answers and, in doing so, situate them in dialogue with other, non-theological ways of talking about moral action. I don't propose a single approach as the one and only true way of understanding moral agency (e.g., virtue ethics, divine command ethics, etc.). Rather, I argue a somewhat untidy, mixed economy of frameworks is necessary to shed light on and help undertake better the ways and means through which humans can speak and act morally.

I begin by discussing the need for and priority of divine agency in enabling human moral action and two conditions that limit human moral agency, namely finitude and fallenness (Chapter 7). Following this, I outline the role of God's call and commands in forming the basis of moral agency (Chapter 8). The focus on call and commands is a formal way of framing how encounter with and responding to God's ongoing communication and self-disclosure in and through creation constitutes humans as moral agents. The subsequent chapters integrate with this framework for envisioning divine-human relations as the basis of moral agency in the following way: we become moral agents through responding to God's call and command to love God and neighbor, this command constitutes the realm of human flourishing, which is lived out in spheres of responsibility through specific vocations. Rules (Chapter 9) and virtues (Chapter 10) specify and enable this in practice. And practical reasoning that begins with listening (Chapter 11) is what we undertake in relation to specific moral questions and issues that arise as we figure out how to bear faithful witness among these people, in this place, at this time (i.e., the reality we discover ourselves situated in).

By way of caveat, the focus in Part II is very much on *human* moral agency. This in no way denies the agency and importance of other-than-human ways of being alive. Rather, it recognizes that like any creature, humans have specific ways of acting that need attending to and accounting for theologically. These may be symbiotic with or parallel to nonhuman forms life but still need describing in their own terms. Conversely, nonhuman ways of being alive have their own distinct modalities of agency: how a fly sees the world is not the same as how a human does; how octopuses think and act is not the same as how humans think and act; how human society experiences time is not the same as how a forest does. Echoing Chapter 2, any theological account of human moral and political agency must move beyond anthropocentric and biocentric approaches to develop a theocentric account of human agency as enmeshed in and woven out of the actions of the rest of creation, living and nonliving. What follows articulates such an account.

7 Finitude and Fallenness

During the height of the COVID-19 pandemic, doctors dealt with scarce resources and overwhelming need. In such situations, they had to engage in triage. A decision must be made, for example, about how to allocate ventilators. But should doctors allocate ventilators on a first come, first served basis? Or do they prioritize the sickest patients? Do they give ventilators to the essential personnel whose presence is most needed (e.g., medical staff or those required for maintaining critical infrastructure)? Or do they grant them to those most likely to survive? In the face of equally terrible possibilities, medical practitioners are still required to discern a morally responsible course of action. And they must act in real time without knowing what the outcome will be. Their actions are constrained both by their own limited knowledge and capacity and by a system that can't or won't give them the resources they need to solve the problem. And no matter what choice they make, someone will suffer. This situation is emblematic of all moral judgments east of Eden. As moral agents, humans are finite, operate in a fallen world, and often face tragic choices.

This chapter reflects on the limits rather than the possibilities of moral agency, arguing that time determines the conditions of our ability to act and live well. Our ability to act morally is torn between two times: temporal, this worldly time, and the eschatological time of the age to come. In this situation, moral agency must navigate how everything *is* changing, everything *must* change if it is to get better, and everything *will* change in the age to come. Within this temporal age, our moral agency is limited by the fact that we are both finite and fallen. Distinguishing finitude from fallenness is hard yet vital since finitude is to be accepted as a liberating constraint, while fallenness is to be struggled against and depends on God's grace to overcome. What is at stake in this distinction can be seen by comparing and contrasting a doctrine of original sin as one way of understanding what it means to be sinners with various modern ways of understanding how and why, despite our best efforts, we are unable to act morally and live well. I end by giving an account of how, as action caught between two times, much moral action in this age is to a certain degree tragic.

MORALITY AS ACTION IN TIME; BUT WHAT TIME?

Forging and sustaining moral ways of being alive involves action in time. As the COVID-19 example above demonstrates, our moral judgments are time bound and time sensitive. The need to act in time raises three central problems that any account of moral and political agency must address. The first is that, as temporal creatures, we discover ourselves responding to a world around us that we did not make and do not control yet can still act in to make a difference. As finite creatures, we live between a past we inherit, a present that is constantly changing, an earthly future we can't determine, and a hoped-for, eternal future that is ever before us.[1] Theologians frame this temporal condition as being caught between "the now and not yet" of the kingdom of God or between Christ's ascension and his return. This is an ambiguous time, a field of wheat and tares, neither wholly profane nor entirely sacred, when the kingdom of God has come but is not yet fully established.

As we inhabit this age before Christ's return, we must grapple with the reality that all human moral action is temporal rather than eternal. The time we live in will pass. Yet it is a time open to healing and redemption and in which the kingdom of God can erupt. Thus our actions today have significance beyond the immediate needs and vicissitudes of the moment. Moral action is thereby contingent yet meaningful. Situated between Christ's ascension and return, moral action is thereby freed to be good but penultimate.

As penultimate rather than ultimate, our moral and political judgments have great value but must not be over-valued. We should not over-invest in what we do here and now. It is not the be-all and end-all of human existence. This age is already fulfilled in Christ and so it's ultimate end and future determination does not depend on anything I do or say here and now. A key implication of living in this in-between time is that Christians do not have to establish regimes to control the time so as to determine the outcome of history. Rather, we can live without control because the resurrection and ascension of Jesus Christ already inaugurated the fulfillment of history, even as its consummation awaits Christ's return.

In this in-between time, when everything is subject to flux, finitude, and fallenness, we must still act to change things so that  they more nearly echo and witness to the meaning and purposes of creation as revealed in Christ. And so we must come to judgments  about what to do and how do it. Yet ethical thought and moral judgments have to reckon with what it means to always already begin  in the middle even as we seek to change things for the better. We never get to determine where we start from, we can only go on from where we find ourselves, acting "today" in answer to God's address (Heb 3:13–15).

The necessity of beginning in the middle leads into the second problem: how to conceptualize change. The basic claim at the heart of Christian ethics is that we should not live with the world as it is: in the light of the life, death, resurrection, and ascension of Jesus Christ we discover this world as so afflicted by oppression, sin, and idolatry that our very ways of being alive disfigure and destroy us. Then the question arises as to how to change, how to move from the world as it is to the world as it should be. How are we to imagine and narrate moral and political change? Is change about returning to or recovering what was lost? Or does it mean progressing beyond or leaving behind the past in order to be liberated from it? To give two contemporary examples: if life in the United States is to improve morally and politically, should its citizens seek to return to or recover a better time ("make America great again") or abolish and abandon all existing social and political structures in order to be "on the right side of history"?

As soon as we recognize the need for change, we encounter a third problem: the need for changed persons *and* changed structures. Given that all ways of being alive are fallen, we have to reckon with how our form of life is a poisoned chalice: it is a chalice that gives us a life, but it is at the same time toxic to the soil, the self, and those we live with and depend on. Distinctions of class, race, sexuality, and gender and the ways we construct differences between human and nonhuman life are the water we swim in and, at the same time, the water that drowns us. While political revolution or changes to legislation or education may, at times, be important mechanisms of change, none of them is ever sufficient or really gets to the core of what needs changing. At a deeper level, if we are to live a more loving and just life here and now, what needs reinventing is everyday life and what needs changing are hearts and minds. In what follows, I discuss further how the need for change that is both personal and structural combine to shape the conditions and possibilities of human moral agency. Chapters 12–14 of this book model what this looks like in practice.

On a theological account of time, Christ's life, death, and resurrection are central. The kind of time the Christ-event represents involves a qualitative rather than quantitative experience of time. *Kairos* is one term used to name this form of time. Experienced qualitatively, this form of time is neither cyclical, linear, nor progressive, nor does it exist as a perpetual perishing present. As with memory, in kairotic time, the past can be alive to the present while what is happening now can vibrate and dance with eschatological possibilities made present by the Spirit.

In becoming enfolded in the Christ-event, all time is now liberated from its entropic movement toward nothingness and can be breathed out in infinite, life-giving variations. By contrast, chronological time is linear, regular, monotonous, and measurable. It is also time devastated by the fall. Chronological time can only be experienced by those existing at this moment, while the kairotic time of Christ is open to enjoyment by anyone at any time, hence talk of the communion of saints as a transtemporal and co-inhering reality.

We can thus experience two times or two histories simultaneously: kairotic time and its aftershocks and chronological time and its duress. Christian moral agency sits on the cusp between these two times. By participating in the kairotic time of Christ, Christians metabolize chronological time so that time accursed may become a blessed time.

FINITUDE AS CREATURELINESS

Finitude is a primary limiting condition of living in this in-between time. Just because the kingdom of God is inaugurated doesn't mean that we cease to be persons constituted through time. Our moral judgments and actions are thereby still subject to the shifting sands of history. Moreover, our knowledge and ability to act is always bounded by temporal and spatial limits: we cannot be everywhere or do everything. Rather than seeing this as a limitation to overcome, finitude is to be embraced. Through it we learn we are not gods but creatures. Encountering limits to what we can achieve in human strength is the beginning point of recognizing how much we need and depend on God and neighbor. In addition, creaturely finitude frees us to do whatever God has given us to do without becoming overwhelmed by how much is beyond our capacity. In fact, it is often our attempts to move beyond the bounds of creatureliness that generate forms of domination and self-destruction.

The church has long struggled to digest one particular hard truth about what it means to be finite creatures. We are fragile, flatulent, sweaty embodied beings. And so was the incarnate Christ. However, a perennial temptation for Christians is to become Gnostics, a primal Christian heresy. But even if not full-blown heresies, the tenets of Gnosticism reverberate through the myriad theologies that separate spiritual and bodily life, exalting the former and denigrating the latter. However, theologically, the truly spiritual life does not overcome or transcend materiality. Rather, the Holy Spirit creates and fructifies it, enabling frail flesh to both be itself and to become something more than itself. Human finitude and corporeal vulnerability are not bad or evil as Gnostics suppose, nor are they a design flaw to be fixed, as techno-utopians assume. They are part of what it means to be creatures. To believe and behave otherwise is to deny the incarnation of Jesus Christ, whose flesh and blood are the bread of life (John 6:43–59). Humans are neither zombies – bodies without spirit – nor angels – spiritual without being material. Rather, to be human is to be a biospiritual creature who can no more be merely material than we can be purely spiritual. In denial of this truth, we often conflate finitude with fallenness and read what is a creaturely limit to be lived through into a problem to be overcome. The discernment is to distinguish what is a condition of fallenness and what is a feature of creatureliness.[2] Our response to the former should be repentance and the pursuit of liberation. Our response to the latter must seek the healing and restoration of what is broken, anticipating now the fulfillment and transfiguration of our bodies in the age to come precisely through our corporeal vulnerability and frailty. When, for example, medicine heals the body it acts righteously. When it tries to solve or overcome frailty or seeks life at any cost it becomes an instrument of idolatry, making human life itself a god. That said, the shift from healing to idolatry is often difficult to discern and requires ethical reflection.

Distinguishing finitude from fallenness is extremely difficult as they are laminated together. This is illustrated by Augustine's discussion of sex in Eden. Augustine tries to imagine sex as existing without lust or shame, unconditioned by domination and violence, and where men and women exist in harmony with God, themselves, and each other.[3] He struggles. Or perhaps more accurately, I struggle to find his account very convincing. But we don't have to accept Augustine's account of paradisiacal sex to learn from his attempt to imagine creatureliness without fallenness. Even though any attempt to do so is hobbled by the reality that in a sinful world, creatureliness is only experienced in the modality of fallenness, each refracting the other.

The Spirit enables true materiality, that is, creation open to eschatological fulfillment. Contrary to how he is often read, Paul takes this view. For Paul, the "fleshly" life refers to patterns that orient us toward death and disintegration and away from relationship with God.[4] To think and act in fleshly ways is to be at once misdirected, superficial, and inconsiderate. On this reading, legalism and license are two sides of the same coin. They constitute a false valorization of the self and an assumption of invulnerability that in turn directs us to nothingness and away from eternal life and communion with God.

The converse of Paul's division between the fleshly life and the Spirit-empowered life in Romans 8 is that the bodily life can either be a witness to or against God. For Paul, there is a battle over the shape and pattern of bodily life. It is a battle fought between the false authorities or principalities and powers of this age and the true and good Lordship of Jesus Christ. Every aspect of bodily life – eating, drinking, thinking, sex, economics, politics – is to be conformed to Christ because, for Paul, our bodies are members of Christ. By this logic, if we are to live according to the truth about ourselves, we must become Christ-like. Paul directly echoes a central theme of the Hebrew Scriptures/Old Testament. As Mari Joerstad notes:

> In the Hebrew Bible, what you wear, how you shave (or not shave), the use of tattoos or scarring, the creation and collection of ornaments, and so on, are not optional bodily practices, but part of what it means to be a person. The body is not a given, nor a neutral reality, but a project that must be maintained in order to continue to be a human person .... Humans become fully human over time, by living in a particular way, and by performing certain deeds and avoiding others.[5]

Likewise, in the New Testament, it is the structure of human life and not some building structure that is the Temple of the Holy Spirit (1 Cor 6:15–19). Conversely, it is other forms of life, and not pagan temples, that constitute the real threat to faithful witness.

Spirituality, materiality, and morality are indexed to each other. Our spirituality must at the same time be moral and material; for example, cutting or starving ourselves (as against fasting) for spiritual ends is forbidden. While moral ways of organizing material life cannot be separated from cultivating our practices of piety (prayer, fasting, etc.). Moreover, we encounter God and the bursting out of the new creation not in some special spiritual time or space of enchantment but amidst the vicissitudes, conflicts, and contingency of ordinary life and its material necessities. This is an important insight of *Latine/ Latinx* theology which prioritizes *lo cotidiano* – that is, everyday experiences on the street, cooking, at work, etc. – as sites for encountering God and generating wisdom about how to survive and thrive amid daily struggle.[6] As Maria Pilar Aquino puts it: "We have no other place than *lo cotidiano* to welcome the living Word of God or to respond to it in faith."[7]

We don't commune with the Holy Spirit by overcoming, escaping, or transcending embodiment and relationality. Such communion enhances and fulfills what it means to be a creature enmeshed in relations with others, both human and nonhuman. The Spirit gives us gifts of speech (e.g., prayer and prophecy) for forming a loving and just common life; gifts of character (notably, faith, hope, and love) that sustain the fragile ecology of relationships essential to metabolizing that common life; and gifts of transformative action (e.g., forgiveness, reconciliation, healing, and deliverance) that herald unexpected or seemingly impossible ways of living together in the face of division or harm.[8] When combined, these gifts can generate new ways of being alive characterized by fellowship/*koinonia* and *shalom* particular to these people, in this place, at this time. Examples of exceptional moral and political heroism spring to mind at this point. One such example is Nelson Mandela and other leaders of the anti-apartheid struggle in South Africa, whose courage, forbearance, and hope led to a completely unexpected, peaceable new beginning for that country amidst unremitting racial violence. But there are myriad quieter, small-scale, and sometimes clumsy acts of grace that also live out this dynamic. One I have experienced is when the right gesture at the right time opened new possibilities for reconciling a broken friendship beyond hurt and recrimination. A truly holy spirituality is one that works with the grain of finitude, seeding its fulfillment in embodied communion with God and neighbor.

FALLENNESS

A Christian ethic entails recognizing that the path to goodness begins by admitting we are not just finite; we are also sinners. But what is sin? Scripture uses a cluster of images to identify what is wrong: we are weighed down, indebted, impure, and enslaved. These images point to how human action is not simply limited (as with finitude) but negatively constrained and disoriented. Despite our best efforts, we cannot do what we need to in order to flourish. What's more, even our best efforts are corrupted or disordered such that they produce something else – a burden, debt, impurity, oppression – that needs repairing or rectifying (it must be removed, paid back, cleansed, or set free) so that our actions may once more generate flourishing.[9]

One of the most theologically influential accounts of sin in the West is the doctrine of original sin, first developed in a systematic way by Augustine.[10] While this is a theologically problematic account in a number of ways, we can still glean important insights from it. It expresses four interrelated statements about sin:

(1) Sin is contingent because it is neither a necessary part of creation nor a consequence of human freedom. Its origin (if not its present reality) resulted from a free act but was neither inevitable nor a reflection of human nature. Rather, it was a distortion of what was originally good.

(2) Sin is radical because it is a condition or state we are in and only secondarily manifested in this or that action. Sin is not momentary or episodic but basic to all we do and say.

(3) Most controversially, sin is communicated to us prior to our becoming personal agents who are capable of independent action and intention. Sin is a pre-personal distortion. Thus, even newborn babies participate in it. That said, this in no way implies that anyone is required to bear the specific sins of others.

(4) Sin is universal. We are all in a situation of sin and we all commit individual acts of sin. There is thus a universal solidarity in sin that is neither simply the product of, nor reducible to, the fact that everyone sins.[11] By implication, no one and no action is innocent or pure. Another way to put this is that given the kind of metabolic vision of agency outlined in Part I, the sin of each constitutes the lives of all and the sin of all feeds into and constitutes the agency of each.

Augustine forged his understanding of original sin in conflict with the Pelagians, on the one hand, and the Manicheans, on the other. The former emphasized the continuing goodness of humans despite the fall (thereby underemphasizing the impact of sin), while the latter claimed that far from being good, creation was evil and needed to be escaped (thereby overemphasizing the nature of sin and mythologizing the nature of evil). The doctrine of original sin was an attempt to negotiate a third way between these two views.

For Augustine, his conception of original sin as a *perversion* of the good is directly related to his understanding of evil as a *privation* of the good. Sin corrupts so that we love good things the wrong way; evil disintegrates our capacity to flourish. They both represent a failure to participate in reality and an attempt to live by a false construct. In doing so, we become less and less able to live truthfully, thereby normalizing the distorting effects of sin and the destructive effects of evil. Our ways of being alive become inversions of a flourishing life so that they take on an active negative force, rendering into nothing what is true, good, and beautiful. In refusing the goodness of God's creation, the sinner catastrophically turns what is gifted for the good of all into private things to be used and exploited for their own benefit – including other humans. Evil, as a negatively constructive force, is action that exploits creational vulnerability and interdependence so that, cancer-like, our ways of being with and for others become the very means of destroying us and creation. What we need to survive and thrive – for example, intimacy, trust, sex, community, and sharing resources at a time of need – become in themselves modalities of exploitation and domination – child abuse, rape, racism, usury – that poison and tear apart the fragile fabric of life together, setting in motion metabolic processes that produce toxicity rather than flourishing.

An Augustinian framework is not so much an attempt to explain sin and evil – they have no efficient cause – as to show up their absurd, unintelligible, but ever-present reality in human experience.[12] However, a theological problem with conceptualizing evil as the absence of being is that it can mask the New Testament sense of evil as an active power that possesses us and our social and political life, subjecting them to the "principalities and powers" (e.g., Eph 3:10).[13] In the light of an apocalyptic reading of sin and evil, one that draws on these elements of the New Testament, we can also see that the doctrine of original sin over focuses on questions of personal morality as well as directs attention backwards to what has been rather than forward to what is coming and the struggle to bear witness to what will be. Sin and evil are not just personal problems; they also produce and are reproduced by systems and structures that need converting. For example, money and the state are human fabrications that only have force because we give them value and authority over our lives. Created to serve human society, they take on a life of their own, generating systems and processes that in turn shape human and nonhuman life together at a collective and individual level, often in ways that actively militate against our flourishing. Turning away from God to secure ourselves by serving either money or the state is a misplaced act of faith in things of human making, and thereby idolatrous and so self-destructive.[14]

A contemporary example of this dynamic that has emerged of late is the use of "big data." Machine learning, artificial intelligence, algorithms, and biometric identification are now integrated to surveil and control us in ways that are mostly unseen and claim to be neutral, but which either replicate, intensify, or create new forms of unjust discrimination and inequality.[15] One result of this confluence is spelled out by Juval Harari who notes:

> Biologists are deciphering the mysteries of the human body, and in particular of the brain and human feelings. At the same time computer scientists are giving us unprecedented data-processing power. When the biotech revolution merges with the infotech revolution, it will produce Big Data algorithms that can monitor and understand my feelings much better than I can, and then authority will probably shift from humans to computers.[16]

For Harari this development will disintegrate what he sees as the "illusion of free will" as we "daily encounter institutions, corporations, and government agencies that understand and manipulate what was until now my inaccessible inner realm."[17] In short, our life can be hacked to serve the political and economic interests of others. Tools that were developed to make life better have become mechanisms creating new forms of oppression and intensifying existing forms of tyranny.[18] As Harari points out, these systems are now all-pervasive and intimately present in our lives. We created them to protect and serve us, but they in turn distort and destroy our common life.

The response to systemic and structural sin and evil cannot merely be personal repentance combined with enduring life in the earthly city. As part of actively bearing witness to what will be in Christ, it must also entail resistance to and a struggle to expose and overcome the occult forces that are parasitic on and metastasize how social, political, and economic life turn away from God here and now and thereby destroy us and our neighbor.

In the West, the doctrine of original sin has been the majority view. However, from the eighteenth century onwards, philosophers and theologians became highly critical of it. These criticisms center on a number of points. First, Augustine is criticized for making sin basic to existence and compromising a view of creation as good and of humans as made in the image of God. Second, it undermines any notion of free will, personal responsibility, and autonomy. In what way can we be free if we are bound to sin? Third, it is contrary to basic morality: How can we be held accountable for things we did not do? How can we be guilty of crimes we did not commit? The backdrop to all these critiques is the view of humans as autonomous, self-reflexive subjects.

In rejecting a notion of original sin, modern conceptions of sin tend to repeat the positions that Augustine was arguing against. Many modern moral and political philosophies are Pelagian, operating with an optimistic assessment of human potential. Humans are essentially good and capable of exercising free choice (their will is not in bondage to sin) and thus they are capable of transcending their limitations. For example, some modern accounts downplay "sin" as reducible to ignorance and irrational prejudice that are best addressed through education. But such accounts struggle to account for and cope with complex and intractable phenomena such as pedophilia or structural racism where greater knowledge and education alone has little effect.

A variation on the Pelagian approach is one that considers humans to be intrinsically good but corrupted by the negative impact of the social, economic, and political systems that condition them. This is to completely externalize sin and locate it in structures rather than persons. Such an approach is exemplified in the opening line of Enlightenment philosopher Jean-Jacques Rousseau's *The Social Contract* (1762): "Man was born free, and everywhere he is in chains."[19] Such a position is a reaction against the ways the doctrine of original sin generates overly individualistic and moralistic understandings of sin that do not account for structures of domination and the need for social reform or even revolution.

Another variation on the Pelagian conception of sin is to say that humans are good but are made bad by the abuse of others. Thus, my misogyny or domestic violence results from my prior trauma. The focus is less on structures of domination keeping us back, than on the ways in which we internalize what others have done to us. On this account, sin is reduced to a psychological condition. Such an approach can be understood as a response to an overemphasis on pride in the Christian tradition. While it is true that many need humbling, others need raising up: "Let the believer who is lowly boast in being raised up, and the rich in being brought low" (Jas 1:9–10). Sin can be both prideful self-assertion and a shame-filled diminishment of a proper self-respect.

If, on the one hand, there are a host of modern Pelagians, there are, on the other hand, a range of modern Manicheans. To them, human flourishing consists of transcending our physical limitations and achieving a higher gnosis/consciousness unbound by present conditions. Contemporary Manicheans include all who see the body as a limitation from which we need release, with technology providing the escape. Techno-utopian accounts that envisage humans as being able to overcome death, download human consciousness onto a computer, merge humans and machines, or reengineer the human to end suffering through biotechnology and genetics all exhibit Manichean tendencies.

There is another stream of modern thought that runs parallel to Augustine's conception of original sin but that errs on the side of being too pessimistic. The "masters of suspicion" – Marx, Freud, Darwin, and Nietzsche – all question the modern faith in the intrinsic goodness of humans and the emphasis on human freedom. They ask how free humans really are: Do we suffer from false consciousness and are we subject to historical forces beyond our control (Marx)? Are we in bondage to our sub-conscious urges (Freud)? Is life really about being good or is it wholly determined by a fight for survival of the fittest (Darwin)? Or is human freedom itself a historical construct that masks a "tyranny of timidity" (Nietzsche)? These critics of modernity helped generate a reappraisal and reappreciation of the doctrine of original sin as a theological tool for making sense of the human condition. However, these "realist" accounts leave little room for redemption and deny any original goodness: violence goes all the way down.

A Christian account of moral agency must reckon with human evil and sinfulness without slipping into various contemporary forms of Pelagianism or Manicheanism and thereby underestimating or overestimating the problem. This is best done by telling the whole story of the Creator's relationship to creation. Theological accounts of sin and redemption provide ways of making sense of the story that creation is good, but something is fundamentally wrong with the human condition within it. Thankfully, God, through Israel and Jesus Christ, has redeemed us – all may now, through the mediation of Christ and in the power of the Holy Spirit, be reconciled and enjoy communion with God, each other, and creation. However, we still await the fullness of that reconciliation and communion to be shown forth at the fulfillment of history when Christ returns.

Misconceptions of moral and political agency omit some part of this story or overemphasize one aspect at the expense of another.

TRAGEDY

If creaturely limits and sin set terms and conditions for moral agency, so does the tragic nature of moral action that arises within these conditions. I use "tragic" here to denote the inescapable ways in which in trying to do good we either cause harm or cannot alleviate suffering. Tragic situations often take place when moral conflicts occur that cannot be resolved or bypassed. Whatever choice is made, even a choice to do nothing, the result is either suffering or harm for someone. For example, take the situation of the social worker who has to make a decision as to whether to remove at-risk children from their substance-abusing parents. No matter the decision, the children will be adversely affected. Despite the inescapable and unmerited nature of the bad outcomes, action (or inaction) to address the situation is haunted by culpability, that is, by a sense that I must act in some way, yet anything I do will be at best inadequate and at worst harmful. Some use the language of moral injury to describe the effects of such situations. This language points to how in such situations, no matter what I do, I will contravene my deeply cherished moral commitments.

Related are situations where a decision must be reached, grave consequences follow from that decision, yet a mistake is highly likely due to either human error, ignorance, or the unjust structures we participate in. Criminal legal judgments can be of this nature: a judgment must be made, but it could turn out to be wrong, and the innocent end up imprisoned. Even if the decision is right, a person is still in prison and a fabric of relations is shattered. And the judgment itself is caught up in reproducing a carceral system that unjustly and disproportionately harms the impoverished and communities of color.

Sometimes what appears as a tragic situation is really a category mistake. For example, in pastoral care, we might have a sense that somehow the caring thing to do, the thing that relieves suffering, is in conflict with the moral thing to do and that what we take to be moral seems to lack compassion or will generate affliction. Such mistakes arise because we lack the imaginative resources, character, or pastoral acumen to understand and frame what is going on in such a way that the ethical and the pastoral are one and the same. To echo concerns addressed in Part I, how we describe, narrate, and thereby frame a problem is key. For example, when counseling and providing pastoral support to parents whose fetus is diagnosed as having Down syndrome, do I see it primarily as a medical problem that makes the child the issue and therefore brings into view the seemingly tragic quandary of whether to abort the child? Or do I see the syndrome primarily as a social problem that challenges whether our community is willing to include disabled people and support those who care for them. The latter is not a tragic situation but an instance of injustice that demands a social and political response in order to generate a more loving and just common life in which people with disabilities may flourish.

There are, however, often genuinely tragic situations where we have to choose between conflicting goods or discern a way forward in the face of intractable evil or suffering. There is much philosophical and theological debate as to whether there can be truly incommensurable conflicts between competing goods or whether a deeper harmony can be sought (thereby making the suffering that results from our actions morally contingent rather than necessary). But while speculatively interesting, in practice, given how human judgments are subject to fallenness and finitude, competing claims have to be confronted and decided between. For example, which should receive priority, the claims of the mother to determine her life course or the claims of the unborn child to have a life? We have to act in deeply ambiguous circumstances, we cannot always predict the outcome of our actions, and what we do may well make things worse or cause great pain. This is part of the tragic nature of human life this far east of Eden. But to acknowledge something is tragic is not then a license to claim that the right thing to do is simply to choose the lesser of two evils, even if this can seem an attractive option as we seek to make sense of difficult choices. Utilitarianism says that when faced with a ticking bomb scenario it is morally required to torture someone if that is the only way to get the needed information that will save thousands of lives. Deontology and command ethics say it is never right, however heinous the situation, to torture someone. We might be tempted to add a third position: we recognize it is morally heinous but, in certain circumstances, such as a choice between thousands of people dying and torturing one individual, torture is the lesser of two evils.

Thinking we can address tragic circumstances as a choice between the lesser of two evils refuses to live between the world as it is and the world as it should be by saying there is only the world as it is. In the name of a faux realism, it thereby renders superficial the moral landscape we occupy and constitutes a refusal to live with tension and ambiguity by falsely resolving the nature and depth of the problem.

To take a historical example, one way to interpret Dietrich Bonhoeffer's involvement in the plot to kill Adolf Hitler is as choosing the lesser of two evils. As a committed pacifist, he was opposed to the use of violence; but in the circumstances, he thought it was the lesser of two evils. Such an interpretation flattens and distorts how Bonhoeffer himself understood what he was doing. Despite his principled commitment to pacifism, Bonhoeffer understood his involvement in the plot to kill Hitler as the right and responsible action. It was not a small evil undertaken to overcome a greater one. He saw his actions as good and right even as it was fraught with contingency, potential risks, and he could be judged morally wrong.[20] Bonhoeffer thereby points to a truth learned of old from the Psalms: we must act without certainty, but in hope and with faith, trusting ourselves to God's mercy if our actions should prove to be wrong.[21]

The possibility of doing something that might cause harm raises the question of whether it is ever right to do evil so that good may come or so we can prevent what is harmful. Bonhoeffer's approach underlines how in Christian ethics the ends never justifies the means.

The means must be good, but that does not imply that the means don't cause negative outcomes. Here we need to make an important category distinction between what is *morally wrong* and what is spiritually, socially, politically or economically *harmful*. Drinking alcohol may be harmful at a number of levels but it is not necessarily morally wrong. Or organic food may or may not be healthier, but it may well be a more moral way to grow food. Arguments about health or risk should never become a substitute for arguments about right and wrong. Risk management and health and safety measures cannot be placeholders for ethics. Equally, harmful means may be, under certain conditions, used to achieve moral ends.

Harming someone is not always the same as wronging them. We can avoid harming ourselves or someone else by acting immorally. Conversely, while it is never right to do evil that good may come, it may be necessary to do what is injurious in some way, either to ourselves or to others, in order to do the right thing. For example, "social distancing" is alienating and economically harmful, but in a pandemic, it is the morally right thing to do in order to care for the vulnerable. Or surgery can cause real harm or result in further suffering or even death, but that result is not inherently immoral or wrong. A surgical intervention is often the morally right act even if it generates permanent disability (as in an amputation) or there is a great risk of death. More controversially, just war theory argues that war, while deeply harmful and violent, is morally required in certain circumstances and under certain conditions. Likewise, violent civil disorder may cause harm, but it is not necessarily immoral. A grief-stricken and chaotic uprising in response to an incidence of racially motivated police brutality is different in kind and end to drunken sports fans rampaging through a town after a game (yet both get labeled a riot).

Beyond technical distinctions between what is moral and harmful, Christ calls us to engage with what we fear, don't understand, or find difficult (death, illness, tragic circumstance, injustice) through *pathos/passio*: that is, a fierce desire to participate in and bear witness to reality as determined by the loving presence of God in a world of suffering. In a fallen world, such passionate engagement may entail great difficulty, pain, and struggle. This passionate or pathic witness contrasts with how we tend to understand compassion or sympathy as an altruistic sentiment.[22] Pathos involves active contemplation, abiding, and waiting, in order to encounter the truth about the world as it is and so be able to act fittingly in response to that world.

Ethical reflection that engages reality must reckon with how sin, tragic circumstances, and creaturely limits mold how we judge what is the right, just, and loving thing to do. The essential frailty and contingency of moral action must shape our moral imagination, without generating despair as to the possibilities of moral action in this kind of world. Moral agency exists within the reality that, this side of Eden, without faith, hope, and love our humanity dies; however, we must also acknowledge that being truly faithful, hopeful, and loving, like Christ, may well get us killed or throw us into the midst of affliction we can hardly bear. There is no solving or movement beyond moral distress amid great suffering, only living into it in ways that hallow the dignity, beauty, and fearsome fragility of those we care for and who care for us.

A combination of fallenness and finitude means we must accept the ambiguity and tension of living between the now and the not yet, between the world as it is and the world as it should be. Given the impact of the Fall on our ability to know or do the right thing, we need the humility to admit we could be wrong, might need to revise what we thought, and are often not the best judges of our own actions. We must also learn to abide with heterogeneity and deep disagreement about what is the morally fitting thing to do here and now. And despite our best intentions, we fail those around us on a regular basis, committing sins of omission and commission. Under such conditions, a desire for moral certainty and clarity is itself morally wrong. Certainty is not a Christian virtue. Rather, we must seek to act in

faith, hope, and love. That said, moral agency is not entirely rudderless, without means of navigation or ballast to stabilize it. Commands, rules, virtues, and practical reason provide means of moral action amid conditions of finitude and fallenness. It is to these I now turn.

ACCOMPANYING READINGS

Augustine, *City of God*, book 14 (various editions). Augustine influentially (and controversially) gives an account of the Fall, the origins of sin in pride, the disordered will (exemplified in sexual lust), and the formation of two cities oriented by two loves: love of self, which seeks its own glory and thereby produces domination, and love of God that seeks to glorify God, which thereby produces love of neighbor.

Fyodor Dostoevsky, "Rebellion" and "The Grand Inquisitor" from *The Brothers Karamazov* (various editions). These sections discuss the relationship between freedom, moral responsibility, and the fragility of love in the face of human suffering and need.

Reinhold Niebuhr, "Christianity and Tragedy," *Beyond Tragedy: Essays on the Christian Interpretation of History* (New York: Charles Scribner's Sons, 1937), 155–169. Niebuhr contrasts a classical and what he identifies as a Christian understanding of tragedy and how these frame the nature of the moral life.

Cornel West, "Subversive Joy and Revolutionary Patience in Black Christianity," *The Cornel West Reader* (New York: Basic Books, 1999), 435–439. Like Niebuhr, West sets out a distinctive, theological understanding of tragedy. But his account is shaped by and focused on the experience of the Black church in the United States. Contrasting the tragicomic vision of Black Christians with that of ancient Greek and modern views of tragedy, West gives an account of "the tragedy in the struggle for freedom and the freedom in a tragic predicament."

Christoph Schwöbel, "Recovering Human Dignity," *God and Human Dignity*, eds., Kendall Soulen and Linda Woodhead (Grand Rapids, MI: Eerdmans, 2006), 44–58. Schwöbel develops a trinitarian and scriptural account of human dignity, sin, and the nature of finitude.

M. Shawn Copeland, "Following the Tears of a Crucified World: A Theological Meditation on Social Suffering, Solidarity, and the Cross," *Knowing Christ Crucified: The Witness of African American Religious Experience* (Maryknoll, NY: Orbis, 2018), 127–147. This is a meditation on social and structural sin, the suffering it generates, and how the moral response to such suffering is solidarity understood as "intelligent and effective compassionate action."

NOTES

1 An influential meditation on exactly this dynamic and its challenge to understanding the need for change is set out in books 10 and 11 of Augustine's *Confessions* where he reflects on the relationship between time, eternity, and memory.

2 The question of whether mortality is a feature of creatureliness or only a sign of fallenness is much contested. I take the view that Jesus's death and resurrection represents not simply the defeat of death as an enemy but also ensures death loses its sting, thereby freeing mortality once more to be a chrysalis-like point of transition to eternal life (Isa 25:8; Hos 13:14; John 11:1–44; 2 Tim 1:10; 1 Cor 15:24–26, 54–55; Rev 21:4).

3 Augustine, *City of God* 14.23–26.

4 The difference between life in the flesh and life in the Spirit is the difference *not* between a wooden ship and a steel ship (i.e., two different kinds of vessel) but between a boat powered by solar energy that is fully operational and has a clear direction and the same boat but this time powered by coal, with a large leak, and without instruments to navigate.

5 Mari Joerstad, *The Hebrew Bible and Environmental Ethics: Humans, NonHumans, and the Living Landscape* (Cambridge: Cambridge University Press, 2019), 23–24.

6 Ada María Isasi-Díaz, *La Lucha Continues: Mujerista Theology* (Maryknoll, NY: Orbis, 2004), 92–106.

7 Maria Pilar Aquino, "Theological Method in U.S. Latino/a Theology," *From the Heart of the People: Latino/a Explorations in Catholic Systematic Theology*, eds., Orlando O. Espín and Miguel H. Díaz (Maryknoll, NY: Orbis, 1999), 39.

8 As Hannah Arendt frames this dynamic in relation to forgiveness: "Forgiving … is the only reaction which does not merely re-act but act anew and unexpectedly, unconditioned by the act which provoked it and therefore freeing from its consequences both the one who forgives and the one who is forgiven." Hannah Arendt, *The Human Condition*, 2nd ed. (Chicago: University of Chicago Press, 1958), 241.

9 Other scriptural and theological images used to describe sin include humans as sick (and so in need of healing), as immature (so in need of growth), as out of right relation (and so in need of reconciliation), as heading

in the wrong direction or falling (and so in need of turning around/ conversion or transcendence).

10 Augustine built on the prior work of Tertullian (c. 155–c. 240) and Cyprian of Carthage (c. 200–258 CE).

11 Alistair McFadyen, *Bound to Sin: Abuse, Holocaust and the Christian Doctrine of Sin* (Cambridge: Cambridge University Press, 2000), 16–17.

12 In doing so, Augustine takes his lead from Scripture. Accounts of sin in the Bible – notably, Genesis 3:1–15 and Isaiah 14:12–21 – are not origin stories so much as descriptions of a condition and its consequences.

13 The debate about how to understand the principalities and powers centers on two questions: first, do the principalities and powers refer solely to material structural dynamics or to cosmic, extra-material forces; and second, are the powers redeemable or not? I take the view that the principalities and powers mentioned in Luke-Acts and the Pauline epistles are both spiritual and socio-political and are created good, presently fallen, judged in the Christ-event, and open to redemption at the eschatological fulfilment of all things.

14 A counter view that confirms my point here is developed by the philosopher Thomas Hobbes. In his influential political treatise, *Leviathan*, he argues that the only way to secure peace is to give over our freedom to the state/ Leviathan/a machine of our own making, trusting ourselves to it, even as he acknowledges that this beast may turn on and devour us.

15 See, for example, Margaret Hu, "Algorithmic Jim Crow," *Fordham Law Review* 86 (2017): 633–696.

16 Juval Noah Harari, *21 Lessons for the 21st Century* (New York: Random House, 2019), 49–50.

17 Harari, *21 Lessons*, 49–50

18 See Shoshana Zuboff, *The Age of Surveillance Capitalism: The Fight for a Human Future at the New Frontier of Power* (New York: PublicAffairs, 2019).

19 Jean-Jacques Rousseau, *The Social Contract and the First and Second Discourses*, ed. and trans., Susan Dunn (New Haven, CT: Yale University Press, 2002), 156.

20 His actions embody what Bonhoeffer called "vicarious representation": that is, taking action in the name of others through representing them in one's own person, this includes taking on the consequences and guilt of that action on their behalf. Dietrich Bonhoeffer, *Ethics*, trans., Reinhard Krauss et al., *Dietrich Bonhoeffer Works*, vol. 6, ed., Clifford Green (Minneapolis, MN: Fortress Press, 2005), 257.

21 See, for example, Psalms 25:6; 40:11; 51:1–6; 119:156; and 123.

22 On this, see M. Shawn Copeland, *Knowing Christ Crucified: The Witness of African American Religious Experience* (Maryknoll, NY: Orbis, 2018), 127–147. Copeland envisages the moral response to suffering as solidarity understood as "intelligent and effective compassionate action."

8 Call and Commands

When my family and I moved to the United States, my eldest son had never played or seen a game of basketball. He was not even that interested in sports. But on arrival, he was invited to join a neighborhood recreational team. That opportunity awakened a love for the game that then became his passion until he went to university. As it turned out, being a serious basketball player in North Carolina is not a trivial matter. It structured much of his life, including how he experienced school, our town, the intersections of gender, class, and race, as well as his own physical development. However, there was neither an identity nor a way of acting as a basketball player that was somehow hidden inside him waiting to jump out. Rather, that identity was called forth and nurtured by a context and set of relations he was embedded within, helped (or hindered) by comments by coaches as well as gendered, racialized, and economic structures and signals. It is also true that his innate capacities, height, prior experiences, and history were taken up and woven into the identity that was called forth, and all these elements came together to open new and unique pathways for future action.

Like my son, we are all in a process of becoming. Our identities and agency are in dynamic relation with and constituted through the world around us. I become a parent through the existence of a child I respond to with bathing, songs, food, and cuddles. The farmer becomes such through tending fields or chickens, the academic through books and students. These material and social relations are mutually constitutive even as many are asymmetric. Learning language (whether through sign language or spoken words) follows the same pattern: without another person and a world to name, there is no one to speak with, learn from, or respond to. Language is a social phenomenon through which we come to know ourselves and the world around us. It exists between us. In a similar way, we learn how to eat, kiss, or walk from and with others, discovering together how to inhabit a shared world. Becoming attuned to and learning how to flourish in this world is a relational and physical process, not just a cognitive or affective one. In Chapter 2, I framed this inductive process of discovery, attunement, and response as a process of metabolizing the world around us.

On a metabolic view of agency, we are animals whose way of inhabiting reality depends on how we are called into it. We do not have a fixed identity or preexisting self that is simply expressed, and which must somehow be recognized by others as already existing. Each person comes to be in and through others, both human and nonhuman, and discovering who and what we are and how we will or can act takes time and discernment. We do not arrive in our world as autonomous, self-directing agents able to make sense of it from an already established point of view. No. We are summoned into and enabled to act in this world through practices of care and communication. We become through a process of reception and response – being swaddled and caressed, being spoken and sung to, being cooked for and fed, being given a world to see and smell. It is through these interactive experiences that our brains form and our own capacity to care and communicate develops.

On a Christian account, becoming a disciple entails being baptized into and learning how to faithfully metabolize God's call to and communication with us. The Word calls creation into being and continues to care for creation and, in doing so, calls creation into communion with God. Our moral and political lives are a response to this call and ongoing processes of care, communication, and interpretation that responding to this call entails. This chapter examines how God's commands constitute us as moral agents. In doing so, I reflect on what it means to be called by God into a particular way of acting with and for others as moral agents through discerning how God acts with and for us through divine commands.

Amid conditions of finitude and fallenness, the good news Christian ethics proclaims is that God acts first so that we may now act well.[1] A significant approach for framing how God's prior action enables human moral agency is in terms of divine commands. So, alongside understanding call and vocation as means of moral agency, this chapter reflects on what divine commands are and what it means to respond to them. Talk of divine commands can be a synonym for cognate terms such as divine law, eternal law, and creation mandates. Each is a way of talking about God's creative, communicative, and self-revealing agency in and through creation. This communicative agency is not static but relational and covenantal in form. And it comes before, authorizes, and catalyzes human moral and political action understood as a means through which humans forge and sustain shared worlds of meaning and action directed to the flourishing of creation.

Understood formally, divine command ethics refers to the position that the good or moral life is one lived in obedient response to God's commands. A command reveals a truth grounded in the nature of God; it is therefore unchangeable. However, what it means to follow the command is always subject to interpretation and further specification. Divine commands are mediated to us primarily through Scripture, such as in the Ten Commandments or the Sermon on the Mount. But we also find them through the orders or spheres of responsibility given in creation – notably, familial, economic, and political life. The commands establish obligations or duties to be fulfilled. Divine commands are those things we are obligated to do or responsible for undertaking if we are to fulfill what it means to be in relationship with God and neighbor and participate in God's love of creation. Given what I have just said, it is easy to see why command ethics is often categorized as a form of deontology (i.e., about doing our duty); but as I will show, this is an inaccurate description.

DIVINE AND HUMAN FREEDOM

Many people see commands as externally imposed regulations. Against such a view, I contend a theological understanding of divine commands requires seeing them as establishing a form of life or generating a shared endeavor. Rather than coming from "outside," they make possible and form the basis of faithful, hopeful, and loving ways of being alive. To put this another way, to follow a command – love thy neighbor – is to engage in something that inhabits, furthers, and is intrinsic to a Christian form of life; to not follow it is to act unchristianly. Commands thereby both establish a way of life and enable the ability of humans to be free *for* that way of life.

I am pushing back here against an ancient view that divine commands are external constraints rather than liberating conditions. At a formal level, philosophers have framed their critique of divine command ethics in terms of what is often referred to as the "Euthyphro dilemma," a version of which is first articulated in Plato's *Dialogues*. Socrates is debating with Euthyphro about the nature of true piety. The central question they argue about is as follows: "Does God command the good because it is good, or is it good because it is commanded by God?" I will unpack this dilemma in some detail as it gets to the heart of understanding how divine-human relations shapes Christian ethics.

One dimension of the dilemma is that if actions are good only by virtue of the fact that God commands them, then God's commands, since no reason is given for them, must be arbitrary. God must be obeyed, not because there are good reasons to follow divine commands but because divine injunction is backed by divine power. Put more sharply, the problem is that if something is good because God wills it, then God can order atrocities and they are still good. The story of Abraham's attempt to sacrifice Isaac is often read in this light, with Abraham's action deemed as justifiable only because God commanded it (Gen 22:1–2).[2]

Related to this problem of divine fiat is the question of how divine commands affect human autonomy. This has been of particular concern in the modern period. If we obey God's command only because God issued it, then we are assenting to an arbitrary will out of fear rather than freely consenting to something we have rationally agreed with. This is the problem of "heteronomy," meaning law that is imposed from above and conformed to without consent. In short, modern philosophers come to see God's command as the brute assertion of divine sovereignty that opposes and undermines human autonomy, freedom, and rationality. It follows that to be free and fully rational we must throw off the overlordship of God and exercise our autonomy to decide what is good or bad by dint of non-arbitrary, rational, and freely chosen criteria.

This modern anxiety about the relationship between divine commands and ethics has a long history, one that goes back to the emergence of the philosophical schools of thought known as "voluntarism" and "nominalism" in the medieval era. The emergence of these ideas is bound up with theological debates about the doctrine of God. Crucially, this anxiety is produced by a shift from understanding the fundamental nature of being as grounded in participating in communion with God to one in which God's sovereign will is the ultimate principle of being (voluntarism). In the modern period, we simply displace God with humans but leave the conceptual structure intact. Instead of God giving laws to humans, the autonomous, sovereign individual with an indivisible will issues laws to him- or herself. In so doing, the human will simply replaces divine will as what we must obey. For example, instead of an individual being recognized as having an intrinsic dignity and set of rights because it is God's will, human rights are founded on the freedom of each individual to will and consent to what is done to them.

Freedom on this account is not the discovery of a form of life that enables us to live, and move, and have our being in communion with God and neighbor (i.e., a participatory metaphysics). Rather, freedom is reduced to a moment of consenting to something, which can be anything, however arbitrary or destructive. Freedom on this account is a zero-sum game and not about mutually responsible social relationships in which the individual's freedom and fulfillment is constituted by the kinds and quality of their relationships with others and with God. Instead, my freedom is asserted at the expense of and in opposition to someone else's: more freedom for me means less freedom for you. This framework can equally apply to God: more of God equals less of me. For example, in medical research, anything can be done with the information or biological material from an individual if that person signs a consent form. Freedom to research is premised on the patient signing away their freedom to object. What this moment of consent ignores is the way the individual is subordinated to the power of the medical-industrial complex whose help they need and how they in turn have very little if any agency to determine the conditions of the help they receive. There is no ongoing, mutually responsible relationship that enables the flourishing of researcher and patient, just a transaction in which the individual patient is entirely at the mercy of those who have all the power to help and heal them yet are entirely unaccountable to and outside of any meaningful relationship with the one in need of healing and help.

Within this logic, self-sacrifice rather than communion becomes the normative expression of Christian love. To truly love someone is to give up our autonomy and dispossess ourselves of our agency. For example, to give up a life of comfort to work in a refugee camp would seem to be good in an uncomplicated way. It involves sacrificing a large measure of freedom and autonomy so as to fulfill a duty of care for others. On closer inspection, however, such an act may be exercising self-assertion through a messiah complex focused on how I can save others, as if my actions are the only ones that count. A true account of the moral relation must recognize that the ability of the aid worker to act is called forth and constituted through relationship *with* the refugees served. Moral agency exists *between* the aid worker and the refugees and not in a one-way relation. Far from sacrificing their freedom and agency, the aid worker is enhanced in their ability to act through their relationship with those served. Moreover, they may come to see how the way of life they left behind was itself built on the oppression of others and so should be renounced anyway. Working with the refugees is thereby a moment of liberation not self-negation.

In the contemporary context, understanding the highest expression of love as sacrificing one's freedom and autonomy for others swings between two poles. On the one hand, it idealizes self-sufficiency and autonomy, understanding freedom as self-assertion and thereby denying the reality of interdependence. On the other hand, it envisions the truly good moral action in terms of renouncing one's freedom and autonomy. This idealizes self-sacrifice understood as self-negation. Both self-assertion (egoism) and self-negation (altruism) are deeply individualistic, as they make the unilateral action of the individual the prime focus of moral agency. Moral agency is thereby divorced from the reality of interdependency, overlooking the way my freedom and dignity are bound up with and constituted through participating in relationship with others.

An individualistic view of moral agency that swings between the poles of self-assertion and self-negation depends on a particularly Western conception of freedom. Such a conception can be contrasted with something like the Southern African concept of *ubuntu*. *Ubuntu* is used as a framework for social ethics by Archbishop Desmond Tutu (1931–2021). It holds that a person is a person through other people (*umuntu ngumuntu ngabantu*). There is no autonomous "I" who acts either in self-assertion or self-negation. Rather, the self is constituted through relationship, and it is the quality and character of these relations that determine whether I am moral or not. There are analogs to *ubuntu* within Western strands of thought. Examples include Martin Luther King Jr.'s notion of "beloved community" that draws on Black church traditions, Christian personalism, and pragmatic philosophy; the constitutive relation between human dignity, freedom, and solidarity in Catholic social teaching;[3] the centrality of interdependency in an ethics of care;[4] the place of community in virtue ethics;[5] and, not unproblematically, the conception of freedom as based on mutual recognition in Hegel's moral and political philosophy.[6] Freedom in these frameworks entails some notion that our ability to act freely arises from the quality and character of our relations with others.

Within these more participatory and mutualistic views of freedom, the relationship between divine commands and human moral agency looks very different. We are not autonomous rational agents who are somehow choosing to bind ourselves to an externally imposed and alien law. God is not some deranged sergeant major ordering us to march up and down on a capricious whim. It is not some random instruction we are obeying but the command of a loving creator God who has healed, redeemed, and fulfilled creation so that we may once more flourish as creatures in relationship with God and neighbor. In hearing God's command, we discover who we are created to be. Through hearing and responding to God's command, we are enabled to inhabit our true nature.

The account of how divine commands generate moral agency given here is exemplified in the stories of social workers, teachers, ministers, or nurses who sense a direct call from God to their vocation. This call deeply shapes the pattern and basic orientation of their lives, determining in everyday ways how they love God and neighbor. As the American philosopher Robert Adams (b. 1937) defines it: "A vocation is a call from God, a command, or perhaps an invitation, addressed to a particular individual, to act and live in a certain way."[7] For Adams, the particular vocation of the teacher or minister is a way they play a part in God's love. In this sense, they experience their vocations as both invitation and imperative. They are directed by God to undertake their vocation but not in the sense of having an alien law imposed or shouldering a burdensome duty. Rather, they are discovering who they are called to be in relation to and with others. With that comes a sense of release and freedom. This dynamic is encapsulated in Jesus's statement that: "If you keep my commandments, you will abide in my love, just as I have kept my Father's commandments and abide in his love. I have said these things to you so that my joy may be in you, and that your joy may be complete" (John 15:10–11; Ps 16). Following divine commands brings joy and a sense of release because it is a way of abiding in divine love in and through love of neighbor. This is good news.

VOCATION AND NEIGHBOR LOVE

Søren Kierkegaard (1813–1855) and Karl Barth (1886–1968) are key figures in the renewal of thinking about the place of divine commands in ethics. In different ways, both challenge dominant modern conceptions of freedom, rationality, and autonomy influenced by the philosophical frameworks of René Descartes (1596–1650) and Immanuel Kant (1724–1804). Kierkegaard held that all genuine moral duties are divine commands and that whatever God commands is morally obligatory. But God's commands cannot be arbitrary because they extend from God's nature and thereby have love and the flourishing of creation as their goal. As creatures, we are most fully creaturely when we respond appropriately to God's command, which is to conform to what Jesus Christ reveals. Failure to do so leads us to despair and nothingness. We will be judged against the criteria of God's self-revelation in Christ, not some other standard. On this account, to make humans a law unto themselves, as the philosopher Immanuel Kant does, deprives humans of the lynchpin by which they can orient themselves morally in the world. Without God's commands, we are adrift.[8] Far from becoming rational and well-ordered because we have supposedly escaped the arbitrary interventions of God's will, morality itself becomes utterly arbitrary.

Like Kierkegaard, Barth also rejects the basic premises of the Euthyphro dilemma. Echoing and expanding on Kierkegaard, he argues that God elects to act in certain, self-limiting ways and humans can only be good through faithful response to God encountered in Christ as Creator, Reconciler, and Redeemer. Thus, for Barth, the command of God enables us to discover what it means to be God's creatures, sinners pardoned by God, and heirs-expectant of the coming kingdom of God.[9] Keeping faith with (i.e., obeying) God's command requires we respond appropriately as creatures, sinners, and heirs expectant. For Barth, the Ten Commandments represent neither an assertion of divine power nor an imposition on human freedom but the delimitation of the sphere in which human life, in relationship with God, may be free and fulfilled. God's commands are not some external constraint but God's personal address, which as command is simultaneously an invitation and a source of empowerment, a demand and a resource, a call and a means to respond. Again, think of the social worker, teacher, minister, nurse, or parent hearing their call: it is both a demand and empowering. Christian ethics is "evangelical" because it proclaims the good news that God is for us and that because of God's prior action, we can once more rightly pursue human flourishing in relationship with God and neighbor.

The flourishing life for Barth is a life of response-ability; that is, a life lived with and for others in response to God's commands. In being confronted by God's command, we are forced to turn away from self and respond to our neighbor. The commands demand recognition that we cannot live alone and that we are not the source of our own being. Like the nurse or teacher discovering their vocation, our freedom means being free *for* relationship *with* others. This is what it means to be responsible: our ability to respond (response-ability) is restored in Christ so that we can once more respond faithfully to God and neighbor. In responding to God's summons heard in the commands of God, we are constituted as moral agents able to act with and for others.

For Barth, the primary vocation humans are called to is to love God and neighbor. Neighbor love transcends and frames all other offices or roles. In his understanding of vocation and its relationship to the call of God, Barth envisages our specific vocations (to be a teacher, engineer, farmer, parent, etc.) as our particular response to the command of God. Our particular response is not random. It builds on and renders fruitful such things as personal aptitude, historical context, and age.[10] In this way, divine commands connect to our everyday arenas of human speech and action. Our specific vocations are the context and "place of responsibility" where we hear God's command in continual interaction with our neighbors, liberating us for what God calls us to do while also releasing us from taking on more than we can cope with.[11] Rather than getting burned out by a sense of duty to respond to all that is wrong with the world, we recognize that we cannot do everything. Instead, we are to do only that which is given into our hands. Or as Adams puts it, our vocations call us into "responsibilities proportioned to our capacities."[12]

Some question whether Barth's approach allows for growth in character over time as it seems to demand we always respond to God in the moment. As one critic puts it, his approach is "radically occasionalist."[13] In response, Bonhoeffer's notion of mandates – arenas in which we hear God's command and discover our responsibility for others – amplifies and supplements Barth's approach. Such arenas as family, employment, and civic life are contexts in which we take on particular roles such as carer, plumber, accountant, or citizen. Each of these spheres can involve different kinds of judgment and emphasize particular constellations of rules and virtues. Put more concretely, the forms of intimacy and virtue required to sustain a marriage are not the same as those needed to sustain a political party. So, for example, we should not expect the same kind of loyalty or faithfulness to a party as we do from a spouse – although some get them confused. That said, while distinguishable, each mandate contributes to and is constituted by the others; for example, familial life is part of and helps constitute economic life and vice versa. In Part III, I explore how kinship, economic, and political relations are interdependent and entangled yet distinguishable domains within which we bear witness to God and form a common life with creation.

God's commands both liberate and establish new possibilities for human action. Commands invite us to particular kinds of relationship: Christ-like ones through which I fulfill who I am created to be. It's not a zero-sum game, as the relationship established by God is a noncompetitive one: the more of God there is, the more of me can exist in relation to others. We are not erased by encounter with the divine. Rather, as the Jewish philosopher Martin Buber frames it, God's "Thou," encountered in the commands, calls forth and constitutes the "I" as an ethical subject able to act with and for others. Commands are thereby not heteronomous (imposed from above) but synergistic (dynamically combining divine and human agency).[14] They generate Christ-led, Spirit-empowered participation with God, neighbor, and the rest of creation in shared enterprises such as education, pastoral care, healing, agriculture, or trade.[15]

THE HOW AND WHERE OF HEARING GOD'S COMMAND

It is important to note that within this framework revelation does not replace or usurp reason. We do not obey God's command spontaneously or without reflection. Rather, the prior action of God inaugurates a specific way of being oriented to the world around us and a particular kind of practical reasoning. And because we are responding in the context of a dynamic, ongoing relationship with a living God, we cannot pre-decide or fix what it means to be faithful to God's call here and now. What *is* rejected is any notion of a blueprint or procedure independent of God's ongoing self-communicating agency. Barth, for example, rejected natural law approaches and all frameworks of ethical reasoning that posit their existence as autonomous from God (e.g., deontological and utilitarian frameworks). Such blueprints and procedures come between the person and their encounter with God. Put another way, there can be no fixed list of dos and don'ts for determining what we should do in any instance. Such lists mean we are following a code rather than following the living God. Rather, we must be faithful to God's self-revelation in Jesus Christ and what that means in this particular moment with these particular people.

When we want to know what we ought to do, our first act is neither to reflect on abstract concepts (about, for example, what is true, good, or beautiful), nor apply a general principle (e.g., what will produce the greatest good for the greatest number), nor begin with vague generalizations (e.g., do no harm). Rather, our first act is listening to and hearing what God is commanding us to do here and now. Through listening for and to God we become specific and concrete. But hearing what God is saying here and now is not straightforward.[16] Given the embodied and relational nature of human creatureliness, hearing is a whole person process. Indeed, even dreams, visions, direct words, and inner promptings may play a part in hearing God's command – Samuel (1 Sam 3:2–15), Joseph (Matt 1:20–21; 2:13, 19–20, 22), Paul (Acts 9:3–6), and Peter (Acts 10:9–23) being scriptural cases in point.

Echoing the sources of authority discussed in Part I, Barth contends we hear the command of God primarily through:

- Engagement with the canon of Scripture;
- active interrogation of what it means to participate in creaturely ways of being alive;
- prayer;[17]
- dialogue with those from other traditions with whom a common life must be forged and in whom the Spirit may be at work (what Barth called "secular parables");
- encountering suffering or hearing from experiences of marginalization and oppression;[18] and finally,
- attending to our fellow hearers of God's Word, both past and present (tradition).[19]

These measures represent *how* we hear God's commands. This process of hearing itself forms us as persons: the more we practice this kind of listening the better we become at hearing and responding to God's imperatives. As a process of discernment and testing, listening is *discursive* (it is done in dialogue with Scripture, creation, strangers, the afflicted and oppressed, and ancestors), *contextual* (it pays attention to history and place), and *synthetic* (it draws all this together in a moment of judgment and decision). Barth called this process a "practical casuistry," a "casuistry of prophetic ethos," and elsewhere a "casuistry of the event."[20] There is thus a central place for moral reasoning and debate in hearing God's commands. Moreover, our moral commitments and judgments must always be open to further challenge and revision. New responses to God's command may well be demanded because the Word of God shatters our predetermined assumptions about what to do. Failure to be open to such reevaluation is a sure path to idolatry as it means trusting in our own fallible and fallen judgments rather than trying to discern what being a faithful witness to God entails here and now.

Within this framework, there is a place for extensive, rigorous ethical reflection on particular issues such as euthanasia, immigration, artificial intelligence, or war. This reflection entails the kind of process of listening just outlined. It produces commentary and counsel that help orient us toward faithful witness. As Barth puts it:

> These directives may help man on to ethical reflection and action, to the finding, studying, honouring, and, God willing, the keeping of the commandments; that is, to his conversion from disobedience to obedience in relation to the divine commanding as it comes precisely to him. To draw these lines, to give these directives, is, in a general way, the task and the theme of special ethics.[21]

In sum, books, articles, podcasts, lectures, and the like that analyze a particular topic or moral question – what Barth calls "special ethics" – should function as guidance on walking a faithful pathway rather than as manuals for determining what to do and how to do it. In addition, historical or ethnographic examinations of previous or current judgments (e.g., Bonhoeffer deciding whether the plot to assassinate Hitler was justifiable) provide examples of special ethics in action that help us reflect on our own processes of moral discernment.

The approach outlined here to the place of divine commands in the moral life needs situating within a covenantal framework: that is, a promise between two parties that forms the basis of a common life that has shared goals pursued together over time. Covenants are *where* we hear God's commands. Divine-human covenants are established by God for whom the indicatives of love always precede the imperatives of command: "I have created you," "I have loved you," "I have saved you," and "I have liberated you," always precede "therefore keep my commandment." The laws of Leviticus and Deuteronomy are prefaced by remembering how God liberated the people from slavery: "For I am the Lord who brought you up from the land of Egypt, to be your God; you shall be holy, for I am holy"

(Lev 11:45; cf. Deut 5:1–33). After a covenant is made between God and the people, the law is given to provide the means for and measure of ongoing relationship.

God's loving call and prior salvific action is the unconditional and unshakable foundation of divine-human covenants. But this prior action calls forth a response, and the ongoing interaction of call and response generates a common life in which both God and creation participate. The specific shape of this common life and what it means in practice to love God and creation varies according to historical, geographic, and cultural context as well as personal capacity and aptitude. It can only be discerned as we cultivate a common life with others. Covenant and command provide the context and conditions within which metabolizing creation can be fructifying and moral agency realized. An account of the virtues – as developed in Chapter 10 – specifies in a more granular way what it actually means to live with and for others and what freedom as responsibility for others entails. However, before discussing the virtues, I reflect on the place of rules and regulations in moral agency.

ACCOMPANYING READINGS

Søren Kierkegaard, "Problema I: Is There a Teleological Suspension of the Ethical?," *Fear and Trembling* (various editions). This is Kierkegaard's influential meditation on the *Akedah* or binding of Isaac story, the ethics or otherwise of Abraham's action in following God's command, and how faith can suspend and thereby, paradoxically, refound the moral life.

Karl Barth, *Church Dogmatics: The Doctrine of God* vol. II/2, trans., G. W. Bromiley et al. (Edinburgh: T&T Clark, 1957), 631–708 (the small print sections can be excluded).

Kathryn Tanner, "A Theological Case for Human Responsibility in Moral Choice," *The Journal of Religion* 73, no. 4 (1993): 592–612. Tanner develops a realist understanding of moral responsibility as the fruit of divine-human relations and shows how, in contrast to parallel conceptions, her account helps respond to structures of oppression that curtail human flourishing.

Ellen Charry, "Asherism in the Pentateuch," *God and the Art of Happiness* (Grand Rapids, MI: Eerdmans, 2010), ch. 9. Charry lays out how the commands of God in the Decalogue and holiness codes are aimed at cultivating what she calls an "asherist" way of life; that is, a flourishing life that accords with covenantal faithfulness. Charry's account overlaps with but also markedly differs from the approach set out in this chapter. Much of the difference arises from her exegetical framework, which contrasts sharply with the five rules for reading Scripture set out in Chapter 3.

NOTES

1 This divine action involves a threefold dynamic: God acts to heal our capacity to act as finite creatures directed to our true end, communion with God; God acts to redeem us from sin so that our actions are no longer wholly determined by the Fall; and God acts to fulfill human actions so that they can anticipate and participate in their eschatological fulfillment now.

2 See, for example, Augustine, *City of God*, 1, 21.

3 See, for example, John Paul II, *Sollicitudo Rei Socialis* (1987), §§32–40.

4 See, for example, Virginia Held, *The Ethics of Care: Personal, Political, and Global* (Oxford: Oxford University Press, 2006).

5 Alasdair MacIntyre, *Dependent Rational Animals: Why Human Beings Need the Virtues* (London: Duckworth, 1999).

6 See Molly Farneth, *Hegel's Social Ethics: Religion, Conflict, and Rituals of Reconciliation* (Princeton, NJ: Princeton University Press, 2017).

7 Robert Adams, *Finite and Infinite Goods: A Framework for Ethics* (Oxford: Oxford University Press, 1999), 301.

8 Søren Kierkegaard, *Kierkegaard's Writings, XVI: Works of Love*, eds. and trans., Howard V. Hong and Edna H. Hong (Princeton, NJ: Princeton University Press, 1995), 115–117.

9 Karl Barth, *The Christian Life: Church Dogmatics IV, 4 Lecture Fragments*, trans., Geoffrey Bromiley (Edinburgh: T&T Clark, 1981), 7.

10 Karl Barth, *Church Dogmatics: The Doctrine of Creation*, vol. III/4, trans., A. T. Mackay et al. (Edinburgh: T&T Clark, 1961), 595–647. Barth echoes John Calvin, *Institutes of the Christian Religion*, 3.10.6. For Calvin, a particular sense of calling was a way of working out a more general sense of the call to be a Christian.

11 This is a generous way to read Calvin's conception of vocation. See Calvin, *Institutes*, 3.10.6.

12 Adams, *Finite and Infinite Goods*, 303.

13 James Gustafson, *Can Ethics Be Christian?* (Chicago: University of Chicago Press, 1975), 160.

14 In calling them synergistic, I draw on texts such as 1 Corinthians 3:9 – "For we are God's fellow workers (*synergoi*)" – and Philippians 2:25, 1 Thessalonians 3:2, Philemon 1, Colossians 1:7 and 4:7, which envisage those who actively participate in the mission of God as co-workers/colleagues and fellow servants (*synergos* and *syndoulos*).

15 An alternative to synergy to describe how divine and human interact to produce moral agency, one used by both Barth and the Protestant theologian, Paul Tillich, is "theonomy." Strictly speaking, this term means direct rule by God. On Barth and Tillich's conception, God elects to work with and through humans, so that Christian ethics is neither heteronomous (imposed from above) nor autonomous (self-generated and independent of God) but theonomous. But synergy captures better the participative and infused nature of divine-human relations in generating moral agency. It is also less prone to creating confusion.

16 Barth, *Church Dogmatics*, III/4, 15.

17 Karl Barth, *Church Dogmatics: The Doctrine of God*, vol. II/2, trans., G. W. Bromiley et al. (Edinburgh: T&T Clark, 1957), 646.

18 Barth had his own version of a "preferential option for the poor." This is particularly evident in three instances: his encounter with the industrial workers he pastored in his first congregation in Safenwil, his response to the persecution and oppression of the Jews by the Nazis, and the influence on his theology of his encounter with the incarcerated he ministered to in Basel's prisons at the end of his career. Each of these encounters shaped his theology in significant ways.

19 Barth's list echoes many other such rubrics for discerning the call of God. One item missing from his framework though is seeking counsel from a confessor, prayer partner, spiritual director, mentor, or friend.

20 Barth, *Church Dogmatics*, III/4, 9.

21 Barth, *Church Dogmatics*, IV/4, 7.

9 Rules and Regulations

The Hippocratic Oath dates back to the fifth century BCE and forms a key part of thinking about medical ethics even today. In it we see various behavioral rules such as promising not to administer poison, not to take sexual advantage of a patient, and not to violate confidentiality. Set within the context of an oath or covenant, such rules were there to ensure medicine was practiced ethically. In the contemporary context, some people have a knee-jerk reaction against any kind of rules. However, they want *their* doctor to abide by the rule of, say, not poisoning them with a lethal drug. In the midst of any misgivings we might have about rules, the Oath points to the importance of rules and regulations in enabling moral agency: they are guides to good conduct and a means of accountability. This chapter examines how rules and regulations can function this way. It also reflects on how following rules goes wrong, becoming an enemy of good conduct by generating forms of legalism. Moreover, rules can undermine moral agency by imposing overly burdensome demands. The Hippocratic Oath speaks to these dynamic as well. It does not provide a long, complicated list of things doctors should and should not do; rather, it is sage guidance that directs those who practice medicine toward minimizing harm and fulfilling the moral good of medicine, which is to cultivate health.

Today, most institutions, including churches, have professional codes of conduct. These address various situations that arise, for example, in ministry or analogous professional settings and lay down rules for how to behave in those contexts. Within any kind of organized and institutional relationship, particularly where there are differences of power and status, there are certain obligations and behavioral expectations. These range from the informal and tacit, such as around questions of etiquette – do you shake hands, kiss on the cheek, or high five when greeting someone – to the formal and more substantive – such as how police should treat suspects or what is appropriate and inappropriate behavior between students and teachers.

There are various approaches to thinking about the need for rules and what the relationship is between them and moral agency. In this chapter, I focus on the place of rules in shaping a Christian form of life. I examine how a theological account of them differs from modern understandings of the place of rules and authoritative obligations in determining moral judgments as exemplified in the deontological and utilitarian approaches to ethics mentioned in earlier chapters.

WHAT IS A RULE?

Rules stipulate, sanction, or prohibit individual or corporate conduct, providing criteria and direction to determine right action within a specific context. Moral rules serve to enable the pursuit and fulfillment of particular moral ends or goods. The use of rules as aids to moral conduct goes wrong when a rule is treated as an end in itself, and thereby ceases to serve its meaning and purpose. Based on practical reason and embedded within and emerging from social practices, rules are contingent and contextual and so subject to variation and even radical reconfiguration over time. For example, the offside rule in soccer was first introduced in 1863. It enables the game to be played fairly. To ensure it continues to serve that end, the rule has been changed and adapted several times since its introduction.

Building on the previous discussion of commands, it is important to distinguish between following a rule and obeying a command. As noted in Chapter 8, a command is the basis of a form of life that constitutes us as moral agents. Since commands reveal something about the nature of God, a command is unchangeable. To use a technical term, it is an exceptionless moral norm. However, what it means to follow the command is always subject to interpretation and further specification. Rules help specify and interpret commands.

To help explain the difference between a command and a rule a distinction can be made between:

- what is commanded (what you must do),
- what is commended (what you should do to flourish),
- what is licit or morally permissible (what you can do),
- what is prohibited (what you should not do), and
- what is evil (what is an inversion of a command and thereby a negation of what you are as a creature, divine image bearer, and moral agent acting responsibly with and for others).

This list echoes a long-standing distinction moral theology makes between counsels (that which is commended but not required) and commands (that which is required).[1] What is required and the inverse of that, what is evil, are the realm of commands. What is commended, permissible, or prohibited are further specifications and developments of a command and subject to rules. For example, "don't murder" is commanded, the obverse of this command is what is commended, which is seek life – while letting die is permissible, manslaughter is prohibited, and murder is evil. Much moral debate centers on judging how to categorize certain kinds of action. For example, is killing in war morally licit, immoral, or evil? Tragically, we often confuse commands and rules, making a command of what is only counseled or the reverse.

It can seem as if rules sit over and above an arena of practice when, in actuality, understanding and applying rules is context-dependent. For example, the instruction to "carry dogs" makes no sense as a general rule but it makes perfect sense when we see it located in front of an escalator at an airport or in a metro station. The context allows us to make sense of the rule. Conversely, the rule aids us in navigating the context well.

Many rules we draw on to navigate the world around us are unspoken and tacit. For example, we have social rules around queuing and not cutting in line. These work without legal or coercive sanction. They operate in the realm of custom and habit and depend on widespread social trust and reciprocity and forms of nonjuridical regulation such as shame, embarrassment, and parental or peer exhortation to be enforced. They can also be suspended by explicit if often unspoken agreement. For example, when someone is in a great hurry or in a wheelchair at an airport, you might let them cut to the front of the security line.

At points of crisis, rapid social change, or when a form of life is found to be oppressive or corrupted, rules then need to be made explicit, or rethought and changed. Relying on virtues or customary practice are not enough. An appalling example of this are the instances of the sexual abuse of women and children in and through situations of pastoral care. Such horrendous contraventions and inversions of what the practice is supposed to generate – namely, love and care – call for deep reexamination of the churches and ministry settings within which the abuse takes place: Are these problems exceptions and aberrations, or is there something intrinsic to the congregational life, ministry, or denomination that is generating them? Whatever the outcome of such questioning, rules for how to behave appropriately given the form and vision of life have to be made explicit so there is no ambiguity about what should be done to protect the vulnerable. This can lead to the creation of codes of conduct, regulations, and procedures that are then enforced by more formal and coercive sanctions, so that abusers are dismissed from their jobs and possibly imprisoned.

If one problem that arises with rules is that they are no longer fit for a particular purpose, another is that instead of a rule better enabling a form of life to flourish, a moral practice is reduced to merely following a rule. This results in forms of legalism that put a program or procedure before the flourishing of a people. Our rules become a Procrustean bed; that is, our practices are made to fit an external and alien framework that in turn corrupts or undermines good practice. A relatively trivial but often frustrating contemporary example are health and safety regulations that end up prohibiting what seem like commonsense actions needed to fulfill a moral end. For example, some years ago, at an elementary school near where I lived, a child managed to climb up a tree and got stuck. The teachers felt they could not rescue the child as doing so would contravene the school's health and safety code. When a passer-by intervened and rescued the child, the school actually prosecuted the passer-by for trespassing. In such cases, we have a conflict between doing the right thing through contextually alert judgments based on practical reason and simply following a regulation or code without any regard for who, what, and where you are located. The rule has become a procedure, that is, a decontextualized, alien, and unilateral means of controlling what happens that is divorced from the vision of the good it is meant to serve. Instead of being subordinate to and serving the good, the rule has become an end in itself.

When thinking about the place of rules in enabling moral action, it is helpful to distinguish between rules that are *constitutive* and rules that are *regulative*. Rules of a game such as basketball or chess are constitutive. Not to abide by them is either to cheat or attempt to play an entirely different game. For example, if I start kicking a ball in a game of basketball, then I have stopped playing one kind of game and am trying to play another. Constitutive rules make a practice possible, so knowing how to follow and apply those rules is vital to rightly conducting and fulfilling that practice. By contrast, an example of regulative rules are health and safety procedures. If I don't wear safety goggles and gloves when doing a chemistry experiment with acid, I've disobeyed the health and safety code and acted foolishly. But nothing in the experiment or chemistry per se is at stake if I don't, so my not wearing them will not necessarily affect the outcome of the experiment. As this example illustrates, a key difference between regulative and constitutive rules is that constitutive rules are intrinsic to good practice, while regulative rules are extrinsic, operating in a preventative and precautionary capacity.

We tend to imagine rules only in regulative terms. Regulative rules can be vital in inhibiting immoral or evil action, but we are rightly wary of the extent to which regulative rules can help positively generate moral action. In Christian ethics, regulative rules raise the twin specters of works righteousness (following a rule correctly somehow makes us holy) and legalism (the merely formal following of the letter rather than the spirit of the law). Both concerns are highlighted in the story of Jesus's debate with some Pharisees about what it means to observe the Sabbath. His response to evident issues of legalism and works righteousness was: "The Sabbath was made for humankind, and not humankind for the Sabbath" (Mark 2:27). But rejection of works righteousness and legalism should not obscure how both constitutive and regulative rules facilitate moral agency even as working out how and when a rule applies demands paying attention to its context as well as the spirit and animating vision a rule is meant to serve.

RULES AS *TORAH*

Protestants have a long history of worrying about how regulative rules inhibit and undermine moral action. The background to this anxiety is a particular way of interpreting the apostle Paul's distinction between "law" and "Gospel." According to this interpretation, following the law is bad, as the law is understood as an external constraint on Christian freedom. In much Protestant theology (as against the Pauline use in the epistles), the law-Gospel distinction becomes a binary that can only see law in negative terms. It also plays into anti-Jewish polemics about law-bound, unloving Jews who are contrasted with supposedly free, loving, Gospel-proclaiming Christians. A law-Gospel binary ignores how law is understood in the Hebrew Scriptures/Old Testament not as a regulative code of conduct but as constitutive for following in the way of the Lord. Law is better understood as *torah*, or teaching and instruction in a way of life. For example, Psalm 119 is awash with synonyms for "law" (e.g., *torah*, *dabar*/word, *mishpatim*/ordinances, *'edut*/decrees, and *piqqudim*/precepts), with most of the 176 stanzas containing one of these synonyms. These terms are consistently linked to either following a pathway or to a dynamic movement such as walking or traveling. For example, verse 5 pleads, "O that my ways may be steadfast in keeping your statutes!" Law understood as *torah* is not a static code or reducible to a set of rational principles extracted from "behind" the text. Rather, law is a guide to an ongoing and dynamic way of life. Instead of demanding conformity to a set of mechanical procedures, it is meant to help us "make straight the way of the Lord" (Luke 3:4–6/Isa 40:3–5).

We do law a disservice when we imagine it primarily in terms of a court room. Law as *torah* is better understood within the context of a *workshop* where rules help constitute a craft into which we are apprenticed. Law/rules/sage guidance enable growth in the skill, capacity, and practical wisdom needed to undertake the craft of living a faithful, hopeful, and loving life. Another common frame of reference is that of a *pilgrimage*. To the pilgrim, rules are instructions about directions of travel, what to pack, where to rest, and what food to eat – all of which combine to enable someone to undertake the journey and reach their destination. The images of a workshop and a pilgrimage connect rules to the account of virtues in Chapter 10. Constitutive rules have a formative and educative role in the cultivation of virtue by providing guidance and being a point of reference and a summary of previous wise judgments. Beyond providing protection and accountability (e.g., health and safety rules and traffic laws), regulative rules can, at times, also be pedagogical.[2]

Theologically, the law court is exactly the wrong frame of reference through which to understand the relationship between rules and moral agency and how they aid moral judgment. The New Testament distinction between *pistis*/faith and *nomos*/law is more helpful than the binary between law and Gospel. *Pistis*/faith denotes enduring commitment to and trustworthiness within the ongoing, future-oriented, and dynamic covenantal relationship with God and the communion of saints. By contrast, *nomos*/law requires obedience and conformity to a static set of external and coercively backed regulations here and now. After Christ, we cannot live by a juridical and thereby coercive form of law (Rom 3:27–31; Gal

2:19–21). Rather, we must live by the law of the Spirit written on our hearts that is constitutive for generating faithful, hopeful, and loving forms of life. But that should not lead us to reject law understood as *torah*. Rather, it should lead us to embrace *torah*; that is, instruction on how to live virtuously. There is a proper wariness about forms of *nomos* (regulative rules) as they have limited value in enabling moral agency. However, we need to delight in and meditate on constitutive rules as a form of *torah* that provide guidance intrinsic to metabolizing a fruitful way of life that blesses rather than curses those around us.

In downplaying a juridical frame of reference for understanding the proper relationship between rules and morality, we should not replace it with a philosophical one. Rules are not timeless principles or axioms to be applied but living wisdom about a way of being alive. Keeping them involves not calculation and application but meditation and contemplation though practices of listening, reading, and other spiritual exercises. This is how the so-called Golden Rule that "in everything do to others as you would have them do to you; for this is the law and the prophets" (Matt 7:12) should be understood. The rule demarcates a shared realm of meaning and action through which we can hear God's call and respond with faithful, hopeful, and loving forms of witness.

A Christian way of life is not a code to be cracked or a problem to be solved. It is a mystery we can inhabit with ever increasing intensity and fruitfulness. As such, we should not expect complete conceptual coherence, certainty, or clarity. Rules, like the Golden Rule, don't provide a schematic framework or blueprint that can be implemented to produce a set outcome or undertake a prescribed duty. Constitutive rules for being fruitful are not like a GPS system or Google Maps where you punch in your moral dilemma and it gives you specific directions to a fixed, predetermined position, all calculated through some clever philosophical or theological algorithm. Rather, they are sage guidance in an ever-changing way of life that can only be lived one step at a time.

THE PROBLEM OF PROCEDURALISM

An account of moral agency must involve understanding how constitutive rules enable moral agency while regulative rules can aid but at times inhibit right action. When rules cease to be guides to how to respond faithfully, hopefully, and lovingly to the world around us and instead become a technique to follow, or a moral algorithm through which to calculate what to do irrespective of the context, then something is wrong. Yet, much of modern ethics seeks to develop universal rules linked to ways of calculating what to do in order to act morally. Rules become an external measure that our moral practices are forced to conform to, and, like a straitjacket, are constrained by. This is a form of *proceduralism*, in which we doggedly keep doing what we have always done or insist on blindly following a rule, irrespective of whether the situation has changed or ignoring the evil it is causing. As the political theorist Hannah Arendt contended, at its extreme, legalistic and bureaucratic proceduralism generate a thoughtlessness that leads millions to be sent to deathcamps or to endure forced starvation.[3] Arendt named this death-dealing thoughtlessness the banality of evil. Its root is a failure to consider what wider moral purpose a rule or procedure serves.

The two dominant forms of modern moral philosophy – deontology and utilitarianism – are, in different ways, forms of proceduralism. We met these terms in previous chapters, but I discuss them here in more detail. Deontological and utilitarian moral philosophies identify what it means to be moral with a unified code generated from a single source. In the case of utilitarianism, it is the "calculation of utility"; in the case of deontology, it is the "categorical imperative."

Utilitarianism claims that the morally right act or policy is whatever produces the greatest happiness for the greatest number in any given society and, conversely, causes the least pain or harm. Utilitarianism is inherently about consequences, for it demands that any moral injunction – for example, "don't commit adultery" – be based on who or what is made worse off by that which is morally prohibited. The reverse is also true: something is good only if someone or a collective is made better off. Hence another name for utilitarianism is "consequentialism."

Utilitarianism has no absolute moral prohibitions and no duties or obligations. Resolving moral questions is a matter of measuring changes in human welfare and not relying on a sacred text, tradition, or metaphysics. For one of its founding figures, Jeremy Bentham (1748–1832), utilitarianism refounded ethics on an empirical basis and involved a measurable calculation of utility: in effect, ethics became a moral cost/benefit analysis.

Utilitarianism involves an account of human welfare, "utility," well-being or happiness. Generally, humans constitute the measure of what well-being consists of, although this can be extended in a more biocentric direction. It also entails an instruction on how to maximize that welfare/utility in a way that gives equal weight to each person's welfare/utility. Utilitarianism generates an algorithmic code that can be applied to everyone, everywhere, at any time: morality is doing whatever will generate the greatest aggregation of happiness (however defined) for the greatest number of people and/or cause the least pain. All the variations of this approach – notably, act, rule, and preference utilitarianism – involve, at some point, a speculative calculation as to what the consequences of a particular action, rule, or preference will be. This calculation constitutes the basis of moral action.[4]

Another form of proceduralism is deontology and, in particular, the hugely influential version of it developed by Immanuel Kant. Deontology, in contrast to utilitarianism, holds that something is right not by dint of its consequences but because we have a duty or obligation to fulfill. Kant's approach entails universalizing and absolutizing a moral rule like "don't lie." As set out in his *Groundwork of the Metaphysics of Morals* (1785), his approach was based on what is called the "categorical imperative." This has several formulations, including that to be moral one should act only on that maxim through which you can at the same time will that it should become a universal law. In other words, whatever I choose to do, I must rationally consider whether everyone else should behave the same way and what would happen if they did. For example, if I live by the principle "don't lie, except when you can get away with it," then if everyone else followed this same maxim truth itself is undermined and no one will be able to trust anyone else and so basic interactions become unworkable. Therefore, my lying, in *any* circumstances, must be unethical. To be moral, I must will what is universalizable so that if my action is to be morally right, it must be morally right for everyone. Conversely, if it is wrong, it will be wrong for everyone, regardless of either the circumstances or the consequences.

This formulation undergirds another of Kant's formulations of the categorical imperative, which is act in such a way that you always treat humanity, whether in your own person or in the person of any other, never simply as a means but always at the same time as an end in itself. Thus, for example, torture is intrinsically and always wrong because it renders someone a means to an end, respect for their body and person ceasing to be an end in itself. Central to Kant is the idea that all humans have an intrinsic and inviolable dignity simply because they are a human. In the example of whether it is ever right to torture someone in order to discover how to stop a nuclear bomb explosion that will kill millions, Kant's deontological approach holds torture is never right, whatever the consequences. The contrast with utilitarianism is obvious: for the utilitarian, torture is justified as the consequences of not doing so will generate more suffering for a greater number of people than the suffering produced by torturing one person. Modern human rights are largely derived from a deontological approach. It postulates that we can arrive at a basic set of universal rights or duties we owe every human because these can be universalized under the rubric of each individual being treated as an end in and of themselves. And conversely, there are certain actions one is obligated never to do, no matter what the circumstances or consequences.

Kant's approach ultimately rests on a particular understanding of human autonomy, free will, and human reason. For Kant, an act of individual will is the only basis of good action, the truly moral thing to do being what a rational, free, autonomous agent would choose. This comes to the fore in another of his formulations: All maxims as proceeding from our own making ought to harmonize with a possible kingdom of ends as a kingdom of nature. Roughly translated, this means that if I choose rationally, then *any* world that I choose must be a "kingdom of ends," meaning a world in which all humans are treated as ends and not means. If it is not, I will be choosing in a way that undermines or even destroys my own capacity to choose. Such a choice would be irrational because it would be self-defeating and inconsistent. A moral principle is only rational and thereby moral if it can be universalized, that is, deployed anywhere and everywhere irrespective of time and place. Conformity to these rationally derived principles determines whether an action is truly moral or not.

Echoing Chapter 6 and the account of ethical frameworks that emphasize the need for ethics to be universal and impartial, Kant's approach is a way of doing ethics without needing to attend to context, revelation, or tradition. This is to ensure that ethics itself is moral, that is, untainted by the partiality that comes with particular and place-based commitments. That said, in his later writing, Kant became concerned with virtue and we can discern in his work a tension between the universalistic and particularistic aspects of ethical judgments.

In many ways, what I have just sketched as the basic features of utilitarianism and deontology are horrible reductions. There are very sophisticated versions of each position, and each is a serious attempt to develop a way to provide a foundation for moral action that is itself moral. But it is important to recognize how the basic logic at work within them generates a form of philosophical proceduralism that treats morality as a kind of algorithmic problem to be solved rather than a mystery to be lived.

In this chapter, I've explored how rules can be vital aids to developing and enhancing moral agency. Whether in the form of either constitutive or regulative rules, rules can provide guidance and boundaries that enable the pursuit of a good life. However, rules alone are not enough. Rules also need contextually attuned forms of practical reasoning if the spirit rather than the letter of the law is to be followed. Indeed, the kind of practical moral reasoning I examine in Chapter 11 contrasts sharply with the kind of procedural moral reasoning that utilitarianism and Kantian deontology represent. But also needed are virtues to ensure rules do not collapse into forms of either legalism or proceduralism. It is thus the virtues that are the focus of Chapter 10.

ACCOMPANYING READINGS

Augustine, "The Spirit and the Letter," *Augustine: Later Works*, ed., John Burnaby (Philadelphia: Westminster Press, 1955), 195–250. Part of Augustine's anti-Pelagian writings, in this text Augustine argues that the human will alone is insufficient to live a good life in accordance with God's commands. Instead, such a life requires the active aid of the Holy Spirit.

Immanuel Kant, "Second Section: Transition from Popular Moral Philosophy to the Metaphysics of Morals," *Groundwork of the Metaphysics of Morals* (1785). Various editions.

John Stuart Mill, "What Utilitarianism Is," *Utilitarianism* (1863), ch 2. Various editions.

Hannah Arendt, *The Life of the Mind*, One Volume Edition (New York: Harcourt, 1978), 3–5.

Richard Miller, "Rules," *The Oxford Handbook of Theological Ethics*, eds., Gilbert Meilaender and William Werpehowski (New York: Oxford University Press, 2005), 220–236. Miller develops a theology of rules and what it means to follow a rule while also discussing the role of rules in shaping and sustaining a moral life with others.

NOTES

1 See, for example, Thomas Aquinas, *Summa Theologiae*, I–II.108.4. This distinction is part of a broader set of distinctions that includes precepts, prohibitions, counsels, and directly effective commands ("Let there be light"). All are forms of divine address. On these see John E. Hare, *God's Command* (Oxford: Oxford University Press, 2015), 32–50.

2 The word "pedagogical" is used deliberately. In the Greco-Roman world, the pedagogue was one charged with both the instruction and discipline of a

child. Without rehearsing the long-standing debate about the moral uses of the law, regulative rules are primarily disciplinary but can be instructive as well.

3 Hannah Arendt's study of the Nazi bureaucrat Adolf Eichmann and her subsequent reflections on thinking and judgment draw out this danger of modern management and administration, whether in private corporations or state-run institutions. See Hannah Arendt, *The Life of the Mind*, One Volume Edition (New York: Harcourt, 1978), 3–5.

4 Crudely put, *act utilitarianism* judges whether an action is good by its consequences, *rule utilitarianism* judges whether the rule is good by its consequences (and then judges actions in accordance with rules determined good by this measure), and *preference utilitarianism* judges the preferences by their consequences.

10 Virtues and Vision

I remember vividly seeing footage on the news of the space shuttle *Challenger* launching on January 28, 1986. Seventy-four seconds after takeoff it exploded, killing all seven crew members. The immediate cause of the explosion was a technical fault. But it was not just a mechanical failure that led to the deaths of everyone on board. The cause was also a failure of character. The *Challenger* space shuttle disaster was investigated by a presidential commission and subsequently the subject of extensive research and analysis.[1] What these assessments reveal is not just problems with the design and engineering of the craft or the management of its construction and launch. On the eve of the launch, four engineers led by Roger Boisjoly remonstrated with those in charge to delay the launch out of concern for identifiable technical problems that could lead to catastrophe. They had tried to do further research on and raise concerns about the issue for months beforehand only to be thwarted due to budget constraints. Despite being told of the dangers, the managers of both Morton-Thiokol, the private company responsible for the solid rocket boosters that had the problem, and NASA, a government agency, chose to ignore the warnings. Instead, managers bowed to social, commercial, and political pressures to launch sooner rather than later. In doing so, their actions demonstrated a lack of courage, patience, humility, prudence, and justice. Despite their espoused ideals, extensive expertise, and numerous protocols, they lacked the virtues necessary to make the right judgment.

The *Challenger* space shuttle disaster is often used as a case study in the ethics of engineering. However, it is mostly taught in a way that makes it seem ethical issues are exceptions best addressed by complying with a code of conduct.[2] In response, a number of engineering schools and departments are beginning to include character education into their curriculum.[3] This acknowledges that truly good engineering takes more than technical proficiency, empirical knowledge, detailed risk assessment, and following rules. It also takes moral purpose, good character, and keeping ethical considerations and social impacts to the fore at every stage of an engineering project, from inception to completion.

Talk of virtue is a way of recognizing that, like the courageous engineers who tried to stop the launch of *Challenger* in 1986, we also need the right character to do the right thing at the right time, especially in difficult circumstances. Accounts of virtue build on the insight that for an action to be moral it is not enough for it to merely conform to a rule or even generate good consequences. Neither make the action itself moral. While particular kinds of action are required for us to be good – for example, caring for the sick – for such actions to be moral, our inner disposition and intention must also be rightly aligned. Hence, the prophets denounce Israel for its sham sacrifices and paying lip service to the commandments (e.g., Isa 29:13; Amos 5:21–24), and Jesus cries woe to those who on the outside look righteous but inside are full of death and filth (Matt 23:27). They were doing the right thing, but their hearts and minds were in the wrong place. For an action to be good, it requires the integration of right action, intention, desire, and affective state (or passion). A name for this point of integration is "virtue." But Christianity adds to this picture the need for right relationship with God: moral agency is somehow infused with God's action and being through Christ and the Holy Spirit.

This chapter advocates for virtue as a key framework for understanding the nature, but also the limits, of human moral agency. Intrinsic to a conception of virtue is the sense that the cultivation of specific habits, actions, and desires both enables and embodies the journey of transformation from where we are to where we need to be if we are going to live well.[4]

SHOULD WE PRIORITIZE WHO WE ARE OR WHAT WE DO?

A conception of virtue helps untie the Gordian knot of whether what it means to be a moral person should prioritize *who we are* or *what we do*? Many ethical frameworks are uninterested in your identity, soul, or ontological status – in other words, who you are. What matters is what you do. Morality in these frameworks is concerned with action – either what consequences will flow from an action (utilitarianism) or what is the dutiful action to undertake in order to do the right thing (deontology).

By contrast, certain streams of Christianity say what matters most is whether your soul is saved. You can lead an immoral life, but if you say the "sinner's prayer" then you are good because goodness or righteousness come from God, not from us. Or you are part of the elect, so you are saved despite your actions. In such accounts, being is prioritized over action and what you do has very little if any effect on whether you are righteous or not.

It is not just certain strands of Christianity that prioritize being over action. Marxists envisage the proletariat as embodying the emancipatory consciousness on which the liberation of all humankind rests, so who the proletariat are is more important than what they do. Evaluating the moral actions of any particular member of the working class is irrelevant since what really matters is someone's status as either a member of the proletariat or the bourgeoisie. Likewise, no matter how well a member of the bourgeoisie acts, nothing they do is right because by their very nature they are on the wrong side of history. There is a parallel in frameworks that emphasize who you are (your identity) as mattering far more than what you do. One's status as someone who is minoritized, stigmatized, or socially excluded trumps consideration of whether this or that action is moral or not. Someone is good or bad according to whether they are a member of an oppressed class.

Conceptions of virtue are a way to steer a path between those who prioritize identity and those who prioritize action. In talk of

virtue, who you are is constituted through what you do and the quality of relations you participate in, so there is a feedback loop between being and doing. Both matter. We come to be through what we do, and who we are enables us to act well.

WHAT IS A VIRTUE? AND HOW DO WE BECOME VIRTUOUS?

What then is a virtue? The Greek word used by Aristotle and most commonly translated as virtue is *aretē*, which is perhaps better translated as "goodness" or "excellence." An excellence is a quality that enables something to fulfill its purpose. For example, it is an excellence of a saw if it enables efficient and effective cutting. An excellence, therefore, is a property or trait whereby its possessor fulfills its purpose. Aristotle, for instance, sometimes speaks of a good moral character as "human excellence" or an "excellence of soul."[5] The idea here is the same as with the saw – having a good moral character (being virtuous) helps its possessor act well and fulfill their nature.

A formal definition is that virtues are those persistent, reliable, and active dispositions or character traits that enable us to nourish and sustain a good life in response to the demands and realities of the world. A virtue involves the integration of actions, intentions, desires, and affective states that direct the whole person toward a good. Moreover, the virtuous person seeks to fulfill the good for its intrinsic value rather than for either instrumental reasons (e.g., for money, status, or power) or because of legalistic adherence to a moral code.

Virtues are good in themselves and enable us to flourish as human animals. This means that a trait like wittiness is not a virtue. It may be something we value but it can be used to bless or curse, to build up or put down. This contrasts with love or courage, which are intrinsically good and enable us to achieve other kinds of good amid the reality of the world we live in. In Christian terms, we should desire moral dispositions such as love and courage for their own sake *and* because they enable us to fulfill who we are as redeemed creatures.

We acquire virtues by engaging in certain kinds of practices that enable the genuine flourishing of ourselves and the rest of creation. Formation in the virtues comes through the following:

- *Apprenticeship* in moral practices. Virtue is a skill we learn through persistent, intentional, ends-directed habituation into moral practices. We can invoke the image of a workshop in which we need apprenticeship in cultivating the requisite skills and practices for crafting a flourishing life. In Christian terms, Jesus is the master we are apprenticed to as disciples. We follow in his way, doing the things he did, and thereby learning how to live well in a fallen yet redeemed world.
- *Socialization* into and experience of specific kinds of relationship, such as friendship. The virtues are inherently social and we acquire them by participating in relations of the quality and character that cultivate virtue in us.[6] If apprenticeship is more like intentional training, socialization points to the communal and more diffuse processes through which we are formed in the virtues. In Christian terms, we are socialized through participating in the people of God into being friends of God and neighbors to creation.
- *Imitation* of excellent practitioners in the craft of a flourishing life. Like socialization and apprenticeship, imitation involves relationship with virtuous others but operates by a specific process of copying moral exemplars. For Christians, the primary exemplar is Jesus Christ. As those made in the image of God, we have lost our likeness through sin and so must regain our distinctive way of imaging God through a process of "mimesis": that is, we desire to be like what humanity will be as revealed in the person and work of Jesus Christ. This participation through imitating converts us so that over time Jesus's way of being alive becomes more deeply sedimented in our characters, and, in turn, we are transformed to become more Christ-like in how we live.[7]
- *Education* through serious talk and thought about matters of substantive concern. An influential vision of such an education envisages it as involving dialogue and argument over time with others about existential questions, studying works of philosophy and literature, watching plays, participating in teamwork (e.g., in sports), and undergoing self-examination. Participating in these things enables growth in character, broadens our understanding of what really matters and why, and fosters further desire to grow in virtue. This was an ideal central to ancient philosophy as articulated in Greek notions of *paidea* and Roman notions of *humanitas*, one that was picked up

> and developed in medieval notions of the liberal arts and modern German conceptions of *bildung*. In the United States, its vestiges can be found in the form of Great Books programs. A parallel vision animates informal traditions of popular education as a vital component of radical social movements for change such as the labor and civil rights movements. Transformation through rigorous reflection, debate, and shared action is captured in the term "conscientization."[8] Both informal and formal versions of this framework envisage education as a form of conversion: it should make you a better person. Those educated in this way do not merely repeat what they are taught. Rather, as the philosopher Julia Annas (b. 1946) suggests, education that cultivates virtue should inculcate what she calls a "drive to aspire," which "enables the learner to ... assess and criticize what he has been taught, and to be able to correct the teacher and the context and culture in which he has been taught."[9] In Judaism and Christianity, the contemplation and study of Scripture is the primary form this transformative education takes. Or it should be.

Apprenticeship, socialization, imitation, and education form us in the virtues. They point to how being virtuous is not simply a matter of becoming what we do. Rather, like driving a car or playing the piano, being virtuous involves a combination of will, desire, moments of reflective deliberation, learning, imagination, creative interpretation, and enfleshed skill. This contrasts with simply being a creature of habit or doing what you have always done, which is sloth. Developing the virtues enables us to metabolize the distractions, temptations, and failures that inevitably afflict us in our relations with the world around us, thereby enabling us as to act morally with and for others.

Apprenticeship, socialization, imitation, and education can, however, all operate without God. A Christian conception of virtue must account for how the virtues are cultivated through divine-human relations and contribute to participating in communion with God and creation. A Christian ethic must situate virtues within the context of divine-human relations or it risks reintroducing a form of works righteousness where we achieve goodness apart from God.

There are those who hear talk of virtues as inherently advocating a form of works righteousness. However, they tend to operate with a competitive vision of divine-human relations whereby divine action nullifies or supplants human action. By contrast, within a participatory, noncompetitive, or symphonic conception of divine-human relations (as outlined in Chapters 2 and 8), virtues are *both* a gift of God given through the power of the Spirit (especially faith, hope, and love) *and* an infused work of the self, cultivated through worship, works of mercy, studying Scripture, and spiritual disciplines such as fasting. Together, these practices are forms of apprenticeship, socialization, imitation, and education.

As an aside, it is worth noting that the centrality of virtue within Christianity as a framework for understanding moral agency has waxed and waned through the centuries. In Roman Catholicism, talk of virtue fell into disuse from the eighteenth century onwards with the emergence of the "manualist" approach to moral theology. The roots of this approach were the penitential manuals for the laity dating back to the twelfth century. These were handbooks for confessors that assigned fixed penances for sinful acts. These handbooks evolved into the moral manuals of the eighteenth century, which were textbooks that applied set principles to specific cases and emphasized moral obligations, rules, and duties. They helped foster forms of rigid legalism.

Beginning at the Reformation, Protestant have tended to emphasize the centrality of God's grace rather than the relationship between character and moral action. For Luther, talk of virtue smacked of self-elevation that denied our total dependence on God's grace to be good. (At one point he scoffed at the idea that by doing good we can become good, calling the notion "bilge water of hell.") For Luther, once humans were saved, their good actions were made possible by the grace of God and had an almost spontaneous character. Luther himself did not counsel passivity in the face of sin, but the way others developed his approach generated what Bonhoeffer called "cheap grace": grace has no transformative impact upon human life as it became disconnected from discipleship.[10] All that really mattered was being saved, with the paradoxical result that sanctification was reduced to a toxic combination of interior personal beliefs and individualized, legalistic external behaviors.

Variations and combinations of legalism and cheap grace run through modern expressions of Christianity, from the holiness movements of the eighteenth and nineteenth centuries to the Prosperity Gospel of today. In recognition of the problems of legalism and cheap grace, and influenced by a turn to the place of virtue in ethics by modern philosophers, most notably Elizabeth Anscombe (1919–2001), Philippa Foot (1920–2010), Mary Midgely (1919–2018), and Iris Murdoch (1919–1999), both Catholic and Protestant ethicists renewed their focus on virtues in discussions of moral agency from the mid-twentieth century onwards. Foremost among those closely identified with the contemporary recovery of virtue ethics are Alasdair MacIntyre (b. 1929) and Stanley Hauerwas (b. 1940). However, they are not alone in turning to virtue to steer a passage between legalism and license. Moreover, what is obscure in their work – namely, the relationship between cultivating virtue and struggles for liberation – is vividly rendered in the work of others discussed below.

THE VIRTUES, CARDINAL AND THEOLOGICAL

An influential set of virtues originates in ancient Greek philosophy. These are known as the cardinal virtues, from the Latin *cardo* meaning "hinge," as these virtues were understood as pivotal to developing a good life. They consist of the following:

- *prudence or practical wisdom*: the ability to reflect on reality so as to determine what is the action most needed to act morally among these people, in this place, at this time;
- *justice*: the ability to give each person and thing their due, including how to order the part in relation to the whole;[11]
- *temperance*: the ability to order one's desires appropriately (particularly toward whatever gives pleasure), exercise self-control, and know what proper enjoyment or appreciation of something entails; and
- *courage/fortitude*: the disposition to constantly pursue a good in the face of what is fearful, dangerous, or difficult while at the same time being aware of one's own vulnerability and limits.

Aristotle argued that virtue lies in the mean between the poles of *excessiveness* and *deficiency*. For example, to be brave is to act in a way that constitutes the mean between cowardice and recklessness. Determining the mean takes prudence as it changes according to circumstances and shifting demands. What courage requires in the emergency room of a hospital is not the same as what it entails at the dinner table when raising an awkward but important family matter. Another instance is temperance as the mean between indulgence and insensibility. In relation to the affective state of anger, the temperate person is neither consumed by blind rage nor apathetic in the face of realities that should properly inspire anger, such as injustice and idolatry. A temperate individual can exercise the passion of anger when it is right to do so in a way that is appropriate and proportionate to the reality of the situation.[12]

To the basic list of "cardinal" virtues, Christianity, drawing on Scripture, added the "theological virtues" of faith, hope, and love. These were understood as perfecting and fulfilling the cardinal virtues and vital for having a life directed toward communion with God. In contrast to the cardinal virtues, faith, hope, and love are not constituted by the mean. There can never be an excess of love.

The theological virtues can be characterized in the following terms. *Faith* as a theological virtue entails loyalty to and a sure trust in God. Faith directs us to follow God's call in the here and now no matter what the circumstances or how we feel, steadily trusting that God is a living and active presence who keeps promises. Beliefs about who God is and who we are in relation to God shape this trust, but faith is not reducible to creedal confession. In prioritizing faithfulness to God above all else, faith as a theological virtue can lead to the overturning of other loyalties and commitments. The Gospels explore this dynamic in the interplay between the ways Jesus fulfills the law and the prophets: Jesus is doing the will of the Father, but the religious authorities of his day view him as a traitor. This contrasts with the Pharisees and others who understand themselves to be paragons of faith yet whose way of life contradicts their espoused commitments.

Hope is an orientation to, expectation of, and identification with reality as ultimately and finally determined by God. This means we understand suffering and injustice as neither the fullest truth about the world we live in nor as the final determination of the meaning and purpose of life. Real hope does not evade the tragic, overlook suffering, or repress injustice by fixating on a future object or time. It faces head on the world as it is but refuses to be governed by it. To put this another way, hope refuses the tyranny of the present. In hope, we act now in the light of who God is revealed to be, who we are in relation to God, and how Christ will fulfill and reconcile all things. It is through hope that we can carry on in the face of affliction knowing that while everything does *not* have a reason, all things can be redeemed in Christ. Hope enables action today that is directed toward and identifies with this promised "eschatological" end – the kingdom of God or new creation. This end cannot be extrapolated from the present. Rather, following the form and pattern of Christ's resurrection, it confounds current experience in its newness and the ways it utterly transforms existing ways of life.

Love is the disposition to an energizing and existential desire for and enjoyment of communion with the triune God that in turn orients and orders our desire for communion with and enjoyment of everything else. Contrary to much modern understanding, true love is not unconditional, all-affirming, and non-preferential (a widespread misinterpretation of *agape*).[13] Divine love may take on these characteristics at times, but at others, divine love is manifested in very different ways. More importantly, we are not God. We can only love others in creaturely ways, ways that are always conditioned by finitude and God first loving us. And our love will prefer specific qualities of relation, such as caring for a neighbor in need, honoring the dignity of enemies, and rightly pursuing particular relations (for example, with our children or spouse).[14] This entails judgments about who should not be preferred at this time, in this place. Moreover, neither is true love necessarily self-sacrificial. Drawing on the rich descriptions of love in the Hebrew Scriptures/Old Testament and its wide array of terms for love, the New Testament portrays how human love for God and neighbor can be embodied in three forms of action: a gift in response to a specific need that seeks no return as exemplified in the parable of the Good Samaritan; asymmetric, reciprocal exchange as when Jesus receives hospitality but gives new life in return such as in the encounter with Zacchaeus, the Samaritan woman at the well, or the travelers on the Emmaus road; and finally, mutual sharing between friends as at the Last Supper. These embodiments of love come into play at different times and contexts so as to rightly determine each person in relationship with and for God and neighbor. The affective states that accompany and energize these actions are multifarious, ranging from fear, sorrow, and longing to reverence, gratefulness, joy, and adoration.

Faith, hope, and love are interrelated. Faith arises from the experience of being loved by God. Learning to trust in and keep faith with God strengthens our capacity to love God and neighbor, enabling us to reach out, in hope, that there is a concrete form that love might take in this situation with these people here and now. Hope is grounded in faith and love as we learn to see that the world is not defined by the sinful status quo but rather is ultimately determined by Christ, the alpha and omega. But faith, hope, and love in God do not arise "naturally" and cannot be achieved through an act of will. They grow up in and through relationship with God.

Talk of virtue is another, more formal and anthropocentric way to frame the metabolic conception of agency I outlined in Chapter 2 and overlaps with the ethics of care I sketched in Chapter 4. Christian virtue ethics as a framework points to how we become moral through a meshwork of caring relations with others. It also shows how moral development must integrate the need for stability and equilibrium with growth and adaptation over time. Implicit in talk of virtue is a conception of the dynamic interplay of our psychological, physiological, affective, moral, and spiritual states. This is perhaps most easily illustrated by a negative example. Gluttony is not just the moral and spiritual problem of grasping at the world through food and drink; it also generates physiological problems with often dire health consequences and treats the world around us as something to be consumed wholly for our individual benefit and pleasure. Conversely, temperance as a virtue enables us to enjoy the world in ways that foster the spiritual, moral, physiological, and psychological growth and development of ourselves and others, including the growth and development of nonhuman life. A temperate people would generate a more ecologically sustainable form of life.

INTEGRATING THE CULTIVATION OF VIRTUE WITH THE PURSUIT OF LIBERATION

There is not one catalog of virtues fixed for all time. Different social and historical contexts emphasize different virtues, and different visions of the good life will generate different conceptions of what counts as a virtue. We can contrast, for example, the virtues and vices that ancient Roman moralists like Livy or Cicero hold dear with those Augustine esteems, noting that what is virtue in the former is vice in the latter.[15] Augustine distinguishes Christian *humilitas* from the Roman pursuit of glory (which he sees as an instance of *superbia* or arrogant pride), viewing this as a fundamental difference between Christian and pagan virtue. Inevitably, as people try to live out a particular vision of the good life in a specific context, disputes will emerge about what it means in practice as well as what virtues best help or hinder its realization. So even within the same moral tradition, different virtues can be emphasized. For example, Augustine sees pride – in the form of self-possession, independence, and desire for an honorable reputation – as the primary sin to be overcome, with humility, sacrifice, and obedience to God its antidote. By contrast, Valerie Saiving (1921–1992), in a seminal text in the development of feminist theological social ethics, regards self-effacement and self-negation as the primary problems to be overcome for both men and women in a modern bureaucratic, consumerist, and industrialized world.[16] Saiving catalyzed ongoing and productive debate about how to understand love, humility, and sacrifice and their role in a

Christian vision of moral and political life. This debate challenges whether humility understood as self-denial and self-emptying is a Christian virtue. It also raises questions about whether humility can be an antidote to pride as the root of domination since humility for some (namely, women and minorities) reinscribes their domination while producing pride in others (namely, white bourgeois men). This debate has reconceptualized love, humility, and sacrifice.[17] Rather than self-abnegation, humility is reimagined as both the renunciation of oppressive forms of power and truthful self-evaluation.[18]

Within Christianity, the theological virtues of faith, hope, and love are recognized as vital for directing humans toward the ultimate good: life with and for God. But there are a host of other virtues that enable us to pursue penultimate, non-eternal goods. To posit a definitive and final list of cardinal virtues hollows out the rich diversity of ways responses to God's creative work in history can be embodied. Moreover, differences of structural location and context bring the need for different virtues into view. For example, the unjustly advantaged must address internalized attitudes of domination that distort and damage them and mask how what they take to be flourishing may really be a form of domination. They also develop callous and cruel attitudes that disable them from being able to relate in just and generous ways to others. Or in the words of the Magnificat (Luke 1:46–55), the privileged and powerful must be brought low and so need humility as their primary virtue. Conversely, the lowly need raising up. Echoing Saiving's concern, the feminist virtue ethicist Lisa Tessman argues that internalized oppression and its distortions of character must be addressed. The oppressed can develop an inferior sense of self that may lead to self-destructive behaviors that inhibit their flourishing in relation to others.[19] And so virtues such as solidarity rather than humility need more emphasis.

As already outlined in Chapter 2, moral action always begins in the middle of a world we did not make. We are constantly navigating forces beyond our control, whether these take the form of the unbidden – for example, when a pandemic strikes – or what philosophers refer to as "moral luck" – for example, the geography of where we are born and how this affects us socioeconomically. And we are always already situated within a meshwork of dependent relations and burdens of care. It is only when we imagine ourselves as autonomous, self-directing subjects that we think certainty and control are necessary to act well and posit being unburdened as an ideal. Yet to live an unburdened life is a sure sign of a life made possible by either the exploitation or abandonment of others. Being virtuous is inherently burdensome and precarious in a fallen, systemically unjust world. To be courageous, for instance, is not to think oneself invulnerable; rather, it is to pursue a good in full knowledge that as a result of one's actions either oneself or others may be wounded (physically, economically, socially, psychologically, etc.). Becoming virtuous entails taking up our burdens rather than avoiding or displacing them on to others.[20]

For those affected by systemic injustice or conditions of chronic deprivation, what counts as a virtue can look like a vice to those operating from a more secure structural location. Pursuit of the virtues is necessary for the pursuit of the good or flourishing life, yet sometimes this necessitates prioritizing survival; and in some contexts, what passes for morality and virtue is a way of enforcing a system of domination. The Black liberation theologian James Cone (1938–2018) poses this challenge with characteristic force when he states that oppressors cannot determine what does or does not constitute Christian behavior.[21] Cone contends that enslaved persons "rejected the white masters'" view of morality, but they did not thereby reject law and morality. Rather, they "formulated a new law and a new morality that was consistent with black strivings for [survival and] freedom."[22] This meant, for example, that "stealing" from their enslavers was not stealing per se but taking what was being unjustly and immorally kept from them under the system of slavery. To run away was not an act of theft (as fugitive slave laws asserted) but a moral act for survival and freedom, one done in obedience to a "higher" or "moral" law.[23] As Womanist social ethicist Katie Cannon puts it: "Racism, gender discrimination and economic exploitation, as inherited, age-long complexes, require the Black community to create and cultivate values and virtues in their own terms so that they can prevail against the odds with moral integrity."[24]

Virtue for the oppressed can look like immorality to those who oppress, since the latter expect civility within and loyalty to an unjust status quo. But, as it was for Jesus, to survive and overcome oppression requires active disloyalty to and distrust of systems and cultures of domination. What becomes a virtue in this case is impatient endurance, which entails righteous anger that points to God's wrath against injustice and idolatry. Such anger is born out of grief for the gap between the world as it is and the world as it should be. It is not vindictive and revengeful fury but the urgent and agitational pursuit of justice, respect, and reparation enfolded within hopeful perseverance in the struggle against systemic injustice. Righteous anger points to a desire for a world beyond the existing order of things, a world undetermined by domination and idolatry.

An example of how experiences of oppression generate the need for a particular set of virtues is developed by Katie Cannon (1950–2018) as part of her reflection on the nature of moral agency under constraint. She posits "invisible dignity," "quiet grace," and "unshouted courage" as virtues necessary for the survival and thriving of Black women in contexts of oppression.[25] Cannon looks to the life and work of the African American novelist and anthropologist Zora Neale Hurston as exemplifying these virtues and sees them as part of a tradition handed down from mother to daughter.[26] Invisible dignity celebrates survival and stays feisty and "unctuous" in the face of oppression.[27] Quiet grace is a type of "functional prudence" that opposes values that alienate self and community and adjusts moral codes until they are "more appropriate to [a Black woman's] needs."[28] Unshouted courage is fortitude in pursuit of self-fulfillment despite situations of "forced responsibility" and oppression.[29]

Cannon's work points to how the cultivation of virtue and the struggle for liberation must go together. It also highlights the need to distinguish between "prospering" and "flourishing."[30] The wicked and idolatrous can be said to *prosper* (which can include wealth, health, emotional well-being, or psychological and affective states of happiness and pleasure), but they do not *flourish*; that is, they do not enjoy the truly good life, a life characterized by *tzedakah u'mishpat* (righteousness and justice). Or as the book of Tobit puts it: "A little with righteousness is better than wealth with wrongdoing" (Tobit 12:8). As per the Prophets, it is only when those with material wealth and concentrations of power turn back to God marked through generosity and justice toward the least, the lost, and the last that they can be said to flourish (i.e., be faithful creatures and covenant partners). True flourishing is built on a loving and just life for all people and conformity to God's covenantal order of shalom, a measure of which is active care for the vulnerable. This is in stark contrast to Aristotle for whom the flourishing community is one that presumes the domination of women, slaves, foreigners, and children and is wholly compatible with disregard for the welfare of those with little status.

Any adequate moral theory must attend not only to the *ends* but also to the *conditions* of human flourishing, which means understanding the systemic barriers to flourishing created by oppression. It should also stipulate that personal and spiritual growth must go hand in hand with structural transformation. Both are oriented to the formation of a common life in which all people may flourish since full flourishing requires both the right structural conditions and the right quality and character of interpersonal relations.

The intersection of personal and structural transformation can be illustrated by the "democratic paradox." Democracy presumes the existence of people and institutions committed to respecting the dignity of each individual. It employs dialogue and persuasion instead of killing and coercion as means of resolving conflicts, and it affirms that people should have a say in decisions that affect them. Yet democracy is forged out of immoral people, dependent upon hierarchal and often authoritarian institutions, and plagued by the despotism of either the one, the few, or the many. The personal dispositions needed for a freer, more egalitarian and democratic society will not be generated through either centralized state mechanisms, revolutionary vanguards, technocratic elites, or an ideological program of social engineering. Moreover, merely changing the immanent structures of power is never enough. Nor is it enough to change which people hold power. To put this in biblical terms: Egypt abolished is not Israel empowered. Alongside legal and institutional changes, new ways of acting, ways not determined by domination, takes converted hearts and habits. People who are atomized and alienated need reconstituting through changes in the quality and character of the relationships between them (i.e., formation in virtue) so that together they may be capable of pursuing life-giving goods in common through democratic means. The democratic paradox is of course an immanent version of a central theological and pastoral challenge, which is the question of how to live into the kingdom of God when the conditions for its realization do not yet fully exist.

DOES BEING VIRTUOUS MAKE YOU HAPPY?

Talk of virtue is often aligned with what is called *eudaimonistic ethics*: that is, a concern for what it means to pursue a vision of the good, happy, or worthwhile life (ευδαιμονικός) and how our relationships and dispositions enable us to pursue and participate in that life. For example, a eudaimonistic approach to understanding the moral life characterizes several of the major philosophical schools in antiquity – Aristotelianism, Stoicism, and Epicureanism. These were not philosophies in the modern sense but schools of life prescribing not just ways of thinking but also ascetic and relational practices through which to become a good – that is, a happier – person. A eudaimonistic approach is also one central to shaping Christian conceptions of the good life.

Augustine is identified as a leading proponent of Christian eudaimonism. The word "Christian" is crucial here, for in many ways Augustine disrupts and subverts the classical conceptions of eudaimonia he inherited. He describes the moral life in terms of the

Summum Bonum (Supreme Good), which provides the *eudaimonia* (condition of happiness, flourishing, good, or blessed life) that all human beings should seek. Christian eudaimonism is different from classical forms because Christ's life, death, and resurrection are the measure of a good life, and the primary concern is eternal rather than temporal happiness.[31] The beatitudes set out what the good/blessed life entails in the here and now (Matt 5:3–12; Luke 6:20–22). Thus, in Augustine's view, humans are created for, and consequently oriented toward, eternal life with God. Following after Christ, a moral/good life involves ordering our loves in such a way that we love God first and thereby fulfill what we are created to be. Vice and immorality follow from loving the right things in the wrong way by prioritizing them over and above loving God. For example, food and sex are good things, but if we desire them above all else, we pursue and consume them in ways that destroy us, our neighbors, and the rest of creation. The challenge is to reorder our loves so as to love God first and thereby know how to *appropriately* and *proportionally* love everything and everyone else. Under conditions of original sin this is a constant struggle. As per Augustine's testimony in *The Confessions*, we only discover what this supreme good is and what it means to participate in it through a process of conversion.

For Augustine, what humans *ought* to do is determined by the kind of creatures that they *are*, namely, beings created for eternal loving union with God and neighbor. And a life that is properly oriented toward the Supreme Good (i.e., love of God and neighbor) is the truly flourishing or blessed life. Jesus's cruciform life – that is, the relinquishing of material, relational, and spiritual attempts to secure his own flourishing apart from union with God – is the pattern and form of such a life. On this account, happiness in this life resides in neither material well-being, self-control, nor personal tranquility. Happiness is being in right relationship with God and neighbor, a struggle that entails much joy but also anguish and little serenity. The pursuit of this kind of happiness is a calling that may lead to poverty and suffering rather than material well-being.

Augustine prioritizes eternal over temporal happiness and communal flourishing over that of the individual. And, while a founder of a monastic rule, he advocates for the need to combine the contemplative and the active life as the means of participating in the *Summum Bonum*.[32] Other eudaimonistic philosophies develop different combinations of the eternal-temporal, individual-communal, contemplative-active axes. One way of reading modern Western developments in moral and political thought is as a shift from the medieval prioritization of a contemplative, communal, and eternal conception of happiness to an active, individual, and this-worldly conception of what constitutes flourishing.

Within a eudaimonistic framework, a virtue is a character trait a human being needs for eudaimonia: that is, to flourish or live well understood not in terms of a mental or physical state of contentment but as living an objectively good life. There are two dimensions to this claim: first, the virtues benefit their possessor by enabling them to flourish; and second, the virtues make their possessor good qua human being (i.e., the virtuous life constitutes the truly good life). These two dimensions accord with the nature of virtue I noted at the outset: namely, that virtues are intrinsic goods and enable us to flourish as human animals. The relationship between virtue and eudaimonia is thus mutually reinforcing. There is no understanding of what the good life is independent of virtue. Conversely, to direct our actions in virtuous ways necessitates a vision of the good life. However, it is not the case that we begin with an idea of what living well is, conceived independently of and prior to the cultivation of virtue, and then peg our conceptions and exercise of the virtues to that understanding. Rather, we come to an ever-deepening understanding of what the good life is by participating in it through the exercise of virtue. Through being virtuous, we know what it means to flourish. At the same time, we can only cultivate virtue through pursuing the good as this enables us to be rightly directed toward our fulfillment and thereby make appropriate judgments about whether a specific action may or may not be rightly directed. For

Augustine, this dynamic implies that because pagans do not seek the ultimate good (love of God), their virtues are ill-founded and disordered: in seeking the glory of Rome as the ultimate good, the virtues cultivated to that end – while of value as virtues – generate pride and domination. Aquinas modifies Augustine on this point, arguing that pagan virtue is imperfect rather than counterfeit, as it rests on an incomplete grasp rather than a wholly fallacious conception of the ultimate good. Salvation thereby perfects (and in the process radically transforms) existing "natural" or penultimate virtues.

In summary, a focus on virtue in ethics employs a concept of excellences of character cultivated through some combination of habituation, socialization, imitation, and education, the pursuit of which is oriented to and participates in *eudaimonia*. A virtuous person is able to act in a way that they are directed toward a truly flourishing life in any given circumstance or context. Within a Christian framework, the vision of the good to be pursued is embodied communion with God and creation through Jesus Christ; faith, hope, and love are the virtues that particularly enable us to participate in communion with God; and other, contingent and contextually determined virtues help us bear witness to and form a loving and just common life with others and with nonhuman life in this age before Christ's return.

However, to act well under conditions of finitude and fallenness we cannot rely on commands, rules, and virtues alone. We also need ways of deliberating and coming to judgment so as to generate practical wisdom about what to do and how to do it.

ACCOMPANYING READINGS

Alasdair MacIntyre, "The Virtues of Acknowledged Dependence," *Dependent Rational Animals: Why Human Beings Need the Virtues* (London: Duckworth, 1999), 119–128. MacIntyre has been a key figure in the contemporary recovery of virtue ethics. In this chapter, he provides an alternative to individualistic understandings of morality and rationality, giving an account of them as based on interdependent relations characterized by "just generosity."

Herbert McCabe, "Teaching Morals," *God Still Matters* (London: Bloomsbury Academic, 2005), 187–198. McCabe develops a pithy, lucid account of what constitutes virtue and why the cultivation of virtues is central to moral description and action by focusing on the nature and form of morality understood in terms of friendship and the sharing of a common life.

Aaron Stalnaker, "Reformations: Spiritual Exercises in Comparative Perspective," *Overcoming Our Evil: Human Nature and Spiritual Exercises in Xunzi and Augustine* (Washington, DC: Georgetown University Press, 2006), ch. 8. A good example of intercultural ethics, this chapter contrasts Augustine and the Confucian philosopher Xunzi's moral anthropology and understanding of virtue in a way that illuminates both Christian and Confucian approaches to the moral life. This kind of comparative work is itself an urgent moral practice of what Stalnaker calls "neighborliness" in a fractured, globalized context of moral, cultural, and religious plurality.

Melanie Harris, *Gifts of Virtue, Alice Walker, and Womanist Ethics* (New York: Palgrave Macmillan, 2010), 49–58, 105–123. Harris builds on the work of the novelist Alice Walker to develop a distinctive Womanist conception of virtue ethics. The book outlines seven virtues Harris takes to be key for such an ethic.

NOTES

1 Report to the President by the Presidential Commission on the Space Shuttle *Challenger* Accident, 5 vols. (Washington, DC: GPO, 1986).

2 Olga Pierrakos, Mike Prentice, Cameron Silverglate, Michael Lamb, Alana Demaske, and Ryan Smout, "Reimagining Engineering Ethics: From Ethics Education to Character Education," *2019 IEEE Frontiers in Education Conference* (2019), 1–9.

3 Pierrakos et al., "Reimagining Engineering Ethics."

4 My advocacy of virtue as an important feature of any account of the moral life should not be heard as advocating "virtue ethics" as *the* determinative framework for doing ethics. As noted earlier, Part II draws on a range of approaches to generate a more synthetic framework.

5 *Nicomachean Ethics* I.13.

6 Cf. Aquinas, *Summa Theologiae* I–II.1–5 (on happiness); I–II.49–54 (on habits); and I–II.55–60 (on virtues).

7 There is a difference between imitation understood as copying in order to approximate a singular ideal form and imitation as being like or recapitulating a prior form. The former is about repetition; the latter is

about participation in Christ's body in ways that are like rather than identical to Christ. We cannot be the same as Christ, but we can be Christ-like through the distinctive testimony of our lives.

8 Key figures who articulate this vision in the Americas are Septima Clark, Ella Baker, Saul Alinsky, Myles Horton, Paolo Friere, and Ivan Illich. For a historical account of its British variant – and the centrality of the Bible in it – see Jonathan Rose, *The Intellectual Life of the British Working Classes* (New Haven, CT: Yale University Press, 2001).

9 Julia Annas, *Intelligent Virtue* (Oxford: Oxford University Press, 2011), 25.

10 Dietrich Bonhoeffer, *Discipleship, Dietrich Bonhoeffer Works*, Vol. 4, eds., Geffrey Kelly and John Godsey, trans., Barbara Green and Reinhard Krauss (Minneapolis, MN: Fortress Press, 2001 [1937]), 40. On Luther's critique of virtue and his conception of moral agency, see Jennifer Herdt, *Putting on Virtue: The Legacy of the Splendid Vices* (Chicago: University of Chicago Press, 2008), 173–196.

11 Practical wisdom and justice are discussed at greater length in Chapter 11.

12 For a discussion of anger and courage, see Aquinas, *Summa Theologiae* II–II.123.10.

13 A classic and influential statement of this misinterpretation of agape is given by the Swedish Lutheran theologian, Anders Nygren in *Agape and Eros* (London: Society for Promoting Christian Knowledge, 1930; 1936).

14 Simon May, *Love: A History* (New Haven, CT: Yale University Press, 2011), 19.

15 Augustine, *City of God*, 19.25.

16 Valerie Saiving, "The Human Situation: A Feminine View," *Journal of Religion* 40, no. 2 (1960): 100–112. It should be noted that whereas Augustine's primary concern is how humility structures relations with God, most feminist critiques of humility focus on how it comes to structure immanent, horizontal relations. For an overview of the feminist debate and how it intersects with understandings of the doctrine of God and Christ's humility, see Sarah Coakley, "*Kenōsis* and Subversion: On the Repression of 'Vulnerability' in Christian Feminist Writing," *Powers and Submission: Spirituality, Philosophy and Gender* (Oxford: Wiley-Blackwell, 2002), 3–39.

17 See, for example, Rosemary Radford Ruether, who rejects an account of humility as self-abnegation used to subjugate women. In its place, she recovers a conception of humility as truthful self-knowledge, something

that contributes to women's realization of their own agency. Rosemary Radford Ruether, *Sexism and God Talk: Towards a Feminist Theology* (Boston, MA: Beacon Press, 1983), 186–189. Ruether echoes the distinction between humility understood as "self-abasement" and modesty as "soberness of mind" made by Mary Wollstonecraft in *Vindication of the Rights of Woman* (1792), ch. 7. See also the account of humility as "poverty of spirit" developed by Latin American liberation theologians discussed in Chapter 5.

18 The internal critique and revisioning of humility as a virtue is different in kind and focus to earlier, philosophical critiques and rejections of humility as a virtue by David Hume and Friedrich Nietzsche.

19 Lisa Tessman, *Burdened Virtues: Virtue Ethics for Liberatory Struggles* (Oxford: Oxford University Press, 2005).

20 The paradox is that in taking up our cross and following Jesus, we discover true, Sabbath rest (Matt 11:28–30; 16:24–26); that is, in the struggle we discover who we truly are and, however tentative and fragile it may be, the joy and peace of communion with God in and through love of neighbor.

21 James Cone, *God of the Oppressed*, rev. ed. (Maryknoll, NY: Orbis, 1997), 191.

22 Cone, *God of the Oppressed*, 191.

23 Martin Luther King Jr.'s "Letter from Birmingham City Jail" is an extended meditation on this theme in the context of Jim and Jane Crow–era apartheid in the United States. For King, justice is not reducible to following the rule of law, and what "law and order" demand can be cruel and unjust. In such situations, justice requires following God's command, not human demand. But this position raises a difficult question: Who decides what God commands? Further to the discussion of tradition in Chapter 6, it is this question that haunted Thomas Hobbes and other early modern political thinkers who sought to reduce justice to law and order and enshrine the sovereign as the one who decides of what law consists in order to curtail the role of revelation in breaking open and disrupting an established political order. The attempt by liberalism as a political philosophy to quarantine religion to the private and the individual follows on from this concern. But as with King, the miraculous and the prophetic break open the lockdown of an unjust legal regime.

24 Katie Cannon, *Black Womanist Ethics* (Atlanta, GA: Scholars Press, 1988), 2.

25 Cannon, *Black Womanist Ethics*, 174. For a parallel account see Melanie Harris, *Gifts of Virtue, Alice Walker, and Womanist Ethics* (New York: Palgrave Macmillan, 2010). Harris identifies seven virtues: generosity, graciousness, compassion, spiritual wisdom, audacious courage, justice, and good community. Similarly, Thelathia Nikki Young identifies "survival/resilience" and "creative resistance" as "virtues of black-queer subjectivity" while recognizing that talk of virtues has not been favored in queer theory. Thelathia Nikki Young, *Black Queer Ethics, Family, and Philosophical Imagination* (New York: Palgrave Macmillan, 2016), 126.

26 Cannon, *Black Womanist Ethics*, 143. Cannon explains that "Hurston, like Black people generally, understood suffering not as a moral norm nor as a desirable ethical quality, but rather as the typical state of affairs. Virtue is . . . that which allows Black people to maintain a feistiness about life that nobody can wipe out" (104).

27 Cannon, *Black Womanist Ethics*, 99, 104–105.

28 Cannon, *Black Womanist Ethics*, 132–135.

29 Cannon, *Black Womanist Ethics*, 143–144, 147.

30 See Ps 37 and 73; Prov 11:28; Jer 12:1–4; Ezek 16:49–50 and 17:24; Mal 3:15.

31 Augustine identifies the Greek term *eudaimonia* with the Latin *beatitudo* (blessedness). A distinction is made later in the tradition between *felicitas* (defined as imperfect, this-worldly, or temporal happiness) and beatitude (perfect, eternal blessedness).

32 *City of God*, 19.19.

11 Deliberation and Judgment

Many students I've taught have been subject to legalistic and harmful forms of judgmentalism in either their church, community, or online interactions. In reaction against that legalism, they tend to practice a relativistic "you do you" approach to moral questions. In the name of tolerance and freedom, they see morality as a purely personal matter and are hesitant to make moral judgments about their own actions, let alone those of others. Yet this "live and let live" mentality undermines the pursuit of love and justice. There can be neither love nor justice in the world without loving and just judgments and the actions that follow from them. Moreover, ethical deliberation leading to moral judgments is a vital element of how we become moral agents.

The legalistic judgmentalism my students suffered and the relativistic license they've adopted in response do not exhaust the available options where moral judgment is concerned. Practical reason provides an alternative to both in a way that avoids the traps of either. It enables us to make a moral judgment about what to do and how to do it in ways that are truthful as well as attentive to the specific circumstances and needs we confront. Moral judgments derived from ethical deliberation based on practical reason are thus different in kind from forms of judgmentalism resulting from either an ideological checklist or a highly abstracted and rigid moral code. Both of these latter ways of coming to judgment are inattentive to the particularities of a person and their context – and thereby untruthful because they fail to attend to what is really going on here and now.

Practical reasoning is the secret sauce or binding agent that brings together all I have been saying so far about commands, rules, and virtues. Without it, the other elements remain separate pieces. They need a process of deliberation to integrate them and generate

moral judgments. Practical reason may sound abstract, but we use it every day. Its wisdom is not speculative or theoretical but enacted. Practical or deliberative reason (*phronesis*) is the process of weighing up relevant factors, evaluating them in the light of the vision or end we seek, and coming to a judgment as to what action to take. A trivial example illustrates the process: a person wants to use a new computer (their end), so they look for an on switch and, finding it, turn on the computer, thereby opening up new possibilities for further action. This judgment incorporated both sensory elements (touch, sight, etc.), desires, and reasoning in the discovery of what to do.

Obviously, as with the example of turning on a computer, not all practical judgments are moral. Neither are all judgments practical; for example, some are purely aesthetic. But my focus here is the relationship between deliberation, judgment, and moral action. I contend that practical reason as against other kinds of reasoning plays a key role in connecting them and thereby constituting us as moral agents. However, to fully understand practical reasoning as a way of coming to a moral judgment, we must first understand the meaning and purpose of moral judgment.

WHAT IS MORAL JUDGMENT?: A CHRISTOLOGICAL FRAMEWORK

Judgment in its broadest sense signifies coming to a conclusion about how to order or value one thing in relation to another. Is this of greater worth than that? Should X come before Y? How is the part to be related to the whole? Judgment thereby involves a process of valuation whereby we sift or assess things. Part of moral and political evaluation is making distinctions – most obviously, discriminating between good and evil or right and wrong. Evaluating and making moral and political distinctions involves two things. It entails determining what needs binding together or reconciling (because it is improperly broken apart) and identifying what needs setting free (because it is falsely bound). This evaluation is a discernment of how things might be rightly ordered and valued both in themselves and in relation to each other. As a part of either binding or loosing, moral and political evaluation can also mean making something public or visible. Through bringing to light what is unseen and giving voice to what is unheard, moral and political judgments either make what is ignored count or render accountable what is hidden.

Theologically, all these elements of moral and political judgment are embodied and enacted in the person of Jesus Christ. Christ is the ground and measure of what is truly valuable. Christ sifts good from bad. Christ rules and orders so as to enable humans to prioritize what is truly valuable. Christ brings what is hidden to light. And, finally, Christ reconciles what is broken apart and sets free what is falsely bound so that it can fulfill its created purpose. It is for good reason that Christ's depiction as the final judge is the underlying motif of a central way in which Christ is understood theologically – namely, as fulfilling the threefold office of prophet, priest, and king (often referred to as the *munus triplex*).[1] Each of these offices represents a different aspect of moral and political judgment that is nevertheless interwoven with each of the others.

Judgment as Ordering

The courtroom has become a governing picture for how we envision moral and political judgment. This frame of reference emphasizes law and justice as the basis for the right ordering of relationships and ensuring each thing or person is directed to its particular good. This emphasis echoes the Hebrew term for judgment – *mishpat* – which means both judgment and justice. Inherent in this term is a normative sense that judgment properly understood and enacted should aim for justice, that is, rightly ordered relations that gives each person their due and enables each to fulfil their own ends.[2]

The courtroom image can be misleading. We often operate with a sense that in making a moral judgment we are like a judge sitting outside of and presiding over the situation being judged. But we are simultaneously defendant, witness, prosecutor, jury, and judge. In his person and work, Christ embodies this dynamic. As Karl Barth frames it, Christ is the judge judged in our place.[3] What is true of Christ is intensified for us. We are immersed in the situations we must come to judgments about, and these judgments are arrived at from within the unfolding story of our lives in which we are the primary participant. Our practical projects, the descriptions and narratives by which we make sense of the world, and the meaning and purpose of our actions are woven into and worked out through discovering what to do and how to do it with others on whose lives our own life depends. Given this dynamic, our moral judgments can be both truthful *and* contingent. By contrast, legalism and relativism constitute failures of judgment: they are neither truthful nor contingent.

In Scripture, covenants frame how judgments that order life with others always begin in the middle of a form of life in which we are participating. That is, moral judgments operate within a context of mutually responsible fellowship oriented toward a vision of shared flourishing. The covenants God made with Noah, Abraham, and Moses are paradigmatic here. An emphasis on covenants recovers a sense of how moral and political judgments are a way to determine how we and others are situated in community with each other and in relation to the community as a whole. Just judgments simultaneously oppose domination as that which disorders and disables right relation *and* seek to enable the building up of a rightly ordered, covenantal form of common life. For example, in the Mosaic covenant (Ex 24:6–8), the law established the framework for fulfilling the covenant through rightly ordering relations between God and the people, between the people themselves, their relationship to the land and nonhuman life, and with strangers in their midst. Central to ensuring the covenantal community of relations was rightly ordered was ensuring each participant (God, the people, land, animals, and strangers) were able to fulfill their specific good as part of a shared common good. Constant judgments were needed to determine how to best follow the law as a means of fulfilling the covenant. But the covenant set the terms and conditions for what it meant to follow the spirit rather than the letter of the law. Within a covenant (e.g., a marriage) there is ongoing need for judgments about how to rightly order relations *and* how to recalibrate relations so as to ensure that the flourishing of each is properly attended to within the flourishing of the whole covenantal community (in the case of marriage, that is the family), and conversely, the flourishing of the whole community is not undermined by each member pursuing their individual good.[4] In trying to fulfill a covenant, judgments can be right and true (here and now) *and* revisable. For example, how I should treat my child aged 4 is different in form to how I should treat them aged 18. The same action that is loving and appropriate when they are aged 4 (dressing and feeding them, restraining them from doing certain things) is abusive if I am still doing it when they are aged 18.

Judgment as Truth-Telling

Alongside a conception of moral judgment as enabling the right ordering of relations within a particular community and context is a notion of judgment as revelation. This is exemplified in prophecy as a form of moral and political judgment. Prophecy speaks to and from a final eschatological order of valuation, pronouncing judgment on present circumstances: amid the world as it is, this is a vision of the world as it will be and so we must act now and value what currently exists in the light of what is to come. Its ultimate expression is articulated in the Apocalypse/Revelation of John. The Apocalypse, the denouement of which is the final judgment, brings to light what is truly going on. In the process, good is sifted from evil, sheep are separated from goats: that is, a right structure of value is identified and imagined. Intrinsic to both prophetic and apocalyptic forms of judgment is a judgment against what prevents true flourishing (e.g., injustice and domination) and a judgment for deliverance into what truly nourishes (i.e., shalom). Moral judgment likewise constitutes a form of revelation that speaks from a vision of the world as it should be. As an act of truth telling, Christian moral and political judgment seeks to wake us up from what is false by giving a true account of reality in the light of how Christ reveals the true meaning and purpose of what is going on.[5] Here moral and political judgment is indexed to right description (as outlined in Part I).

Judgment as Blessing

If we only have juridical and revelatory forms of judgment, then there is little sense of how our moral and political judgments can bring healing and enable new life. This is why we also need to keep in view images of Christ as priest, temple, and sacrificial lamb. As frames of reference, they bring to the fore the repairing, purifying, redeeming, merciful, and reconciling elements of moral and political judgment. Practices such as confession, penitence, absolution, forgiveness, and blessing, all of which constitute words of judgment, enable new, loving patterns of life to emerge. The focus of such judgments is not so much ordering or truth-telling but healing, holiness, and righteousness. Such acts of judgment transfigure life so that it ceases to be determined by sin and idolatry and can again be fruitful.

For example, forgiveness as a judgment re-signifies events rather than erases them, so that we come to understand and experience ourselves and others in a new way. We move beyond being determined by relational and structural dichotomies such as "friend-enemy" or "victim-oppressor," the word of forgiveness opening up new relational possibilities.[6] As fallen creatures, we cannot always avoid making poor judgments and mistakes or suffering the effects of others' bad or evil actions. This means that alongside justice and truth-telling, we need words and gestures of healing, forgiveness, and reconciliation (i.e., merciful acts of loving kindness) if we are to move toward a more *shalom*-like common life. Indeed, the pursuit of loving kindness/steadfast love/mercy (*ḥesed*) must come before and be a condition of the pursuit of righteousness and justice (*tzedakah u'mishpat*). I take this to be a deep logic of Scripture incarnated in the life, death, and resurrection of Jesus Christ. If the order is reversed, then the pursuit of justice becomes a zero-sum game that degenerates into the settling of scores or cycles of revenge with the past overdetermining the future, while the pursuit of holiness collapses into either puritanical zealotry or legalistic moralism.

An event I discussed in the book's Introduction (Chapter 1) helps demonstrates how these three forms of judgment can operate together even as they exist in tension with each other. The response to the evil actions of Dylann Roof in murdering the nine members of Mother Emmanuel Church in Charleston in 2015 involved judgment as ordering, truth-telling, and blessing. In the courtroom, Roof was tried and imprisoned through a process that reordered relations between himself, those he wronged, and society as a whole in a way that held him accountable for his actions. The judgment also sought to tell the truth about what happened, purposing a pathway forward that determined the outcomes for society and the criminal. But the juridical process focused on the truth of the murders alone and the subsequent reordering of how Roof – as an individual – related to society as a result of his actions. Another kind of truth-telling happened outside the courtroom in the widespread demonstrations as part of the Movement for Black Lives. These demonstrations had a prophetic quality, revealing how the murders were not an isolated act of a lone wolf but part of a systemic, society-wide, and historic devaluing of Black life. The call for Black lives to matter sought a fundamental reordering of the social, political, and economic structures of esteem so that Black people along with others subject to racialized structures of inequality and violence are treated with equal dignity. Like the courtroom judgment, the BLM protests enacted judgment as ordering and judgment as truth-telling. In contrast, the statements by some of the victims' families saying they forgave Roof enacted judgment in a priestly register. In doing so, they witnessed to new, seemingly impossible possibilities for relationship beyond murderer-victim and friend-enemy relations.

In summary, echoing the threefold office of Christ, good or wise moral and political judgments rightly order relations, reveal the truth, and open out new, life-giving possibilities from what currently exists. Christ as the one who embodies and fulfills what it means to be a prophet, priest, and king enacts this threefold form of judgment at the Last Judgment. But we are not Christ who combines the threefold office in one person, so for us, each of these elements of judgment may be undertaken by a different party. And in this age, before Christ's return, we must also enact judgments that rightly order relations, reveal the truth, and open out new, life-giving, and loving possibilities under conditions of finitude and fallenness. Practical reason is the way we do that.

My account of practical reason here builds on and assumes all that is covered so far in Parts I and II: commands, virtues, and rules, along with listening to creaturely life, Scripture, strangers, those crying out for liberation, and our ancestors combine to generate a shared world of meaning and action. That shared world constitutes the basis of communal and individual practical reasoning and the wisdom such reasoning generates.

COMING TO WISE JUDGMENT THROUGH DELIBERATION

Judgments that generate wise action look back to understand what the situation is, and forward to determine a way ahead, opening out new possibilities. Wise judgment thus has both a *retrospective* element and a *prospective* one. As a discernment it evaluates an existing state of affairs and as a decision it points to a pathway for action. In short, moral judgments as forms of enacted and embodied wisdom are the hinge connecting the questions "What's going on?" and "What is to be done?" Moral judgments provide an answer to both questions simultaneously. That said, this is not a straightforward process and can involve both great struggle and complex discernment. For example, what role does prior experience or ongoing commitments play in reading a situation and framing possibilities for a way ahead in response to complicated questions: Are genetically modified crops a good way to address food insecurity? Or is euthanasia a moral response to those who suffer when dying? At the same time, we can heed the words of Jesus: "Seek, and you shall find" (Matt 7:7).

Practical reasoning is a means of making moral and political judgments that puts people, place, and history before any particular theory or program. It fosters both *wily wisdom* (the local knowledge, intelligence, and practical skills necessary to respond appropriately to a constantly changing and ambiguous environment) and a *sense of occasion* (the determination and evaluation of what to do today that is best for these people, in this place, at this moment in time).[7] Practical reason is thereby as much about thinking with and through our bodies as it is about thinking with our brains.

For many, however, practical reason is a foolish way of generating moral and political judgments. Some call for decisions based on empirical evidence alone, prioritizing technical over practical rationality. Rather than determining what is good through embodied, communal, and contested reflection and deliberation, a technocratic approach assumes that the best way to improve the world is through efficient and effective procedures for managing resources. Such an attitude was heard during the COVID-19 pandemic from those who advocated "following the science," as if the data and medical science alone could determine what to do and how to do it divorced from any wider economic, social, or political considerations. A more everyday example also makes the point: any use of Google or other internet search engines reveals that data by itself, even vast amounts of data, does not generate truth, let alone wisdom; indeed, searches based on data-driven calculations alone often amplify disinformation, lies, and conspiracy theories. The contrast with practical reason could not be starker. Within a technocratic frame of reference, judgment is reduced to calculation that ignores how wise moral and political judgments require paying attention to context, looking at the bigger picture, and attending to questions of meaning and purpose. In short, technical rationality separates practical means from moral ends. By contrast, while practical reason incorporates matters of technical knowledge, it also asks *why*, not just *how* we should do something.

The decisions artificial intelligence (AI) machines can make illustrate the difference between, on the one side, technocratic and managerial forms of judgment and, on the other, those based on practical reasoning. There is much discussion about how AI is replacing human decision making in such areas as military and medical systems and how to morally evaluate the decisions algorithms generate. What this discussion often misses is how AI can only calculate according to prescribed sequences and forms of pattern recognition. AI reasoning is mostly probabilistic rather than ethical. The decisions AI produces are also in no way equivalent to moral and political judgment based on practical reason. If such judgments are to be wise, they must involve a holistic range of factors including attention to context and inferences, a sense of timing, muscle memory, pursuit of a moral purpose, consideration of counsel, and the exercise of virtues like patience. AI machines can contribute to moral judgments as part of a cooperative human-nonhuman community of deliberation. But on their own, they lack the kind of ethical understanding required for moral judgments in any meaningful sense of that term. By implication, areas of decision making that involve moral and political judgments rather than procedural calculations – for example, whether to launch an attack or admit a patient – should not be left entirely to an AI machine. To do so is to replace morality with technical rationality.

Alongside technical rationality, practical reason also contrasts with basing moral and political judgment on forms of deductive, philosophical reasoning. Within such frameworks, the problem with practical reason is that it is too contextual and contingent, too subject to changing circumstances to be a reliable basis for moral and political judgments. Plato represents this kind of concern. For Plato and those who echo his position, moral and political judgments should be deductive, derived from first principles that construct a mental ideal that is then related to practice. For Plato, we come to know the world through rational contemplation of ideal forms. Moral and political knowledge can be separated from the world of flux and change and a rationally demonstrable account of what is true, good, and beautiful can be developed. The ideal ruler is thus the philosopher king who can make judgments about what to do in accord with rationally derived principles. Similarly, for Kant, moral judgment is about a formal process of deductive reasoning divorced from contextual and communal discernment. Likewise, utilitarianism precludes a concept of practical reason because it subsumes all judgments under a universal rule, that of the quantitative calculation of utility. These kinds of frameworks impose an ideal program, like a cookie cutter, on the ambiguities and fragilities of living, breathing people.

Accounts of moral and political judgment that prioritize theory over practice (whether Platonic, Kantian, or utilitarian) fail to reckon with how moral and political judgments entail action in time. The ideal ruler is not a philosopher king but a ship's captain who is able to safely navigate the tumultuous and mercurial sea by means of experience, craft, and quick-wittedness. Moral and political action requires a means of coming to judgment suited to putting people, place, and history before any particular theory or program. That means is practical reason.[8]

Before proceeding, I should note that like all forms of reason, practical reason has its limits. Ultimately, the truth or otherwise of our moral judgments is validated not by how well they generate wisdom about how to act here and now. Rather, theologically, their veracity and worth are measured by the extent to which they recapitulate and contribute to the fulfillment of all things in Christ – an end we can only act toward in faith. Our moral judgments reach toward what is fitting given the nature and purpose of being alive, but because of our finitude and fallenness, these judgments are contingent and revisable. Definitive judgment on and knowledge of what is and what will be are Christ's alone. As the alpha and omega, Christ is the only one who can break the seals and give definitive judgment on the order of things (Rev 5:1–14). To put this another way, we can act prudentially based on what we have discovered through listening to creation, Scripture, the cries of those struggling for liberation, etc.; however, we must also act in hope of what has been and will be done for creation as a whole in and through Christ. But to act prudentially, confidently, and with hope is not to act with certainty or security, neither of which are possible here and now. But also, certainty is not something to be expected or realizable in moral ways of knowing and relating. Moral knowledge is not that kind of knowledge. Ethics is not a natural science. For example, we cannot know with certain knowledge that we are loved or forgiven. We can only trust that we are. Like King Lear exacting proof of love from his daughters in return for his favor, to demand certainty of any form of moral relation or judgment is to

undergo a tragic failure of understanding and character that marks one as unable to give or receive from others in moral ways.

PRACTICAL REASONING IN PRACTICE

As with the example of working out how to turn on a computer that I began with, practical reasoning involves apprehending a good (affectively, kinesthetically, and cognitively), desiring and intending that good as an end, deliberating about ways and means to attain it, and finally, acting to attain that end. To see what this involves in practice let's consider the example of deciding how to get to church. I need some sense of what church is in order to apprehend it as a good I seek. Moreover, before coming to a decision about how or why I go to church I must have a vision or goal I am trying to fulfill by going to church and a story to tell about what church is. Do I (a) go to meet with people I enjoy spending time with; (b) go to worship God in the company of fellow believers; or (c) go because I find the liturgy a rich aesthetic experience? Each of these goals – and the stories I tell to make sense of them – will organize the information and answers to questions about how to get to church in a different way. By reflecting on the goals we seek, we can put the relevant factors in an intelligible order. Discerning the *telos* – that is, how things should be ordered so that an end can be fulfilled – enables us to know how we should act in relation to the reality we have discerned.

However, that does *not* mean we cannot determine anything until some overarching good has been identified. Neither should we begin with an ultimate good and then work backwards from there. Our sense of the end we seek is already present in the meshwork of relations we participate in. I can determine what friendship as a moral end entails because I have participated in and have stories to tell about friendship. I can also better determine how to be a friend by reflecting on that experience and stories about friendship – real or fictional – and thereby determine how to implement the goal of friendship better. The same process is involved in pursuing the good of church, family, education, health, and the like. Fulfilling these penultimate goods is an iterative process. The more we reflect on and analyze our experiences of them, the more we are able to realize their intrinsic ends. The same goes for developing a desire for and sense of what communion with God and creation entails. These can be enhanced through further theological reflection and engaging in the process of listening outlined in Part I.

Coming to judgment through practical reason is not just a matter of apprehending and desiring an end. I must also attend to the reality of my situation by asking what is going on. In relation to a judgment about going to church I must determine how much time I have before the service starts, how far do I have to go, what is the weather and traffic like, can I walk, or do I need to bike to get there on time? I must reflect on my context and build up a picture, albeit in greater or lesser detail, about my situation. All of these questions focus on understanding my context, reflecting on or theorizing about my situation, and, where possible, ascertaining accurate information.

Making a decision – whether about going to church or needing surgery – is not a subjective exercise. To be truthful, it must take account of the world as it really is, rather than my ideological aspirations about what I think it should be like or my anxieties about what it might be like. Ascertaining the reality of my situation, so far as is possible, is vital to discerning what to do because it directly informs how I understand the available possibilities for action. In relation to going to church, if I say I will drive, but my car is broken, or if I decide to walk, but my church is ten miles away and I have half an hour to get there, I have failed to properly describe my situation. Hence, searching for and discovering what to do requires some reflection on the factors affecting what can and cannot be done. The more complex the context relating to the decision – for example, historical and political relations between Israelis and Palestinians – the more difficult it is to describe and make intelligible the situation in which a particular way ahead must be discerned (and so the more contingent and revisable one's judgments should be about that situation).

As already noted, a key element of searching for and finding wise judgments is having access to reliable knowledge and information. Thus, when we reflect on our context in order to describe it and make it intelligible, we draw on science, history, anthropology, and the like. However, the quest does not end there, as so many people seem to think. Merely being able to accurately describe our situation does not automatically give us wisdom about the right course of moral or political action. For example, President Trump had more information and accurate analysis available to him than anyone else in determining how to respond to the Coronavirus pandemic as it emerged in 2020, but his course of action was not necessarily wise. Making sense of information depends in large part on the story we situate that information within. Moreover, we tend to assume the knowledge we derive from science, or history, or geography is neutral or value-free. We derive it from an "objective" standpoint, outside the picture we are trying to describe. But, of course, we stand within that picture, which affects our understanding. Moreover, how something is described will depend on what we think is being portrayed. When contemplating nature, do we think it is raw material from which we extract what we need to power our life? Or is nature God's creation? Data always needs interpretation, and that interpretation depends on the quality and character of our relationship to the world and the descriptions and narratives we use to make sense of the world around us. It also depends on the ends we seek. To describe our situation truthfully, we must ask questions about meaning and purpose. To not merely depict but also to make sense of what is going on we must ask ends-orientated, vision-type questions: "What is the good life?," "What is justice?," "What is peace? And why is peace better than war?" Or in the case of our example: "What is church? And why go to church?"

Moral and political judgments cannot rest with good intentions, understanding, or description. To generate action, there must be a purposing that maps out what to do and how to do it. For this we must ask "what is to be done in the light of the reality discerned?" Given the reality of our situation, the good or moral vision we are trying to fulfill, and a weighing up of various possible courses of action, we must decide what action most fittingly enables our purpose in this situation at this time. The result of our judgment is the action we eventually take.

A slightly more complicated example illustrates the same process. A budding chef reads about a new dish that sounds delicious. They apprehend it as good based on their prior knowledge and experience of cooking but realize it will stretch them to cook it as it requires more advanced techniques than they are used to. But they desire to try to create it and serve some friends who they think will enjoy eating it. They observe others cook versions of the dish on YouTube and take counsel from more experienced cooks about how to prepare the dish while also reading some recipe books as part of deliberating about the optimal tools, equipment, and ingredients for the task. They weigh up various ways they might go about cooking the dish, eventually finding one that most suits their purpose as well as the constraints of time and resource they are working with. They cook the dish, which necessitates tasting, a sense of timing, and aesthetic perceptions in judging when it is ready. They eat the meal with friends, which incorporates an affective and moral dimension of conviviality, trust, solidarity, and care (or, if it is a bad form of eating, distrust, resentment and the like). If they employ the wrong technique, are impatient, or use the wrong ingredients then they will fail to achieve their goal. Something will have happened; yet the action was not fit for the specific purpose sought. The same applies to more obviously moral actions such as caring for the sick. The wisdom of practical reasoning in pursuit of a moral end is evaluated against the quality, character, and fittingness of the action it generates to the ends it seeks.

Evaluating a moral action by its fittingness to the ends it seeks should not be taken to imply the morality of an action is vindicated by its consequences as utilitarianism assumes. Consequences are contingent on a range of factors beyond the control of the agent and the purpose of their action. It is the not the consequences of the action that are primary in evaluating it but whether it was good and fitting given what was purposed. Telling the truth when asked to betray the Gospel is good, fitting, and congruent with a desire and intention to be faithful to God, even though it may lead to martyrdom, a consequence that is neither desired nor intended even while it might be anticipated.

As the example of the chef suggests, the ways and means of coming to judgment are key. Whether personal or institutional, judgment that culminates in wise action takes the humility to listen. And as set out in Part I, if our deliberation is to be shaped by Christian concerns, who and what we listen to is creation, Scripture, strangers, the poor, and our ancestors in the faith. This process of listening is an apprenticeship in the virtue of wise judgment. But even as wise judgment entails attention and attunement to the world around us, we must be mindful of how, as Scripture reminds us, the fruit of Christian moral reasoning can seem like foolishness to the very world we are listening to (1 Cor 1:21–25).

Part of good deliberation involves seeking and listening to counsel. We need the counsel of others to make wise decisions. This points to the fact that no one has a monopoly on wisdom. Aquinas, following Aristotle, called the ability to seek good or right counsel leading to sound judgment the virtue of *euboulia*. Being *euboulos* involves the ability to deliberate well about what truly benefits you or your community as well as the ability to recognize and receive good advice from others, even those you disagree with or who oppose you. As a virtue, *euboulia* (the disposition to wise judgment) entails being able to consider different options and viewpoints empathetically. As a virtue, it points to the symbiotic link between listening, communicating well, giving and receiving advice, and coming to make wise judgments.

In an institutional or communal setting, the deliberative process of coming to judgment entails a complex interplay of factors. It entails (a) listening to everyone affected by a decision, especially those mostly likely to be negatively impacted by its effects; (b) the capacity and means for those consulted to speak freely and truthfully; and (c) the need for coherent arguments that make a clear case. These three elements must be in play if institutional processes of coming to judgment are to be directed to the good of all or the common life rather than privileging the interests of the one, the few, or the majority.

DELIBERATION, COMMANDS, RULES, AND VIRTUES

As should be clear, moral judgments involve the whole person (including their senses and affective relations) and are situated within a set of ecological, social, political, economic, and historical relations. Making wise judgments is not a question of an individual's capacity for abstract reasoning, or their raw intelligence, or even knowing a great deal. These may or may not help. Moral judgment that enacts wisdom involves the formation of persons who have the right priorities, desires, and intentions – in other words, virtues. Becoming a moral person therefore has as much to do with the quality of our relationships and the behavior we learn as it has to do with what we do or don't know. Formal education is often irrelevant to practical reasoning. Unless I am well nurtured and so learn how to love, how to be patient, how to restrain my lust, I will not develop into the kind of person who has the necessary virtues to discover with others what the good and wise thing to do is. In other words, character shapes judgment. If I am a prudent person and I decide to walk to church then I leave enough time, wear clothes appropriate to the weather, and find an interesting or quiet route. If I decide to walk but don't know the way, get soaking wet because I didn't bring a coat or umbrella, and am late because I didn't leave enough time, then I am an imprudent person, which may be connected to other character flaws such as being impatient or reckless.

It is not just a question of having to be a certain kind of person to make good judgments. Some structural locations better orient us toward truthful discernment and the ability to receive good counsel than others. Our ecological, social, political, and economic situation can open up or close down particular kinds of agency. Geographic isolation, trauma, addiction, or an elite lifestyle closed off from relationship with others unlike oneself constrain possible courses of action and people's ability to discuss, deliberate, and discern what to do and how to do it. Moreover, discovering moral ways of being alive involves social and political struggles through which we expand our ability to tell the truth about our world and ourselves. So, alongside virtue, becoming "otherwise" is part of how to discover wise moral and political judgments.

Alongside virtue and becoming otherwise, we also need commands and rules. All of these combine together in forms of practical reasoning, which enacts wisdom about what to do and how to do it under conditions of finitude and fallenness. This framework can be summarized as follows: God's commands manifest God's ongoing participation in and sustaining of creation and establish the possibility for moral ways of being alive. Responses to God's ongoing communicative agency generates particular, covenantal forms of life (which themselves are intricate webs of creaturely life). Virtues and rules sustain the practices that make these covenantal forms of life possible over time, and which in turn form the basis of practical reasoning that enables loving and just judgments about what to do and how to do it. Covenantal forms of life are arenas in which we discover, play with, and metabolize creation and live out Christian ways of being alive while at the same time cultivating a generous and just common life in dialogue with others and through which we may become increasingly otherwise.

So far in this book, I have primarily focused on the individual moral agent as one enmeshed in relationship with various human and nonhuman others. In Part III, I analyze moral agency from a communal angle. In it, I examine how any form of social, political, and economic life is an inherently moral endeavor and, conversely, how living well entails social, political, and economic processes and conflicts. Any discussion of ethics must include such an account of how human flourishing takes shape in and through social, political, and economic relations.

ACCOMPANYING READINGS

Thomas Aquinas, *Summa Theologae,* II–II qu 60 on "Judgment." Question 60 sets out Aquinas's account of judgment, indexing it to the pursuit of justice.

Roberto S. Goizueta, "Rediscovering Praxis: The Significance of U.S. Hispanic Experience for Theological Method," *We Are a People! Initiatives in Hispanic American Theology* (Minneapolis, MN: Fortress Press, 1992), 51–77. Goizueta reviews the development of US Latinx theology and develops an account of practical reason as praxis that is orientated to social and political transformation.

Stanley Hauerwas, "How I Think I Learned to Think Theologically," *The Work of Theology* (Grand Rapids, MI: Eerdmans, 2015), 11–31. The personal nature of this account of practical reason is central to Hauerwas's argument that who we are as persons directly affects how we come to think theologically and that thinking theologically requires being formed within a community that tells a story about God as revealed in the life, death, and resurrection of Jesus Christ.

NOTES

1 While central to many accounts of Christology, Karl Barth is the modern theologian most directly associated with a focus on Christ as prophet, priest, and king. For Barth, Christ is "the strange Judge that allowed himself to be judged" in our place. Karl Barth, *Church Dogmatics: The Doctrine of Reconciliation*, vol. 4/1, trans., G. W. Bromiley (New York: Charles Scribner's Sons, 1956), 227.

2 This sense of justice includes justice as a rightly ordered state of affairs with justice as a binding moral or legal precept that directs action. It contrasts in a complementary way with justice as a virtue.

3 Barth, *Church Dogmatics*, 4/1, 222.

4 A formal way of framing this dynamic process of recalibration is in terms of commutative and distributive justice and how together these enable the flourishing of each and the flourishing of the whole. Commutative and distributive justice are ways of conceptualizing how to order relations so that these people or this person are appropriately valued or esteemed in relation to these others. Commutative justice denotes equivalent exchange, like for like, or one to one parity. We are most familiar with commutative justice in market transactions where an equivalent value of money is exchanged for a product with the price constituting a judgment of value.

It is also expressed in the motto of the American Federation of Labor, which is "a fair day's wage for a fair day's work": pay constituting a judgment on the value of the work. This ties into broader question about the extent to which workers should share in the profits of a company or whether they should be paid according to what the market value decides. By contrast, distributive justice denotes ensuring each person is given a proportional share of the whole as a member of the wider community so as to ensure they can participate with parity and fully realize who they are in relationship with others. It necessitates evaluating how to recalibrate each part so as to ensure the justice/right ordering of the whole. It is articulated in the labor movement slogan that has as its root the communal vision of Act 4: "From each according to their ability, to each according to their needs."

5 Oliver O'Donovan suggests that the biblical and philosophical metaphor of "wakefulness" is key for conceptualizing ethical judgment. What is it we awaken to through our processes of ethical reflection? We awaken to the "world," the reality that is "the condition of all moral awareness" (10), to the "self," that is, one's own agency and presence in the world with and for others, and to "time," that is, how self and world are co-present "only in the moment of time which is open to us for action" (15) and thence the contingency and historicity of our thought and action. Oliver O'Donovan, *Self, World, and Time: Ethics as Theology*, vol. 1 (Grand Rapids, MI: Eerdmans, 2013). O'Donovan is right but he over-determines ethical judgment in relation to truth-telling, thereby downplaying how moral judgments are also indexed to justice and blessing. This is something he does attend to elsewhere in his work (see Oliver O'Donovan, "The Act of Judgment," *The Ways of Judgment* [Grand Rapids, MI: Eerdmans, 2005], 3–12).

6 Restorative justice is a contemporary example of this form of judgment in action. In late antiquity, it frames the distinction between ecclesial and secular legal judgment. The language used by bishops during the late Roman Empire to arbitrate disputes in their formal court-like "audiences" is permeated with talk of mediation, reconciliation, forgiveness, and charity. Episcopal judgment was not envisioned in juridical terms but as the act of a physician healing a broken body. (Jill Harries, *Law and Empire in Late Antiquity* [Cambridge: Cambridge University Press, 2001], 192–208).

7 My use of the term "practical reason" in the context of forming moral and political judgments should be understood as combining *phronēsis* and *mētis*. According to Marcel Detienne and Jean-Pierre Vernant, *mētis* entails a body of attitudes and behaviors that combines flair, wisdom, forethought, perspicuity, subtlety, resourcefulness, vigilance, opportunism, and experience acquired over years that enables one to navigate circumstances of conflict, change, and instability. See *Cunning Intelligence in Greek Culture and Society*, trans., Janet Lloyd (Chicago: University of Chicago Press, 1991). By contrast, *phronēsis*, at least for Aristotle, more directly emphasizes the moral dimensions of practical reasoning.

8 Absent from my discussion of practical reason is any consideration of conscience understood as either an innate awareness of right and wrong or the capacity to grasp the first principles of moral reasoning to seek the good and avoid evil (what medieval Scholatics referred to as *synderesis*). However, tacit within my account is a conception of conscience as a cultivated disposition for right moral reasoning as well as the act of such reasoning (*conscientia/syneidesis*) articulated through the virtue of prudence. Conscience has been a key category in Christian moral thought, yet it is not an inherently theological category. For accounts of its varied intellectual history and uses, see Mika Ojakangas, *The Voice of Conscience: A Political Genealogy of Western Ethical Experience* (London: Bloomsbury, 2013); and Richard Sorabji, *Moral Conscience through the Ages: Fifth Century BCE to the Present* (Chicago: University of Chicago Press, 2014).

Forgive me, Father,

For what I
have done &
what I have
left undone

PART III Living Well with Others

Sojourner Truth was an abolitionist and women's rights activist who combined her own experience of slavery, empirical evidence about slavery, and a fervent theological vision to summon others to change. As she put it: "The Lord has made me a sign unto this nation, an' I go round a-testifyin', an' showin' on 'em their sins agin my people."[1] Sojourner Truth prophetically revealed what was going on as a prelude to demanding that those who heard her change how they lived and then join with her to abolish the system of slavery. She was a witness.

Witness continues the communication and reception of the Word made flesh. As in a court of law, a witness both reveals the truth of the matter and gives authority to the judgment that is made about how to proceed. We trust the judgment because we trust/believe/have faith in the witness who we ourselves deem trustworthy. To be a witness is also a way we become answerable for what we see and hear by making sense of and narrating it to others, and in doing so, we become accountable for how we act or fail to act. Another, theological word for witness is of course "martyr": one who witnesses to an order in which all may flourish in communion with God and each other.[2] The Christian martyr/witness is not an expert or third party who impartially observes and speaks out on behalf of another. Rather, like Sojourner Truth, the martyr is someone who experiences or encounters firsthand what is described, challenging others to see things in a new way and join with them to create something different. They call others to go and do likewise through embodying in their life and action a trust/faith/belief that loving God and neighbor is the only true way to live well, no matter what the cost.

Echoing Sojourner Truth and building on the New Testament, witness, confession, and testimony are important ways Christians conceptualize both the form of the moral life here and now and the role of the church in relation to the world. Through these final chapters, I reflect on what it means to be a Christian witness today, both as individuals and congregations. Through reflecting on the nature and form of contemporary Christian witness, Part III addresses the question "how should we live together?" Any account of a good life must set out a vision of social, economic, and political life with others in which the flourishing of each is interdependent with the flourishing of all, especially the weak and vulnerable and the ecologies from which our life is woven. Being a witness who calls forth faith in others thereby demands two things. On the one hand, it requires judgments about either abolishing, recalibrating, upholding, or transforming existing systems and structures. On the other hand, it entails prefiguring and pointing to what forms of common life are needed if life is to be lived well – which is to say, if God and neighbor are to be truly loved.

At the outset of this book, I suggested that Christian ethics is theology with people in it. In that spirit, these final chapters add up to a theological anthropology that attends to the material, structural, and social conditions of life as lived. Other terms for this kind of analysis include social ethics and political theology. These chapters also constitute a form of pastoral and practical theology. This broad canvas is necessary because the chapters in Part III reflect on ethics at the intersection of the personal and the political; that is, they address how individual and communal moral agency both creates and is constituted by broader systems and structures.

In what follows, I focus on the quality and character of intimate (Chapter 12), economic (Chapter 13), and political (Chapter 14) relations as I take them to be foundational to human flourishing in its social and material dimensions. There are other topics such as war, technology, incarceration, or medicine that could be addressed and that may have a more urgent appeal. However, the three areas I focus on here provide a basic orientation to living well with others. If intimacy, the provisioning of life through work, and the negotiation of a common life through politics are more loving and just, much else follows from that.

Each of the chapters in Part III draws on the categories and frameworks developed in Parts I and II. In doing so, they are case studies of how the three questions that have shaped this book come together in an integrated analysis of specific areas of moral concern. Building on each other, the chapters also form a symphonic piece in three movements. For although I treat intimacy, work, and politics as discrete topics I am *not* suggesting they are completely separate from each other. While each subject has distinct concerns and dynamics, the reality is that intimacy, work, and politics are braided together in our lives. Faithful witness involves weaving them together in distinctive ways, ways that in turn repattern the quality and character of each.

NOTES

1 Quoted from an article by Harriet Beecher Stowe titled "Sojourner Truth, The Libyan Sybil," first published in the *Atlantic Monthly* (April 1863). From *Narrative of Sojourner Truth* (New York: Penguin, 1998 [1884]), 104.

2 My expansive and communal use of the term "martyr" draws on its etymology rather than its association with individual sainthood. That said, it shares with the latter the importance of resolute resistance to unjust authority and steadfast fidelity in the face of suffering and death.

12 Intimacy

Intimacy is a basic building block of a flourishing life. A lack of intimacy and the resulting loneliness and sense of isolation can cause dire physical, mental, and public health problems that in turn diminish our ability to act with and for others.[1] This chapter begins by focusing on intimacy in general, which then frames a more specific focus on sexual intimacy and the intimacies of home. My argument is that vulnerability is an inherent feature of creatureliness that can be metabolized in ways that produce either intimacy or precarity. On my account, intimacy is a moral relation that specifies what love and justice mean in practice. Yet because intimacy entails vulnerability, inherent in intimate relations is the possibility of their inversion and exploitation such that intimacy can both make and unmake us. In addition, I contend that all forms of intimacy – not just sexual intimacy – involve erotic desire and attunement.

This last statement will seem counter-intuitive or even alarming to some. But whether it is love of God, food, sport, or place, love properly understood involves an erotic dimension. Eros is simply a way of naming the sensual, physically energizing, and passionate elements of love. Rather than pathologizing, suppressing, or compartmentalizing it, the erotic/physically desiring/passionate aspects of how we participate in and relate to creation and to God need metabolizing in fruitful ways, ways that generate care and concern for others. This chapter unpacks what it might mean to metabolize the erotic element of life with others in ways that bless rather than curse.

The structure of this chapter echoes the framework set out in Parts I and II. I begin by asking what is going on by listening to creaturely life, Scripture, strangers, those crying out for liberation, and ancestors. I then ask what is to be done, drawing on notions of call, command, rules, and virtues, with the chapter as a whole being an exercise in moral deliberation. The final section considers the question of how to live together in relation to sexual and domestic intimacy, while attending to the material and political dimensions of these aspects of living well.

In writing this chapter, I found myself remembering those close to me who have suffered sexual violence in one form or another and wanted to keep in view their witness to me. So I have tried to attend to the forms of abuse, sexual and otherwise, that can permeate intimate relations. I am also aware that I write this against a backdrop of an almost unyielding emphasis in Christianity down the centuries on male-female relations, how such relations provide the model for relating to God, and the ways this emphasis has denied or delegitimized the joy of other kinds of physical intimacy to so many. I hope that by placing intimacy rather than sex at the center of my discussion, what is said here might enable non-queer folk to be open to listening to and learning from others not like themselves about intimacy – something everyone struggles with yet needs in order to flourish.

INTIMACY DEMANDS AND FULFILLS VULNERABILITY

Intimacy is possible because a condition of being alive is that we are vulnerable. Vulnerability makes possible and finds its fulfillment in intimacy. Theologically understood, vulnerability is a basic condition of creatureliness: to be human is to be mutually vulnerable and connected to God, others, and the rest of creation. Other species too enjoy the good of intimacy, but my focus here is human intimacy.

Vulnerability is often understood only in negative terms as being in a condition susceptible to wounding (its etymological roots). Yet vulnerability per se is not bad. It is an openness basic to creaturely existence that flows out of what I named in Chapter 2 as the metabolic condition of being alive. However, even though vulnerability is not necessarily negative and is a constitutive condition of being a finite creature, it is, in this age before Christ's return, deeply ambivalent and risky. To be vulnerable under conditions of fallenness *is* inherently to be open to wounding and exploitation. Nevertheless, we cannot survive let alone thrive without living into vulnerability. Attempts to deny or overcome it in order to render ourselves autonomous inevitably destroy us, the world around us, and our relationship with God.

An increase in vulnerability can be a positive gain. For example, becoming more emotionally vulnerable is a sign of maturity, enabling us to experience greater compassion and connection and to in turn receive love and reassurance. Intimacy with God emerges through greater vulnerability and openness. As discussed in Chapter 4, wisdom begins with openness and vulnerability to others or what we fear or don't understand. And as explored in Chapter 9, vulnerability is a condition of virtue: for example, courage as a virtue means being constant in pursuit of a good in the face of what is fearful, dangerous, or difficult while at the same time being aware of our own vulnerability and limits. Refusal to acknowledge or be aware of our vulnerability is recklessness, not courage. To pursue invulnerability is to pursue alienation rather than intimacy. Intimacy requires embracing rather than denying interdependency and our entanglement with and need to metabolize human and nonhuman creation. As the wisdom shared across myriad ancestral traditions frames it, all thriving is mutual.

However, in a fallen world, vulnerability can also generate precariousness. That is, it becomes an experience of the fragility of a life open to harm and death. This precariousness in turn becomes unevenly and unjustly distributed. The precariousness of some is deliberately and systematically exploited so that others might render themselves immune. As the philosopher Judith Butler argues, precariousness thereby becomes what she calls "precarity": the politically and economically induced condition whereby some are exposed to insecurity and injury so that others might be less so.[2]

In a fallen world, faithful witness entails cultivating intimacy while alleviating precariousness and seeking to abolish precarity. Such witness recapitulates Christ's life, death, and resurrection. Christ's incarnation renews the possibilities of intimacy through indwelling and healing what it means to be vulnerable. At the same time, as incarnate, Christ was not immune to precarity. In his life and ministry, he was constantly exposed to violence and death through the deliberate actions of others. Through his death and resurrection, conditions for intimacy with God, neighbor, and creation are reestablished amid ongoing precariousness and precarity. In the light of Christ's death and resurrection, precariousness loses its sting and becomes instead an occasion for new forms of intimacy made possible here and now with the sending of the Spirit, forms that prefigure and anticipate the intimacies of eternal life when we shall behold each other face to face and without tears.

Responses to precariousness can generate very different moral and political gestures. For example, buying a handgun is one kind of response to a justified sense of precariousness. But it is one marked by an individualistic attempt to secure the world around me by defending myself or those in my immediate circle of care.[3] Or my justified sense of vulnerability amid a pandemic causes me to stay home, ordering what groceries I need to be delivered. In both instances, my response displaces my precariousness onto others, rendering them subject to precarity. By contrast, joining with others in forms of collective action to ensure better street lighting, responsive and accountable policing, decent education, healthcare, and social welfare is another response to precariousness. But it is one that recognizes how my own security is found in the context of relationships and systems that enable mutual flourishing.

INTIMACY REQUIRES PARTICULARITY

Unlike precariousness, which is a generalized condition, intimacy only emerges through particular kinds of interpersonal and associational life such as friendship, marriage, or ecclesial fellowship. But whether experienced over a candlelit dinner for two or the excited frenzy of watching with fellow fans your team win a close match, intimacy is beset by the scandal of particularity: we cannot be intimate with everyone, everywhere. It is specific and bounded because it demands proximity, whether that proximity is mediated in some way through technology or involves being physically present. Intimacy with these here and now necessitates a lack or refusal of intimacy with those not here. That said, experiences of intimacy can be transformative, enabling the inhabitation of vulnerability and interdependency in creative and life-giving ways in other settings and within forms of non-intimate relations.

The structure of intimacy entails *differentiation without separation.* As a specific form of relation, intimacy generates a sense of both closeness to and distinctness from others. My attuned awareness of being present with my child when reading them a story while they sit on my knee is at the same time and in the same gesture an awareness that the child is not me; we are not the same even as we are enfolded into each other's sense of being present to the world. Or even more intensely, the experience of pregnancy and birth exemplifies creaturely intimacy as entailing bounded participation and individuation.[4]

Intimacy as the experience of coming into one's distinct personhood in and through shared relation is basic to an experience of flourishing. I become fully myself through intimate relations with God, human and nonhuman others, and particular places. Their calling forth of me and my response to them enables me to know myself and to know them. Through intimacy, I come to be and know myself and we build a shared life, both at the same time. But neither I nor the other possesses or grants intimacy. It only exists between us. I can only discover it and in that discovery, I find out something of who I am and who this other or these others are in relation to me.

The form of human intimacy, both between humans and with other species and places, means that true intimacy has a moral not just an affective dimension: it requires mutuality, cooperation, and trust. For this bit of earth to give forth its fruit requires that I don't poison but cultivate it. The wet snout of a dog sniffing my hand as a sign of greeting presumes I will not strike the dog and, in turn, I assume I will not be bitten. A lover's caress trusts the beloved will not return the gesture with scorn. Talking over personal struggles with a close work colleague presumes the conversation will not be aired as gossip the next day or shared on social media. Something is terribly wrong with the quality and character of the relationship in all these instances should the latter happen.

Precisely because intimacy involves insider knowledge, close familiarity, and a sense of self through being enfolded into the presence of another or present to a particular place, it is open to abuse, betrayal, and exploitation. Intimacy inherently entails risk. Theologically, the ambiguities and risks of intimacy emerge from the ambiguities of being creaturely. Our creaturely flesh is frail and can be hurt. It is mortal and impermanent; like the grass, it decays and dies.[5] Yet there is no human way of being alive that is not fleshly. And while, by itself, flesh cannot inherit the kingdom of God, *all* flesh is a gift from God and Spirit breathed.[6] Flesh becomes the incarnate Word and is resurrected to eternal life. Thus, to be human flesh is to be open to wounding and a site of wonder. And, like the disciple, Thomas, we always encounter wounds and wonder together in our intimacy with the risen flesh of Christ, through whom and in whom we discover our own humanity. This is enacted at the Eucharist where the church liturgically rehearses the death and resurrection as the context for the Word becoming flesh in our lives so that we in turn might be living sacrifices, that is, signs of communion with God who, through this intimacy with God, are able to bless creation.

The ways in which intimacy, east of Eden, is woven from threads of woundedness and wonder presents us with an acute experience of finitude and fallenness. We need intimacy with others if we are to come to a sense of who we are as persons, yet those intimate others can hurt and disfigure us precisely at our points of deepest need: the need for love and recognition. Even at its best, intimacy in the earthly city has a mercurial quality. It can be spontaneous and carefully nurtured, intangible and visceral, a gift and a work, intuitive and deliberate. It can be discovered with either friends or strangers. It is both desired and feared, comforting and awkward. It takes us out of ourselves in ecstasy while also making us acutely self-conscious.

For most of us, most of the time, intimacy is difficult. Through it we both come together and come undone. In our quest for intimacy, we discover our own inability to connect, our rejection of others, our defensiveness and preference for illusions of control and autonomy that keep us from intimacy. We long for intimacy but too often we cannot bring ourselves to say the words or make the gesture that would bridge the gap between yearning and connection. We remain silent out of fear of rejection, contempt, or exposure; or because our own anger, sloth, shame, distraction, or preening self-regard prevents us from reaching out. But such inaction tastes of death, entombing us as we hold back and betray ourselves and others through these silences. Do we have the courage and hope to discover between us the words and actions that would bring healing and turn loneliness into companionship, recrimination into forgiveness, discord into reconciliation? Discovering the right gestures and words is ethical (and often political) work that brings new life, but it is fragile, emotionally arduous work that can leave us drained, and which is more easily if tragically left undone.

Intimacy goes wrong, often in grotesque and evil ways, when we fail to respond appropriately to how, as a creaturely moral relation, intimacy looks two ways at once. Either we deny how it involves mutual participation or we deny how it entails individuation. In the first case, we exploit the ways intimacy establishes connection and closeness, refusing interdependence, so that the other emerges as an enemy to be defeated or destroyed. In the second case, we fail to recognize the distinctiveness intimacy brings into being, denying or silencing the otherness of the other. This has the same effect of breaking down the pattern of interdependence. The difference is that in this second case, the other emerges as either an inferior who can be preyed upon and exploited or is seen as an extension of me and so can be assimilated and used for my own purposes. The subjugation and exploitation of Hagar by Abraham and Sarah is one of many examples from Scripture of this latter failure.[7] By contrast, true intimacy values differentiation without separation, maintaining generative boundaries within interdependent patterns of relationship.

DIVINE AND HUMAN INTIMACY

A full cataloging of how Scripture portrays and describes intimacy with God, neighbor, and creation is beyond the scope of this chapter. However, a few texts drawn from across the Bible help delineate what is going on when it comes to intimacy in the earthly city.

The iconic depiction of primal intimacy between God, humans, and the rest of creation given in Genesis 2 haunts the rest of Scripture. Here is a time and place when humans can stand naked and unashamed before each other, the rest of creation, and God. Ever after, and always for us, intimacy carries the risk of betrayal, violation, and shame even as it is necessary for healing and flourishing. Something of this ambivalence is spoken of in the Song of Songs, a Scripture the Jewish and Christian traditions have turned to repeatedly, both for celebrating human sexual intimacy and as an allegory for the erotic nature of divine and human intimacy.[8] With its complex poetic structure, the text invites highly figural, multilayered interpretations. However, I present here a more "plain sense" reading.[9]

From its opening verse – "Let him kiss me with kisses of his mouth, for your caresses are better than wine!" – the book explores a fierce desire for but also the risks of intimacy in a violent world. It opens with an almost Edenic picture where the sexual intimacy of the lovers is woven out of and into creation that itself blossoms in ecstatic abundance.[10] But in Chapter 3, we find one of the lovers frantically searching for the other in the city at night while evading capture by nightwatchmen (3:3). This is a context where the lovers' precariousness is contrasted with the royal invulnerability of Solomon, who can travel through the wilderness and the city in luxury and without threat because he has a large armed guard (3:6–11). This scenario is played out again in Chapter 5, only this time sanctuary is not found with the beloved; instead, the nightwatchmen capture, strip, and beat the woman (5:7). At this moment of desolation, she calls to the "daughters of Jerusalem" for help. And over and against the violence used to police her behavior through publicly humiliating her, she reclaims her body as a meeting point of pleasure and play through her exuberant poetic descriptions of her beloved's physical appearance and how this calls forth from her visceral delight and joy. These descriptions, declared out loud to the daughters of Jerusalem, boldly speak forth her continued desire for her beloved and constitute a refusal to be defined by the brutality meted out to her at the hands of the militia (5:10–16).

There are three responses to the threat of violence in this earthly city and the ways the lovers' social and structural situation tear them apart. One is escape. The lovers themselves contemplate fleeing the city to the villages where they can be together without threat or censure (7:11–13). Another is security and control. The woman's siblings try to intervene to protect her but also to control her, cutting her off from risk but also from the erotic energy that is life-giving. In a vision of paternalistic violence, the siblings consider walling her in (8:8–9). But with a bawdy humor, the woman refuses to be made secure under their terms, which is to say, imprisoned. Over and against the demeaning designation of her as a "little sister" (8:8), she asserts she is her own person who can determine her own actions. In doing so, she recognizes that in the eyes of her beloved she is called forth as one who brings peace, not a chaos that needs containing (8:10).[11]

The final response is the one that characterizes the standpoint of the poem. It is her determination toward a risk-laden mutual intimacy with her beloved. The vision of creational flourishing and abundance that is woven through this vision contrasts with the characterization of the royal political economy as one of extraction based on unliteral power that brings money but no intimacy (8:11–12). In contrast to the earlier depiction, Solomon, the supposed lover-king par excellence, is portrayed in this chapter as living in a cold world of predictable, contractual relations that stands as a counterpoint to the erratic and erotic physical intimacy of the lovers.

Commentators point to the dream-like, fractal quality of the book, its fragmentary form and enigmatic imagery speaking to the fugitive, episodic nature of our experiences of intimacy, whether with God, a beloved, or the places we inhabit. The book's dialogic form speaks to how intimacy is not something I possess or can control but must be discovered and carefully cultivated – not only between myself and another but also with a wider social context, signaled in this poem by the "daughters of Jerusalem" who stand as witnesses to the lovers' relationship. For all its elaborate poetry, the book is clear-eyed and direct about the fact that intimacy must be sought and nurtured amidst a constant threat of violence and many constraints – both personal and societal – that keep us from either finding or realizing the intimacy we yearn for, whether with God or another human. Others can try to protect us from harm, but that cuts us off from what we need to flourish and is more often than not paternalistic and patriarchal in form and intent. We can try to flee to a solipsistic world of safety or comfort but that itself is a fantasy. Instead, we have to risk ourselves to a love that is undeterred by the threat of death and to a closeness that money can't buy (8:6–7). Trusting ourselves to this intimacy, for all its fragility, is the condition of *shalom*, signified in the poem through the blossoming of creation.

It would be an easy mistake to interpret the Song of Songs through the grid of the romantic myth, wherein someone else completes us. This is *a* if not *the* dominant narrative by which many today understand the ordering of sexual relations and intimacy. The classic formulations of the romantic myth in the West are Tristan and Iseult, Lancelot and Guinevere, and Romeo and Juliet; but in myriad variations it is retold in advertising, TV series, movies, plays, operas, pop songs, and novels. The basic elements of the story involve true love falling like a spell or cataclysm and not as something cultivated over time. The couple on which it falls is special, yet their love goes against the grain of their immediate social circle and is thereby ill-fated. Their romantic love is realized fitfully and clandestinely or against great adversity – or in the romcom and sitcom versions against adversity played to comic effect (will Rachel and Ross in *Friends* get it together or not?). Sexual union is the mark of that fleeting fulfillment. And rather than unfolding commitment, romantic love can only end in death, for true love is too good for this sordid world. Quintessentially, love is understood as desire exquisitely deprived. The romantic myth offers a powerful "good news" story about individual transcendence and rest from our longing for fulfillment. But it is a very different passion narrative to one about a God who out of desire for relationship with us endures pain, struggle, and death so that we might find rest and fulfillment in communion with God, neighbor, and all creation.

Within the romantic myth, sexual intercourse takes on a redemptive quality as it breaks the individual out of their solitariness through a return to an original wholeness experienced fleetingly in sexual ecstasy with the beloved. When two lovers come together, the wound of division is healed. Thus, sexual ecstasy ceases to be a creational pleasure and is given metaphysical or ontological value, thereby becoming over-burdened with significance. This is where the taking up of the Song of Songs as an allegory for divine-human intimacy, an intimacy both situated in and serving the flourishing of a wider meshwork of human and nonhuman relations, is so important. And it is this connection to redemption in and through Jesus Christ rather than a self-serving sexual ecstasy that I now turn. In the salvation story of the Gospels, eros and intimacy are neither exclusively sexual nor reserved for the domain of romantic relations. Intimacy and eros are central to any and all forms of flourishing life.

As an allegory, the Song of Song foreshadows the Gospels.[12] Like the Shulamite woman, Jesus is stripped and beaten yet is undeterred in his pursuit of love, the fruit of which is *shalom* for all creation. At a more granular level, the Gospels depict Jesus enjoying moments of intimacy in his ministry in ways that echo the Song of Songs. To take but one example, the friendship Jesus enjoys with Mary, Martha, and Lazarus is set within a context of precarity and death. In John's Gospel, Jesus is constantly under threat of being stoned or imprisoned. One such incident occurs in John 10 when once again Jesus evades arrest and takes flight (John 10:39–40). It is against this backdrop that Jesus hears that his beloved friend Lazarus is mortally ill (11:3). The delay in Jesus traveling to be with Lazarus is perplexing unless read against the backdrop of his recent escape. The disciples are reluctant to go whatever the circumstances. Their response to Jesus when he proposes going back to Judea to be with Lazarus is one of astonishment that he would return to a context where the people there had just tried to stone him (11:8). They realize that upholding the bonds of friendship entails a direct threat to their lives. Jesus insists on going and so the disciples resign themselves to possible death: "Thomas, who was called the Twin, said to his fellow-disciples, 'Let us also go, that we may die with him'" (11:16). Later, when Jesus is arrested, they lose their nerve and flee or lie to avoid capture. In anticipation of his eventual arrest and as a consequence of Lazarus being raised, the authorities intensify their plans to kill Jesus such that Jesus and his disciples must once again hide (11:45–57). As part of their deliberations the authorities give a classic utilitarian justification for intentionally exposing someone to death for the sake of the immunity and security of others: "it is better for you to have one man die for the people than to have the whole nation destroyed" (11:50).

A further incident involving Mary, Martha, and Lazarus speaks to the nature of intimacy and its enemies. In John 12, amid the setting of friends sharing a meal, Mary of Bethany anoints Jesus's feet with nard. It is an erotically charged gesture of extravagant abundance and physical affection that at the same time is haunted by Jesus's coming death (John 12:2–3, 7). Its reception echoes the Song of Songs. But instead of nightwatchmen and family to police what is happening, there is Judas Iscariot's scolding dismay. Rather than being moved by a beautifully tender act between friends, Judas reacts with an aggrieved sense of entitlement: Mary is sharing what, misogynistically, Judas thinks is not hers to give, and she has taken from him what he considers his to receive. Like the political economy of Solomon, it is money and its effects that are Judas's focus, yet it is just such an economy that Mary's intimate act disrupts and transfigures: nard becomes a gift of anointing and sign of care rather than being used as either an adornment signifying social status or sold to generate the means of patronage to secure clients and thereby political influence (12:4–6).[13] Following Jesus's consistent response to how the social conventions and established authorities try to constrain or narrate him, Mary refuses the terms and conditions of agency the world offers her. She reframes the world and its possibilities through her gesture. We see reality differently through her actions. And like the lovers in the Song of Songs, Mary and Jesus, accompanied by

witnesses, are mutually vulnerable together without shame. In a world exposed to death at every turn, it is this mutual vulnerability with others – whether as lovers, family, friends, church members, or colleagues – that Jesus's life, death, and resurrection opens as "the way" and, like Mary, the church is to bear witness to this way of being in the world. Refusing the terms and conditions of action as offered by the world and instead walking in this intimacy-generating, Christ-like way requires conversion. For what that entails, Paul's conversion is emblematic.

As readers, we first meet Paul as Saul, one who is raising himself up in the world through persecution (Acts 8:1–3). The prospering of what he cherishes is secured through the death and imprisonment of others. Then on the road to Damascus he is knocked down. In Caravaggio's famous Renaissance painting of the conversion scene, Paul is thrown off a horse. There is no horse in the text, but Caravaggio captures well the figural elements of Paul's descent. The horse symbolizes Saul's reliance on state power and the markers of elite status to gain standing and prestige. As New Testament scholar Brittany Wilson contends, fundamental elements of Paul's identity, particularly his masculinity, are recalibrated and transformed through his conversion as he goes through a process of dis-identification with hegemonic signifiers of power – which in his day as in ours emphasized the need to be invulnerable and exercise self-control.[14] He is blinded. Such disablement is a sign of stigma. He must be led by Ananias and so lacks self-mastery, which is a source of shame. He loses command of the soldiers and fails in his mission, so lacks military honor. He must be cared for and financially supported by others and so is a client rather than a patron, which is to be without political power in the Greco-Roman world. And finally, he is not a father and is celibate, so lacks virility and has no children to carry on his name. Thus his conversion transforms his relationship to the world around him. He cannot rely on worldly means to achieve his goals or to gain status. Quite the reverse: the means of earthly power become instruments of his persecution.

Paul's encounter with Christ does not lead him to transcend or escape the world. Rather, he becomes more vulnerably enmeshed within it even as he ceases to be of it. He can no longer watch impassively while another is stoned to death and consider this a righteous and just act. Instead, he is saddled with care and becomes prepared to suffer extreme hardship for the sake of others. His letters are suffused with compassion, tenderness, frustration, and anxiety for those he is called to love. He endures shipwreck, imprisonment, and other dangers for people he names and communities he knows. In short, his conversion renders him vulnerable to the risks, tragedies, betrayals, and joys of finite and fallen relationships.

As the example of Paul's conversion suggests, freedom in Christ is not based on escaping relations of dependency and care. And contrary to how it is so often understood in both the ancient and the modern world, neither is it premised on a movement *from* the household understood as a private realm of necessity and nurture, *to* the public arena of politics understood as the realm of liberty, autonomy, and equality. Rather, becoming free involves cultivating the ability to inhabit relations of dependency, intimacy, and care more justly and lovingly, wherever they occur. The realization of human freedom comes through, not despite, relations of dependency and care.

INTIMACY WITH OTHERS AMID CRIES FOR LIBERATION

Under fallen conditions, intimacy tends to be indexed to domination so that, as Scripture bears witness, we must hear the cry of those subject to conditions of precarity if we are to understand what true intimacy entails here and now. An acute historic example of this is chattel slavery as it emerged in the early modern Atlantic world. For example, the world of intimacy and frivolous domesticity Jane Austen depicts in her novel *Mansfield Park* is dependent on maintaining slave-worked sugar plantations in Antigua to supply and resource it.[15] Intimate domesticity for some required the brutal exploitation of others and the destruction of the ecologies they called home. Conversely, those subject to regimes of exploitation and extraction are denied the conditions for cultivating and sustaining intimacy. Intimacy for the slaveholder and his wife in the plantation house was premised on refusing intimacy to the enslaved mother and her children who were property to be bought and sold and so could be parted at any moment. The 1662 British colonial law in North America of *partus sequitur ventrem* dictated children of enslaved women inherited the mother's status. Consequently, children were not kin but property to be bought and sold. As the Black feminist scholar Hortense Spillers puts it: "The child, though flesh of her flesh, did not 'belong' to her, as the separation of mothers and children becomes a primary social motif of this 'peculiar institution.'"[16] In the eyes of the slaveholder and the system of racial capitalism he operated within and reproduced, slaves did not get to have family life (that was reserved for white slave owners) and men and women did not get time together to be intimate (slaves had no leisure time). However, slavery could not annihilate intimacy between those treated as slaves: kinship and the shared sociality of spirit breathed flesh are always more basic and in excess of that which desecrate and violate them.[17] But the brutal conditions under which intimacy was found between those enslaved were "stolen moments" and the intimacy they cultivated with God in the brush harbor was secret and seditious.

Echoing my distinction between prospering and flourishing in Chapter 9, a question mark hangs over whether what the slaveholder and his family enjoyed was really intimacy at all. Austen suggests as much in *Mansfield Park*: the protagonist Fanny repeatedly observes how what passes for intimacy is really enactments of selfish ambition and solipsistic self-concern. What Austen envisages as authentic intimacy is contrasted with unvirtuous forms of domesticity and can only emerge in the novel through overcoming its false, ill-founded forms. More broadly, the spiritual, psychological, interpersonal, and material conditions required to maintain the system of exploitation and extraction slashes and burns the conditions of meaningful intimacy for the slaveholder: racism assaults the possibility of intimacy between Blacks and Whites, sexism and paternalism render it brittle between men and women, class differences keep rich and poor apart, ideals of masculinity as impervious and self-controlled prohibit male intimacy, capitalism put everyone in competition with each other, and an extractive economy renders toxic relations between humans and the rest of creation. All these were features of the system, mobilized to keep it in place, and acted as catalysts and pathways for overt violence used to enforce its norms (lynching, domestic abuse, beatings, etc.).

Trying to render oneself immune to precariousness through exploiting the vulnerability of others destroys the possibilities of intimacy for the oppressor as much as if not more so than for the oppressed. As Harriet Jacobs observes in her 1861 memoir *Incidents in the Life of a Slave Girl*: "slavery is a curse to the whites as well as to the blacks."[18] This is the perversity of systemic injustice: oppressors count as a blessing what is a curse of their own making. Martin Luther King Jr.'s invocation of beloved community – itself a vision of revolutionary intimacy – is an explicit counter to this dynamic. For King, the proactive nonviolent overcoming of injustice that culminates in beloved community as its end represents at the same time the liberation of oppressors as well as the oppressed.[19] That is why it is so radical in both its analysis of the problem of racism and what it prescribes as the response.

Slavery may seem like an extreme example, but the modes of alienation just outlined are still present today and continue to act as vectors of violation. Moreover, it illustrates in a stark form how conditions of injustice and oppression prohibit intimacy through promoting ideologies of autonomy and solipsistic self-concern. The tragic irony is that the invulnerability and alienation generated through violently redistributing precariousness is only possible because of a more basic interconnectedness. Complex meshworks of trade, political alliances, and linguistic, agricultural, and culinary borrowings made the development of the Atlantic slave trade and plantation system possible even as this political economy/ecology generated exploitative and extractive relations at every level. Alienation, exploitation, and extraction are premised on and feed off a more basic connection. And this brings me to a vital theological insight: intimacy is not reducible to just another combination of power and pleasure and humans don't find intimacy despite domination. Domination – even in its most brutal forms – distorts and is parasitic on a more basic interdependency of which intimacy as a moral relation is an expression.

Ideologies of autonomy invert what is going on by denying a more fundamental interdependency and the innumerable ways intimacy can be articulated through it. But the problem of valuing autonomy and independence over the realities of vulnerability and interdependence is not just ideological. It is also a matter of affective ideals and regimes, particularly of masculinity. Standing in stark contrast to the conversion of Paul outlined earlier, these take manifold form, including the ideal of the magnanimous self-sufficient man, Stoic visions of the man who is above being affected by and suffering with those around him, chivalric conceptions of honor, the British stiff upper lip, the North American self-made man, and notions of machismo. These and numerous other iterations of "true manhood" entail emotional invulnerability, self-control, self-sufficiency, and a self-regard manifested in hypervigilance about matters of pride and honor. Each of these iterations is better characterized by how Dante's *Inferno* envisages Satan: an isolated figure suspended in ice, unaffected by the world around him, yet radiating evil effects. Crises of intimacy more often than not have their roots in visions of the ideal human as an autonomous and detached subject (mostly coded in masculine terms) struggling to maintain a world of competition and status acquisition rather than cooperation and thereby destructively rather than fruitfully metabolizing creation. Hearing the cries of those subject to conditions of precarity punctures such fantasies, revealing the absence of intimacy in a world where prospering for some is ideologically redescribed as flourishing for all.

This need to listen to those crying out for liberation and healing cuts deep into what it means to be church, as the very attempt to utter the words or make the gestures that move us toward intimacy with God can themselves be weaponized to do evil. For example, sexual abusers may deploy the concept of forgiveness to secure a victim's silence. Forgiveness thereby becomes a weapon to inflict deeper wounds. Hilary Scarsella and Stephanie Krehbiel cite a disturbing incidence of this dynamic. The following is quoted from someone abused by their father: "My dad would come into my room and fondle me at night. Before he'd even leave, he would demand that I forgive him. He said that if I ever told anyone, even when I was an adult, it meant that I hadn't really forgiven him. I would go to hell because God wouldn't forgive me."[20] Here intimacy is exploited to prey upon the vulnerability of the child. Instead of a site of disclosure nurtured through care by which the child becomes a distinct person in relation to others, the child's body is turned against the child. The sexual abuse of children is a particularly horrific example of how exploitation desecrates a prior vulnerability and connection.[21]

In the above instance, recourse to the language of forgiveness as a means of silencing points to the way in which this kind of exploitation depends not on dehumanizing the one violated but on seeing them as fully human, as one capable of forgiveness. As examined in Chapter 4, dehumanizing or objectifying others can be a prelude to their brutalization. But intimate partner violence and child abuse operate in a different register. The abuse depends on and feeds off seeing the abused as owing human care and affection to the abuser. Commenting on domestic violence between heterosexual couples, the philosopher Kate Manne notes:

> In this economy of moral goods, women are obligated to give to him, not to ask, and expected to feel indebted and grateful, rather than entitled. This is especially the case with respect to characteristically moral goods: attention, care, sympathy, respect, admiration, and nurturing. The flipside of this is his being entitled to take much in the way of these moral goods, including – it would seem – the lives of those who can no longer give him what he wanted in terms of moral succor.[22]

Manne points to acid attacks on women as an extreme example of this everyday dynamic. The reasons given for the attacks are the refusal of marriage, the denial of sex, and the rejection of romance.[23] The attacks both punish women for not providing the desired intimacy and disfigure them so that they are unable to enjoy intimacy with others.

COVENANTAL FAITHFULNESS

God calls the whole person into intimacy with God, neighbor, and creation, and we hear and respond to God's call in and through our intimate relations. The theologically normative way of framing how humans are to respond to God's call to intimacy is the need for forms of covenantal faithfulness. Covenantal faithfulness is the context in which mutuality, cooperation, and trust can be cultivated and intimacy pursued as a specification of love and justice.[24] But, while covenantal faithfulness lends itself to these things, it cannot guarantee them.

Too often, the need for covenantal faithfulness as a fruitful context in which to cultivate intimacy translates into the attempt to create specific zones or bounded territories within which intimacy is legitimate and outside of which it is illegitimate. These zones are constructed along the lines of what in Chapter 4 I called the logic of approximation, whereby the good is identified with a fixed ideal or singular way of acting to which all must approximate. Being moral is constituted through taking up a particular position on a hierarchy of status with some representing the ideal, some more closely approximating the ideal, and others representing its perversion.[25] Rather than openness to vulnerability being a measure of moral maturity – with all the risks this entails – being moral is evaluated by invulnerability to sin marked by self-control and boundary keeping (a common ethical operation in legalistic forms of Christian morality). However, attempts to fix intimacy within a bounded territory or identify it with a limited set of actions fail to understand that, as with a need for food, none can flourish without intimacy. Moreover, like what counts as good food and ways of eating, intimacy takes myriad forms. There are ways that a need and desire for food can be abused or exploited.

Moreover, eating has limits. However, no one doubts that food is a basic good of being alive or asks whether it is worth taking the moral risk of eating. It should be the same with intimacy. The questions to ask of intimacy are about its form, quality, and character not whether there can or should be intimacy between persons.

A prevalent example of the territorial approach is fixing intimacy within marriage alone, with marriage framed as a bounded territory. Legalistically setting up fixed terms and conditions for intimacy (as against the rules of thumb discussed in Chapter 10) absolves me from the need for prudential judgments about what form intimacy should take in these circumstances if the flourishing of each is to be cultivated. To territorialize intimacy also generates a form of sanctioned license by saying that whatever happens in that territory is automatically good, thereby masking or legitimizing abuse within it. Setting fixed boundaries for "good" intimacy ironically prevents the complexities of true intimacy.

On the other hand, attempts to overcome legalism by saying intimacy with anyone, anywhere is possible deny the ways that intimacy requires proximity and vulnerability over time. Which brings us back to covenantal faithfulness as the context for cultivating intimacy over time with others. However, rather than a territory to be defended or a narrowly prescribed set of actions to be performed, such covenantal relations are a way of talking about a set of virtues and practices through which we learn to relate fruitfully and truthfully and through which we metabolize creation in ongoing, dynamic ways. Marriage understood in this way, as an expansive social practice and vocation, is very different from marriage understood as a bounded territory. Echoing Chapter 9, virtues and practical wisdom are needed to determine what gesture or word at this time with this person will either generate or sustain intimacy and bear truthful witness – whether between those who are married or not. Some may consider the following example either foolish, prudish, or trivial, but it speaks to the quotidian nature of these practical judgments and how intimacy as a form of mutual care resists codification. It seems entirely appropriate that, when meeting a beloved friend for coffee at a conference at 11 a.m., a friend who is also a junior female colleague (with all the dynamics of institutional power that our relative positions entail), I give her a hug and express effusive delight in seeing her. The same gesture after talking through the day's events over a few drinks in the hotel bar at 11 p.m. may or may not be appropriate. The combination of banter, serious conversation, drink, touch, and praise can take on a very different social signification at 11 p.m. than at 11 a.m., even if done in the same spirit. The same person and gesture but different circumstance of realization requires a different judgment about what is and what is not appropriate. At the same time, legalistic avoidance of either situation for the sake of conventions of either professional or religious propriety is a refusal of intimacy and a choice for alienation.

Jesus is constantly interpreted by juridical authorities and customary conventions as being intimate with the wrong people in the wrong places, yet this intimacy upholds and bears witness to what covenantal faithfulness with God and neighbor looks like. Likewise, as part of the 1906 Azusa Street revival, Black men laying hands on White women and vice versa in Jim Crow America so that each could receive the Holy Spirit contravened racial, gender, and class norms in order to restate covenantal faithfulness in a way that, judging from newspaper reports at the time, was scandalous in its day. To many it still is. With respect to marriage, it is worth remembering that the New Testament is decidedly ambivalent about it, suggesting its moral value is not automatic or simply given but must be understood by how marriage relates to God.[26] Rigid adherence to a prescribed set of rules or code of conduct will not give us the right words or gestures. Sometimes the word or gesture to make is one that transgresses a conventional norm because how we have come to understand that norm – say about who can and who cannot get married – is so bound up with an unjust status quo that the norm itself needs radically reconfiguring.

The forms of intimacy Jesus and the Azusa Street revival embody are at once scandalous and revolutionary because they overturn at the inmost level what is alienated. It is also why such acts of transgression are so vehemently policed and surveilled, miscegenation laws being but one example. Intimacy between Blacks and Whites punctures the affective veil of racism that keeps one set of people untouchable and undesirable to another, thereby stigmatizing ecclesial, political, and other forms of solidarity that cross the color line. Intimate touch can thus be a simple but profoundly revolutionary gesture. As with the woman afflicted with bleeding, rather than becoming a source of pollution through touching the wrong people as convention dictated, touching Jesus brought healing (Mark 5:25–34). Holiness and wholeness, not defilement and violation, are called forth through her transgressive gesture. That said, intimacy that transgresses conventional pieties is not inherently or inevitably moral. Transgression should not be made into a procedure: it cannot make something automatically good, just as conforming to existing social norms is not automatically bad. What matters is the pursuit of intimacy with virtue and keeping the ends of love and justice in view. Both transgressive and conventional forms of intimacy can render the other a thing to be instrumentalized for my own self-gratification.

Fornication is but one instance of a dynamic that exploits vulnerability, pursuing intimacy without virtue. I use the term fornication in its broadest sense and in a way that draws on its etymological roots to refer to sex that exploits others to extract self-gratification from them. It pays no regard to their flourishing and divorces sexual pleasure from actively fostering a shared world of meaning and purpose with another.[27] The sin of fornication renders the other an object to be used rather than a person to be enjoyed, with sexual caresses, penetrative or otherwise, becoming opposed to rather than fostering intimacy over time. Like the insatiable and destructive desire for money that renders everything for sale (*pleonexia* – another sin that exploits and explodes the conditions of intimacy), fornication names an extractive desire to possess. It knows no limit and instrumentalizes others, thereby denying distinction and disabling differentiation. Far from an attuned, enfolded presence with and for another, fornication obliterates the otherness of the other and in the process demeans them and defaces oneself.[28] This obliteration can be reciprocal. Fornication forecloses the possibility of true intimacy because it centers entirely on my self-directed desires rather than the discovery of a shared desire through becoming attuned to another who might challenge, redirect, or transform my existing desires. In this way, the fornicator shuts out both God and the desired one in a gesture of domination. The contrast is with intimacy that draws forth both oneself and another to be more than and at the same time fully each other. Neither transgression nor a particular state such as marriage guarantees such intimacy.

The opposite of fornication is communion. Indeed, fornication can be seen as communion trying to happen but being misdirected to alienating ends.[29] Fornication is desire truncated. It is desire that lacks the imagination and capacity to be liberated for communion, thereby refusing its own possibility to reach out beyond the self, settling instead for the shriveled pleasures of solipsism.[30] Hence the use of fornication as an analogy in Scripture for idolatry (e.g., Jer 2:20; Ezek 23). Fornication is not merely an analogy for idolatry but, as a bodily gesture, a form of apostasy from the covenant with God. Idolatry/fornication dissolves the conditions for divine-human communion and covenantal faithfulness by instrumentalizing creation for projects of self-glorification that in turn deny God and generate domination. On this account, fornication is not first and foremost a matter of personal morality but one of idolatry and political economy.

Arguably, in light of the above account, bourgeois notions of intimacy are intrinsically characterized by fornication. As cultural critic Lisa Lowe argues, intimacy has become a site for the reproduction of the autonomous, self-reflexive, property-owning subject.[31] I have intimate experiences that I possess. They are particular to me and cannot be understood without my dictating them in my own terms. Far from being discovered between us, and thereby its meanings and purposes existing beyond me, no one else can tell me what intimacy means or what its purpose is. I see intimacy as my possession to bestow. Within such a conception, the otherness of the other is irrelevant, because intimacy is merely a means of self-realization. Intimacy understood in this light – that is, as means of expressing one's identity – is indexed to the home conceptualized as a private domain constructed as a site of consumer display. The home marks who I am through the furniture I buy, the TV I watch, the kitchen counters I install, and what I do for pleasure in that private space. The home is the place where I am released from the impersonal, bureaucratic world of work and the fractious world of politics. As we increasingly work at home and politics divides households, intimacy itself is somehow under threat. Conversely, intimacy outside the home, particular in the form of touch, is now either sexualized or medicalized and in both instances, pathologized.

Without question, any conception of a flourishing life – Christian or otherwise – must reckon with sex and kinship structures as part of the fabric of being alive. Everyone comes from someone. Theologically, familial relations are a key realm within which we hear and respond to God's address, even if this is a call to renounce the ties of a biological family so as to serve God in the intentional family of a monastic or some other kind of community. As an inherent part of being alive, relations with kith and kin (biological or otherwise) need metabolizing in sustaining and fruitful ways. Yet, in the contemporary context, churches and society in general are deeply divided over questions about how best to order familial and sexual relations. While important, those arguments deflect attention away from addressing the ethics of intimacy, which I contend is a more basic and universal dimension of human flourishing. Not all need or desire sex, but even the solitary hermit desires intimacy with God. And we can radically disagree over judgments about the ordering of sexual relations even as we learn from each other about how better to sustain faithful, hopeful, and loving intimacy. A form of life without sex – as monasteries demonstrate – can be a meaningful and purposeful enterprise. A life without intimacy is either a brittle and short-lived affair or a sign of an all-encompassing domination, as in a prison isolation wing. That said, it is to questions of sexual and domestic intimacy that I now turn.

SEXUAL INTIMACY AS A MORAL RELATION

To be intimate with someone is a euphemism for sexual intercourse. As a euphemism, it points to how intimacy is often conflated or wholly identified with sex. As an experience of mutual vulnerability, physical closeness with another through touch, smell, and taste, emotional entwining, and sensate pleasure, sex can be a profound moment of intimacy. But as I have argued here, forms of intimacy can be discovered in myriad other kinds of encounter as well. And contrary to a bourgeois view of intimacy, sexual intimacy is not something I possess or choose. As with other forms of intimacy so with sexual intimacy: it is not something that can be generated from one side. It only exists between oneself and another, and it is reciprocal in form. Anglican theologian Rowan Williams puts it this way:

> I cannot of myself satisfy my wants without distorting or trivialising them .... For my body to be the cause of joy, the end of homecoming, for me, it must be there for someone else, be perceived, accepted, nurtured; and that means being given over to the creation of joy in that other, because only as directed to the enjoyment, the happiness, of the other does it become unreservedly lovable. To desire my joy is to desire the joy of the one I desire: my search for enjoyment through the bodily presence of another is a longing to be enjoyed in my body.[32]

Sexual intimacy and its joys are discovered with and through another. As Williams goes on to argue, the perversion of sex rests on the denial or refusal of one's need for the other. True intimacy does not seek to control the other or bypass the risks of vulnerability inherent in sexual relations.

How sexual vulnerability is experienced is coded along gender lines. In the West, women are generally perceived as sexually vulnerable and passive (and thus either available or in need of protection) and men as invulnerable, active agents (and thus either initiators or in need of restraint). A heightened version of this structure operates in much heterosexual pornography where women are portrayed as submissive, powerless objects constantly available for sex, serving men while receiving pleasure from them. Whereas men are portrayed as dominant, active agents who give pleasure. And pornography often portrays this dynamic in physically violent terms, not only normalizing inequality but also eroticizing sexual violence and invulnerability over and against intimacy. It is notable what does not appear in porn: miscommunication, disappointment, negotiating differing expectations, an inability to be present to the moment, the distractions of housekeeping or crying children, and the need for trust. Porn can function as both entertainment and compensation because it divorces coitus from one's own personal vulnerabilities, the intricacies of coexistence, and the role of sexual intimacy in building a shared world of meaning and purpose.

In the contemporary context, where sexuality is often perceived as a personal possession to be spent or saved, there is an inner coherence and connection between seemingly opposed points of view. Some advocate abstention until marriage and chastity within marriage as means of mastering and controlling sexual desire while others press for a kind of entrepreneurial self who exercises self-control through mastering techniques and accumulating sexual experiences as part of taking control of and freely expressing their sexuality. Both stances share an ideal of self-mastery. Yet, as feminist philosopher Erinn Gilson notes, actual experiences of sex reveal how no one is invulnerable and we cannot control or wholly determine who we are sexually.[33] All can heal or harm others through how they respond to another sexually, and sex is situated within and constituted through the flow of communication and webs of signification we inhabit and through which we interpret our sexuality and make sense of our sexual experiences.[34]

Who we become sexually and how our sexual experience shapes our experiences of intimacy is reciprocally related and intertwined with the form, quality, and character of our relations with others.[35] Like all forms of intimacy, sexual intimacy exists within limits and needs structures of formation if it is to be metabolized fruitfully. Conversely, as a way our body takes on and expresses social significance, the ways sex is open to abuse means that abuse is not just physical but also social. As well as inflicting physical and psychological harm, sexual violence attacks a person's standing and significance in a wider web of social relations. A horrific expression of this dynamic is the systematic use of rape in warfare to humiliate not just an individual but also an entire population.

The church has contributed to how intimacy is reduced to sexual intimacy. It has also frequently made the mistake of both isolating sexual desire from the rest of life and conflating erotic desire with sexual desire. Desire for peace, playing sport, food, friendships, etc. all involve erotic but not necessarily sexualized desires. Yet in the contemporary context, we struggle to imagine non-sexualized forms of erotic desire for friends, food, or home. Instead, as per a popular form of Freudianism, desire for these kinds of things is understood to be a repressed form of sexual desire that needs liberating. Consequently, not only is everything seen to be really about sex, but sex is seen to be about nothing else but itself. In this respect, a puritanical church and a libertine culture share the same worldview.

Reframing sex or sexual desire as a means for and directed to cultivating intimacy raises the question of how to desire someone rightly in a way that can behold them nakedly and without shame. Drawing on the full semantic range of the term "naked," this means asking how we encounter ourselves and others as those who are vulnerable. It entails asking what it means to live without pretense, to speak and live truthfully with others. Theologically, this desire to behold and be beheld nakedly and without shame can only be fulfilled eschatologically when we shall see each other with unveiled faces. Until then, we can only catch glimpses, and to do so demands learning to see ourselves and others as first and foremost those who are desired and called by God – who can already see us as who we really are.

Understanding how the whole person is desired and called by God should reframe our moral vision of sex and erotic desire, situating both as a way we might participate in communion with God and neighbor. Theologian Sarah Coakley develops this insight. She suggests that right thinking about sexual desire should not begin by thinking about sex but about what it means to be desired by God and to desire God. Only then can we locate sexual relations and what it means to desire and be conjoined with another through the prism of what it means to desire and be conjoined with God.[36] For Coakley, attention to late antique and medieval mystical theologies (e.g., Gregory of Nyssa, Dionysius the Aeropagite, and, I would add, Dante) demonstrates that, building on Plato, most premodern theologies saw erotic desire as a crucial part of a positive movement toward God.

An important additional point to make here comes from an influential essay by Audre Lorde, who self-describes as a "black, lesbian, mother, warrior, poet." Lorde expands and reframes how to understand the erotic. She rejects limiting the erotic to sexual intimacy. Rather, she sees it is a form of creative, life-giving energy that is generated out of sharing deeply and joyfully any pursuit with another person. For Lorde, erotic energy requires physical, psychic, spiritual, and emotional discipline in relationship with others if it is to be fruitful. Erotic energy and the knowledge that comes through this kind of connection with another person is a way of overcoming numbness and self-negation. It unsettles us from accepting what is convenient, shoddy, or conventionally expected. It is for Lorde the "forerunner for joint concerted actions not possible before."[37]

What Lorde and Coakley bring into view is the need to avoid pathologizing erotic desire and in particular sexually erotic desire. Instead, it needs metabolizing so as to direct it to life giving ends. They also outline how erotic desire is not everything, as in the Romantic myth, but it is something good that, if properly directed and metabolized, finds its fulfillment in communion with God and fruitful relations with creation. Christian ethicist Cristina Traina synthesizes the points Coakley and Lorde make and at the same time connects their vision of erotic desire to a conception of virtue. In naming a virtuous conception of the erotic, Traina rejects the language of temperance as too solitary, chastity as too narrow and inward, and sensuality as too physically exclusive. Instead, she puts forward "erotic attunement," stating that it "possesses both boundaries (there is such a thing as too much, too little, wrong quality) and an extraordinary adaptability to personal taste, immediate situation, and cultural custom." For Traina, erotic attunement

> implies a rhythm of feast and fast, intensity and withdrawal, indulgence and restraint, and it not only permits but demands that we truly enjoy the goodness of touch. But unlike the Thomistic version of temperance and chastity it is centrally, rather than peripherally, interpersonal. That is, it is about sustaining sensual relationship, not only about governing sensation. Attunement – the dance answering the partner's needs and desires – is the substance of the virtue.[38]

Traina contends that part of addressing the prevalence of violent, addictive, and depersonalized expressions of sexuality involves cultivating a wide array of non-sexual forms of intimate erotic sensuality and the kinds of attunement these entail.[39] Eating, singing, dancing, and playing games together with others are all forms of sensuality that generate intimacy and require erotic attunement to go well. The Christian faith wisely contends that intimacy as a moral good realizable in numerous forms of association is one best practiced in relations of covenantal faithfulness. Like erotic desire, covenantal faithfulness is not restricted to marriage as many assume. It is needed between workers and bosses, politicians and voters, ministers and laity, students and teachers, and myriad other institutional and social arrangements in which there is mutual vulnerability and an unequal distribution of precariousness.

One such context for metabolizing erotic desire, whether for food, friendship, or sex through cultivating the virtue of erotic attunement, is that of the home.

HOME AS INTIMACY MADE MATERIAL

I remember taking part in a workshop some years ago with a number of political activists who were far from conventional in their lifestyles. We were asked to draw a picture of home. Almost everyone created some version of what most Western six-year-olds draw: a house with a pitched roof, four windows, a chimney, a door, a path, and a smiling sun in the corner. This image of the single-family dwelling as the picture of home rests on the separation of reproductive and productive labor; that is, living with others, along with the nurture of children, is separated out from the world of paid work and occupies a private space. Only work that takes place outside the home is valued politically and economically, with the result that this separation devalues homemaking as either something done in one's spare time or as an unpaid support structure for "meaningful" work. Moreover, this separation is coded along gender lines, so that homemaking is seen as women's work (which lacks status and visibility) and is done to support male and "public" work, which is often coded with masculine projects of self-realization, such as being a professional, political activism, or achieving recognition in sports. Critics of modern capitalist and patriarchal conceptions of home argue that to treat the household as the primary context for cultivating sexual intimacy is to reproduce this separation and thereby reinscribe a capitalist and patriarchal social order. Yet, as feminist political theorist Iris Marion Young notes, this critique, while in many ways true, misses the creative agency in homemaking and how a sense of home and what it takes to create and provision a household is part of human flourishing.[40] In a similar vein, Black feminist bell hooks points to the importance of a "homeplace" to building and preserving the kinds of meaning vital to generating agency, sustaining dignity, and fostering resistance in the face of oppression.[41]

Conversely, a major form of powerlessness, particularly in the contemporary context, is to be unhomed through displacement. The experiences of the unhomed can be wholly different in kind, ranging as they do from exile, forced migration, kidnapping, enslavement, fugitivity, and imprisonment, to the vagrant, the émigré, the nomad, the troubadour, and the pilgrim. But what unites them is precariousness – whether temporary or permanent – and lacking a place within their immediate context. To be unhomed is to lack status and worth within a place and thereby to have a highly diminished agency and be vulnerable and easily exploitable by others who have the right connections and whose bodies and ways of life have status and worth in that place. Yet it is the unhomed that Jesus likens himself to and asks others to identify with: "As they were going along the road, someone said to him, 'I will follow you wherever you go.' And Jesus said to him, 'Foxes have holes, and birds of the air have nests; but the Son of Man has nowhere to lay his head'" (Luke 9:58).

A homeplace is not to be conflated with or reduced to a physical house or dwelling place. Truck drivers on the road can feel at home even though they are not resident in one place. Home is about the things, places, and people we are intimate with. Familiar objects, landscapes, foods, and smells are vital to constituting a sense of home and a sense of self, even as, for some, these must be transplanted, as is the case for migrants. The homeplace – of which a physical house can be a key part – helps constitute our biography. It is a place through which we come to narrate and describe ourselves and others. As Young notes:

> Dwelling in the world means we are located among objects, artifacts, rituals, and practices that configure who we are in our particularity. Meaningful historical works that embody the particular spirit of a person or a people must be protected from the constant threat of elemental disorganization. They must be cleaned, dusted, repaired, restored; the stories of their founding and continued meaningful use must be told and retold, interpreted and reinterpreted. They must also be protected from the careless neglect or accidental damage caused by those who dwell among and use them, often hardly noticing their meaning as support for their lives.[42]

In other words, domestic housework and cooking make a life and are works of imagination and attention that render love material and tasty.

Homemaking as the ongoing ways we cultivate and preserve space and time for intimacy is always a work in progress and vital moral labor, as it constitutes a basic context and condition for human flourishing. But this biographic sense of home is enfolded into and woven out of fallen and idolatrous constructions of home and this entanglement speaks to the ambivalence of home as a space and time of domestic intimacy. My homeplace is both precious – it helped make me, me – yet it also enmeshes me in reproducing oppressive as well as ecologically destructive ways of dwelling with nonhuman creation. To put this theologically: home as a place where life is created and nourished is also a site that produces sin and idolatry. But as such, it can become a point of repentance and homecoming to God and neighbor, including the rest of creation. In the light of eternity, we can never be fully at home in this fallen world, as it is not our ultimate place of rest and the intimacies we enjoy here are riven with precariousness. At the same time, just and loving homemaking is a way of participating in the reweaving of creation as a homeplace for God, a God who seeks to tabernacle with us amidst our cultures and systems of domination, anticipating here and now eternal Sabbath intimacy and the *shalom* of the new creation.

On this account, home as a site and set of practices for the cultivation of intimacy does not merely serve as a platform for our moral and political lives. Rather, the quality and character of our homeplace is a constitutive way we come to inhabit more just and loving forms of political life. The relationship between homemaking and politics in the cultivation of intimacy is exemplified by how enabling children to have a good childhood takes political struggles for a more just common life.

Childhood is not a modern phenomenon; but it comes to be understood and lived out in specifically modern ways. Central to the modern construction of childhood is that it is distinct from the world of economic production (even as childhood is a key site of consumer display). The ways modern childhood is separated from productive labor is the result of the agricultural and industrial revolutions. But it also emerges through struggles to free children from industrial labor. Most children in the West no longer have to work plantation fields, be sent down mines, or up chimneys. The freedom of all children – not just those of the elite – to be nonproductive members of a household who have the possibility of enjoying intimacy with family and friends rather than being subject to regimes of hard manual labor was a political struggle, one that continues in many parts of the world. To have time and spaces to play and learn, the political and economic conditions necessary for the common good of a childhood – clean air to breathe, roads that are safe to cross, a neighborhood in which you will not be shot at, food that will not poison you, parks to play in, schools that teach rather than act as a pipeline to prison – must be secured through politics.[43] Ensuring the freedom to enjoy childhood as a common good requires resistance to certain political and economic forces "from above" and "from below" that refuse to recognize children as persons either capable of or in need of simply being children (e.g., they are delinquents in need of surveilling, consumers to be targeted, or sexual subjects to be groomed). The need to defend and tend childhood as a shared good through politics points to how a sense of being at home is woven from a common life with and for others far beyond the immediate circle of domestic intimacy.

Home is the materialization of intimacy and a place within which covenantal faithfulness and erotic attunement can be cultivated. My discussion of home leads into Chapter 13, which examines the nature of work, what it means to provision a flourishing life, and how householding is a constituent element of any such endeavor. Like home, the economics of creaturely flourishing cannot be considered as somehow a separate realm from politics, and so this and the next chapter anticipate the consideration of politics in the final chapter.

ACCOMPANYING READINGS

Karen Lebacqz, "Love Your Enemy: Sex, Power, and Christian Ethics," *Annual of the Society of Christian Ethics* 10 (1990): 3–23. Lebacqz reflects on the ethics of intimacy between men and women, with a focus on sexual violence.

David Matzko McCarthy, *Sex and Love in the Home: A Theology of the Household* (London: SCM Press, 2004). In Chapter 5, McCarthy discusses the moral purpose of shared households.

Cristina Traina, *Erotic Attunement: Parenthood and the Ethics of Sensuality between Unequals* (Chicago: University of Chicago Press, 2011), ch. 7. Traina reflects on the ethics of intimacy, and the virtues it requires, with a particular focus on relations between primary carers and children.

James Wetzel, "The Original Sin: Sex and Christian Ethics," *Parting Knowledge: Essays on Augustine* (Eugene, OR: Cascade, 2013), 199–208. Wetzel provides an analysis of the debate between Augustine and Jerome on the relationship between marriage and celibacy.

Thelathia Nikki Young, *Black Queer Ethics, Family, and Philosophical Imagination* (New York: Palgrave Macmillan, 2016), ch. 4. Young examines the ethics of family life and the differing shape and form families can take.

Alberto La Rosa Rojas, "A Migrant at the Lord's Table: A Reformed Theology of Home," *Reformed Public Theology: A Global Vision for Life in the World*, ed., Matthew Kaemingk (Grand Rapids, MI: Baker Academic, 2021). Drawing on the Reformed tradition and his own experiences of migration, this essay sets out a theological framework for narrating what it means to be at home in a world on the move.

NOTES

1 See John Cacioppo and William Patrick, *Loneliness: Human Nature and the Need for Social Connection* (New York: W. W. Norton, 2008).

2 Judith Butler, *Precarious Life: The Powers of Mourning and Violence* (London: Verso, 2004); Judith Butler, *Notes Toward a Performative Theory of Assembly* (Cambridge, MA: Harvard University Press, 2015); Judith Butler, "Rethinking Vulnerability and Resistance," *Vulnerability and Resistance*, eds., Judith Butler, Zeynep Gambetti, and Leticia Sabsay (Durham, NC: Duke University Press, 2016), 12–27. Butler tends to conflate precariousness and vulnerability.

3 The mere fact of recognizing vulnerability does not generate solidarity with others. It can equally generate exclusionary, often violent measures designed to remediate the threat of vulnerability perceived as being caused by others (e.g., immigrants) that then generates a solidarity among those who see themselves as threatened fostered through active opposition to those others.

4 For an exploration of this dynamic in pregnancy and motherhood, an exploration done in dialogue with Augustine, see Natalie Carnes, *Motherhood: A Confession* (Stanford, CA: Stanford University Press, 2020).

5 Lam 3:4; Isa 40:6; Ps 73:26; Ps 78:39; 2 Cor 4:11; Jas 5:3.

6 1 Cor 15:50; Rom 8:5.

7 See Delores Williams, *Sisters in the Wilderness: The Challenge of Womanist God-Talk* (Maryknoll, NY: Orbis Books, 1993), 15–33.

8 In the Christian tradition, Origen (c. 184–c. 253), Gregory of Nyssa (c. 335–c. 394), Bernard of Clairvaux (1090–1153), and Teresa of Ávila (1515–1582) are notable examples of theologians who read the Song of Songs in this way.

9 The reading of the Song of Songs and John 11–12 given here is an instance of theology done *en conjunto*, shaped as it is by studying these texts with Sarah Jobe, Ryan Juskus, Casey Stanton, and Felipe Witchger.

10 The book is read by some as a commentary on Genesis 2–3.

11 Her identification as a Shulamite (6:13) reinforces her self-designation: Shulamite is a derivative of *šlm* from which the word Solomon and *shalom* are derived. I take there to be a figural contrast between the peace the woman represents and that which Solomon does.

12 Other depictions of intimacy in Scripture also echo the Song of Songs. Ruth and Naomi cultivate an adoptive filial intimacy amid famine, interethnic/interreligious conflict, and destitution; Jonathan and David foster an intimate friendship amid war and punitively divided loyalties; and the picture of divine-human and familial intimacy between Jesus, Mary, and Joseph has as its backdrop the slaughter of innocents, imperial systems of domination, and refugeehood.

13 Rather than care being a gesture of accommodation and tacit complicity in a system of domination that patches up the one subject to that system so they can continue within that system and the system can continue unchecked, Mary's gesture reframes care as a sign of resistance and counter-practice to the structures of domination.

14 Brittany Wilson, *Unmanly Men: Refigurations of Masculinity in Luke-Acts* (New York: Oxford University Press, 2015).

15 Against Edward Said's groundbreaking postcolonial reading of *Mansfield Park*, which took Austen to be silent on the question of slavery, much recent research shows it to be an active and explicit theme in the novel. For example, Marcus Wood contends that the novel "contains a caustic assault on the moral basis of British colonial slavery." Marcus Wood, *Slavery, Empathy, and Pornography* (New York: Oxford University Press, 2002), 298. Austen knowingly portrays the connection to question the legitimacy and standing of the aristocratic household.

16 Hortense Spillers, *In Black, White, and in Color: Essays on American Literature and Culture* (Chicago: University of Chicago Press, 2003), 233.

17 This point draws on the work of Hortense Spillers.

18 Harriot Jacobs, *Incidents in the Life of a Slave Girl* (Boston, 1861), 81.

19 Martin Luther King Jr., "Stride Toward Freedom (1958)," *A Testament of Hope*, ed., James Melvin Washington (New York: HarperCollins, 1991), 482–490.

20 Hilary Scarsella and Stephanie Krehbiel, "Sexual Violence: Christian Theological Legacies and Responsibilities," *Religion Compass* 13, no. 9 (2019): 96.

21 On this, see McFadyen, *Bound to Sin*, 57–79.

22 Kate Manne, *Down Girl: The Logic of Misogyny* (New York: Oxford University Press, 2018), 22.

23 Mann, *Down Girl*, 72–73.

24 Mutuality is not a synonym for equality. There is a tendency in Western sexual ethics to assume that as long as sex is between equals and involves consent it is thereby legitimate and ethically unproblematic. This can be its own kind of proceduralism and does not in every instance apply to intimacy, particularly non-sexual intimacy. To put this another way, mutuality in intimacy can involve relations between those of equal agency but does not require it. For example, non-sexual relations between doctors and patients, or students and teachers, or parents and children can be mutual while involving an asymmetry of agency. Rather than the equality of commutative exchange, mutuality involves reciprocity of gift relations where what is exchanged can involve great asymmetry, but which is fitting for and builds up each. For example, what the parent receives from the child in no way matches what the child receives from the parent, but it

is nevertheless fitting and needed by the parent from the child. Abuse involves either giving what is not fitting for this person in this kind of relationship (e.g., sexual attention and touch by a parent to a child) or demanding what is not fitting or needed as a response to what is given (e.g., sexual touch in response to physical or emotional care).

25 The New Testament constantly destabilizes established social hierarchies. This is not necessarily egalitarian in the modern sense of that term, which tends to imply sameness. There is still hierarchy, but it is one of holiness where power is marked by service not domination. Unlike European aristocracies, the status as the best, the most excellent, the most honored, or dignified and virtuous (i.e., the *aristos*), is not tied to blood, gender, or property ownership. Holiness exceeds and is unbound by material conditions. Righteousness is obtainable by anyone who follows Christ with all their heart. This is the witness of the saints whose status as a saint is not dependent on birth or biology and is available to anyone regardless of ethnicity, class, sexuality, or gender.

26 Just to take the Gospels, those verses that value marriage include Matthew 19:3–6 ("Therefore what God has joined together, let no one separate") and the story of the wedding at Cana. There are also those that portray the messiah as a bridegroom (Matt 9:15; Mark 2:19–20; Luke 5:34–35) although these relativize marriage as secondary to relations with God. Likewise, in Jesus's response to the Sadducees, marriage is seen as a created but not an eschatological good (Matt 22:22–33; Mark 12:25; Luke 20:27–38). More negatively, it is envisioned as one possible obstacle to total devotion to God. For example, it is cited as a hindrance that prevents joyful acceptance of the invitation to the messianic banquet, being one of the excuses cited in Luke 14: "I have married and cannot come." Similarly, marriage provides an image of preoccupation with the world when it will be surprised by Christ's return (Luke 17:26–30). And continent singleness is advocated as the best way to serve God (Matt 19:12). With the exception of Clement of Alexandria, most Patristic theologians followed this latter line, championing celibacy over marriage as the truly righteous way. Modern theology has tended to invert this advice, championing marriage over and against celibacy. But as with most moral questions, while Scripture is a vital reference point and catalyst, it alone does not answer the question of what to do and how to do it here and now. We have to make theologically reasoned, practically wise judgments about what to do and how to do it in

response to God's call to us in this place at this time and develop the kinds of loving, faithful, and hopeful character that enable us to make those kinds of judgments.

27 *Porneia* (πορνεία) is often translated as "fornication" or "sexual immorality" in the New Testament. Fornication derives from the Latin translation of *porneia* in the Vulgate, which itself is derived from *fornix* meaning arch or vault (which were places to meet prostitutes). In Greek and Roman contexts, these terms were associated with prostitution, brothels, and the selling of sex. For example, *fornicatio* was a general term for visiting a prostitute. The social context of its meaning was bound up with a political economy of slavery (most prostitutes were male or female slaves) and systems that rendered moral the sexual exploitation of women and men who lacked status and were subject to precarity. Under the influence of the Septuagint and the New Testament, particularly Paul's letters, in Christianity fornication comes to refer to all forms of sexual immorality and carries a valence of that which violates and defiles through misusing one's body and exploiting the vulnerability of another (see especially 1 Cor 6:13–18 where Paul explicitly refers to sex with prostitutes). However, it often takes on a narrower reference to any sexual relations outside of marriage as the counterpoint to adultery (sexual infidelity within marriage).

28 In contrast to intimate partner violence and child abuse, which constitute forms of violent oppression that may or may not take a sexualized form, but which are parasitic on human care, fornication is dehumanizing and objectifying and is constitutively sexual.

29 How fornication is understood needs situating within a wider understanding of erotic desire, which in the Christian tradition is caught between those who see it as inherently irrational and socially disruptive and so in need of strict regulation and those who see erotic desire as serving and finding its fulfillment in communion with God and neighbor (and so is socially generative), even as it can be misdirected to fallen ends. I tend to the latter view.

30 As C. S. Lewis points out, the problem is not yearning for earthly pleasures but that what we desire is too weak. As he puts it: "We are far too easily pleased." C. S. Lewis, "The Weight of Glory," *The Weight of Glory and Other Addresses* (New York: HarperCollins, 2001), 1.

31 Lisa Lowe, *The Intimacies of Four Continents* (Durham, NC: Duke University Press, 2015).

32 Rowan Williams, "The Body's Grace," *Theology and Sexuality: Classic and Contemporary Readings*, ed., Eugene F. Rogers (Oxford: Blackwell, 2002), 313.

33 Erinn Gilson, *The Ethics of Vulnerability: A Feminist Analysis of Social Life and Practice* (New York: Routledge, 2014), 150–151.

34 One thing modern critical theories of sexuality share with religious prohibitions about sex is that both understand sex to be as much a system of social communication and signification as it is a set of physical actions. Its meanings and purposes are held collectively rather than individually. Like food, sex has to do with the generation and sustenance of life and so, as existence itself is in play, it inevitably takes on a moral significance and becomes symbolically freighted activity. Fights over the meaning and purpose of sex and who can have sex with whom, where, and when are inevitable as its symbolism and significance changes, indexed as these are to changes in how existence itself is imagined and narrated. As with birthing practices and parenting – also constitutive and necessary biological features of human ways of being alive – how we do sex and norms and expectations about sexual behavior are historically conditioned and contested, change over time, and vary between cultures. The church itself has also changed how it makes sense of the social and theological significance of marriage and will continue to do so as part of its argument over time about the meaning and purpose of life in the light of the revelation of God in Jesus Christ.

35 Gilson, *The Ethics of Vulnerability*, 150–151.

36 Coakley builds on a combination of Patristic and feminist thought to explore this theme, pointing to unexpected resonances (and points of dissonance) between them. Echoing a broad swathe of feminist theology, part of what she argues against is a false opposition posed in modern theology between *agape* and *eros*. Sarah Coakley, *God, Sexuality and the Self: An Essay "On the Trinity"* (Cambridge: Cambridge University Press, 2013).

37 Audre Lorde, "The Uses of the Erotic: The Erotic as Power," *Sister Outsider: Essays and Speeches* (Freedom, CA: The Cross Press, 1984), 53–59.

38 Cristina Traina, *Erotic Attunement: Parenthood and the Ethics of Sensuality between Unequals* (Chicago: University of Chicago Press, 2011), 241.

39 Traina, *Erotic Attunement*, 243.

40 Iris Marion Young, "House and Home: Feminist Variations on a Theme," *On Female Body Experience: "Throwing Like a Girl" and Other Essays* (New York: Oxford University Press, 2005), 123–154.

41 bell hooks, "homeplace: a site of resistance," *Yearning: Race, Gender, and Cultural Politics* (Boston: South End Press, 1990), 41–50.

42 Young, "House and Home," 142.

43 This is a theme taken up in discussions of and activism around reproductive justice that focus on the right to parent children in safe and healthy environments.

13 Work

In this age, there is no human life without labor. We need someone, somewhere to work so that life can be provisioned and sustained. Work is a central way, as human animals, we metabolize creation. To understand this requires analyzing the purposes of human work, the conditions of good work, and how work is situated within broader economies, both human and divine.[1] This chapter addresses each of these in turn. In doing so, it analyzes whether work is an intrinsic and good feature of creaturely life that can be eschatologically transformed or a symptom of fallen life that will cease in the new creation.

At its most basic, human work is a form of agency. Through work we respond to and make something out of our environments. As such, work is a mode of interpretation and communication: through work we make sense of and do something with the flow of signs and signals – whether biochemical, spiritual, linguistic, or otherwise – that constitute our relations with our surroundings and other species. As a way of purposefully metabolizing creation, work is thus a number of things all at once: it is activity that has material effects, a means of building up a shared world of meaning and action with others, and a way of realizing who we are through relationship with the world around us.[2]

For better or worse, we make something of ourselves and of our world through work. However, work does not make the world. Echoing what I say in Chapter 2, human work can generate new combinations or innovate different pathways, but as a form of purposeful agency it operates in the middle term. It brings to the fore what is there, both affected by and affecting what is already happening. Through an interactive process, human work discerns and draws out the potentialities and energies of other things so as to redirect them. Rather than creating out of nothing, it gathers, preserves, adapts, mixes, crafts, catalyzes, and cultivates. In short, to enable human life to go on, our work brings forth or releases the potential of those things that are to hand.[3] To do this in a way that enables both humans and nonhumans to flourish requires being attuned to creation and promoting generous and just forms of common life.

Work not only remakes and metabolizes the world around us. It also makes *us*. How, where, and what we work at shape our sense of self and the quality and character of our relations with others and creaturely life in general. This means that work is secondary to workers. Rather than only valuing labor and what it produces, we need to prioritize the laborers: who they are as persons and the ways they relate to each other that their shared work mediates and constructs. When the conditions of work are exploitative, they produce deep forms of both personal and communal oppression and alienation.

WORK IN THE CAPITALIST SYSTEM

Work is a universal feature of human existence. However, work is only ever undertaken in historically and culturally specific forms. In the contemporary moment, the form and nature of work in the West is largely imagined and determined by some form of capitalism and the experience of wage labor (with domestic work marked as unwaged labor). And by capitalism I mean an economic system in which the accumulation of capital through profit maximization is the primary and overarching criteria by which judgments about what to do and how to do it are made. There are many versions of this system, but one thing they share is that the need to be paid in order to live dominates the conditions of life. Work within such a system, determined as it is for most people by dependency on either an employer or market-based exchanges, often lacks significant purpose, institutionalizes forms of licensed despotism, reproduces oppressive and ecologically destructive processes, and causes death by overwork. Yet our identities and sense of moral worth are sought within it.

Work generates and is enveloped within a broader economy. A key problem with how modern economies are imagined and narrated is that economic systems and structures are thought to be self-constituting and autonomous. Economies, and thence paid labor, are treated as separate spheres and thereby seen to be a law unto themselves. Yet economies and the labor that drives them are enmeshed within and contribute to a broader common life. The view that economies are a law unto themselves is an anomaly. In previous eras, economic activity served society, not vice versa. The emergence of a modern global market system inverted that relation. In contrast to hunter gatherer and largely agrarian economies, social and political relations are now organized around the demands of the market and the need to produce for gain, a development that depended on massive amounts of state intervention to impose it, intervention that was often colonial in form.[4] The result of this process is that, as the economic historian and anthropologist Karl Polanyi (1886–1964) summarizes it: "Instead of economy being embedded in social relations, social relations are embedded in the economic system."[5] The sociologist Max Weber (1864–1920) puts this more sharply still, saying that humans are now "dominated by the making of money, by acquisition as the ultimate purpose of life."[6] What Polanyi and Weber point to is how society has become ruled by financial considerations rather than the other way around. One outcome of this inversion is that what the market rewards (celebrities, hedge fund managers, etc.) is rarely what society needs (teachers, farmers, nurses, etc.).

Polanyi contends that historically the formation of a capitalist system inherently led to spontaneous counter-movements to re-embed economic relations within social and political relations as governments struggled to cope with the deleterious impact of an unregulated market on society and nature. Some counter-movements are anti-democratic and authoritarian, such as fascism; others are democratic in form. Examples of the latter include political movements such as the labor and environmental movements that help generate regulatory checks such as employment legislation, the formation of welfare structures, and environmental protections. Whether authoritarian or democratic, each counter-movement seeks to prioritize society and nature as having an independent and greater value than profit margins.

Whether one agrees with the specifics of Polanyi's historical account or not, his broader point stands. The production, distribution, and consumption of material and social goods, along with the use of money and debt to enable this, cannot be placed over and against everything else that makes up life with others. Life together should not be subsumed within and made to serve market systems and reductively economic modes of valuation. Moreover, the ways in which relations of reciprocity and gift are braided into and necessary for the proper functioning of all aspects of economic life needs recognizing and strengthening.[7] Conversely, any account of neighbor love that does not keep in view the material and social conditions of work is a false one as it is a failure to reckon with how love of God, neighbor, and all creation is constituted by and contributes to a political economy.

To illustrate these points, let us consider healthcare as a form of neighbor love. The value of what a nurse does cannot be articulated or valued in purely economistic terms. It is not reducible to efficiency in producing, distributing, and consuming healthcare. And no one wants to be cared for by nurses who view their job only in these terms. The prior and overarching goal of nursing is to cultivate the health of those cared for, which means the nursing must be evaluated first and foremost by the quality of care given. That said, care as gift and money as payment for services are not opposed in the work of the nurse. Both are needed in the production of good healthcare. However, a wholly materialistic and profit-driven vision of medicine is a highly reductive way to imagine the provision of healthcare. Yet healthcare is often talked about in reductive, economistic terms, and this model has led to health systems around the world more driven by the bottom line than concern for the health and physical flourishing of the people served. This inversion, whereby healthcare serves commercial considerations rather than the other way around, is tasted in eating hospital food (which in my experience is mostly a penance to be endured rather than a pleasure to be savored). All the evidence points to how nourishing and tasty food contributes to healing, and it's entirely feasible for a health system to produce such food. Yet it is not done because rather than seeing food as care and those that produce it as healthcare workers, it is produced as cheaply and efficiently as possible. Those that produce and serve it are given little value and paid accordingly.

Material security, work, and economics are not the sum total of the meaning and purpose of life. And when we make them our ultimate horizon then we have made an idol of them so that instead of imaging God, we refashion ourselves and our world in their image. The consequence of such idolatry is that the fabric of what makes up a human life is quickly shredded. Instead, economic life must be made to serve the meaning and purpose of life, which is to love God and neighbor and bless creation. We get confused about that, but the Bible is not. We do not live by bread alone and the call is to serve God not Mammon. And as a way of pointing to eternal life, the people of God should generate forms of life here and now that are in excess of and don't fit well within current economic systems.

HUMAN WORK AND THE COMMAND TO BE FRUITFUL

Theology frequently draws on language associated with work to depict God. For example, God creates and delivers. That said, a theology of work needs grounding in theological anthropology rather than a doctrine of God. Situating a theology of work in this way goes against many modern theologies of work that proceed by naming God as a worker and envisaging God's "work" as the model for human work.[8] This move should be resisted. It represents a problematic analogy that over-identifies the nature of God with human work. In doing so, it makes work a definitive feature of imaging and relating to God and the "work" of creation necessary to God rather than a contingent, gratuitous gift. Moreover, in addition to conflating divine and human agency, it is contrary to the scriptural witness, where God's agency is unlike and beyond the work of human hands. In the

Bible, it is relations of gift that constitute divine-human relations, and a movement unto Sabbath rest, not yet more work, is upheld as the true end of human and divine fulfillment.

Key texts repeatedly drawn on to frame the meaning and purpose of human work are Genesis 1 and 2 where humans are commanded to "fructify" life (Gen 1:28) and appointed to fulfill this command through *`ābad* (tilling, serving, working) and *shamar* (keeping, preserving, protecting, treasuring) creation (Gen 2:15). What follows can in many ways be taken as a meditation on what it means to follow this command, after Christ.

Drawing on Genesis, work can be envisioned as a facet of creaturely life, one oriented to blessing creation as part of a thankful response to the prior gift of life. In the earthly city, however, work takes place out of right relationship with God and creation and so, more often than not, it curses rather than blesses. In short, while work can bring blessing, all human work stands under God's judgment (Gen 3:16–19). Yet, as the prophetic literature envisages, there are better and worse forms of work; liberated working conditions are marked by ordinary workers enjoying the fruit of their labor in feasting and resting (e.g., Micah 4:4; Isa 65:21–23). As with bread and wine, the fruits of human work can become signs and mediators of divine presence. And in Revelation, the New Jerusalem is said to incorporate the good fruits of human work (Rev 21:26–27). Scripture thereby both values but also relativizes the place of human work as a penultimate contribution to living a good and holy life. Human action matters, but divine action matters more. At the same time, Scripture is marked by a deep realism about work, depicting it as often painful and arduous. Its fruits are ephemeral and its conditions exploitative, and it is unable to either overcome human limitation or save us from sin.

Through the course of its history, Christian theology takes up the scriptural portrayal of work and its conditions and possibilities in a variety of ways. These can be summarized in the following terms. Positively, work is envisioned as:

- a way to bless creation through enabling fruitfulness;
- a means of participating in and witnessing to God's healing and renewing of creation;
- a vocation through which we may enact the call to love God and neighbor;
- a way to realize human personhood and build community; and, more ambiguously,
- an ascetic discipline that forms disciples.

Negatively, work is seen as:

- a curse, characterized by toil, alienation, and exploitation;
- a means of false righteousness and the opposite of grace; and
- limited by Sabbath rest.

In what follows, I touch on each of these, focusing on some more than others, to sketch a constructive theology of work, including the nature and form of ethical working conditions.[9]

Good work is directed toward blessing creation, which means enabling creation to be fruitful in *shalom*-like ways. While penultimate, work that brings blessing witnesses to and participates in the work of the Spirit in healing creation and bringing it to eschatological fulfillment. We tend to think of the Spirit in ethereal, otherworldly ways. But in Scripture, it is the Spirit who hovers over the formless void, bringing creation into being. It is the Spirit who is breathed into dust to create life. It is the Spirit who acts to set the Israelites free by blowing as a mighty wind to part the waters. It is the Spirit who anoints judges, prophets, and leaders to call forth new capacity among the people to live a more generous and just life. It is the Spirit who overshadows Mary, bringing forth Jesus, enabling him to be fully human and fully divine. And as the Son takes human form, it is the Spirit who takes the animal form of a dove to anoint Jesus's ministry to creation. Jesus then breathes the Spirit on the disciples who empowers them to be embodied witnesses to the ends of the earth. In other words, it is the Spirit who brings into being what is truly material – matter that really matters, matter that can bear the fruit of eternal life.

The scriptural narrations of the Spirit's action reveal a threefold work. First, the Spirit actualizes creation, enabling creation to be itself through animating, healing, and delivering it (in the double sense of bringing life to birth and liberation). Each part of creation is thereby enabled to be truly what God created it to be. Second, the Spirit fructifies creation, making what exists fruitful in a way that is generative so that something unexpected, new, and transformational comes into being. Even as the third person of the Trinity builds on and intensifies what already exists, there is a surprising departure, a rupture even. The Spirit adds to nature more than is expected or seems possible, generating new ways of being alive. A wandering Aramean couple can be a source of blessing to all peoples, swords can become plowshares, Jebus can become Jerusalem, the Word of God can become frail flesh, bread and wine can become the body and blood of Christ, and what is a source of shame or foolishness can reveal divine wisdom and glory (1 Cor 1:20–31). Third, as at the ascension, the Spirit fulfills creation through enabling creation to participate in communion with God. Good work witnesses to and can participate in this threefold work of the Spirit.

As a witness to the work of the Spirit who brings into being glorified matter, work should not treat creation as an inanimate collection of objects or as an inert resource waiting to be extracted. Rather, creation is a place of Spirit-filled activity, redolent with divine meaning and purpose, signifying more than itself, and connected to what is beyond itself. To be *good*, work must communicate with and be attuned to creation rather than imposing itself upon creation. In contrast, unethical work brings creation to naught, rendering it less than it was: toxic rather than life-giving, alienated and broken apart rather than symbiotic and intricately woven. Such work renders creation unable to bear eternal fruit, making of it matter that no longer matters because it has lost or been turned against its meaning and purpose. Bad work turns creation toward nothingness and away from eschatological fulfillment.

WORK AS CURSED

In this age, it is a struggle to undertake work that blesses rather than curses. At a mundane level, under conditions of finitude and fallenness, work now involves toil and drudgery. But beyond being a struggle, there is the constant temptation to view work as a means to dominate the world around us and thereby create tools and systems that impose our will on creation, extracting resources from it, and exploiting our neighbors through expropriating the fruits of their labor. Rather than asking how work cultivates and metabolizes the world around us, and thereby participates in and fructifies creation and our common life with others, our work alienates us from ourselves, from others, and from the rest of creation.

Instead of generating blessing, work that alienates will exacerbate general conditions of precariousness, which can be particularly devastating to specific groups. In Chapter 12, I examined how slavery is just such a form of work and how, as an economic system, it enables material security and prosperity for some through the brutal exploitation of others and the destruction of whole ecologies. A contemporary example is migrant farmworkers from Central America and elsewhere vital to the production of cheap and accessible food in the United States.[10] Attempts to secure ourselves by forcing others to carry the cost of our burdens exploits our neighbors, renders toxic the habitats on which we depend, and alienates us from ourselves. Such work is a curse trading under the guise of being a blessing. Even if we materially benefit from it, we are personally and spiritually impoverished through either requiring or orchestrating such work to make our way of life possible.

There is another form of alienation that is part of the engine of our current financialized, debt-fueled economic systems. This system treats your home as an investment, your education as an asset, and the firm that employs you not as a means to produce goods and services to provision a common life but as a debt leverage instrument. This system is driven by the insatiable and rapacious desire for more

money (*pleonexia*), the pursuit of which becomes an end in itself. All else is subordinated to its accumulation and everything is valued only in monetary terms.

Money is good as either a medium of exchange, a store of value, or a means of accounting. However, as a form of work, moneymaking renders everything into a financial instrument and degrades all other forms of work. It undermines the pursuit of virtue and goods in common, and thence the formation of a flourishing common life, because making money becomes the sole measure and goal of work.[11] The pursuit of money/capital as the overriding end of work means everything is for sale and nothing is sacred. Health, education, and even piety itself become products with no intrinsic value or end and are sought solely for monetary considerations. Commodification names this particular form of alienation; that is, the treating of that which is not a product (a child, your liver, faith, air) as a commodity to be bought and sold. The monetization of our personal lives and emotional connections by social media platforms is a case in point. These platforms render friendship and connection into a commodity to be sold off to the highest bidder and in doing so undermine the fragile fabric of social trust that makes a common life possible. As noted earlier, Scripture has much to say about commodification as a manifestation of idolatry.

One response to laboring under fallen conditions is to envisage work as itself an ascetic and penitential discipline that trains us to look beyond ephemeral things that rust and invest in things of eternal value (Matt 6:19–21). An influential expression of this vision was articulated in Saint Benedict's monastic rule. Through manual labor, study, and prayer the monk cultivates the humility that is the antidote to pride, which, as per Augustine, is the root of the human lust to dominate. In the Benedictine tradition, penitential regimes of laboring for the glory of God rather than working to improve one's own lot is the therapy for a disordered love of the world. Work in such a vision is not good in and of itself but is an instrumental means of serving a beneficial end: learning to love God and neighbor more truly.

The Benedictine vision sees neither alienation nor exploitation as the primary threat to doing good work. Rather, it is idleness, whether forced or chosen. Idleness (often associated with the vice of sloth) is a problem for a number of reasons. The first is that it disorders the moral use of time. This can sound like a bureaucratic demand for effective time management. But the efficient use of time is not a *moral* concern: doing what is moral is often inefficient and sometimes we need the grace to do nothing. Rather, the moral use of time is a question of how a flourishing life needs a rhythm of work and rest (as distinct from leisure). In Shakespeare's *Henry IV*, Prince Hal gets at this when he rejects Falstaff's vision of the good life as consisting of idle dissipation: "If all the year were playing holidays, to sport would be as tedious as to work."[12] But beyond the human need for temporal rhythms, idleness is either the refusal or forced inability to participate in cultivating shared worlds of meaning and action and thereby represents a loss of dignity (something Shakespeare's portrayal of Falstaff draws out).

As a state of involuntary idleness, unemployment is often a source of anguish. The suffering arises not only through the loss of income, status, and established temporal rhythms but also because of how unemployment functions as a mode of exclusion from contributing to a shared world, thereby representing a diminishing of one's agency and dignity. A sense of being diminished can be expressed through experiences of loneliness due to loss of familiar patterns of life and camaraderie with colleagues.

Physically hard and dangerous work such as mining or firefighting, or tedious work such as cleaning, can be a source of meaning through the sense of solidarity they can generate and the way they may build up a shared world. As Martin Luther King Jr. noted in one of his last speeches, given in support of striking sanitation workers in Memphis in 1968: "The person who picks up garbage is as crucial to the health of society as is the doctor." King insisted that "professional jobs" might be better rewarded but were no more significant, stating:

> "Let me say to you tonight that whenever you are engaged in work that serves humanity and is for the building of humanity, it has dignity and it has worth. One day our society will come to respect

> the sanitation worker if it is to survive, for the person who picks up our garbage, in the final analysis, is as significant as the physician, for if he doesn't do his job, diseases are rampant.[13]

That said, those who perform sanitation and other "dirty work" that is either menial or morally injurious must be properly compensated and the hours they spend doing it limited. This is a basic way to recognize their vital contribution.[14] Moreover, such essential workers need the freedom and time to organize so as to achieve good working conditions.

WORK AS VOCATION AND THE NATURE OF WORTHWHILE WORK

Intrinsic to a Benedictine understanding of work is the sense that work should be an expression of one's vocation to serve God and neighbor. As the Protestant Reformers realized, envisaging work in terms of vocation can be applied beyond the walls of the monastery. As Luther puts it in his lectures on Genesis:

> All our actions in domestic life are pleasing to God and that they are necessary for this life in which it becomes each one to serve the one God and Lord of all according to one's ability and vocation .... Let them know that a woman suckling an infant or a maid sweeping a threshing floor with a broom is just as pleasing to God as an idle nun or a lazy Carthusian.[15]

For Reformers such as Luther and Calvin, Christians had a vocation to love their neighbor as part of their response to God's call and this overarching vocation transcends and frames all other offices or roles. As noted in Chapter 8, this understanding of vocation and its relationship to the call of God is developed by Karl Barth for whom a specific vocation (to be a teacher, engineer, farmer, parent, etc.) is the context and "place of responsibility" where we hear God's command in continual interaction with our neighbors. Whether in the household, field, factory, or office, work is a central means through which humans exercise their vocations and gifts and in doing so respond to the call to love God and neighbor. That said, a number of dangers lurk at the door in talk of vocation.

One danger is the over-identification of personal identity and sense of worth with a professional role and/or paid employment. This can generate both workaholism and "workism" whereby work becomes the lynchpin around which one's life and relationships revolve. Looking to work as the foundation stone of self-worth is an idolatry of production and achievement as opposed to an idolatry of consumption (i.e., one that looks to status symbols and lifestyle as the basis of standing and dignity). In previous generations, the arc of a life and a sense of vocation came together in doing a single job often undertaken within the same organization, whether a hospital, General Motors, or the army. Paid employment and vocation were conflated. Today, when many people undertake multiple jobs or work as independent contractors in the "gig" economy, the focus and purposes of work are not indexed to the means of employment. Vocation provides a way of thinking about the structure and coherence of our work independently of paid employment. However, in this context, there is a different danger: a fatuous and solipsistic "do what you love, love what you do" understanding of vocation that ties it to individual fulfillment and ignores both the conditions of work (exemplified in the figure of the unpaid intern) and how doing "what you love" is made possible by the labor of others who have to do whatever pays the rent and puts food on the table.

As a means to answer the call to love God and neighbor, work must strike a delicate balance: it is a social and material condition through which personhood is actualized even as it neither exhausts nor defines what it means to be a person. The Roman Catholic encyclical *Laborem Exercens* summarizes this insight as follows: "Since work in its subjective aspect is always a personal action, an *actus personae*, it follows that the whole person, body and spirit, participates in it, whether it is manual or intellectual work."[16] On this account, work is not only toil; it can also, in the same gesture, be a gift. Like all gifts, the fruit of human labor is a way in which the person is present to and recognizes others. Work, worker, and the objects and services produced are symbiotic. As part of the provisioning and circulation of things that constitute life together, work helps generate a *habitus* or form of life. To make work degrading is to desecrate the personhood of the workers and demean a way of life. Likewise, to make labor serve and be subject to capital is to invert the moral order by making persons serve money. When conceptualized and inhabited as part of how humans exercise their call to be a person in relation to God and creation and participate in the work of the Spirit in doing so, work can be part of how humans forge a common world of meaning and action and come to realize their dignity as persons. And no work is merely economic. Work is always social, political, and spiritual as well.

The connection between work and the realization of one's personhood (the movement from merely existing to having a life) calls into question modern visions of a leisured society made possible by technologies that free humans from the need to labor. Long predicted but never realized, such a society may be a fantasy, but there is the real prospect that technologies like artificial intelligence and increasing automation will render obsolete many existing sectors of work, from taxi drivers to accountants. One response is to advocate a Universal Basic Income (UBI): a universal, unconditional, regular payment to every citizen by the state. Whether viewed as a social democratic panacea to increasing automation, a libertarian policy by which to dismantle the welfare state and public services, or as an attempt by corporate capitalism and Silicon Valley to buy off "surplus populations" while giving them just enough to keep buying consumer products, such a policy accepts and merely offsets the societal impacts of technological changes viewed as inevitable. Yet UBI is insufficient as a response to technologies that are designed to serve the interests of capital, concentrate economic and political power, increase surveillance, and render people idle (in the sense just outlined). In place of advocating for a UBI, a "solidarity economy" approach would be to design alternative, nonproprietary, open-source technologies with affordances that increase social, political, and economic agency, distribute resources, generate greater participation in meaningful work, and enable attunement to, not alienation from, creation. And rather than view technological development as inevitable, it would be situated within and subordinated to democratic debate about what kind of human future was sought and thence what technologies were needed to enable such a future.

It is not necessarily the activity itself that determines whether work is worthwhile or not. As philosopher Alasdair MacIntyre puts it:

> Most productive work is and cannot but be tedious, arduous, and fatiguing much of the time. What makes it worthwhile to work and to work well is threefold: that the work that we do has point and purpose, is productive of genuine goods; that the work that we do is and is recognized to be *our* work, *our* contribution, in which we are given and take responsibility for doing it and for doing it well; and that we are rewarded for doing it in a way that enables us to achieve the goods of family and community .... [This conception] stands in the sharpest opposition both to the conception of productive work as something that can best be done by a machine, so that the human worker is, so far as possible, to perform her or his tasks in mechanical routines, and to the closely related conception of productive work as no more than a means to the ends of profitability and of consumption, so that the measure of human work is its cost effectiveness. Every workplace is a place of potential conflict between these rival conceptions of work.[17]

Contrary to what John Ruskin and early Christian socialists argued, artisanal, craft-based ways of producing goods are not inherently worthier than factory-based forms. Neither is intellectual work (law, academia, accounting, poetry, etc.) more meaningful than manual labor, whether in the factory or care home. Work that is focused on people is not necessarily of greater value than work focused on producing things and, as per the Reformers, nor is "spiritual" work of either the minister, the monk, or the missionary necessarily more important than that of the mechanic.[18] Rather than distinctions based on the intrinsic worth of the work, such hierarchies of value and status are more often than not shaped by class distinctions, the inequalities these reinscribe, and a long history of aristocratic disdain for manual labor. MacIntyre's criteria point to the way good work demands that the work contributes to building up and provisioning a shared world of meaning and action. And that workers must have some measure of control over their working conditions so that they can determine what is safe, how they should be treated, and how their work should be valued. This includes having a say in what constitutes "a fair day's wage for a fair day's work," for a wage is not about income alone. It is also a medium for honoring the value of someone's contribution to a shared enterprise and thence their dignity.

A commitment to worthwhile work necessitates upholding the agency of workers in having a say in their conditions of work, whether in a household, call center, shop, farm, or hospital. Whether or not they are empowered to determine their living and working conditions points to wider questions about how power is organized and what it takes to transform an existing form of life into a more loving and just one. Today, in practice, this entails a commitment to forms of economic democracy (trade unions, representation of workers on boards, worker ownership, and other forms of codetermination and shared governance of workplaces). It also means developing means of production – whether of goods or services – that prioritize the quality and character of workers' agency over the demands of either shareholders for a profit, customers for cheap goods, or managers for efficiency. Finally, it means both ensuring workers are paid enough and that there are limits to how much time they devote to paid employment so there is time and energy for other kinds of meaningful activity. In theological terms, the firm should be seen as a covenantal relation requiring both mutual cooperation and mutual accountability between all its stakeholders.

To restructure paid employment along the lines sketched here would inhibit the formation of immiserating and exploitative systems of work and go some way toward addressing the maldistribution of good work and the need for good working conditions. And given the connection between exploitation of workers and extractive, instrumentalizing ways of treating nonhuman life – for example, in meat processing plants – it would also help ensure our economies are more attuned to and serve the good of creation.

WORSHIP, REST, AND PLAY AS THE LIMIT OF WORK

As should be clear, meaningful work should not be equated with paid employment. For example, intentional acts of gathered worship are a form of work; that is, worship is a purposeful activity that has material effects, is a form of interpretation and communication that builds up and contributes to a common life, and is a way for people to realize their personhood through cooperative action.[19] And as a form of work, gathered worship also exemplifies how human labor can be taken up into the work of the Spirit. Etymologically, liturgy is a term derived from the Greek word *leitourgia*, meaning a public work of service or duty undertaken by the citizen and done for the benefit of the people or wider community. And, as Jacob Neusner points out, the Hebrew word for work (*abodah*) is the same word used for "divine service," "liturgy," or the labor of priests in the Temple making offerings to God.[20] Work covers all forms of labor, including acts of worship and piety. As a work of the people of God and a work of the Spirit within the world, gathered worship is a mode of non-alienated work born out of the shared labor of God and humans. The fruits of this work are distributed and consumed both by the participants, as each has need, and by the world, which the working people represent before God in their prayers, songs, and words.

The work of worship is paradoxically a form of Sabbath that relativizes all other forms of work. Worship witnesses to how provisioning a life is not all there is to life. We are also formed as flourishing persons through rest and play (understood as something more like recreation than amusement or entertainment), which means that we must limit and interrupt the provisioning of material needs and wants through work. Gathering for worship, celebrating feast days, saying grace before a meal, or praying during the day are just such interruptions. These moments of Sabbath offer time to contemplate and celebrate what lies beyond meeting material needs and desires.[21] They reorient us to a posture of thanksgiving and remind us that humans did not make the world. Rather, it is a gift from God we depend on and cannot live without. As a gift, creation is to be enjoyed and delighted in, not exploited or destroyed for short-term material security. Observing times of interruptive Sabbath-keeping is a way of insisting that, in the last analysis, not everything is reducible to human work. Rather, human work finds its fulfillment in the kingdom of God, which is beyond what humans can bring into being through their actions. The command to keep the Sabbath is thereby fundamental as it sets the terms and conditions of human flourishing (Ex 20:8–11; Deut 5:15; Ps 92). Failure to abide by it reduces life to a desultory scramble to get an education, take on debt, get a job, get a house, buy and consume stuff, raise kids to repeat the cycle, and then die.

The distinction between work and rest is important but not absolute, since rest is not necessarily the cessation of industry even if it is the ending of paid work. Rest can entail imaginative and creative activity, but crucially, such purposeful activity is directed beyond provisioning material needs. It feeds the soul, not the body. Contemplation and play are but two examples of such activity. Rest is defined by the quality, character, and end of the activity rather than by what kind of activity is involved. For example, recreational fishing is a form of rest, but someone who makes their living by fishing is working when they fish.

The church, by being the church, should hold open times and spaces for wonder, prayer, rest, festivity, and play, all of which regenerate the human spirit. Through such times and spaces, churches also keep open the need to ask questions about the meaning and purpose of life and especially of economic activity and work. They thereby keep in view the transcendent ends of what it means to be a person, ends neither reducible to nor attainable by economic activity. Work can be a way of hallowing creation in relation to God and fulfilling the purposes of being a human creature (which is to love God and neighbor); but this requires keeping many things in tension: worship and laboring, contemplation and action, grace and effort. Such tensions are irresolvable but necessary ones for the health and integrity of each. To focus on one to the exclusion of the other, or to collapse them into each other, is to lose both.

A POLITICAL ECONOMY OF BLESSING

In dominant narrations of modern economics, the purpose of an economy is not first and foremost about provisioning, let alone enabling love of God and neighbor. Its purpose is growth. Growth creates profit, and profit, understood in monetary terms, drives economic development which in turn enables humans to fulfill their needs and desires. However, this was not always the story told. Moreover, there are myriad alternative economic visions and ways of doing business to those advocated by contemporary mainstream economics and most of the financial services industry. For example, echoing Aristotelian and Thomistic views of the economy as ordered to the promotion of happiness/flourishing, there are attempts to make well-being and quality of life a metric of economic health in recognition that, after a certain level, greater material abundance and increases in GDP do not generate greater happiness.[22] To this end, since 2012, the United Nations has issued an annual World Happiness Report as an alternative, more holistic index to GDP to measure economic development. Alongside these alternative ways of measuring economic strength at a national scale are businesses such as "B-Corps" (e.g., Athleta sports clothes), cooperatives (e.g., Mondragon, founded by a Catholic priest), and fair-trade companies that measure economic success in terms of the "triple bottom line," which includes people (social equity bottom line), planet (the ecological bottom line), and profit (the financial bottom line). Such initiatives build on a long history of church-related mutual aid societies, cooperatives, and covenantal forms of business that provided alternative means of wealth creation to purely profit-driven forms. These efforts question all economic visions, practices, and systems that put abstract growth and reductive visions of material development over and above what economist Kate Raworth calls "human prosperity in the flourishing web of life."[23]

In order to replace anthropocentric and extractivist driven growth – whether framed in capitalist, communist or other terms – as the criteria of a healthy economy, a Christian economic vision should emphasize blessing. Blessing equates prosperity with God's *shalom*. As noted in the Introduction (Chapter 1), the Hebrew word *shalom* denotes wholeness, flourishing, fruitfulness, abundance, peace, and well-being. Movement toward blessing includes repair and regeneration of creation (whether human or nonhuman) and is marked by fulfillment of one's personhood in and through life with others, including other kinds of creatureliness. Blessing is obviously not synonymous with monetary profit, which may or may not be a blessing, and redefines economic success in terms of how economic systems and structures serve *creational* not simply human flourishing. Concern for prosperity and abundance understood in terms of *shalom* also speaks to a vision of salvation as including ecological, social, political, and economic flourishing – and the redistribution of power that enables this flourishing.[24] But such a vision emphasizes how the good life – and the health and wealth this can include – is one lived *with* the rest of creation and attentive to the needs of the poor and marginalized. When unhooked from concern for creational flourishing and a generous and just common life, it is not blessing that is produced but a curse masquerading as a blessing.

A number of distorted visions of blessing can be identified. One influential example is the early modern philosopher John Locke's vision of how God's call to be fruitful and multiply is focused on the cultivation of land. For Locke, making active use of land and the creatures found there through one's labor converted common land into private property. As property it was then the exclusive possession of the owner/cultivator. On this account, private property is the basis of flourishing and enclosure a source of unalloyed blessing.[25] In a similar vein, another distorted vision is Prosperity Gospel teachings that align sanctification with the ascetic disciplines demanded by capitalism and reduce divine-human relations to a contractual, mechanistic relationship: so much "faithful" action produces a requisite amount of God's "blessing." Both the Lockean and the Prosperity Gospel visions are a cruel parody of a holistic, *shalom*-based vision of blessing.

Alongside and aligned with an obsession with growth and prosperity understood in wholly materialistic terms, consumerism is another distorted and idolatrous vision of blessing, one which also confuses material abundance and the possession of many things with flourishing. In addition, it conflates happiness with pleasure. Drinking bourbon and eating donuts are enormously pleasurable, and are not wrong in themselves, but when divorced from the pursuit of other goods and made an end in themselves they become wrong. It is loving good things the wrong way. Such disordered love will not make me happy in the sense of cultivating my flourishing. Indeed, pleasure seeking for itself is a forgery of happiness. Reducing happiness to pleasure is, however, a favorite ruse of the advertising industry and an economic system wholly orientated to profit, which can package and sell pleasure but not flourishing. Flourishing depends on myriad goods such as intimacy and wisdom that can neither be bought nor sold.

In response to this conflation and following the lead of Christian moralists down the ages, it would be easy to strike an apocalyptic note and denounce the widespread pursuit of pleasure over flourishing. But pleasure in itself is good. Moreover, the church often ignores how seeking pleasure as an end in itself can provide solace in the absence of a fuller and more holistic experience of flourishing under oppressive or tragic conditions. As should be clear by now, cultivating a flourishing life is hard. It entails struggle, coping with limits, and the need to make difficult judgments. Pleasure can provide a ready substitute in the face of life's woes. In saying this, I am neither legitimizing consumerist means of cultivating desire for the world nor condoning making sensate pleasure the end goal of human happiness. As with Nietzsche's *übermensch* and last humans examined in Chapter 6, the pursuit of material prosperity and of pleasure to the exclusion of everything else is driven by a kind of practical nihilism that destroys creation in order to extract solipsistic and fleeting gains. That said, consumerism is as much a pastoral and political question as a moral problem. A pastoral and political response to consumerism entails not jeremiads but, echoing what I say above, enacting a different vision of work, rest, and play to that which a consumerist and profit orientated economy dictates.

ECONOMIES ARE ABOUT MORE THAN MARKETS

Alongside an emphasis on growth rather than blessing, another dominant story told about modern economies is that markets are the best and most effective means by which humans can meet their needs and organize work. Indeed, as already noted, paid employment valued according to market exchanges is the primary framework through which work is understood. And the predominant story told about markets is that they are self-regulating, finding their own equilibrium, that the state is bad for them, that the cultivation of care and intimacy is not part of them, that the environment is an "externality" to them, and that the only way to organize them is through regimes of private property. But this is a narrow and inaccurate story. Echoing what I said earlier, while vital, markets, like fire, are not self-regulating: they can get out of control and destroy everything around them. They need limits: for example, citizenship and children are not things to be bought and sold, and something is fundamentally wrong if they are treated as commodities.

A market is a social practice with intrinsic moral ends the fulfillment of which entails the practice of certain virtues. An absence of virtue leads to a breakdown in the reciprocity, trust, and cooperation a market needs to function (e.g., a breakdown in social trust leading to a run on the banks will quickly tank a national economy).

Conversely, increases in the quality and character of social relations – for example, in trust, honesty, and prudence – improves the efficiency and productivity of market transactions.[26] As the causes of the 2007–2009 Great Recession powerfully demonstrated, recklessness combined with deceit and hubris in the highest echelons of banking brought economic devastation.

Humans cannot live by markets alone. Indeed, if markets are the only institutional mechanism for provisioning life and structuring work, then what is generated is an economy that curses rather than blesses. Diverse institutional forms are needed. Moreover, a singular focus on markets deflects attention away from the other means through which our work is currently organized and valued. These include the household, the commons, forms of association, and the state. Each of these is a vital institutional tool for solving collective problems, structuring our work, and providing, fulfilling, and ordering the goods necessary to sustain a common life over time and at scale.[27] And, like markets, each of these "tools for conviviality" needs moral relations to undergird its practice if it is to enable flourishing.[28] Modern political economies – whether predominantly capitalist, communist, democratic socialist, or agrarian in form – assemble these elements differently, but they are present in one way or another in them all, the world over.

In what follows, I examine each of these different forms of economic institution that, alongside markets, organize work and enable the provisioning of a common life.

Households

Historically, the household was not a solely human entity. It incorporated the animals with whom the humans of the household shared a common life. The things managed could be material but also what we now designate as religious and cultural. For much of history, households, great and small, nomadic and settled, have been the basic unit for organizing and providing the material needs and wants of humans. Even with the industrial revolution, and the separation of paid work from the household economy, households are still a primary means for organizing and valuing material and social life. They produce basic goods such as intimacy, socialization, and a homeplace, while current economic systems continue to depend on the unwaged care that takes place in households. To put this at its most basic, a workforce with no potty training is not going to be very productive. In the ancient Greco-Roman and early Christian conceptions of the household as an economy, to be counted as good, the management of the household was directed to the flourishing of its members. And as noted in Chapter 12, the flourishing of a household can necessitate engagement in political struggles in order to reorientate a common life so it serves the needs of a household. Internally, the duties and responsibilities of the household are more directed to distributive justice, in contrast to those of the market, which are more directed to commutative justice.

Commons

The commons curates shared material and social goods such as language and water. A commons is made up of a shared social and material good (a mountain pasture), a human community (shepherds and the villages of which they are a part), and a set of formal and informal customary practices, rules, processes, and priorities for governing and administering that good (practices for rotating access to the pasture between shepherds). A commons is produced through the interaction of human cooperation, nonhuman ways of being alive, and material processes. Each commons is distinct and adapted to specific conditions such that the moral and social norms for managing a commons cannot be easily transferred (e.g., a forest commons in Germany will be different from one in Indonesia). There are three basic types of commons: (i) the natural commons of fisheries, forests, watersheds, irrigation systems etc.; (ii) the cultural and knowledge commons of a community's language, ancestral wisdom, stories, music, scientific techniques, rituals, and cultural practices such as games; and now (iii) the digital commons of open-source software, information, and technologies (e.g., Wikipedia, Linux, and TCP/IP protocols). Like the household, the commons is a non-state, non-market, agency-centric means of provisioning human needs and desires, one that entails highly participatory, self-organized, and distributed forms of management, and peer-to-peer governance. That said, a commons can be guaranteed by the state (e.g., the influential 1217 Charter of the Forest – the complement to the earlier Magna Carta of 1215 – formally recognized many ancient rights to graze and forage in "forests," which included wood, heath, and wetlands).[29] The duties and responsibilities for governing a commons combine distributive and commutative justice but emphasize the former over the latter.

States

The state produces public goods such as laws, roads, parks, libraries, and social welfare provision for the people of a polity. Public goods are goods and services that everyone needs such as sewers, the use of which neither excludes others nor entails competition. Public goods are provided or protected by state-centric means. They stand in contrast to both a commons and private property. These differences are made explicit in the influential set of distinctions Roman law makes. Operating with a natural law framework, the sixth-century Justinian Code states: "Of these [things] some admit of private ownership, while others, it is held, cannot belong to individuals: for some things are by natural law common to all, some are public, some belong to a society or corporation, and some belong to no one."[30] For example, in the Justinian Code, a port was a public thing built and maintained for the public good (the use of which was at the discretion of the public authority), but the sea and seashore were a commons owned and controlled by no single authority and available for use by everyone at any time.[31] To take a modern example, Yosemite National Park is a public good, as its boundaries, institutional form, and access to it are determined and controlled by state authorities.[32] In contrast, Maine lobster fisheries are a commons with certain legal recognition but its scope, means of governance, and organization are not derived from or created by the state. Rather, the state responds to and sanctions something that already exists, and which is constituted independently of the state. Generally, while the modern state supports commutative justice, its own duties and responsibilities should be directed toward distributive and social justice. Social justice entails the responsibility to generate the systems, institutions, and general conditions (e.g., peaceableness) for individuals and communities to be able to act with social, economic, and political parity in relation to other members of that polity so that each may realize their own good and contribute to the flourishing of the whole. Providing unemployment insurance is one example: it stops fellow citizens from starving and ensures they have basic needs met so as to be able to act both for themselves and with others.

Societies and Corporations

Echoing the distinctions made by the Justinian Code, in addition to the commons and the state as means of providing for social and material needs and addressing collective problems, there are also forms of association that take the form of societies and corporations. Business conglomerates like Amazon, Koch Industries, Disney, Maersk, Unilever, and Boeing are overwhelmingly associated with the term "corporation," but alongside trading companies are corporations and societies such as monasteries, cathedrals, guilds, professional associations, universities, trade unions, and cities (e.g., the Corporation of the City of London). Consociations of various kinds have been a central feature of both the ancient and modern world, indeed their standing in ancient Greek, Roman, and Germanic legal traditions are the backdrop to their form today in the West. For example, the joint stock trading company – the early modern archetype of the contemporary capitalist firm – was based on the *corpus politicum et corporatum* or *communitas perpetua* that went back to Roman law. Corporate associations of various kinds stand between the household, market, state, and commons as another core institutional tool for providing, organizing, and governing the use of material and social goods and constructively addressing shared challenges.

Property

Finally, alongside public, associational, and common things, providing and managing the resources needed to live can also be done by means of property. Property can be institutionalized and understood in various ways and is made use of by all the institutional forms outlined so far. Here I explore two regimes of property and their respective moral economies: private property and property envisaged as a social and communicative good. And against both its critics and advocates, I examine how property is neither an unadulterated blessing nor an unequivocal curse. Rather, my contention is that within a Christian frame of reference, property should be understood as a prudential and contingent means for provisioning a common life. I recognize, however, that property is both an emotive issue and a central way modern economies are secured. Against that backdrop, many will find what I say counterintuitive, paradoxical even. I simply ask that the implications of what I write are fully considered rather than dismissed at first glance.

There is, quite properly, a skepticism within Christianity toward notions of *private* property understood as the total and exclusive possession and use of a thing. Raising a permanent question mark over the moral worth of any notion of exclusive ownership are, first and foremost, Jesus's rejection of property, his teaching about earthly riches, and his instructions to his disciples (e.g., Matt 19:21–30; Mark 6:7–9; Luke 9:3; 21:1–4). There is then the communalism of the early church and monastic and radical Protestant communities (e.g., the Hutterites and Diggers) and groups such as the Franciscans advocating voluntary poverty. However, suspicion about private property does not give way to Manichaean conceptions of property ownership as inherently immoral and in need of abolition. Rather, there is an ongoing debate about what constitutes right use. For this, New

Testament disavowals of private property are situated in relationship to Old Testament conceptions of property as a communicative good.

In ancient Israel, possession of land did not entitle the holder to exclusive use; rather, one had rights and responsibilities to land that were themselves situated in relationship with a wider community. One *held* land in trust for a time, an idea still echoed in the terms leasehold and freehold. Human ownership and use of created goods were limited because ultimately the territory and its fruit – like creation itself – was God's homeland: humans are trustees and priests receiving, sharing, and offering back to God what they have received as a gift. To claim complete and exclusive control over something is to usurp God who gives gifts for the good of all.

Treatment of the poor is a touchstone that marks whether property relations are properly situated within and orientated to covenantal relations of faithful, mutual responsibility that generate life with and for others. Land as property was to be used to provide the means of life and build up the commonwealth, not converted through exploitation or monopolization into a means for one's own aggrandizement and the destitution of one's neighbor. Within this theological vision of land, property was a communicative and not an absolute good. This communicative vision of property relations as the basis for a shared life premised on the ability of each having agency and gifts to share contrasts with both privatized and nationalized (i.e., state-centric) conceptions of property. In the former, the use of property is solely determined by the sovereign individual or corporate owner, whereas in the latter its use is determined by the sovereign state.

Within the theological framework sketched here, property is not inherently private. Individual and corporate ownership withdraws a good (e.g., land) from the wider community. However, that does not mean the wider community ceases to have any claim to its use. For example, as in cases of eminent domain, under the auspices of the state, the wider community can reclaim property to serve public goods as the need arises (e.g., to build a railway or road). Or in countries with freedom to roam laws (e.g., Sweden, Austria, and Scotland), members of the wider community can make use of land for limited purposes. All property claims depend on the legitimization by and consent of a wider community. For the most part, within Christianity, property is morally licit and is seen as enabling the pursuit of important goods and virtues (e.g., responsibility). Yet it can only do so when situated within and serving the development of a common life and goods held in common.

Critics of property who call for its abolition are responding to a conception of property as an inviolable and exclusive right that generates competitive and often violent relations. Yet, as indicated already, there are alternative conceptions of property that prioritize the communicability and sharing of goods rather than their private or exclusive use. One influential, alternative, theologically grounded conception is Thomistic.[33] Aquinas's social conception of property derives from a notion of the prior common gift of the earth to all humanity. For Aquinas, all ownership arrangements are contingent, resulting from historical, legal developments, and should be subordinated to serving the "common good."[34] It is a tradition of conceptualizing property that is echoed in modern Catholic social teaching. The latter view is encapsulated in the following statement from *Laborem Exercens*:

> Christian tradition has never upheld this right [to private property] as absolute and untouchable. On the contrary, it has always understood this right within the broader context of the right common to all to use the goods of the whole of creation: *the right to private property is subordinated to the right to common use*, to the fact that goods are meant for everyone.[35]

Prudential judgments are needed as to which institutional tool – household, market, corporation, state, commons, property – should be prioritized in order to provision a need or address a challenge through shared work. If monopolies and the domination these foster are to be avoided or curtailed, then there must be a basic commitment to a plurality of institutional forms and what it takes to sustain that plurality. Creativity comes in discerning the relative weight to be given to each element if flourishing is to be adequately and appropriately provisioned in any given context. For example, ignorance is a collective problem that education as a common good addresses. The provision of education can involve households, commons, state, markets, and corporations such as a university. Treating the provision of education as the exclusive domain of any one of these over concentrates power for it in one sector, thereby creating a monopoly, and cuts off education from vital resources. Instead, a vibrant mixed economy of educational provision is needed, one that involves a range of institutional means.

RELATING DIVINE AND HUMAN ECONOMIES[36]

As already noted, in the ancient Greco-Roman world, economy was understood to serve a vision of the good life. The management of the household as a site of flourishing was situated within concentric circles of moral and spiritual relations extending upward to the whole cosmos. Early Christianity drew on but also radically recalibrated this understanding of economy to frame God's providential ordering of the cosmos, referred to as God's *oikonomia* (economy). Its use in this way intersects with a whole range of scriptural and theological metaphors for divine-human relations as forms of work: the shepherd caring for a flock, the vigneron tending a vineyard, the farmer cultivating the land, the teacher educating students, and the physician attending to the health of a patient. Rather than the modern, bureaucratic sense of administration or management, these biblical examples suggest cultivation as the picture for how God orders the cosmos. Analogously, God's *oikonomia* seeks to create and sustain conditions in which creaturely life might grow and be fulfilled. In the formative period of Christian theology, God's economy referred to the Trinity's cultivation of salvation throughout creation, coming to a head in the incarnation of Jesus Christ (e.g., Eph 1:7–14).[37] Christ was both the means of cultivation and the embodiment of flourishing.

The theological conception of God's economy developed an innovative understanding of God's action in history. It represents a movement out of a cyclical view of history, with its cycles of growth and decay, to one of historical development and eschatological fulfillment beyond the iterative cycles of nature.[38] This innovation emerged by combining a conception of divine action as evolving through history (providence) with one of divine action as occurring in particular events or as the end point of history (eschatology). God's economy is the condition for the possibility of all human economies. Conversely, all other economies are good or bad to the extent to which they are attuned to and participate in God's economy (which transcends human economies). To borrow a distinction from Wendell Berry, when these "little" economies are rightly ordered, they prioritize participation in God's "great" economy.[39] Human economies make, exchange, distribute, and consume things, but such activity must work from the basis that humans are first and foremost members of God's economy and that the things manufactured, exchanged, distributed, and consumed are first received as gifts to be shared and are neither things wholly produced by human labor nor objects entirely under human control. When economic life ceases to serve right participation in God's economy, and instead serves the perpetuation of little economies divorced from membership of God's cosmic economy, then these little economies have become idolatrous and self-destructive. Little economies turned in on themselves are manifested in, for example, the idea that the sole purpose of economic activity is making money and the competitive pursuit of private interests.

Human little economies are made up of three intersecting and oftentimes contradicting ways of ordering and organizing life together (see Figure 13.1). Extending further my earlier theme that economies are about more than markets, my use of the term economy in what follows draws on an ancient sense of the term. "Economy," in origin, denotes more than merely the production, distribution, and consumption of material and financial goods and services. Economies necessitated the cultivation of what today are separated off into distinct realms: namely, the ordering of desire, the formation of a moral life, and the organization of religious devotion.[40] The household could not

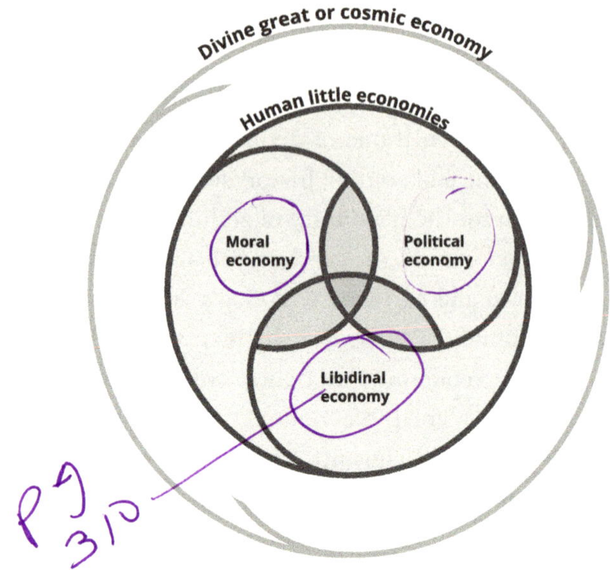

FIGURE 13.1 Human economies within God's cosmic economy

thrive without all these elements being cultivated. My contention is that every economic judgment in the modern sense is also at the same time a judgment for or against how to participate in an economy in the ancient sense; that is, as one that is reproducing a way of ordering our life with God, tending a moral form of life, and directing our desires to life giving ends.

In accord with what we associate with the term economics today, human little economies are in part made up of a political economy. Political economies are the material, institutional, and social means of structuring and administrating modes of production, distribution, and consumption. A political economy is a way of provisioning human life through assemblages of government, markets, societies, commons, and households – and the labor, material exchanges, and financial transactions that connect them. However, all political economies are material displays of moral commitments, with accounts and credit card statements a moral ledger as well as a record of financial transactions. As the New Testament puts it:

"for where your treasure is, there your heart will be also" (Matt 6:21). But beyond being moral investments (or lack thereof), political economies also trade off and depend on a "moral economy." They cannot function without an ethical register and way of ordering and shaping moral relations. For example, financial credit/debt relations rely on a moral framework in which to be moral, righteous, and just is to be personally responsible for what you borrow and to pay back what you owe. Or to reiterate a previous example, banking entirely depends on moral relations that produce trust, absent that trust and there will be a run on the banks that can undermine a whole political economy. Political economies are thus enfolded in a prior moral system and framework that itself needs cultivating if a given political economy is to be sustained.[41]

In accord with the ancient sense of economy, all economic judgments are thus producing, distributing, and consuming a "moral economy" that shapes and makes a form of life.[42] A moral economy is realized through upholding ethical norms; practices of care; the virtues that are esteemed (e.g., honor or humility); relations of trust, reciprocity, and mutual obligation; the ends that are pursued (e.g., health or wealth); the narratives and ritual processes through which meaning is made; and the visions of the good life that direct and give purpose to a form of life (e.g., *shalom* or material prosperity). These elements have been the focus of Parts I and II. However, building on what I say in Chapter 7, it is important to remember that human moral economies operate in fallen ways. Fallen moral economies are a field of wheat and tares that can deprave and deprive even as they enable and sustain forms of common life. Whether that common life is at the scale of Babylon and the United States or my school or neighborhood, all need conversion. Nevertheless, transgressing the ways a moral economy is operating – for good or ill – generates a sense of outrage because what is valued or considered sacred is desecrated. Depending on what is considered sacred, these responses can be democratic or anti-democratic. An uprising in response to police killing a Black person and protests over imposed plans to build a motorway through an underserved neighborhood are examples of the former. An example of the latter is a march to defend a public statue scheduled for demolition when the historical record shows the monument symbolizes racist norms, narratives, and ends but in the memory of those marching it is said to represent family, faith, and flag.

Central to the formation and ordering of all moral and political economies are economies of desire (or what some refer to as a "libidinal economy").[43] These are ways in which life together is governed through our appetites and emotions. This can be the desire for intangible, psychic goods like respect, security, recognition, or a sense of self-worth as well as manufactured hungers for material things like fashionable clothes or fast food. It includes structures of feeling that shape responses to and desire for others or the world around us. These feelings can be positive or negative; for example, fear, anger, disgust, or pleasure. Whether it is the advertising industry, Fox News, MSNBC, or the arrangement of the sights and smells of a supermarket, a great deal of investment goes into producing such feelings and desires so that whole populations can be either managed or mobilized. Libidinal economies also include aesthetic desires for the images, signs, and symbols that generate forms of identity and modes of representation. For example, the desire for a particular house or job is not merely the desire for a place to live or means of employment but also the desire for a status symbol and a conscious or unconscious desire to be identified with a certain class or social group.

Many contemporary accounts of human economies focus on only one of these ways through which life together is organized and governed. Most systematic theologies focus on the divine economy but never connect this to questions of political economy. Scientific Marxists and most contemporary economists focus on the political economy but ignore or treat as externalities the divine, moral, and libidinal economies. Many Christian virtue ethicists focus on the divine and moral economy but ignore how these are always already wrapped up with libidinal and political economies. Yet any ethical analysis of a common life necessitates attention to all four and the ways they intersect with and refract each other. For example, pornography is a libidinal economy of image and representation that trades on moral values of freedom and tolerance even as it transgresses other moral norms while being a multibillion dollar industry. It also disorientates us from participating in fruitful ways in God's cosmic economy. Another example is racism, which, as noted in the previous discussion of intimacy, renders certain bodies exploitable through a combination of the moral, political, and libidinal economies at work in slavery and capitalism, ways that distort and deprave God's great economy of creaturely life.

Churches often reproduce rather than contradict the ways fallen little economies are assembled and operate. They remake the world as it is, albeit with a Christian coat of paint. However, the church, in all its forms, is meant to be a little economy in tune with and bearing witness to the divine economy through reweaving fallen moral, political, and libidinal economies in *shalom*-like ways, ways that are to be represented and enacted in the sacramental life of the congregation.

This chapter focused on the question of how work can metabolize creation so as to provision a common life in ways that participate faithfully in God's *oikonomia*. In Chapter 14, I focus on how to form and sustain a *shalom*-like life through politics.

ACCOMPANYING READINGS

Gustavo Gutiérrez, *A Theology of Liberation: History, Politics, Salvation* (Maryknoll, NY: Orbis, 1973), chs. 2 and 9. Gutiérrez offers a critique of economic growth as the only measure of human development and unfolds an account of how economic and political liberation are intrinsic to a divine economy of salvation.

Wendell Berry, "Two Economies (1983)," *The Art of the Commonplace: The Agrarian Essays of Wendell Berry*, ed., Norman Wirzba (Washington, DC: Counterpoint, 2003), 219–235.

Pontifical Council for Justice and Peace, "Human Work," *Compendium of the Social Doctrine of the Church* (Cittá del Vaticano: Libreria Editrice Vaticana, 2004), ch. 6. Also available online. This section summarizes and synthesizes a broad range of encyclicals to articulate how Catholic social teaching understands work and its place in fostering human dignity and solidarity.

Vincent Miller, *Consuming Religion: Christian Faith and Practice in a Consumer Culture* (New York: Continuum, 2004), chs. 3 and 4. Miller reflects on how consumerism reshapes religious belief and practice through the interaction of political economies and economies of desire. Miller pays particular attention to how desire for God and participation in the divine economy is misdirected and commodified through consumerism.

Emilie Townes, *Womanist Ethics and the Cultural Production of Evil* (New York: Palgrave Macmillan, 2006), ch. 3. Townes examines how moral, libidinal, and political economies intersect to produce racism using the example of the marketing icon, Aunt Jemima, and the role of the Mammy figure in American history.

Jonathan Tran, "Deep Economy," *Asian Americans and the Spirit of Racial Capitalism* (New York: Oxford University Press, 2022), 192–243. Tran offers an account of how the intersection of racism and capitalism contrasts with the divine economy of creation, incarnation, and redemption and the work necessary to live into the latter so as to dismantle the former.

NOTES

1 What it takes to provision a way of life so it can survive and thrive falls under the heading of a theology of work and economic ethics, although as will be seen, these terms are problematic given the contemporary conflation of work with paid employment and economics with capitalism.

2 In some ways what I say echoes Karl Marx's notion of "social metabolism," but as per Chapter 2, human work does not simply act on nature to make human life possible but acts with nonhuman life through a meshwork of relations in order to generate human ways of being alive. All human economies are at the same time human-nonhuman ecologies.

3 An influential statement of this conception of work is given in Martin Heidegger's essay "Bauen, Wohnen, Denken [Building, Dwelling, Thinking]" (1951).

4 Karl Polanyi, *The Great Transformation: The Political and Economic Origins of Our Time*, 2nd ed. (Boston: Beacon, 2001 [1945]), 59–70.

5 Polanyi, *The Great Transformation*, 60.

6 Max Weber, *The Protestant Ethics and the Spirit of Capitalism*, trans., Talcott Parsons (London: Routledge, 2001 [1930]), 18.

7 Accounts of this dynamic are developed by feminist economists, those advocating for a civil economy, and recent developments in Catholic social

teaching. See, for example, Julie Nelson, *Economics for Humans* (Chicago: University of Chicago Press, 2006); Luigino Bruni and Stefano Zamagni, *Civil Economy: Efficiency, Equity, Public Happiness* (Bern: Peter Lang, 2007); and Benedict XVI, *Caritas in Veritate* (2009).

8 For examples of the "God as worker" approach, see Douglas Meeks, *God the Economist: The Doctrine of God and Political Economy* (Minneapolis, MN: Fortress Press, 1989); and David Jensen, *Responsive Labor: A Theology of Work* (Louisville, KY: Westminster John Knox Press, 2006).

9 Modern theologies of work tend to divide between those that emphasize how work is part of a creation mandate, those that ground good work in its eschatological possibilities, and those that envisage work as a co-creative act with God. I draw on elements of all these approaches without plumbing for one as definitive.

10 See, for example, Seth Holmes, *Fresh Fruit, Broken Bodies: Migrant Farmworkers in the United States* (Berkeley: University of California Press, 2013).

11 To put this in terms of an equation, this is the shift from commodity-money-commodity (CMC) to money-commodity-money (MCM).

12 *Henry IV*, Part 1, Act 1, scene 2.

13 Martin Luther King Jr., "All Labor Has Dignity," *The Radical King*, ed., Cornel West (Boston: Beacon Press, 2015), 246.

14 Dirty work is not only that which is unpleasant or unsanitary. As Eyal Press defines it, dirty work is also that work which is in some way morally suspect, shameful, or injurious and thereby demeaning, yet required by society for it to function. Such work is largely hidden from view and mostly undertaken by those who themselves exist in conditions of precarity with few other options. Ethically, we must question the conditions that make some jobs seem essential when they are so physically dangerous or morally compromising. The examples Press discusses are prison custodial staff, military drone operators, and slaughterhouse workers. Eyal Press, *Dirty Work: Essential Jobs and the Hidden Toll of Inequality in America* (New York: Farrar, Straus and Giroux, 2021).

15 Martin Luther, "Lectures on Genesis," *Luther's Works*, 55 vols., eds., Jaroslav Pelikan and Helmut Lehmann (Philadelphia; St. Louis, MO: Fortress; Concordia, 1955–1986), vol. 3, 218.

16 *Laborem Exercens*, §V.24.

17 Alasdair MacIntyre, "Where We Were, Where We Are, Where We Need to Be," *Virtue and Politics: Alasdair MacIntyre's Revolutionary Aristotelianism* (Notre Dame, IN: University of Notre Dame Press, 2011), 323.

18 While advocating a vocational egalitarianism, the Reformers, echoing medieval guild practice, rightly emphasized that vocation cannot be separated from connection to the life of the church, which can be marked through sacramental and institutional linkages such as prayers, services of thanksgiving, and chaplaincy.

19 Under this definition of work, children, the severely disabled, the elderly, and all those in situations of radical dependency do work just as they can all contribute to the sacramental life of the church through being present with others in worship.

20 Jacob Neusner, "Work in Formative Judaism," *The Encyclopedia of Judaism*, vol. 4, eds., Jacob Neusner et al. (Leiden: Brill, 2005), 2829.

21 Contemplation, rest, and play do not imply solemnity or quiet. The Jesus who plays ludic games with loaves and fishes and turns water into wine, thereby conjuring up plenty amidst dearth, needs celebrating as much as the Christ who calls on the rich young ruler to see that true value does not reside in wealth and luxury or Christ the suffering servant. In their feasting and carnivals, medieval peasants could be more faithful than their monastic contemporaries to the incarnation.

22 Technically, this is referred to as the Easterlin paradox after the economist, Richard Easterlin, who first discovered it in the 1970s.

23 Kate Raworth, *Doughnut Economics: 7 Ways to Think Like a 21st Century Economist* (White River Junction, VT: Chelsea Green, 2017), 47.

24 Walter Brueggemann, *Living toward a Vision: Biblical Reflections on Shalom* (New York: United Church Press, 1982), 100–101.

25 There is much debate about how to interpret Locke's influential theory of property and how this connects to his conception of natural rights that itself became a foundational part of liberal moral and political thought. What is often missed is the role of Genesis in its inception, particularly the exegesis of Genesis 1:28, and how his account of property is driven by a sense of the need to respond to God's blessing "to be fruitful and multiply." See especially John Locke, "First Tract on Government" (1660).

26 Luigino Bruni and Stefano Zamagni, *Civil Economy: Efficiency, Equity, Public Happiness* (Bern: Lang, 2007).

27 In pointing to the importance of households, state, commons, and corporate forms of association, I am building on the work of Karl Polanyi,

Elinor Ostrom, Ivan Illich, David Bollier, Kate Raworth, Julie Nelson, and the field of institutional economics.

28 Ivan Illich, *Tools for Conviviality* (New York: Marion Boyars, 1985 [1973]). On Illich's account, tools for conviviality enable fellowship and are technologies, systems, and structures that strengthen the agency of ordinary persons, are "open source" in that they are available to everyone and easily replicated and distributed, and are highly adaptive. On my account, the household, commons, corporate forms of association, and the market are just such tools for provisioning human ways of being alive and addressing shared problems. Democratized state systems can share some of these elements but not all.

29 Economist Elinor Ostrom demonstrates empirically that a commons, as a cultural-ecological-political construct, is often the fruit of a negotiation between and interweaving of public authorities, market processes, property rights, and nonpecuniary forms of organization and association based on customary practice and tradition. Elinor Ostrom, *Governing the Commons: The Evolution of Institutions for Collective Action* (Cambridge: Cambridge University Press, 1990).

30 *The Institutes of Justinian*, trans., J. B. Moyle, 3rd ed. (Oxford: Clarendon Press, 1896), 36.

31 *The Institutes of Justinian*, 36–37.

32 This reflects the existing reality. Whether US national parks should have been understood as a commons developed in dialogue with and respecting the native Americans who lived there is another matter.

33 A parallel conception of property as a communicable and shared good can also be found in the work of John Wesley and early Methodism. Wesley, while in many respects a Tory, rejected an account of property as an inviolable right. See Randy L. Maddox, "'Visit the Poor': John Wesley, the Poor, and the Sanctification of Believers," *The Poor and the People Called Methodists, 1729–1999*, ed., Richard P. Heitzenrater (Nashville, TN: Kingswood, 2002), 59–81.

34 *Summa theologiae* IIa–IIae, qu. 66. See also John Finnis, *Aquinas: Moral, Political, and Legal Theory* (Oxford: Oxford University Press, 1998), 187–210. For a general account of Aquinas's economic vision in dialogue with contemporary economics, see Mary Hirschfeld, *Aquinas and the Market: Toward a Humane Economy* (Cambridge, MA: Harvard University Press, 2018).

35 John Paul II, *Laborem Exercens*, §14. See also John Paul II, *Centesimus Annus*, §43.

36 For my discussion of the relationship between theology and economics, debt, money, economic democracy, the need to distinguish markets as a social practice from capitalism, and the nature of capitalism and the ideology of libertarianism as a theological problem, see Luke Bretherton, *Christ and the Common Life* (Grand Rapids, MI: Eerdmans, 2022), 323–358.

37 The primary focus was not divine-human relations so much as the relation between the Father and the Son, within which all other relations were situated.

38 It could be argued that this shift is the conceptual backdrop to modern ideas of progress and aligned notions of economic growth without limits. A cyclical view of history has a notion of limits built in whereas some eschatological conceptions of history can lead to either the material world not mattering (as in premillennial accounts) or a sense of ever-unfolding progress (as in postmillennial accounts). The Irenaean view outlined here stands as a critique of both a gnostic undervaluing of creation and materiality and a wholly immanent protological and progressive view of God's action in history.

39 Wendell Berry, "Two Economies (1983)," *The Art of the Commonplace: The Agrarian Essays of Wendell Berry*, ed., Norman Wirzba (Washington, DC: Counterpoint, 2003), 219–235.

40 See, for example, Xenophon, *Oikonomikos*.

41 A classic study of the dependency of a political economy on a prior moral ethos is Weber, *The Protestant Ethics and the Spirit of Capitalism*.

42 Use of the term "moral economy" originates with the work of E. P. Thompson and James C. Scott.

43 My use of the terms "economy of desire" and "libidinal economy" draws on a broad range of work that includes feminist and patristic theologies of desire (e.g., Sarah Coakley); Augustinian critiques of consumerism as driven by misdirected desire (e.g., Vincent Miller); the role of desire in Latinx theological aesthetics (e.g., Roberto Goizueta); the cultural, affective, and aesthetic dimensions of racial capitalism identified by womanist and black feminist writers (e.g., Emily Townes and Keri Day); affect theory (e.g., Sara Ahmed); and critical theories of the libidinal economy (e.g., Jean-François Lyotard and the Afropessimist thinkers Jared Sexton and Frank Wilderson).

14 Politics

When most of us hear the word "politics" we think of either fights between political parties, fractious policy debates, or a manipulative and self-interested form of negotiation expressed in the phrase "they're playing politics with the issue." But underneath the polarization, rage tweets, and backroom deals is the reality that politics is the description of a moral and existential good. Politics embodies the recognition that some kind of common life with others must be cultivated and sustained over time if life is to go on. Politics is the name for generating this common life and the stark alternative to three other options. When I meet someone I disagree with, dislike, find strange or threatening, I can do one of four things. I can kill them. I can create a structure of domination so I can control them. I can make life so difficult that they run away. Or I can do politics. That is to say, I can form, norm, and sustain some kind of common life – amid asymmetries of power, competing visions of the good, and my own feelings of fear or aversion – without killing, dominating, or causing them to flee. These really are the only options. Human history and the contemporary context are awash with examples of the first three approaches. Faithful Christians should be invested in the fourth one for both theological and practical reasons I'll sketch here.

This chapter recovers an understanding of politics as a moral good. It begins from the recognition that politics is essential to live, let alone live well. It is through politics that we determine whether our life with others – at whatever scale, from the local to the global – is just or unjust, generous or heartless, peaceable or violent, attuned to or destructive of creation. In what follows, I examine what it means for humans to be political animals and for Christians to be a particular kind of political animal through reflecting on the quality and character of good political relations as well as their meaning and purpose. My contention here is that politics is a primary way we discover and fulfill what it means to be a creature, answer the call to love God and neighbor, and witness to distinctively Christian forms of life called church. In relation to this last point, to be a Christian political animal is to be a member of the people of God – a distinctive kind of political community that can only be formed and sustained through politics.

The overarching argument of this chapter is that the aim of politics is to pursue the moral good of association and that an ethical politics cultivates loving and just forms of association. But I begin by setting out why talking about politics in a theological key necessitates attending to how such talk must have a tragic, apocalyptic, and pastoral register if it is to articulate the conditions of political life in this age.

THE APOCALYPTIC, TRAGIC, AND PASTORAL DIMENSIONS OF POLITICS

Theologically, politics takes place between Christ's ascension and return. This orientation means Christians must trust that history is open to change, a new creation is coming, and that the Spirit can bring into being a radical, surprising, and unanticipated newness, often in response to the cry for justice and love by those on the underside of history. So Christian political witness must have an apocalyptic register. An apocalyptic register is born out of a revelation of what is really happening from a heavenly perspective and a discernment of the active and living presence of God here and now. An apocalyptic register also sounds a note of judgment on the present order of things, making clear that the world as it is is not the world as it should be, and so we should repent and humble ourselves. It demands reckoning with how our lives now are subject to the judgment to come and that we live in a time when the kingdom of God is present, creating moments of transformation and rupture. New beginnings are possible, and so established ways of doing things need reevaluating. It is not good enough to simply go with the flow because the messianic age is dawning, so we must act now as if the present order of things does not have the last word and is coming to an end. This apocalyptic orientation calls for judgments that both provide prophetic critique of current arrangements and proclaim new visions of what flourishing could mean for these people here and now in the light of the end of *this* world, that is, the form of life we currently inhabit.

Alongside an apocalyptic register, a Christian conception of politics must also attend to the tragic nature of politics in this age before Christ's return. As noted throughout this book, we are always already having to act in a world we did not make and do not control. One implication of this today is that Christian political witness must wrestle with what it means to act together with others in a context shaped by the violence and brutality we inherit from ages past. That may be the legacies of the Atlantic slave trade and its afterlife in racial capitalism, anti-Semitism and the Holocaust, the history and ongoing reality of discrimination based on gender or sexuality, or the destruction of ecosystems because of deeply entrenched forms of extractivist production and consumption. And as the inheritors of various brutal histories, we must also wrestle with the dilemma of how to balance the pursuit of justice with the need for order if the world around us is not to collapse into violent chaos through the settling of scores. To wrestle with what it means to do politics amid histories of violence and structures of domination means understanding the tragic nature of political action amid suffering, loss, the randomness of evil, intractable injustice, and the fragility and folly of life with others. Echoing Chapter 7, a tragic orientation involves a certain realism about what can and cannot be achieved through earthly politics.[1] And in keeping with the account of judgment in Chapter 11, the tragic nature of politics in this world corresponds to the need for judgments and institutional arrangements that restrain evil and either uphold or move toward a more equitable order. So a tragic register must be woven together with an apocalyptic one if we are to realize a full account of politics.

A third condition of politics is that it takes place through and serves the ordinary life that must be cultivated if children are to be raised, crops planted, and life is to go on. Thus, Christian political witness must also have a pastoral register.[2] The Old Testament is awash with pastoral imagery and concerns (e.g., the laws around land and sabbath keeping and divine rule envisioned in creational and pastoral terms). Likewise, Jesus's teaching and parables are permeated with agricultural and pastoral imagery, populated as they are by shepherds, sowers, and vine keepers. Jesus's rule is likened to that of a shepherd whose simple life, exemplary virtue, and moral teachings contrast with the sophistry and cowardice of Pilate as well as that of the decadent quisling, Herod. But alongside the world of work and politics through which we cultivate shared realms of meaning and action, the pastoral also refers to the everyday world of family life, another stream of scriptural reference: sons run off and return, children are healed and nursed, food is prepared and eaten. The pastoral encompasses the mundane joys and struggles that make up the ordinary time of our lives.[3] These too are crucibles of divine disclosure and constitute part and parcel of political life. In contrast to the apocalyptic and tragic, the pastoral as a genre is not pressed for time. It can depict a present in which humans, animals, and the landscape are intimately connected and reciprocally related.

C. S. Lewis captures the role of the state in relation to the pastoral dimension of political life when he says:

> The state exists simply to promote and to protect the ordinary happiness of human beings in this life. A husband and wife chatting over a fire, a couple of friends having a game of darts in a pub, a man reading a book in his own room or digging in his own garden – that is what the state is there for. And unless they are helping to increase and prolong and protect such moments, all the laws, parliaments, armies, courts, police, economics etc. are simply a waste of time.[4]

But beyond the duties of the state, a pastoral register attends to the *social* practices that reweave life together through gestures of hospitality, reconciliation, and forgiveness and provide the nourishment necessary to sustaining life with others. As noted in Chapter 13, the classical and modern relegation of the domestic life in which such nurture mostly takes place to the "private" is not one Christian ethics should subscribe to. A pastoral register, no less than a tragic and an apocalyptic one, is vital for a faithful, hopeful, and loving approach to politics. Attention to the pastoral needs of a community calls for judgments and forms of organization that cultivate nourishing patterns of life that bring everyday kinds of blessings and help nourish virtuous people capable of life-giving mercies.

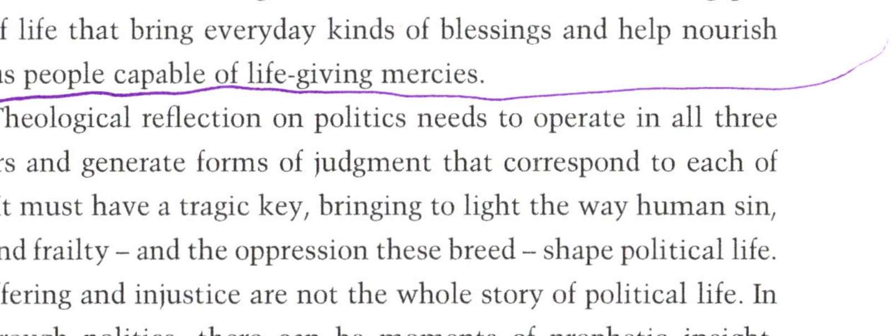

Theological reflection on politics needs to operate in all three registers and generate forms of judgment that correspond to each of them. It must have a tragic key, bringing to light the way human sin, folly, and frailty – and the oppression these breed – shape political life. But suffering and injustice are not the whole story of political life. In and through politics, there can be moments of prophetic insight, repentance, and transformation, as well as disclosures of the active work of the Spirit making all things new. So political speech and action must find ways to speak of hope cradled in grief, love swaddled in death. But to only speak of hope and grief, without being able to consecrate the common joys and activities that make up a life, Christian witness will be anemic and disconnected from the realities of how life is actually lived. Likewise, to speak in only one register – as if we are only in the end times, or there is only tragedy or nothing of concern beyond the everyday – is to render ourselves prone to grotesque misjudgments that cause great harm to ourselves and those around us. Apocalypticism alone produces violent polarization that dehumanizes enemies. A tragic sensibility left unchecked baptizes the status quo, breeding fatalism rather than hope. And a solely pastoral concern generates disregard for systemic injustice and the misery of those outside my immediate circle of care. As I explore in what follows, to be wise, political speech and action must attend to all three registers.

HUMAN CREATURES ARE POLITICAL ANIMALS

To be a human creature is to be a political animal. Humans are not created to be alone. As noted throughout this book, we are vulnerable, interdependent animals whose very survival depends on the care we give to and receive from others. And beyond mere survival, our flourishing depends on being embedded in loving and just forms of common life. Politics is the work of forming, norming, and sustaining that common life with others. As shared communication and action, politics is purposeful activity that has material effects. Through doing this work together, we actualize who we are individually and collectively. Like all forms of work, we need rest from it, and so there must be times when politics stops and we either rest or do other kinds of work to ensure life carries on. And as a form of work in the earthly city, politics is undertaken within the tension-filled and ambiguous time between the world as it is and the world as it will be in the age to come.

Just because politics operates under conditions of finitude and fallenness does not mean politics is necessarily a corrupt or dirty business, as many assume. It does mean that a distinctive feature of how humans are political animals is that humans can decide to act against their ability to live well. Despite being able to adapt to the ecosystems we depend on and having social relations suited to our thriving, we often turn both against ourselves, thereby destroying the conditions of human flourishing. As Aristotle argued, tyranny is one such way of making life unlivable. It is a catastrophic failure of what it means to be a human attuned to the material and social conditions of what it takes to thrive as animals.[5] The scriptural insight is that before the messianic age politics will always be a struggle that involves negotiating asymmetries of power and often divergent or conflicting visions of what it means to be good. Doing politics well involves discovering ways and means of shared flourishing in the midst of the often intractable disagreements that emerge in this age. Discovering how to flourish together through politics reveals the ways all forms of common life are founded on and a response to a prior and more basic form of shared creaturely life.

Contrary to modern origin myths of humans as lone individuals who contract together to form polities, the account of politics given here assumes that no one is or can be an island. Human animals are interdependent creatures, enmeshed in forms of shared life. The nature, shape, and ends of our political, moral, and libidinal economies change, but all forms of life and the identities they generate are simply reworkings of a prior, more basic, created sociality. However, as is often the case, we can make a life together that either benefits the few and burdens the many or exploits a minority to benefit a majority. Yet, what is made can be remade. For example, racist and sexist political economies are produced. They are neither inevitable, timeless, necessary, nor inherent features of human existence. They assemble material and social relations in particular ways that can be disassembled and reorganized. Like all forms of domination and exploitation, they are parasitic on the created sociality of human existence. They are a privation and depravation of creaturely goodness, a falling away from how things are created to be in God's divine economy as well as a turning away from how things will be in the new creation. Christians are to work with others through politics to remake the world as it should be and bear witness to how it will be in Christ. In other words, Christians are to be salt and light. Being salt means identifying and conserving what is good in our society that we receive from those who came before us, tending and cultivating it so that it can be handed on to the next generation. Christians are also to be light, which exposes the deeds of darkness and brings understanding. Being light means identifying what needs changing if we are to move from the world as it is to a more generous and just one. But being light also means nurturing and forming new practices and institutional arrangements that point to and exemplify the kingdom of God.

Politics is a necessary condition for transforming the world, but by itself it is not sufficient. Echoing previous chapters, *shalom*-like transformation also requires people to be formed in virtues, guided by wise laws and rules, and provisioned by institutions that enable them to act together in more loving and just ways over time and at a fitting scale. And if politics is to be directed to ends that bless rather than curse, it requires reflection and deliberation on the meaning and purpose of our common life and the goods we seek to sustain it. Theologically, this entails reflecting on the significance, purpose, and ordering of forms of common life in response to the address of God we hear in creation, Scripture, encountering the stranger, cries for liberation, and the wisdom of our ancestors, Christian or otherwise.

Just as medicine serves the moral good of health, so politics serves a moral good: the good of association. Participation in and fulfillment of this common good is constitutive of human flourishing. It is through politics that we build up a shared world of meaning and action that makes for thriving forms of life together. Association is both an intrinsic good and the primary means through which to fulfill other substantive common goods, such as health and education. Indeed, association is arguably the most basic and important common good as no other good, public or common, can be achieved without it. Moreover, it is only through politics that collective needs and problems can be addressed peaceably and justly.

A key dimension of association as a good is that it represents what is common or shared by all. Other terms for this common life include the "commonwealth," "commonweal," "public life," or *res publica*. To pursue this common good, politics must be directed to the flourishing of the whole rather than the part, the common rather than either a factional or private interest. When political life serves only the interests of the one, the few, or even the many rather than what is common or shared, then politics is corrupted into a form of tyranny such as a plutocracy, oligarchy, or majoritarianism.

Politics is also corrupted when it is viewed in individualistic terms. Contrary to utilitarian accounts, as political animals we are not utility maximizers. Such a view reduces politics to a process of aggregating individual choices into a collective interest. Neither are we individual contractors bound together by nothing more than market and legal exchanges. Rather, we are persons who come to be in the pursuit of shared goods (e.g., education and health) on which the flourishing of each depends and through specific kinds of relationship with others (as mothers, brothers, citizens, nurses, etc.) that entail virtuous relations if they are to go well.

To expand on an earlier point, to be sustained over time and at scale, politics requires institutional forms that enable the pursuit of association amid disagreement and diversity. These institutions (and the rules and regulations that help constitute them) take the form of laws, constitutions, the means of governance (e.g., bureaucracy), and electoral systems. As a name for the institutions of a polity, politics is a synonym for statecraft: that is, the exercise of sovereignty and the governance of state apparatus. At its best, statecraft is an instrumental and functional good that helps to order and maintain a common life. Failure to serve the good of association and instead make the state an end in itself means statecraft is disordered and oppressive, which will thereby render life unlivable for many.

Statecraft includes formal, institutional practices for sustaining commonality amid difference. But statecraft does not exhaust the ways and means of doing politics. Alongside statecraft, politics also refers to the participatory and collaborative social practices through which a common world is cultivated. Politics as an informal, relational craft takes place in multiple settings and is not coextensive with control of the state or even dependent on there being a state. Nomads in the desert outside of any formal state structures still generate a rich form of political life through customary practices of hospitality, greeting, etc., through which they sustain a common life based on shared goods (e.g., access to water). Elders and pastors negotiating changing service times in a church are practicing the craft of politics. Boardroom negotiations without recourse to litigation are a form of politics. Neighbors sorting out complaints about noise between themselves without calling the police are likewise doing politics in this informal dimension.

Politics as a craft for collaboration and making shared judgments about what is common entails acting in a way appropriate to the time/*kairos*. Hence it entails the need for prudential judgments about what is best in a particular situation: How, when, and where should we act and what should we do? And as action in time, politics involves questions of power and so requires answering questions about how to act, who does what to whom, and how to achieve our goals. This, in turn, raises questions about legitimacy: Why should we act this way rather than that way, who gets to act, and what is the meaning and purpose of our actions? And finally, politics involves wily wisdom: the local knowledge, strategic analysis, and practical skills necessary to respond appropriately to a constantly changing and ambiguous environment. In combination, this is what it means to be "shrewd as serpents and innocent as doves" (Matt 10:16).

The account of politics outlined here suggests that politics is categorically not war by other means. The bullet and the ballot box are mutually exclusive routes to solving shared problems.[6] At a basic level, politics as a means of negotiating conflict is the alternative to unrestrained violence and cycles of revenge. Politics entails a commitment to conditions in which worlds of shared meaning and collaborative action can be created or sustained. By contrast, the proactive use of physical violence – beatings, kidnapping, torture, bombing, and the like by state and nonstate actors – represents the destruction of the institutions, customs, practices, and habits that enable communication, trust, and reciprocal relationships to be sustained.[7] Consequently, it is inappropriate to use "politics" as a synonym for talk of power understood as a wholly negative and inherently violent phenomenon.[8]

If politics is not war by other means, neither does it depend on sharing the same ideology. Politics does not begin once everyone I disagree with has left the room. Rather, it presumes difference and diversity. It begins from the assumption that we are all complex bundles of competing, often contradictory loyalties and loves whose personhood cannot and should not be reduced to a singular set of commitments or beliefs. An implication of this assumption is that a political position is not a placeholder for character. People with views I abhor have shown me love and kindness beyond what I deserve; while others I agree with on most things have stabbed me in the back in the blink of an eye. To do politics and thereby forge some kind of common life, it matters far more how someone actually treats those around them than whether they share the same beliefs or worldview. Multiparty parliamentary systems and their attendant practices of loyal opposition embody this understanding of politics.

In the same vein, the moral basis of a common life is politics and *not* "family, faith, or flag." There are of course myriad attempts to circumvent the need to have a robust form of politics through saying a common life is based on something else: the "we" in "we, the people" is constituted by sharing the same blood, history, culture, or religion. However, envisioning the body politic as living and moving by one of these is inherently exclusionary, as it is closed to and denies the contribution of those who are not part of the same ethnicity, history, culture, or religion. Such things inevitably and quite properly inform and shape the identity and character of a polity, invoking bonds of loyalty and a sense of belonging to it. But anchoring public life in anything other than pursuit of common goods and the conciliation of different interests through politics refuses the fact of plurality and can quickly lead to killing, dominating, or persecuting those who are not considered like "us." Understanding the commonwealth as constituted through politics means that its nature and form is only ever as good as, and must be persistently remade through, the quality and character of its political relationships, modes of communication, and institutional processes.[9] Without constant tending, a task for which all citizens are responsible, the common life of a polity becomes brittle and is easily shattered.

POWER IN POLITICS

Politics necessarily involves power. But power should not be a scary word. It simply means the ability to act. At its most basic, political power takes the form of either relational power (power with), or unilateral power (power over), or some combination of both. There is a third source of political agency: "soul power" or the power from within. This is the subjective, internal element that enables individual action over, with, or for others. It includes drive, motivations, gifts (including spiritual gifts), will, dispositions (whether toward virtue or vice), sense of vocation, and personality/charisma/spirit.[10] But my focus here is relational and unilateral power.

Statecraft primarily deploys unilateral, command and control forms of power, whereas politics as a participative and collaborative craft depends on relational power. Both can be used to oppressive ends. However, attention to relational power foregrounds agency, while focusing on unilateral power directs attention to structures and systems. Attending to the ordinary ways people are able to relate to and act with each other is important because otherwise there is little to say other than wolves eat sheep, power corrupts, and the strong triumph over the weak. Overly deterministic accounts of unilateral, "command-obedience" conceptions of power and the domination of structural forces such as capitalism and racism deny the kinds of individual and communal agency that can enable social movements and other forms of political action to bring about change.[11] Through ends-oriented and conscious action in concert, the structurally weak can resist the unilateral power of money and the state in order to establish shared goods. The early labor and civil rights movements are paradigmatic examples of such relational power in action, and both depended on traditions of popular piety such as those found in Black-led churches, Methodism, and Roman Catholicism. A faithful politics does not renounce power, it converts it. Power redeemed is power shared and reconfigured so that each person's agency and gifts might be exercised to bring blessings to all as part of a collaborative endeavor.

There is a key divide in theological reflection on politics as to whether political life is understood as a post-Fall development or whether it is an original part of creation (a division often mistakenly attributed to a difference between Augustine and Aquinas). If the former, the need for politics is a symptom of the introduction of sin into creation; if the latter, politics is a good in itself rather than at best a providential good that inhibits things getting worse. A lot follows from this division. If the former, political authority and political life are primarily about restraining evil. If the latter, politics is part of human flourishing, even though, after the Fall, it is caught up in and manifests idolatrous and sinful patterns.

I split the difference. Politics is a creational good, the goal of which is cultivating *shalom*-like forms of common life that, post-Fall, should seek to restore and repair the goodness of creaturely life and bear witness to the coming kingdom of God. Statecraft, which necessitates the use of coercive, unilateral power, is a postlapsarian enterprise that at its best inhibits evil. Inhibiting evil is not, however, only a negative act of restraint. It includes enabling a common life to be so ordered that it can be sustained over time through such measures as providing public goods like sewers and roads, as well as common goods, like healthcare. That said, if our common life is to be loving and just, then something more than statecraft is needed. That "something more" is a rich and diverse associational life – and the relational power it enables.

The character and form of a distinctively Christian vision of political relations is based on neighbor love. I spell out below what I mean by neighbor love and how it incorporates love of the stranger, the enemy, and the friendless. In so doing, neighbor love fulfills the basic moral commitment for politics as the cultivation of a common life to be possible: that is, a commitment to the dignity of friends *and* those not like "us" (however that "us" is defined) or whom we don't like or find objectionable.

POLITICS AS A MODE OF NEIGHBOR LOVE

The constructive way in which Christians frame relations with others in a fallen world is in terms of loving one's neighbor. The parable of the Good Samaritan is the paradigmatic scriptural passage for understanding neighbor love. In the story, the neighbor loved has three identities: he is a stranger, an enemy, and someone who, in his suffering, is without either friends to help him or the capacity to care for himself. In the light of the parable, neighbor love is a vocation to love strangers, enemies, and the suffering, excluded, and impoverished who lack the resources to meet their needs. Chapter 4 addressed the imperative to love strangers, while Chapter 5 reflected on the preferential option for the poor; so here I focus on how folded into neighbor love is love of enemies (Matt 5:43–48; Luke 6:27–28).

In the call to love enemies as neighbors, the New Testament addresses a central moral problem of politics. In the Greco-Roman world, those judged to be outsiders/noncitizens, whether resident within the boundaries of the polity or living elsewhere, were potential, if not actual, enemies. Their way of life threatened the very existence of the *polis*. And since the physical, moral, and spiritual flourishing of the individual citizen was coterminous with the flourishing of the city, this meant that outsiders not identified with or contributing to the life of the polity were necessarily either potentially seditious (if they were resident aliens) or a threat (if they were foreigners). It was necessary to guard against alien forms of life, and if they disturbed the peace, they were either repressed (if inside the walls) or repelled (if outside). Violent reactions against Paul's preaching and miracles in cities like Philippi and Ephesus exemplify these responses (Acts 16:12–40; 19). Internal and external "others" were also a means by which the common life of "our" polity came to be defined and understood. "We, the people" were not like "them," and all that the other was imagined to be (effeminate, uncivilized, treacherous, cruel, etc.) was all that "we" were not (virile, loyal, brave, honest, rational, etc.). See, for example, numerous ancient Greek depictions of the Persians.

Notoriously, the Nazi jurist and political thinker Carl Schmitt made a virtue of friend-enemy relations, seeing them as the basis of political life.[12] We should neither make a virtue of them nor see them as the basis of politics, but neither can we ignore Schmitt's insight that they are a central feature of political life from the ancient to the modern world. Different civilizations have imagined themselves over against different internal and external others, and friend-enemy relations deeply shape fallen political life. This is no less true of Christendom than of city-states like Athens, or the Roman, Ottoman, or Ming empires, or atheistic states like the former Soviet Union. European, confessionally Christian civilization historically imagined itself over against the internal other of Jews and the external other of Muslims. This self-understanding thereby justified the repression or subjugation of Jews and Muslims and formed the thought world that subsequently justified the subjugation of various "pagan" and nonwhite peoples.

Theologically, friend-enemy relations need converting so they are ordered according to neighbor love. The universal scope of God's love and presence calls into question any attempt to make the "friend-enemy" binary definitive. The heretic Samaritan and the pagan Syrophoenician woman, no less than the faithful Jewish man, can teach us something about God, how to live well, and that God can be present in "their" form of life, despite it being very different from "ours."[13] This is not to deny that Christians have a distinctive vision and form of life that others can threaten and seek to destroy, but it should prohibit any attempt to set in stone distinctions between Christians and non-Christians. Friend-enemy relations are fallen rather than created; thus, they can be converted. Indeed, love of neighbor embodies the redemptive possibilities of politics. It disrupts how we imagine and construct friend-enemy relations by extending our sense of who to include in our common life.

The neighbor contrasts with other ways of imagining and narrating the relationships that constitute our forms of shared life. One way of conceptualizing good political relations, which mostly draws inspiration from Aristotle, is as public friendships. But unlike being a friend, being a neighbor does not depend on liking, having a rapport with, or being equal to others. Neither is being a neighbor a condition, state of being, or preassigned role. Unlike such things as family, class, or ethnicity who my neighbor is cannot be predetermined. Neighbors have neither assigned social identities (e.g., father, sister) nor institutionally constructed roles (e.g., doctor, police officer). We only discover our neighbor within contingent and contextual relationships. Moreover, we can encounter a neighbor in any one of our roles and beyond the boundaries of those with whom we identify. Indeed, the encounter with a neighbor confronts us with a need to interrogate our own settled identities and the ways these inhibit our ability to treat others as neighbors. Neighbor love can therefore disrupt ways of constructing a common life through hierarchies of status or identity. It also cuts across vocational and ideological lines, superseding prior commitments and loyalties. The dynamics of neighbor love can, at times, demand greater intensity of devotion to distant neighbors than to family and friends, whether that distance be cultural, ideological, economic, or geographic. For example, when out walking in the park with my kids and I see someone has fallen into the pond, the imperative to help them in that moment supersedes my vocation as a parent to prioritize care for my children.

AGITATIONAL SOLIDARITY AS LOVE OF ENEMIES

Christian enemy-love tends to fall into one of three traps. Either we make everyone an enemy (the sectarian temptation to denounce anyone who is not like "us"). Or we make no one an enemy, denying any substantive conflicts and pretending that if we just read our Bible and pray, things like racism and economic injustice will get better by means of some invisible process (the temptation of sentimentalism). Or we fail to see how enemies claim in problematic ways to be our friend (the temptation of naïveté that ignores questions of power). In relation to this last trap, we must recognize that the powerful mostly refuse to recognize they are enemies to the oppressed and claim they are friends with everyone.

A loving act in relation to those in power who refuse to acknowledge their oppressive action is to force those who claim to be friends to everyone (and are thereby friends to no one) to recognize that their actions perpetuate domination and need renouncing. This involves struggle culminating in an ongoing dance of conflict and conciliation. With too much conflict, we cannot hear each other. Politics thereby dissolves into sloganeering, polarized denunciation, and eventually violent strife. With too much conciliation, we paper over real points of disagreement, foreshortening the debate and concealing the truth of what is going on. Like any good dance, politics as a form of neighbor love requires cultivating a sense of motion in balance through learning certain moves, fostering specific dispositions like patience and courage, and developing the ability to live with tension. It is also important to remember that tumult can be a means of grace no less than times of calm. But for a dance of conflict and conciliation to be formational of holiness we must learn to see enemies as neighbors capable of change and recognize that we ourselves must move and change.

Building any form of loving and just common life through a dance of conflict and conciliation entails reckoning with a hard truth: everyone must change, and in the process, we must all lose something to someone at some point. Change is part of what it means to live as frail, finite, and fallen creatures who are nevertheless open to new ways of being alive. If some kind of shared flourishing is to emerge, loss – and therefore negotiation and compromise – is inevitable.[14] The temptation for those with concentrations of privilege and power is to fix the system so that they lose nothing and others always lose, no matter how hard they work. The fight is to ensure that the loss is not borne disproportionately by the poor and marginalized. And, as James Baldwin articulated with such force in the context of getting White folk to realize their complicity in racism, central to this fight is agitation that punctures the entitled innocence of those who "have destroyed and are destroying hundreds of thousands of lives and do not know it and do not want to know it."[15] The fight also includes holding accountable those who train "their tongues to speak falsely (Jer 9:3–4), who humiliate and demean others, and who intend evil to secure themselves. Such a fight is a critical part of what it means to love our neighbor in a way that is faithful to the life, death, and resurrection of Jesus Christ. To use Martin Luther King Jr.'s formulation, such agitation and protest is "love correcting that which revolts against love."[16] Political struggles for a more loving and just common life are thereby a defining feature of neighbor love. Explored below is how agitational democratic politics can embody such love.

The divine call to listen to and learn from strangers discussed in Chapter 4 should prohibit Christians from turning conflicts over material needs (oil, water, land, etc.) and penultimate common goods (education, health, etc.) into ultimate, Manichaean conflicts of good against evil. When Christians do this, it is because they are overinvested in worldly projects of salvation, having lost sight of the ultimate by making a god of the penultimate. The theological term for this kind of overinvestment is idolatry. Standing against such overinvestments is the crucified Jesus who shatters all attempts to stabilize a single way of life as the ideal way of being human to which all others should conform. Everyone needs conversion, and the church is always in need of reformation. Conversely, building a common life with strangers and enemies is a way to bear faithful witness to Christ as the one in whom all things are created and through whom all may be reconciled. Thus, virtuous resistance to tyranny is not only oppositional; it also requires pointing to an inherent interdependency and the possibilities of a common life beyond conflict. This is a key theological insight that shaped Martin Luther King Jr.'s political ethics and his vision of beloved community. This creational interdependency renewed and fulfilled in Christ's life, death, and resurrection prohibits absolutizing friend-enemy relations in any form, whether between proletariat and bourgeoisie, men and women, blacks and whites, straight and queer, citizens and foreigners, or any other historically constructed binary.

RESPONDING TO THE FRIENDLESS AS NEIGHBORS NOT ENEMIES

It follows that anyone anywhere is a potential neighbor to be loved, and a person's status as a creature made in the image of God and neighbor for whom Christ died is prior to and transcends the status ascribed to them by a nation-state. Refugees and the provision of sanctuary are a case in point. The practice of sanctuary for refugees witnesses to the claim that the authority of Christ transcends any political boundary. If Christ is king, then no fallen sovereign or state has the right to utterly exclude anyone from the status of a creature called to new life in and through Christ. They are neighbors to be loved, not enemies to be feared. Sanctuary for refugees witnesses to this confession. It also exemplifies how such witness can simultaneously combine a gesture of pastoral care with a form of prophetic action amid a tragic situation.

Echoing the parable of the Good Samaritan, the practice of sanctuary embodies how politics as a form of neighbor love includes love of friendless strangers in need. However, as in the parable, where the Levite and Pharisee pass on by without stopping, those suffering or impoverished are often treated as a threat by those with the capacity and resources to help. Like refugees, those in need are perceived as enemies to be avoided or resisted rather than neighbors to love.

The irreducibly relational nature of being a creature – we come to be through relations with others – means that to be without friends is to lack agency, that is, the power or ability to act with and for others. To be friendless is to lack the necessary conditions for surviving, let alone thriving. In political terms, the friendless are those with a severely constrained capacity to either act for themselves or speak in their own voice. Another term for the friendless is "the poor." To be friendless is also to be without standing or recognition in a community: you just don't matter to those with privilege and power. They can pass on by at no cost to themselves, either social, political, or economic. Scripturally, the paradigmatic examples of the friendless are the orphan, the widow, and the resident alien. They lack status, endure endemic insecurity, and are situated in relations of dependency. In the contemporary context, the friendless include socially, economically, and politically marginalized or excluded groups. Like the enslaved, colonial subjects, or Jews under the Nazi regime, to be friendless is to be one whose face is locked inside an iron mask of stereotype and stigma and who is without either rights or recognition. While neighbor love for the friendless should include works of mercy, it is primarily a political relation. As a political relation it demands the "binding and loosing" spoken of in Matthew 16:19. Politics as neighbor love entails making judgments about what is alienated or broken apart and so needs reconciling, and what is in bondage or falsely tied together and so needs releasing. As exemplified by the abolition movement and the work of its leaders such as Sojourner Truth and William Wilberforce, politics as a process of binding and loosing counters the dynamics of exclusion, erasure, abuse, and exploitation. Amid fallen conditions, such struggles reweave the fragile fabric of reciprocal relations upon which a livable common life depends.

Through the work of politics Christians are to restore the ability of all persons to be creatures, that is, to be persons who are neither killed, dominated, nor forced to flee but are responded to as neighbors. But what of the nonhuman ecologies in which humans are enmeshed and depend on for life itself? Do these also count as part of the polity? If so, do they have agency to shape the common life or are they simply acted upon? As noted in Chapter 2, nonhuman creation is not a mere platform that humans make use of for their moral and political lives. Whether we acknowledge it or not, nonhuman ways of being alive are part of our common life and contribute to its formation and character. That said, other species are not political animals in the same way as humans are. Like cooking, human politics and the institutional formations it generates over time and at scale are part of the distinctive way humans participate in and metabolize creation. But human politics must be attuned to nonhuman forms of life and the ways these can constitute distinct communities within the common life of a polity, such as a bird colony.

Against the backdrop of what I say in Chapter 2, I contend that the way to conceptualize political relations with nonhuman life is also in terms of neighbor love. This love needs to be specific to each kind as well as to nonhuman life as a whole. As neighbors, nonhuman life can be a friend (as with companion animals like dogs and cats), an enemy (as with predators and viruses), a stranger (for example, most species whose animal ways are not human ways), or counted among the friendless in need of care and recognition (for example, endangered species or habitats). There will inevitably and properly be disputes about what neighbor love for nonhuman life entails – for example, whether humans should eat animals or not – and this will form part of the dance of conflict and conciliation through which shared visions of flourishing emerge.[17]

BEING THE PEOPLE OF GOD IS A POLITICS

As creatures seeking to bear faithful witness to the healing and redemption of creation in and through Christ, Christians not only love neighbors (whether as strangers, enemies, or the friendless) but also form distinct patterns of common life called church. Without politics there is no church. Indeed, the church *is* rather than *has* a politics.[18] It is through a particular kind of politics that Christians become a people, the people of God. In the New Testament, the people of God are portrayed as incorporating elements of an *ekklesia* (a public assembly of the people) and a *polis* (the form and structure of a political community). However, as a people the church is not restricted by history or geography but exists across histories and places as a communion of saints. It is not, therefore, a territorially bounded polity. Rather, it is a distinctive pattern of relating together and to God, one that radically reconfigures all other social distinctions. For example, gentiles become grafted into Israel, yet, in other ways, they remain gentiles. Likewise, Christians are at once a distinct people yet also citizens of existing polities, strangers in their own land, yet strangers to no land (Eph 2:19; Jas 1:1; 1 Pet 1:1; 2:11).

Technically, as a political community, the people of God are a theocracy. But this should not be understood in the modern usage of the term as denoting a polity ruled by a priestly caste. The scriptural portrayal of theocracy is meant to prevent rule by a single person or class, priestly or otherwise. Rather, the people are ruled by God, which means no human ruler or class can claim sovereign control and God is to be obeyed rather than any human authority (Acts 5:29). Theocracy in this scriptural sense means something like "no master but God" – a sensibility turned to revolutionary ends in Protestant resistance theory from the sixteenth century onwards. As Augustine noted, God's sovereignty is distributed throughout the people rather than concentrated in a single figure or group.[19] Sovereignty is thereby structurally divided. Even with the ambiguous installation of a monarchy, the legitimacy and authority of the king was institutionally negotiated and contested by prophet and priest. As distributed, God's sovereignty is not imposed from above (heteronomous): that is, the people are not passive recipients of the commands of God. First, covenant precedes command; that is, the obligation to obey God's law is founded on the prior agreement of the people generated through a covenant. Second, the fullest expression and paradigmatic form of God's rule are the assemblies where God and the people speak and hear each other, albeit, often mediated by Spirit-anointed leaders such as Moses, David, Nehemiah, John the Baptist, or Peter. These public assemblies involve various kinds of Spirit-anointed speech, including reasoned deliberation, prophetic indictment, legal proclamation, exhortation, cries of repentance, and shouts of acclamation, all of which help constitute the people of God as a distinct people in relationship to other "nations."

Pentecost represents the moment when the mediation of God's presence, whether by Temple, priest, ruler, or territory, is ruptured and relativized. The Spirit is poured out on all flesh so can be manifest in any place or form of life without distinction, and anyone can receive the anointing needed to speak for and with God (Acts 2). The popular, the ordinary, and the vulgar can mediate God's presence, and

God's presence can be articulated in one's own idiom, however uncouth it is perceived by others. Indeed, at Pentecost, it is those from the periphery that speak forth God's Word, not those from the center. There is thus a paradoxically populist and universalizing undercurrent to a Christian understanding of what it means to be a people: anyone can and should speak with and for God and God may speak to anyone in any place.

The politics the church embodies – being the people of God – is not a stable category that inherently generates separation from "the world." To be the people of God is to be formed from, by, and with the world while on pilgrimage through the world. The people of God are therefore unlike other peoples in ways that cannot be predetermined, only discovered in the midst of building a common life with other kinds of people. In building a common life within and without the church through politics, the ways the church is like and unlike the world, for better or worse, can be discerned and acted on. Conversion generates degrees of identification with and participation in how the Spirit is making Christ present in the world. Personal and communal attunement and reorientation to the work of the Spirit create patterns of identification and disidentification with the world. Indeed, one way of understanding penitence as a central feature of Christian piety is as a process of disidentification with what is worldly through reorientation to the work of the Spirit. At times, who or what is to be identified with lies outside the church, and at other times the call is to identify with the church over and against the world. Making judgments about what to say "yes" to and what to say "no" to, what or who to identify with and what or who to disidentify from, are ever before the church as it seeks to become the people of God and cultivate a more generous and just common life between neighbors.

A problem arises when what it means to be the people of God is conflated with what it means to be a nation-state. There is an obvious theological ambiguity between people and nation deriving from the uses of these terms as synonyms in Scripture (people of God/holy nation). In modern nation-states, what it means to be a people is mostly conflated with what it means to be a member of a homogenous ethnic, racial, or cultural group. Conflating what it means to be the people of God with a particular nation-state is idolatrous. This idolatry can be overhead in talk of this or that country being a "Christian nation." In such talk, the nation-state and not the church becomes the primary community of belonging and shared memory. What it means to be a Christian becomes untethered from any doctrinal or ethical content. By becoming a nationalistic symbol easily manipulated by demagogues, Christianity is thereby reshaped into a form of identity politics.

As the church is prone to sin and idolatry, it needs to undertake particular kinds of political work if its own common life is to be faithful, hopeful, and loving. Names for this work are reformation and renewal. Reformation and renewal mean that Christians must be ready to narrate Christianity against itself when faced with the complicity of Christians, acting in the name of Christ, in generating forms of life that warrant such things as ecological devastation, sexual abuse, racism, and genocide. Addressing the question "what is going on?" necessitates contemplating the tears, spilled blood, and shit that suffuse all forms of common life, including those called church. But as per the need to combine a tragic, apocalyptic, and pastoral register outlined above, histories and current realities shaped by brutality need to be addressed in a posture of repentance as well as a voice of hope even as the work of cultivating an ecclesial common life through prayer, preaching, worship, pastoral care, and mission carry on.

PLURALITY AS A MORAL GOOD

To be a creature is to be someone who needs a common life with human and nonhuman others to survive, let alone thrive. This common life is cultivated through politics, which requires not merely the recognition of difference but an active commitment to plurality.[20] Without such a commitment there can be no politics and so no real basis for association and collaboration.

Plurality, or the need for others *not* like me and a commitment to everyone *not* being the same, is a condition of association. The internal structure of association is difference-in-relation, characterized by patterns of reciprocal relation between distinct others. These differences operate across a broad spectrum, ranging from personality and biography to differences of worldview and identity. At a rudimentary level, anyone who has ever engaged in team building exercises or taken a test to determine your personality type understands that recognizing and navigating differences constructively is basic to any form of collaborative endeavor. Yet we often live in denial of this fact of life.

Forms of shared life that demand everyone becomes the same subsume differences into a single identity. Likewise, the demand for loyalty to a single set of commitments constitute either assimilation or subordination, not association. Pursuing policies of homogenization rather than association is anti-political and oppressive. It is also imprudent: political monocultures are no less toxifying and unsustainable than agricultural ones. In addition, ideological monopolies concentrate power and generate corruption no less than economic ones. Conversely, the assumption that there can be no shared life, or that polarization and division go all the way down, or that there is no such thing as society, only individuals pursuing self-interested exchanges, are also anti-political. They are refusals of association, since a condition of being humans made in the image of God is that solidarity across differences of experience, structural location, and culture can be discovered and that discovery is a revelation of a prior and more basic creaturely interdependency.

The often-made contrast between Babel and Pentecost is instructive here. The former entailed a false unity based on a totalizing uniformity; the latter represents differences coming into a choir of many voices, each singing a different part. One symbolizes totalizing concentrations of power premised on the denial that there are strangers by assuming everyone is the same; the other demands welcoming the stranger as one who speaks God's word in a strange tongue. Part of the work of politics is the pentecostal labor of gathering speakers of strange tongues into a common life that can bear witness, however weakly, to the reconciliation of differences in and through Christ.[21] However, reconciliation generates communion not sameness: that is, difference in fruitful association.

A moral commitment to plurality also recognizes that, as finite and fallen creatures, no one has a monopoly on wisdom about how to live well. All are fallible and all can learn something from someone (technically referred to as the need for "epistemological humility").[22] The refusal to listen to others on the presumption that your own dogma, ideology, or education is so all-encompassing or superior that it alleviates you of the need to hear from others is also anti-political and immoral.[23] The moral problem is one of pride. The political problem manifests itself in self-righteous vanguards who presume to know better how everyone should live and assume they themselves can do no wrong. These vanguards can take the form of either technocratic experts, plutocratic philanthropists, ideological fanatics, or religious zealots.

For freedom to be possible in practice it needs a complex, pluralistic political space. Such a space is one where myriad institutional configurations (household, commons, market, civic and other forms of association) and multiple visions of the good are present.[24] The church is a vital component of this complex space. Theologically understood, eschatology disqualifies any absolute claims of a political sovereign to shape human life and reasserts the need for a thicket of institutional and social forms in the wider body politic. A complex, pluralistic cultural and political space is theologically necessary to hold open the existence of *times* (e.g., festivals, holidays), *spaces* (e.g., family, church, trade unions, the commons), and *practices* (e.g., social customs such as greetings and gift exchange) that are not subject to total determination by state or market processes. On this account, part of the church's vocation as a *res publica* is to bear witness within this age to the possibilities of a common life that is in excess of and beyond this or that worldly order.

For a complex institutional ecology to exist, institutions need the autonomy to determine their own form, character, and ethos, which in turn contribute to and express associational liberty and genuine plurality. Demands for procedural uniformity and ideological conformity across institutions closes down the material, epistemic, and social conditions of freedom of association. It also thereby threatens freedom of expression, since, if individual freedom of expression is to be more than symbolic, the individual needs somewhere to stand and institutional support in order to exercise their agency in speech and action in ways that are neither wholly dependent on nor over-determined by market and state processes. In short, to ensure there is a meaningful "worldview diversity" or a "pluriverse" there must be an array of political and economic possibilities and experiments that institutionally embody and sustain plurality.

Diverse religious traditions in the same polity may have radically different understandings of human flourishing, but they share a sense that, as humans, we participate in a cosmos that is meaningful, that political ends require moral means, and that humans are not reducible to administrative units or commodities. In my view, a plurality of religious imaginaries and institutions is the basis of a genuinely plural politics that can challenge the monopolization of state and market in determining the shape and character of life together. The mere existence of a plurality of religious institutions disrupts totalizing, technocratic systems that demand uniformity and the determination of a common life by wholly immanent and materialistic goals. At the same time, the centralizing tendencies of the modern nation-state and the socially liquefying effects of surveillance capitalism pose a direct threat to an independent, pluralistic, associational life that is a necessary condition for the realization of freedom of association and freedom of expression (and thence, religious freedom).

The way to ensure ongoing plurality at scale is to enable conditions for diverse ways of life and their institutional formations to exist while at the same time building connections between them. This is a central task of politics-as-neighboring. Politics as defined here enables the pursuit of the good of association in ways that enable distinction without atomization. For Christians, politics also entails faithful pursuit of the kingdom of God. I contend that this is inseparable from pursuit of a loving and just common life with non-Christian others through the work of politics. In practice, in the contemporary context, both a commitment to plurality and the faithful pursuit of the kingdom of God require a commitment to three things: (i) the secular nature of politics (i.e., that politics is provisional and penultimate); (ii) engaging in small "d," participatory forms of democratic politics; and (iii) cultivating virtues that enable agitational solidarity across lines of difference. I consider each of these in turn. In doing so, I reflect on and address a central question confronting the church, one I first posed in Chapter 4, and which has been a theme throughout: In loving my neighbor, how can I keep faith with my distinctive commitments while also forming a common life with neighbors who have a different vision of life than I do? Another way to put this question is, how should our sense of what counts as home, identity, or belonging be coordinated with and ordered in relationship to those we find strange or who don't share our beliefs and practices? What follows is a way to answer this question in practice.

Secular Politics as a Theological Commitment

In complex societies, numerous accounts of the meaning and purpose of life emerge, which may or may not be religious. We must find some way of living together amid this diversity. Failure to do so leads to either civil strife or an oppressive hegemony whereby one fallen and contingent account over-determines all others. The constructive way to frame this dilemma theologically is to say our common life is secular yet open to multiple substantive truth claims. But when we call something secular, what do we mean? Rather than that which is not religious, the secular – as a theological term – means *that which is not eternal*. This theological meaning contrasts with and does *not* justify either "secularism" as an ideology or "secularization" as a sociological process.

Secularism is an ideological commitment to the active exclusion of religious beliefs and practices and their aligned institutions from having a voice in determining patterns of common life, whether locally, nationally, or internationally. This takes the form of state and organizational policy frameworks (e.g., in a university or hospital) that render religion a wholly private and individual choice. Secularism is often justified as the enforcement of neutrality and a means of leveling religious differences. In practice, it generates the regulation of religious life, including intervention in substantive issues of doctrine and practice.[25] Advocating for politics to be secular does *not* mean advocating for the ideology of secularism.

Secularization as a sociological framework of analysis assumes that as the world becomes more modern there will be a decline in religious adherence. The "secularization thesis" foretold that religion would become increasingly private and personal. It also contended religion would be separated out from other spheres such as the economy, art, and politics so that these areas would cease to be shaped by religious beliefs and practices. It presumed a progressive model of change, where history was moving in one uniform direction, one that displaced and replaced religious beliefs and practices with nonreligious ones.[26] The reality is very different. Instead of a linear march from faith to rationality, we have the more intuitive recognition that cross-pressures are pulling at one moment toward religion and at another away from it, unmooring all patterns of belief and practice, including those of radical skepticism. These cultural and political cross-pressures generate a wide range of responses, including self-conscious reassertions of orthodoxy, militant unbelief, and hybrid expressions of spirituality. In sum, rather than secularization, the defining feature of the contemporary situation is one of fragmenting diversity and the rise of deinstitutionalized and pluralized patterns of piety.

Theologically, secularization is an impossibility. To parse the poet Gerard Manley Hopkins, "The world is charged with the grandeur of God" even if human eyes are too dimmed to see it.[27] A fractured and fragmented society is a pastoral and political challenge but not an inevitable historical process. Conversely, nostalgia for Christendom and a more culturally homogenous society when Christianity was a hegemonic power should have no place in faithful responses to the contemporary context. Plurality can and should agitate Christians to unwrap tightly bound and fiercely grasped packages of belief and practice and rediscover them as gifts to share rather than possessions to defend.

The secularization thesis and secularism as a hegemonic ideology both assume that the moral way to address conflicts and disagreements is by creating *neutral* ground. This assumes questions of power and partiality can somehow be suspended or avoided. Instead, the moral way of addressing difference amid asymmetries of power and conflicting visions of the good is building up *mutual* ground, not neutral ground.[28] This depends on the quality and character of relations between those with different visions of what it means to live well. It also requires sustaining the material conditions of freedom, namely institutional plurality, so that others can act for themselves.

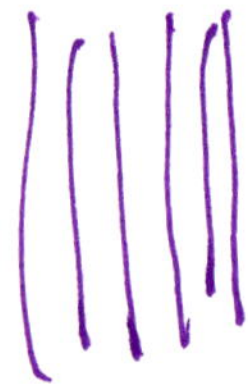

A theological commitment to politics as secular means relativizing all earthly political projects. To use Bonhoeffer's categories, this entails seeing politics as a penultimate activity that can point to but not fully embody the ultimate.[29] It might be objected that the kingdom of God must be pursued above all else. But while pursuing the kingdom of God is a divine imperative, we misunderstand what this means if we pursue it at the expense of penultimate common and public goods like public health and potable water. Conversely, the work of politics is worthy and vitally important, but it is not a work that saves. Casting this-worldly projects in soteriological terms generates false messiahs who dress destruction in the clothes of salvation.

But lest what I've just said is heard as inherently conservative, a key implication of a theological understanding of this age as secular and not eternal is that the current order of things is neither inevitable nor necessary. It can and should change. Our contingent and fallen ways of ordering time and space are not inscribed with an immutable character. They are neither inevitable, natural, nor "just the way things should be." However, the tension between the world as it is and the world as it will be in the kingdom of God gives rise to a dilemma at the heart of Christian political witness. We must strive to see present political arrangements from the standpoint of eternity so that we can understand them as contingent and needing to change. Yet we must also accept the contingency and fallibility of our own moral and political judgments (however righteous the cause), admitting they are temporal and not eternal. To be faithful, political judgments must be held lightly (thereby resisting making this age a final home), even as they are made with the intention to live now in the light of eternity. In practice this generates a constant need to judge what to say yes to and what to say no to in any earthly political proposal.

One way politics as a secular activity has manifested itself is through a division between church and state. In the medieval era, monarchs and the "lords temporal" wielded temporal power (the sword), while popes and bishops wielded spiritual power. But how ecclesial and temporal power were coordinated was much contested. Historically, some called for the total separation of church and state, others for the primacy of ecclesial over temporal authorities, others for the subordination of ecclesial to temporal authorities, and some for a symphony between ecclesial and temporal authorities whereby each limited the other.[30] But *both* ecclesial and temporal authorities were political, and both served the right ordering of this time before Christ's return.[31] How to understand the contribution of the church today to the right ordering of penultimate forms of common life is a key challenge. My argument here is that it needs to be undertaken in a democratic way if it is to be faithful.

Democratic Politics as Faithful Witness

Alongside a commitment to associational plurality and an understanding of politics as operating in secular, non-eternal time,

I contend that democracy is another means of loving neighbors and thereby cultivating a more loving and just common life here and now. Like all politics, democratic politics has two dimensions: statecraft and collaborative social practices. As statecraft, democracy entails systems for sustaining some form of legal-constitutional order that guarantees certain liberties and equality before the law. Such an order is articulated through various procedures and institutions for securing these liberties, for example, an independent legal system and voting. These freedoms – which, against most current thinking, do not have to be conceptualized in terms of human rights – include positive freedoms such as freedom of worship, freedom of assembly, and freedom of speech. They also safeguard negative freedoms, such as freedom from torture and inhuman punishment, freedom from slavery, and freedom from arbitrary arrest and wrongful detention.

Democracy as a mode of statecraft is not necessary to practice the Christian faith, but it does institutionalize four key Christian commitments. The first is to the sanctity of each person as made in the image of God. Honoring the dignity of each person means that no one should be rendered passive or voiceless. Rather, everyone should have agency in cultivating shared worlds of meaning and action through which their personhood is actualized in and through relationship with others. The second is a commitment to loving strangers and enemies as neighbors marked through listening to and dialogue with them as the primary means of either resolving conflict or addressing problems rather than killing, coercing, or causing them to flee. This commitment is institutionalized through parliaments, councils, and other formalized modes of nonviolent assembly through which shared problems are addressed and judgments reached through debate. And the third is to the rule of law, a basic premise of which is that nobody is above the law and government is bound or limited by law and due process. A key tenet of Scripture is the claim that human political orders should be determined not by the personal fiat of a single ruler or by an oligarchy but by law and covenant (that is to say, committed, faithful, mutually responsible social relationships oriented toward fulfilling a shared vision of the good). Finally, a commitment to democratic checks and balances to limit concentrations of power embodies a theological understanding that all human speech and action is finite and fallen, and so require structures that allow for contesting and changing unjust arrangements.

But democracy is not first and foremost about the state and its institutional arrangements. It is primarily a way of nonviolently collaborating with others so as to cultivate a common life. As a social practice, small "d," participatory democratic politics embodies and enables each person to have some say and agency in determining their living and working conditions as well as determine, participate in, and benefit from shared goods. Such practices emerge in many cultures and historical periods, including ancient India, ancient Mesopotamia, and precolonial Africa and America.[32] Examples include West African practices of *palavar*, Islamic practices of *shūrā*, Indonesian modes of shared deliberation and consensus-based decision making known as *Musyawarah Mufakat*, the Carib *wiku*, and the Viking *thing* or *folkmoot*.

In the contemporary context, most institutions and systems, whether governmental or corporate, exclude ordinary people from exercising agency, rendering them passive recipients of decisions taken by others. In such situations, democratic politics entails struggles to realize one's agency either within the system or by alternative means through forms of organized knowledge, money, people, and action. The first, organized knowledge, generates the frameworks of understanding through which to reimagine the world, destabilizing the dominant scripts and ideas that legitimate oppression. It entails informal forms of "popular education" that aim to help those involved to discern and describe their political, economic, and social conditions, helping them move toward alternative ways of understanding themselves and solving specific problems. In the civil rights movement, "citizenship education" pioneered by Septima Clark, Ella Baker, and Dorothy Cotton was a vital if often overlooked element of the movement's success. Crucial to this process of discernment is enabling people to reflect on their conditions through broader frameworks of interpretation. Such "consciousness raising" is vital for generating an alternative community of interpretation, one with the organized knowledge to identify and analyze concrete issues and articulate a position or set of focused demands.

The second form, organized money, is shorthand for generating the material and economic resources to act independently from the state, one's employer, or the patronage and philanthropy of elites. The third – organized people – builds the networks, trust, affective registers, and cooperation that generate and sustain relational power over time. Such ties are necessary to produce movement from the world as it is to a more compassionate and just one. One strand of such work is place-based (e.g., community organizing, residents associations, and block clubs), while the other is work-based (e.g., cooperatives and unions). And in the contemporary context, online forms of mobilizing can contribute to this work alongside on-the-ground forms of organizing. The fourth – organized action – symbolically and physically contests oppressive, corrupt, or unresponsive structures, groups, and practices. This contestation aims at delegitimizing existing arrangements through various kinds of direct action: marches, demonstrations, occupations, boycotts, and the like.[33]

Some combination of organized knowledge, money, people, and action is the engine of democratic politics as a social practice rather than as a mode of statecraft. Echoing the reflections in Chapter 13 on the need to re-embed market systems through economic democracy, democratic politics is a way to ensure both markets and states serve a prior and more fundamental social existence. In modern Europe and the Americas, a new commitment to democracy as a social practice emerged from the nineteenth century onwards with the need to defend and tend social relations against commodification and exploitation by capitalism and instrumentalization by modern nation-states.[34] This is embodied in the emergence of Christian *social*ism, Catholic *social* teaching, and the *Social* Gospel, along with the formation of numerous *social* movements. The insight that faithful witness in the contemporary context entails some kind of active engagement in democratic politics is now shared by many Christian traditions.[35] However, today, there is a pressing need to revitalize democratic politics as a means to respond to new technocratic and totalizing systems and the ways these atomize, surveil, exploit, and polarize society. Faithful democratic politics should take the form of involvement in first, penultimate, small "d" democratic politics that converts unjust concentrations of power by ensuring such power is shared and distributed. The next stage is engaging in statecraft that enables structures of mutual care through policies that promote distributive and social justice while also limiting the reach of the state and private corporations by securing space and time for associational plurality.[36] However, democratic means for cultivating a more generous and just common life are not sufficient. It also takes more loving and just people.

Politics as a Virtuous Endeavor

Politics is never reducible to legal, technical, and bureaucratic processes. As a human endeavor, it arises from a rich symbolic realm suffused with ritual, myth, passions, existential questions, and metaphysical commitments. It is also fundamentally about people and the relationships between them. This means that if politics is to enable flourishing it entails virtue.

One virtue politics requires is faith. Faithfulness is vital to developing any kind of common life and to dismantling corrupt or oppressive structures. Faithfulness denotes reliability, commitment, and trustworthiness. Without it, promises are broken and relations of trust dissolve, thereby eroding our ability to deliberate and act together and the long-term, collaborative relations needed to sustain relational power and engage in the social practices of democratic politics outlined above. The importance of faith to democratic politics is but one example of the centrality of virtue and moral considerations to doing politics well. Alongside faith, other virtues, notably tolerance and hospitality, are vital for navigating plurality in a way that cultivates a common life as opposed to killing or coercing those with whom we disagree.[37] As set out in Chapter 9, there is a crucial relationship between formation in the virtues and liberation. As I note in that chapter, forging a freer, more equitable, and just society is never solely a matter of changed structures. Neither is it merely a question of changing the identity or status of who holds power. Real change requires changed people. That takes the formation of virtuous relationships between people so that new forms of shared action are possible.

Alongside the questions "what is going on?" and "what is to be done?" the question of how to live together is one of the most basic questions ethics asks. The moral answer to this question is always the same: if humans are to live together without killing, oppressing, or persecuting each other, then some kind of common life must be formed and sustained through politics. Politics is the means through which we cultivate shared speech and action through which we discover a life with strangers, enemies, and the friendless. Like language, politics can take many forms depending on the geographic, cultural, and historical context within which it is practiced. But what is universal is that we need politics to live together as human creatures called to love God and neighbor – with our neighbors including other, nonhuman forms of creaturely life on which humans depend. The goods we pursue through politics and the quality and character of our political relations determine whether or not we live well.

ACCOMPANYING READINGS

Martin Luther King Jr., "Letter from a Birmingham Jail" (1963). A classic defense of direct action and agitational democratic politics as a means of faithful change.

Rosemary Radford Ruether, "Communitarian Socialism and the Radical Church Tradition: Building the Community of Liberation," *Liberation Theology: Human Hope Confronts Christian History and American Power* (New York:

Paulist Press, 1972), ch. 10. Ruether portrays a radical vision of a prefigurative nonviolent community of witness acting as a leaven within society. Her account of a non-statist form of democratic socialism as a mode of faithful politics combines tragic, apocalyptic, and pastoral dimensions.

Peter C. Phan, "Kingdom of God: A Theological Symbol for Asians?" *Gregorianum* 79, no. 2 (1998): 295–322. Phan reviews an array of Asian theologies of the kingdom of God, investigating how they operate at the intersection of inculturation and liberation. Through this examination, Phan develops not only an intercultural understanding of the kingdom of God but also a rich theological exposition of a key term in political theology.

Gelasius, "From *The Bond of Anathema*" and "From Letter to Emperor Anastasius," *From Irenaeus to Grotius: A Sourcebook in Christian Political Thought, 100–1625*, eds., Oliver O'Donovan and Joan Lockwood O'Donovan (Grand Rapids, MI: Eerdmans, 1999), 169–179. This early statement of the "doctrine of the two" envisions a separation of powers between ecclesial and political authorities.

Oliver O'Donovan, "Communication," *The Ways of Judgment* (Grand Rapids, MI: Eerdmans, 1999), 242–260. O'Donovan gives an account of the basis of all political bodies in communication situated in a specific place and the ethical relations necessary to sustain such communication over time and so generate the condition for the possibility of politics.

NOTES

1 In modern Christian ethics, Reinhold Niebuhr gave one of the most developed accounts of the tragic nature of politics. Another important account is given by Donald MacKinnon.

2 In terms of literary genre, the pastoral can be aligned with the georgic, derived from Virgil's poem *The Georgics*, which depicts scenes of farming and cultivation. The georgic as a genre emphasizes the place of productive work and fruitfulness. Both the pastoral and the georgic situate human life as enmeshed in and a response to a common life with other creatures and as situated in wider ecologies and particular geographies.

3 I am using "ordinary" here in the liturgical sense of that time between feasts and fasts.

4 C. S. Lewis, *Mere Christianity* (New York: HarperOne 2001 [1952]), 199.

5 On this, see Sara Brill, *Aristotle on the Concept of Shared Life* (Oxford: Oxford University Press, 2020), 86–127.

6 As the tradition of just war theory contends, war is still an arena of moral concern. My contention is that rather than being either constitutive of politics or on a spectrum with politics, war represents a disjunctive arena of moral concern and human endeavor even as the line between war and politics is often blurred in practice. Conversely, at some point, if life is to go on, there must be a shift from war to politics, such that politics sets the limits of war: if we are killing each other, we are not forming a common life; and if we are in dialogue together trying to address shared problems (i.e., doing politics), then we are not killing each other.

7 Against skeptical approaches, I am advocating an understanding of politics as an intrinsically moral activity that contests so-called realist views that suspend ethics in the name of politics, collapse politics into statecraft, and reduce power to violence thereby denying the reality of relational power. The division here is *not* one between ideal and non-ideal theories. The account I give is more pragmatic and attuned to the reality of politics and its possibilities than the truncated account of politics advocated by realists.

8 On the contrast between political relationships and violence, see Hannah Arendt, "On Violence," *Crises of the Republic* (San Diego, CA: Harcourt Brace, 1972), 103–184.

9 Given that humans are political animals constituted through shared communication and action, the tools we use to act and communicate shape the quality and character of our social, economic, and political relations. The technologies through which we construct and reproduce our common life will profoundly affect not only how politics is done but also what is and can be said. To parse Marshall McLuhan, the medium does in part determine the message. It matters whether our common world of meaning and action is mediated through letter or emails, speeches or TikTok.

10 Some social theories that envisage individual subjectivity as the product of wider cultural or material processes or regimes of "governmentality" problematize a notion of soul power. However, outside of wholly deterministic frames of reference, individual agency can be socially constructed and an emergent property, yet still constitute a source of power.

11 Or as Martin Luther King Jr. put it in his "All Labor Has Dignity" speech: "We can all get more together than we can apart; we can get more

organized together than we can apart. And this is the way we gain power. Power is the ability to achieve purpose, power is the ability to affect change." *The Radical King* (Boston: Beacon Press, 2015), 250.

12 Carl Schmitt, *The Concept of the Political*, trans., George Schwab (Chicago: University of Chicago Press, 2007).

13 The New Testament echoes the logic of the Hebrew Scriptures. It is Tamar (Gen 38) and Ruth who are the forebears of David. Childless widows, these two marginal and acutely vulnerable figures, from peoples despised by the Israelites – the Canaanites and the Moabites – are nevertheless paradigms of faithfulness. And before Tamar and Ruth, it is Rahab, a marginal and vulnerable woman of questionable status (a prostitute) from an avowed enemy, who is the first person to recognize what God is doing in the promised land and respond faithfully, not the male Israelite spies (Josh 1–2). Enemies and those we find scandalous can know better who God is and teach those self-identified as the people of God what it means to be faithful, loving, and just.

14 Derived from the Latin, the etymological roots of compromise mean promising something together. The word denotes reaching an agreement or settling a dispute in the face of different interests, values, or objectives. This can involve the more negative association of making concessions, sacrificing something, or being put at risk in some way.

15 James Baldwin, "My Dungeon Shook: Letter to My Nephew on the One Hundredth Anniversary of the Emancipation," *Collected Essays* (New York: The Library of America, 1998), 292.

16 Martin Luther King Jr., "Address to the First Montgomery Improvement Association Mass Meeting" (1955), *A Call to Conscience: The Landmark Speeches of Dr. Martin Luther King, Jr.*, eds., Clayborne Carson and Kris Shepard (New York: Warner Books, 2001), 11.

17 Framing human-nonhuman relations in terms of neighbor love, with neighbor love understood as a political relation, is radically different from an increasingly common move to frame this relation in familial or kinship terms. (See, for example, *Laudato Si'* §228; and Donna Harraway, *Staying with the Trouble: Making Kin in the Chthulucene* [Durham, NC: Duke University Press, 2016]). Understanding this relation as one of kinship collapses the different interests and forms of life each embodies. If everyone is of the same family, then there are no real differences to be negotiated. And there are no asymmetries of power to be transformed

because, as brothers and sisters, we are notionally all of equal agency and standing. Moreover, if we are family, then the existential threat human and nonhuman can at times pose to each other is denied, meaning there are no friend-enemy relations to be converted. When framed in terms of kinship or family the human-nonhuman relationship is also rendered pre- or apolitical since relations are simply given rather than constructed and so cannot be contested or remade.

18 In a way that is somewhat critical of his formulation, I am parsing Stanley Hauerwas's maxim that that church is rather than has a social ethic. While envisaging the church as a body politic, Hauerwas tends to collapse its politics into its sacramental life. What he lacks is a robust account of the distinctive practices and histories by which Christians faithfully negotiate a common life amid asymmetries of power and conflicting visions of the good in ways that simultaneously constitute the church as church and contribute to cultivating a more loving and just common life between neighbors. Invocations of baptism, eucharist, liturgy, or even nonviolence are no substitute for a conception of politics as itself a distinct practice and moral good.

19 Augustine contends that the divine law was given not to "a single man or even a select group of wise men" but to the people as a whole. Augustine, *City of God*, 10.7.

20 This is a point the political theorist Hannah Arendt makes repeatedly throughout her work.

21 1 Corinthians 12 can be read as a meditation on exactly this dynamic in how plurality constitutes the church. Riffing on a common piece of ancient political rhetoric, Paul does not see diversity as a threat, since different members with different gifts and experiences are constitutive of the body. These members are interdependent on each other, with special regard needed for weaker members and those who are dishonored or stigmatized (22–23). Unity requires the exercise of different gifts and how these give voice to different experiences of being embodied (Jew, Greeks, slave, free). Unity is a gift of the Spirit and expressed in mutual care (25–26).

22 Otto Maduro, "An(other) Invitation to Epistemological Humility: Notes toward a Self-Critical Approach to Counter-Knowledges," *Decolonizing Epistemologies: Latina/o Theology and Philosophy*, eds., Ada Maria Isasi-Diaz and Eduardo Mendieta (New York: Fordham University Press, 2012), 88–104.

23 See the discussion of epistemic justice in Chapter 5.

24 Sustaining meaningful material conditions of plurality can involve state funding of religiously based schools, hospitals, and the like. Although if processes of institutional isomorphism and co-option are to be avoided, something like endowment is a better form than direct grants.

25 See Saba Mahmood, "Secularism, Hermeneutics, and Empire: The Politics of Islamic Reformation," *Public Culture* 18, no. 2 (2006): 323–347.

26 As the anthropologist Talal Asad argues, the secular "should not be thought of as the space in which *real* human life gradually emancipates itself from the controlling power of 'religion' and thus achieves that latter's relocation." *Formations of the Secular: Christianity, Islam, Modernity* (Stanford, CA: Stanford University Press, 2003), 191.

27 Gerard Manley Hopkins, "God's Grandeur" (1918).

28 As noted in Chapter 12, mutuality does not necessarily entail equality. It involves reciprocity of gift relations where what is exchanged can involve great asymmetry but is fitting and builds up each party. For example, what the patient receives from the nurse in terms of care in no way matches what the nurse receives from the patient in terms of a word or gesture of thanks, but such a gesture is nevertheless fitting and something is remiss if it is not given (unless of course the patient is incapacitated).

29 *Dietrich Bonhoeffer Works*, vol. 6, *Ethics*, ed., Clifford Green, trans., Reinhard Krauss et al. (Minneapolis, MN: Fortress, 2005), 153–157.

30 For example, Giles of Rome's *On Ecclesiastical Power* (1302) argues for papal supremacy, John of Paris's *On Royal and Papal Power* (1302) argued for a mutually disciplining relationship between church and state, Dante's *De Monarchia* (c. 1312) and Marsilius of Padua's *Defensor Pacis* (1324) argued for versions of church-state separation, and John Wyclif's *On Lordship* (c. 1373) argued for the effective subordination of the church to temporal authority.

31 The key early statement on this was Pope Gelasius's *The Bond of Anathema* (c. 495). Gelasius envisaged the church as able to decide its own affairs and as having a dual responsibility with political authorities for fostering good order. The dual responsibility and division between the two authorities was to safeguard the modesty of both: only Christ could be both priest and king.

32 Temma Kaplan, *Democracy: A World History* (New York: Oxford University Press, 2015); David Stasavage, *The Decline and Rise of*

Democracy: A Global History from Antiquity to Today (Princeton, NJ: Princeton University Press, 2020).

33 Gene Sharp, a leading theorist of civil resistance, lists 198 forms of nonviolent direct action: www.aeinstein.org/nonviolentaction/198-methods-of-nonviolent-action/ (accessed May 12, 2022).

34 The need to protect and tend the social is intensified by the ways the conditions of life itself, from the genetic level up, are now subject to commodifying and governmental regimes of surveillance or what Michel Foucault calls biopolitics: the control of entire populations through diverse techniques for achieving the subjugation of bodies.

35 See Luke Bretherton, *Christ and the Common Life: Political Theology and the Case for Democracy* (Grand Rapids, MI: Eerdmans, 2019), 51–198.

36 On this account, one shared by a broad array of both Catholic and Protestant political theologies, the state secures social justice by means of such measures as social insurance or national healthcare. But against Hegelian and Marxist-Leninist visions of the modern state as the means of realizing human freedom and fellowship in history, it is the body politic or political society constituted through myriad forms of consociation that is the means of realizing freedom and fellowship, albeit in temporal, non-eternal/secular forms. In short, statecraft can tend justice, including social justice, but it cannot generate love; that is the domain of non-state centric forms of covenantal association.

37 See Bretherton, *Christ and the Common Life*, 238–288.

Epilogue

To be a moral person is always a struggle. Converting one's temptations into virtue and foolishness into wisdom is a part of the struggle, as is transforming places and peoples accursed by abuse and injustice into a realm of blessing. But we cannot do either alone. Nor should we. The gift of coming together with others in a shared struggle to live well is that, in doing so, we discover who we are already in Christ and forge more loving and just forms of common life that anticipate and witness to the world as it will be in Christ.

This book narrates a way of understanding what we are doing when we come together with others in a shared struggle to live well and how to engage in that simultaneously moral, spiritual, and political struggle faithfully, hopefully, and lovingly. In doing so, each part addresses a question fundamental to ethics; namely, what is going on? What is to be done? And how should we live together? Focusing on the first of these questions, Part I set out how we become rightly orientated to reality and able to name and pursue a flourishing life through a combination of listening to creation, Scripture, strangers, cries for liberation, and our ancestors. Part II then addressed the second question by focusing on how we become moral agents and the nature, character, and purpose of moral action. This entailed reflecting on what limits moral agency and the place of commands, rules, virtues, and practical reason in forming us as persons able to act morally. Part III provides case studies that model different ways of synthesizing the schema established in Parts I and II. The chapters in Part III also combine to provide a framework for answering the third question of how to live together in ways that bless rather than curse. The book as a whole casts a vision for what Christian ethics is and how to do it today.

I am aware that throughout this book I raise more questions than I answer. That is intentional. Part of what this book seeks to do is cultivate a desire to ask questions even if the answers elude us. Learning to ask good questions is the vital first step in the struggle to live well. If we are not asking questions, it means we are neither asking what is going on nor deliberating about the meaning, purpose, and character of our actions. Which is to say, we are not struggling to live well but conforming to a fallen status quo.

To ask difficult questions is to confront the ways and means death and destruction are at work within us and in the world around us. The response to what we find should not be attempts to control or transcend how we bring life to nothingness. Neither can we fight, flee from, nor freeze when facing the abysmal void we encounter in ourselves and others. These are all missteps that seek to either escape or render oneself invulnerable to the tormented realities of the world we inhabit and that inhabits us. Rather, following in the way of the life, death, and resurrection of Jesus Christ, the right, if risky path is to metabolize our wrecked and accursed ways of being alive into ways that bring blessings through loving God and our human and nonhuman neighbors.

Index

Made in the USA
Monee, IL
30 July 2025

22180310R00225